KT-564-855

BRIEF

Contents

A Guide to
Help Desk Concepts
Second Edition

Donna Knapp

THOMSON

COURSE TECHNOLOGY

Australia • Canada • Mexico • Singapore • Spain • United Kingdom • United States

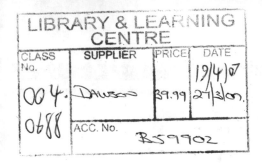

THOMSON

★

COURSE TECHNOLOGY™

A Guide to Help Desk Concepts, Second Edition
is published by Course Technology.

Senior Vice President, Publisher:
Kristen Duerr

Executive Editor:
Jennifer Locke

Acquisitions Editor:
Bill Larkin

Development Editor:
Robin M. Romer

Product Manager:
Janet Aras

Editorial Assistant:
Christy Urban

Marketing Manager:
Angie Laughlin

Associate Production Manager:
Christine Freitas

Cover Designer:
Julie Malone

Compositor:
GEX Publishing Services

Manufacturing Coordinator:
Laura Burns

Photo Researcher:
Abby Reip

Photo credits: Figure 1-2: Courtesy of Nokia. Courtesy of Motorola. Courtesy of Handspring, Inc. © 2003 Eyewire/Getty Images. © 2003 PhotoDisk/Getty Images. © 2003 PhotoDisk/Getty Images. Figure 1-5: © 2003 Eyewire/Getty Images. © 2003 PhotoDisc/Getty Images. Courtesy of Plantronics, Inc. © 2003 PhotoDisc/Getty Images. Courtesy of Telex Communications, Inc. Figure 1-7: Courtesy of Applix, Inc. Figure 3-3: © Walter Hodges/CORBIS. Figure 5-2: Courtesy of Siemens Business Communications Systems. Figure 5-5: Courtesy of Shutterfly.com. Figure 5-7: Courtesy of Applix, Inc. Figure 5-8: Courtesy of Remedy, a BMC Software Company. Figure 5-9: Courtesy of XO™ Communications. All rights reserved. XO™, the XO™ design logo are trademarks of XO™ Communication, Inc. All other trademarks are the property of their respective owners. Figure 5-12: This image compliments of and is Copyright © 2003 LANDesk Software, Inc. All rights reserved. Figure 5-13: Courtesy of SilverBack Technologies. Figure 5-14: Courtesy of Spectrum Corporation. Figure 5-16: Courtesy of Telecorp Products, Inc. Figure 7-2: © 2003 PhotoDisc/Getty Images. Figure 7-7: Courtesy of Relax the Back. Figure 7-8: Courtesy of Sony Electronics, Inc. Figure 7-9: Courtesy of 3M. Figure 7-10 courtesy of Balt, Inc. Figure 7-11: Courtesy of Plantronics, Inc. Figure 7-12: Courtesy of Dazor Manufacturing Corp. Figure 8-3: © DiMaggio/Kalish/CORBIS.

TABLE OF
Contents

Preface

For the past fifteen years, I have provided help desk-related consulting and training services. As a consultant, I work with companies both large and small that have the desire to improve the quality of their help desk services. As a trainer, I have had the opportunity to meet and interact with hundreds of help desk managers and analysts who have the desire to learn new skills and make their help desk a better place to work. I learned as much from these engagements as they learned from me, and I hope our combined experiences enable you to see the tremendous opportunity this field presents. Preparing this second edition has enabled me to reflect on how dramatically the help desk industry has changed in the past five years. A function that once received little respect is now the shining star of many organizations. Processes and technologies previously found in only the most sophisticated help desks are now making their way into even the smallest organizations. The role of help desk analyst has been elevated from an entry-level position to that of a respected profession. Although a lot has changed, one constant remains the same—the help desk is first and foremost a customer service organization. More than ever, customers expect the help desk to be responsive, caring, and capable. They want and expect to encounter a *can do* attitude each and every time they need support.

The heroes of this industry are the front-line service providers who day in and day out and maintain that *can do* attitude do the best they can to help their customers. This book was written with these heroes in mind. It was also written for all of the people who are bringing about the positive and lasting change that is enabling this industry to thrive and for the people who are reaping the benefits of their efforts. Through this book, I hope to shed light on this exciting and challenging field and provide the information people need to pursue not only a job, but a career in customer support. This book explores all aspects of the help desk and the help desk industry. It is designed to provide a solid foundation upon which analysts entering the help desk industry, or striving to advance in the industry, can build their skills and knowledge.

Intended Audience

This book is primarily intended for three kinds of readers.

- Readers who are considering career opportunities in a help desk, and who want an introduction to the field. They can use this book to explore the different types of help desks, the available help desk career paths, and the kinds of knowledge, skills, and abilities they need to be successful.

- Readers who are working in a help desk and want a better understanding of how people, processes, technology, and information affect the typical help desk. They can use this book to obtain additional knowledge and depth about how these components enable the help desk to operate efficiently and effectively as well as clear definitions and explanations of key concepts.

- Readers who are taking a course in help desks and customer support or a related degree program. They can use this book to obtain a high-level overview of the help desk. These readers will especially benefit from the end-of-chapter activities that provide practical experience with the concepts and skills they will use on the job.

Help Desk Curriculum

This book is designed for a first course in any Help Desk Curriculum. It is intended for use in community and technical college courses, such as Introduction to Help Desks, Help Desk Concepts, Customer Service and the Help Desk, and Problem Solving for the Help Desk. These courses are part of rapidly emerging programs that aim to prepare students for the following degrees or certificates: IT Support Professional, Computer Help Desk Specialist, Computer Technical Support, Help Desk Support Specialist, Computer User Support, and Computer Support Technician. As the need for and the quantity of help desks grows, companies are turning to community colleges, technical colleges, training centers, and other learning institutions to prepare their students to fill new and existing entry- and higher-level positions in the help desk industry.

No longer are technical skills the only requirement for the field of technical support. Companies now want to attract individuals who have the appropriate balance of business, technical, soft, and self-management skills that contribute to making their help desks successful. Increasingly, organizations that are committed to providing quality customer support view their help desks as a strategic asset. These companies are seeking individuals who have the desire and skills needed to acheive the help desks mission. Whether the help desks provide support to the customers who use their companies' products or the help desks provide technical support to the companies' employees, the need for help desk professionals is on the rise.

Approach

This book is designed to provide an overview of each of the topics relevant to working at a help desk. My goal is to provide an in-depth understanding of the concepts that the reader needs to understand to succeed in the help desk industry and to bring these concepts to life by providing real-world examples of these concepts in action. To this end, separate chapters are dedicated to subjects such as people, processeses, technology, and information. Collectively, these chapters offer one of the most current and inclusive compilations of help desk-related information available today. These chapters also show how the people, processes, technology, and information components—when well designed and managed—come together seamlessly in the workplace. Like a puzzle, each piece is required, and when all of the pieces are assembled, the picture comes into view. If one piece is missing, the picture is incomplete.

To derive the maximum benefit from this book, the reader must be an active participant in the learning process. The end-of-chapter activities are designed specifically to develop the reader's knowledge and help the reader assimilate the chapter concepts. They encourage the reader to expand his or her knowledge through self-study as well as prepare the reader for the team-oriented help desk environment by having the reader work with other students in project groups or teams. Many of the end-of-chapter activities encourage the reader to utilize information resources and solve problems—skills that are essential in the dynamic help desk industry.

Assumed Knowledge

This book assumes that readers have experience in the following areas, either through course work, work experience, or life experience:

- Basic customer service concepts

- Basic computer concepts or computer literacy

- Internet and World Wide Web concepts

Overview

The outline of this book takes a holistic view of the help desk. Each chapter explores a particular component of the help desk in detail and builds on the information presented in previous chapters.

Chapter 1, Introduction to Help Desks Concepts, explains the historical context of technical support, the role of help desks within a technical support department, the components of a successful help desk, and why customer service is the bottom line for help desks.

Chapter 2, Help Desk Operations, describes the different types of customer service and support organizations, the roles and operations of internal and external help desks, and how size influences help desk operations. It also explores the benefits and challenges of centralized and decentralized help desks as well as of managing help desks as cost centers and profit centers.

Chapter 3, The People Component: Help Desk Roles and Responsibilities, describes the business, technical, soft, and self-management skills and job and professional responsibilities required for both the principal and supporting job categories at a help desk. It also explains the necessity of working as a team.

Chapter 4, The Processes Component: Help Desk Processes and Procedures, describes the evolution of business processes and the leading quality improvement programs that enable continuous process improvement. It also describes the most common processes used in help desks and discusses how they are integrated along with their importance and their benefits to the help desk.

Chapter 5, The Technology Component: Help Desk Tools and Technology, covers the wide array of tools and technology used in help desks. It introduces the primary help desk technologies, remote support technologies, help desk communications tools, and help desk management tools. In addition, it provides a seven-step method for evaluating, selecting, and implementing new help desk technology.

Chapter 6, The Information Component: Help Desk Performance Measures, explains how information is used in the help desk as a resource, describes the most common data categories captured by help desks, and discusses the most common team and individual performance metrics.

Chapter 7, The Help Desk Setting, briefly examines the factors that influence the location and layout of help desks and describes how analysts can improve the ergonomics of their personal workspace. It also explores how to design and maintain work habits that enable analysts to stay organized and achieve personal success.

Chapter 8, Customer Support as a Profession, explores help desk industry trends and directions, explains the role of certification in the help desk, and provides ways to prepare for a future as a help desk professional. It also provides transition tips for individuals who choose to pursue a help desk management position.

Features

To aid you in fully understanding help desk concepts, there are several features in this book designed to improve its pedagogical value.

- **Chapter Objectives.** Each chapter in this book begins with a list of the important concepts to be mastered within the chapter. This list provides you with a quick reference to the contents of the chapter as well as a useful study aid.

- **Illustrations, Photographs, and Tables.** Illustrations and photographs help you visualize common components and relationships. Tables list conceptual items and examples in a visual and readable format.

- **Notes.** Notes expand on the section topic and include resource references, additional examples, and ancillary information.

- **Tips.** Tips provide practical advice and proven strategies related to the concept being discussed.

- **WWW pointers.** WWW pointers direct you to the Internet for more information about a topic, an example related to the chapter content, and other points of interest.

- **Bulleted figures.** Selected figures contain bullets that summarize important points to give you an overview of upcoming discussion points and to later help you review material.

- **CloseUps.** CloseUps detail real-life examples of the chapter topic. Taken from actual experiences, CloseUps confirm the importance of the topic and often contribute related information to give additional insight into real-world applications of the topic.

- **Chapter Summaries.** Each chapter's text is followed by a summary of chapter concepts. These concise summaries provide a helpful way to recap and revisit the ideas covered in each chapter.

- **Key Terms.** Each chapter contains a listing of the boldfaced terms introduced in the chapter and a short definition of each. This listing provides a convenient way to review the vocabulary you have learned.

- **Review Questions.** End-of-chapter assessment begins with a set of approximately 25 review questions that reinforce the main ideas introduced in each chapter. These questions ensure that you have mastered the concepts and have understood the information you have learned.

Hands–on Projects. Although it is important to understand the concepts behind help desk topics, no amount of theory can improve on real-world experience. To this end, along with conceptual explanations, each chapter provides eight to ten Hands-on Projects aimed at providing practical experience in help desk topics. Some of these include applying help desk concepts to your personal life and researching information from printed resources, the Internet, and people who work in or have experience with the support industry. Because the Hands-on Projects ask you to go beyond the boundaries of the text itself, they provide you with practice implementing help desk concepts in real-world and help desk situations.

Case Projects. There are three case projects at the end of each chapter. These cases are designed to help you apply what you have learned to business situations much like those you can expect to encounter in a help desk position. They give you the opportunity to independently synthesize and evaluate information, examine potential solutions, and make recommendations, much as you would in an actual business situation.

Instructor Support

The following supplemental materials are available when this book is used in a classroom setting. All of the supplements available with this book are provided to the instructor on a single CD-ROM.

Electronic Instructor's Manual. The Instructor's Manual that accompanies this textbook includes:

- Additional instructional material to assist in class preparation, including suggestions for lecture topics.
- Additional discussion questions.
- List of Web references.

ExamView®. This textbook is accompanied by ExamView, a powerful testing software package that allows instructors to create and administer printed, computer (LAN-based), and Internet exams. ExamView includes hundreds of questions that correspond to the topics covered in this text, enabling students to generate detailed study guides that include page references for further review. The computer-based and Internet testing components allow students to take exams at their computers, and also save the instructor time by grading each exam automatically.

PowerPoint Presentations. This book comes with Microsoft PowerPoint slides for each chapter. These are included as a teaching aid for classroom presentation, to make available to students on the network for chapter review, or to be printed for classroom distribution. Instructors can add their own slides for additional topics they introduce to the class.

Solution Files. Solutions to end-of-lesson questions can be found on the Instructor Resource CD-ROM and may also be found on the Course Technology Web site at **www.course.com**. The solutions are password protected.

Distance Learning. Course Technology is proud to present online testbanks in WebCT and Blackboard to provide the most complete and dynamic learning experience possible. We hope you will make the most of your course, both online and offline. For more information on how to bring distance learning to your course, contact your local Course Technology sales representative.

ACKNOWLEDGMENTS

I wish to thank the staff at Course Technology who contributed their talents to the creation of this book, including Bill Larkin, Acquisitions Editor; Janet Aras, Product Manager; and Christine Freitas, Associate Production Manager. Thanks also to Abby Reip, who was instrumental in obtaining many of the pictures that brought this book to life.

Robin Romer served as developmental editor on the first edition of this book and so having her assume that role for the second edition as well was a great comfort. Although we live on opposite sides of the country, Robin and I have managed to carve out a style of collaboration that's uniquely our own. She offers guidance and structure, and I listen—most of the time. I occasionally vent and whine, and she ignores me. It works for us. Thank you, Robin!

I want to express my great appreciation to the industry professionals and educators who reviewed the draft manuscript and made suggestions that significantly enhanced the readability of the book. Their experiences in the help desk industry and in education contributed considerably to the quality and completeness of the book and to its usefulness as a learning tool. The reviewers are Dennis Ford, Central Texas College; Jorge Gaytan, Richards College of Business, State University of West Georgia; John Nadzam, Community College of Allegheny County; Carol Okolica, Dowling College; and Harry Woloschin, Wake Technical Community College. Special thanks to reviewers Joyce Parker and John Ross, Fox Valley Technical College, who contributed their talents to the first edition as well as this edition.

I am also very grateful to the following people for their valuable contributions to the CloseUp sections that offer a "real-world" view of the subject matter presented in each chapter: Whitney Brown and Mike Landreth, Shutterfly, Inc.; Harriet Chavez, Kass, Shuler, Solomon, Spector, Foyle & Singer, P.A.; Meg Franz, CompuCom Systems, Inc.; Elaine Frost, Island Pacific; Malcolm Fry, FRY-Consultants; Calvin Hastings, MOUSE; Walter Hundley, Science Applications International Corporation (on behalf of Entergy Corporation); David Liss, Southwest Missouri State University; Pete McGarahan, STI Knowledge, Inc.; Danny Morse, Schulte Roth & Zabel LLP; Ron Muns, Help Desk Institute; James Pullen, Sykes Enterprises, Inc.; and Bill Rose, Service & Support Professionals Association.

Special thanks also to my family who have learned to tolerate the clutter, neglect, and forgetfulness that a book project inevitably brings. I love you all very much, and greatly appreciate your support and encouragement.

Finally, I want to dedicate this book to the thousands of professionals who are currently working in the help desk industry. Your efforts have enabled this industry to become what it is—an exciting and growing professional career choice. I hope this book will further elevate the help desk as a profession and encourage the knowledgeable and enthusiastic students who complete this course to enter the field and help it continue to grow.

Donna Knapp
Tampa, Florida

1

INTRODUCTION TO HELP DESK CONCEPTS

> **In this chapter you will learn:**
> - The evolution of technical support
> - The role of the help desk within a technical support department
> - The components of a successful help desk
> - Why customer service is the bottom line for help desks

In today's fast-paced and fiercely competitive business environment, companies and people increasingly depend on complex computing technology to do their work. This dependence and complexity result in an enormous challenge: to support the growing number of technology users when they need help. The **help desk**—a single point of contact within a company for managing customer problems and requests and for providing solution-oriented support services—provides this support.

And the need for support is great. Hardware manufacturers and software publishers receive millions of help requests annually from frustrated users of today's increasingly complex personal computer (PC) systems. The number of requests made to help desks within companies is estimated to be larger still. Why? Just a few of the factors that contribute to this increasing demand for support include:

- New computer users, many of whom have never used a computer before.

- The seemingly constant installation of new systems such as antivirus and firewall, collaboration and messaging, and so forth.

- Upgrades to existing systems, such as office systems (database management, spreadsheet, word processing), operating systems, and so forth.

- Problems with legacy systems, such as mainframe-based accounting and human resources systems.

- Systems once used only in offices are now being used at home and in schools; these include presentation tools, photo-editing tools, tax software, money-management systems, travel and trip planning systems, and so forth.

Of the help desks surveyed by the Help Desk Institute (a member organization that focuses on the needs of internal and external support organizations), 83.5 percent report that the monthly number of service requests they receive is remaining the same or increasing.

This huge demand for support, coupled with a shortage of information technology (IT) professionals, has created a tremendous career opportunity in the field of customer service and technical support. According to the United States Department of Labor, computer support is projected to be among the fastest growing occupations through the year 2010 ("Computer Support Specialists and System Administrators," U.S. Department of Labor Bureau of Labor Statistics, June 2002).

To work at a help desk, you must understand what is involved in delivering technical support services and the role of the help desk within a support department. You must have excellent communication and problem-solving skills as well as applicable technical skills. Above all, you must understand that the help desk is first and foremost a customer service organization that contributes to a company's bottom line by delivering services that meet the needs of its users.

EVOLUTION OF TECHNICAL SUPPORT

As people and companies worldwide struggle to manage costs and justify the benefits of their technology investments, they are finding that technical support is one of the most significant costs. **Technical support** refers to the wide range of services that enable people and companies to continuously use the computing technology they have acquired or developed. Technical support is a considerable part of the **total cost of ownership** (**TCO**) of computing technology, which is the total amount that a company or person spends on computer technology over its lifetime.

In the early 1970s, companies did little to support technology users. They considered technical support a necessary evil that disrupted the development of new products. This perception came about because the same highly skilled developers of the software or hardware also handled technical support questions and problems. They viewed these technical support calls as a distraction from their primary jobs of product development and programming. Developers often answered the same, sometimes simple, questions over and over because few companies captured and reused the responses to frequently asked questions. The developers sometimes treated users rudely and frequently lost or forgot problems because no system existed to specify how they should handle a call or record the resulting information. When a user located someone who gave them a satisfactory response, they would continue to call that person for a variety of problems, even if a problem was outside the developer's area of expertise. For example, a customer with a jammed printer might contact a developer who had previously assisted him with an account system problem. Having a developer leave their programming duties to clear a jammed printer is a costly, inefficient use of time.

As the computer industry grew, people used more and more systems—often, on different computer platforms—to do their work. Some people used mainframe-based systems developed internally by their company's information technology (IT) department. Others used PC-based **off-the-shelf** products—personal computer software products developed and distributed commercially. Increasingly, people used systems on both platforms. This growing complexity made technical support even more challenging and time-consuming.

Users often had no idea where or whom to call for help. Sometimes, companies gave users a list of numbers to call—one for hardware problems, another for telephone- or network-related problems, and others for help using mainframe-based systems or PC-based software packages. As shown in Figure 1-1, users were bewildered. When in doubt, users would contact anyone or everyone they thought could help resolve their problem.

Outside	555-4321
Vendors Network Support	x5310
PC Support	x4571
Mainframe Support	x9722
Security	x7411
Accounting Application Support	x6552
Accounting Department Supervisor	x5397
Payroll Application Support	x4726

Figure 1-1 Obtaining support without a help desk

The costly, negative effects of companies' prolonged failure to recognize the need for technical support accumulated. Developers missed deadlines because they were diverted to technical support calls, leaving little time for their primary job of programming. Information was not being collected, so developers had to discover the same solution again and again. Recurring problems were neither identified nor resolved. Finally, technology users, who expected quick and accurate solutions to their problems and requests, were extremely dissatisfied when their demands were not met.

Companies began realizing that they had to distinguish between **development**—the construction of new systems—and **support**—services that enable the continued use of a system once it is released for distribution. In addition, companies learned that they had to support not only technology, but also the *users* of that technology. They recognized that each user should be treated and referred to as a **customer**, a person who buys products or services. They realized that their highly skilled developers often lacked the diplomacy, interpersonal skills, and communication skills required to interact directly with customers. Developers' skills were better suited for projects, product-planning and design activities, and the day-to-day running of systems.

As a result, many large companies established an information center to support their employees. An **information center** was a place within the company where employees could receive training and help using personal computers. A forerunner of the help desk, the information center fostered computer literacy and made it easier for people to use computers to get their jobs done.

At about the same time, some vendors (most notably, IBM) began to offer discounts to customers who "screened" problem calls internally before calling the vendor. Calls were screened to determine the nature of the problem. If the problem required the services of a field engineer, the company would contact the vendor who would then **dispatch**, or send, a field engineer to the customer's site. Otherwise, the company would handle the problem internally. Although the vendor's goal was to minimize the number of times a field engineer was dispatched unnecessarily to a customer site, it introduced technology users to the idea of calling a central point of contact for help. This trend paved the way for a concept that IBM called the "help desk."

In the early 1980s, a number of factors caused even more companies to focus on supporting the users of technology, not merely the technology itself, and to view technology users as customers. These factors included:

- The explosion of PC tools and the accompanying increase in the number of companies competing in the computer industry.

- The quality movement, a business trend that began in the late 1970s and challenged companies to measure and monitor quality and to take corrective action when products or services failed to satisfy customers' requirements.

- The high number of increasingly sophisticated, yet frustrated technology users who were willing and able to take their business elsewhere.

- A business realization that a broader set of support services, delivered efficiently and effectively, could reduce the total cost of owning technology, enhance customer productivity, improve customer satisfaction, and, ultimately, increase revenue by helping to sell more products.

The quality movement introduced the concept that a customer can be either external or internal to the company. Today, the service industry recognizes an **external customer** as a person or company that buys another company's products and services. An **internal customer** is a person who works at a company and at times relies on other employees at that company to perform his or her job.

This increase in customer focus prompted companies to expand their definition of technical support to include a set of activities known as customer support. **Customer support** includes services that help a customer understand and benefit from a product's capabilities by answering questions, solving problems, and providing training. The term *technical support* has taken on new meaning and now includes services that span the complete lifecycle of information technology. Technical support begins with selecting and installing the hardware, software, network, and application components that enable technology users to do their work. Ongoing support includes keeping the system in good repair, upgrading hardware and software when needed, and providing customer support. Ongoing support also includes proactive activities such as having a regular maintenance schedule with steps such as backing up data and using system utilities such as Scandisk and Disk Defragmenter. Technical support for a particular piece of hardware or software ends when the technology becomes unusable.

In the 1990s, the World Wide Web was established, resulting in the rampant expansion and commercialization of the Internet. The **World Wide Web** (**WWW** or **Web**) is a collection of documents on the Internet with point-and-click access to information that is posted by government agencies, businesses, educational institutions, nonprofit organizations, and individuals around the world. The **Internet** is a global collection of computer networks that are linked to provide worldwide access to information.

The rapid commercialization of the Internet, coupled with increasingly more affordable and portable computing technology, led to an explosion in the number of people using computers on a daily basis—and therefore in the number of people who need technical support. Over 544 million users have access to the Internet (NUA Internet Surveys, February 2002). Millions more people regularly use computers at home, in schools, in libraries, and while traveling. Portable Internet-enabled devices such as laptop computers, two-way pagers, personal digital assistants (PDAs), and cellular telephones make it possible for people to interact with computers at any time and in any place.

The sheer and growing number of computer users and the constant influx of new technologies have solidified the concept of technical support and its importance. Companies that once had little need for technical support are now giving serious thought to how and by whom technical support services are delivered. Figure 1-2 illustrates the evolution of technical support.

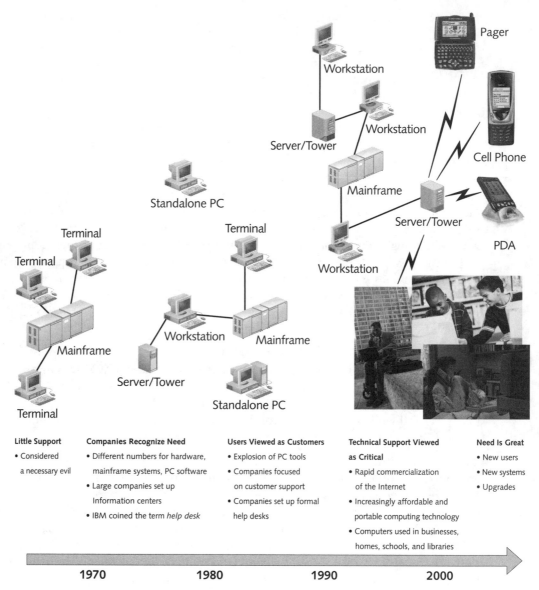

Figure 1-2   Evolution of technical support

The technical support services that a company delivers, as well as how and by whom those services are delivered, vary according to company size, company goals, and customer expectations. Some companies, particularly smaller ones without a help desk, deliver technical support informally by people who are knowledgeable about computers (perhaps because they have one at home) but who have little or no specialized training. Coworkers direct their computer-related questions or problems to these resident "experts." Technical support in such companies is often highly personalized. For example, a computer expert may go to the desk of a user and provide one-on-one support. Or, a user may track down an expert in an effort to obtain immediate assistance. Although users tend to greatly appreciate such "high touch" service, the computer expert may quickly become overburdened. After all, technical support is not his or her primary job function. As a result, most companies take a more formal approach to technical support. For example, they often have an "official" help desk that users can contact. This practice enables the company to maximize its technical resources and ensures that the people providing support services have the required skills.

Most companies that have a help desk offer customers a choice of ways to contact the help desk, such as the telephone, voice mail, e-mail, and the Web. These various routes of communication to and from the help desk are typically called **channels**. Many help desks maintain a Web site that customers can access to request services, obtain answers to frequently asked questions (FAQs), search for solutions to common problems, and, in some cases, download software. Figure 1-3 shows a part of the Cisco Systems Technical Support Web site. Although this "lower touch" approach to delivering services via multiple channels may not be personalized as one-on-one support, many users appreciate being able to get the help they need, when they need it, using the method of their choice.

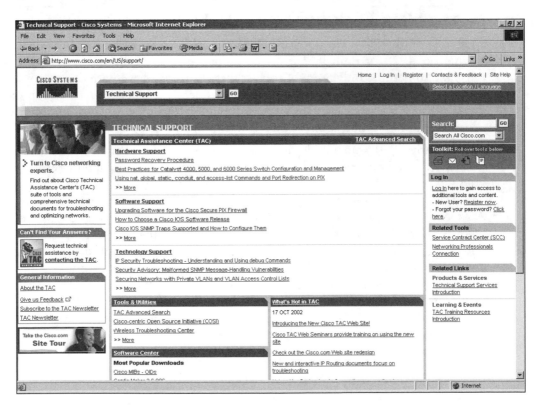

Figure 1-3   CISCO Systems Technical Support Web site

The informal support delivered by companies that don't have a help desk can occur within companies that have an established help desk. For example, users occasionally may turn to **peer-to-peer support**, a practice in which users bypass the formal support structure and seek assistance from their coworkers or someone in another department. Peer-to-peer support is effective when a coworker can help a person in the same department understand how to use a product to do their work. Peer-to-peer support has its drawbacks, however. For example, when a person asks a coworker for help solving a complex technical problem that neither one has the skill to resolve, they not only waste time trying to solve the problem, they could also make the problem worse. Or they may "fix" the problem incorrectly so that it is likely to recur. Also, because the help desk does not know about problems that coworkers solve, it cannot help others who experience similar problems.

As the computer industry has evolved, so has the concept of technical support, which has moved from a narrow focus on fixing technical problems to a much more comprehensive focus on supporting customers and helping them use technology to achieve business goals. The help desk is one result of this evolution.

ROLE OF THE HELP DESK IN TECHNICAL SUPPORT

The role of the help desk has changed dramatically since IBM coined the term *help desk* in the late 1970s. Originally established simply to screen calls, the help desk is now the first and sometimes only point of contact that customers have with a company or a company's IT department. Many companies consider the help desk a strategic corporate resource because of its constant interaction with the company's most important asset: its customers. This section looks at the evolution of the help desk.

In the early 1980s, support departments—not help desks—handled questions from customers who did not know how to operate their computers. The support department either did not know the answers or was told not to provide them, so it dispatched, or routed, even simple questions to highly skilled developers or field engineers. As in the early days of technical support, this misuse of highly skilled resources was costly, to say the least. Slowly at first, companies implemented, then expanded, the role of the help desk. The help desk began to answer simple questions and *resolve* problems instead of just passing them on. Support organizations and customers both realized the benefits of a well-implemented help desk, prompting companies to expand the help desk's role further. During the mid-1980s, many companies redesigned their help desk support processes. Some help desks began to acquire and use sophisticated telephone systems, problem management, and resolution technology. Some help desks took on new activities, such as:

- Conducting and scheduling training sessions.
- Coordinating hardware and software installations.
- Distributing software electronically.
- Creating reports for customers and managers that detailed opportunities to improve the company's products and services, problem areas, training needs, and trends.

- Maintaining system and network status and availability information.
- Managing programs designed to attract and keep customers.
- Marketing help desk services as well as the services offered by other departments, such as training.
- Monitoring the efficiency and effectiveness of delivered services to ensure customers' needs are met.
- Participating in the development of hardware and software standards.
- Performing customer satisfaction surveys.
- Processing service requests, such as orders for new products or services, enhancement requests, and requests to move, add, or change equipment.
- Resolving complex problems.

All these activities meant that the help desk role was more *proactive*—that is, better able to anticipate problems and prevent them—than *reactive*—that is, merely responding to problems. A proactive help desk meant better training, relevant information, timely system status information, fully resolved problems, and feedback. As a result, customers were less likely to have problems, and when they did, they had a much better chance of the help desk resolving those problems quickly. This trend toward proactivity led to more effective help desks than ever before.

In the 1980s, some organizations began to **outsource** their help desks—that is, to have services provided by an outside supplier instead of providing them in-house. Some help desks outsourced all of their services, whereas others outsourced only a portion of their services. For example, some help desks outsourced only their support for off-the-shelf products, such as Microsoft Office products, or only their after-hours support. This outsourcing trend, which continues today, had a profound effect on the support industry because it forced companies to recognize and determine the real costs associated with delivering the support services needed by their customers.

By the early 1990s, it became evident that help desks could positively affect the bottom line of their companies by delivering efficient and effective support services. In an effort to demonstrate their contribution, help desks began to assess their efficiency and effectiveness by creating performance measures, or **metrics**, and measuring customer satisfaction levels. They ranked their performance in relation to their own past performance and in relation to other help desks. Having a "world class" help desk became a goal for the most ambitious and progressive companies. The term **world class** describes a company that has achieved and sustains high levels of customer satisfaction. For example, a world class manufacturing company is considered excellent by its customers when compared to other companies, regardless of what industry they are in. World class is different than **best-in-class**, which describes a company that is the finest in its relative industry peer group. For example, a best-in-class manufacturing company is considered excellent by its customers when compared only to other manufacturing companies.

World class help desks resolve a high percentage of problems and try to avoid dispatching or sending problems to other support groups. Also, their practices are proactive, rather than reactive, in nature. Figure 1-4 illustrates these characteristics of a world class help desk.

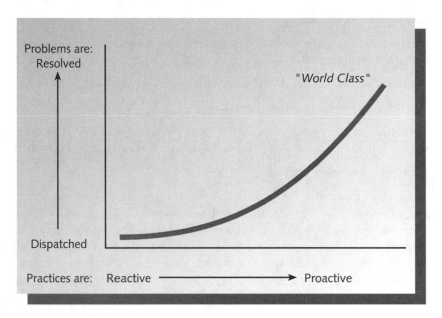

Figure 1-4   Characteristics of a world class help desk

By the late 1990s, help desks began to fully realize the benefits of problem management and resolution technologies and some began to capitalize on the capabilities of the World Wide Web. They worked hard to streamline and automate their key business processes and to empower users to help themselves by reviewing FAQs and searching knowledge bases on the help desk's Web site. To accommodate increasingly mobile users, some help desks instituted remote control and diagnostic systems. These systems enable the help desk to take remote control of the keyboard, screen, or mouse of connected devices, and troubleshoot problems, transfer files, and even provide informal training by viewing or operating the customer's screen.

Today, help desks are in the midst of another shift, this time toward the concept of a support center. The **support center** is a help desk with a broader scope of responsibility and the goal of providing faster service and improving customer satisfaction. In addition to its traditional services, responding to inquiries and handling problems, today's support center uses technology to perform tasks that various other support groups performed historically. For example, network management tools make it possible for the help desk to perform proactive network monitoring. Also, in an effort to reduce the time required to satisfy a customer's request, some help desks perform certain system and network administration tasks. Table 1-1 summarizes how the role of the help desk has evolved.

Table 1-1   Evolution of the Help Desk Role

Decade	Role of the Help Desk
1970s	▪ IBM coined the term *help desk* ▪ Help desks simply screened calls
1980s	▪ Help desks dispatched even simple questions ▪ Help desks began to answer simple questions and resolve problems ▪ Companies redesigned help desk processes ▪ Help desks began to use sophisticated telephone systems and problem-management and resolution technologies ▪ Help desk role became more proactive than reactive ▪ Some companies outsourced their help desk services
1990s	▪ Companies realized help desks could positively impact the bottom line ▪ Help desks began measuring performance and customer satisfaction levels ▪ Help desks ranked their performance with other help desks ▪ Becoming "world class" became a goal ▪ Help desks began to exploit the capabilities of the World Wide Web ▪ Help desks began empowering users to help themselves
2000s	▪ Help desks are evolving into support centers ▪ Help desks are using technology to perform tasks such as: - Network monitoring - Remote diagnostics - System and network administration

Companies are in varying stages of this transition from reactive help desk to proactive support center. Some companies have invested heavily in help desk services. Other companies provide only basic or minimal help desk services—either because they have yet to fully recognize the help desk opportunity or because other priorities take precedence. Others still are taking the next step, which is to focus on problem elimination rather than problem resolution. As with the technical support services, the role of the help desk varies based on the company's size, goals, and customers' expectations.

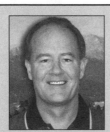

RON MUNS
CEO AND FOUNDER
HELP DESK INSTITUTE
COLORADO SPRINGS, COLORADO
www.helpdeskinst.com

The support industry has evolved considerably in the past decade and is entering a maturation phase. Ten years ago there was confusion within the industry about the role of the help desk and issues such as how to organize and staff the help desk and the skills required. Today it's become clear that the help desk must focus on business productivity. Support organizations must learn new business-management skills in an effort to better communicate with and gain the support of corporate executives. They must understand and align their services with the strategic goals of their companies.

Help desks must also take advantage of the numerous tools that are available, and focus on integrating those tools and using them to solve business problems. Technology trends such as the proliferation of mobile devices, the growing acceptance and availability of self-service and knowledge-management technologies, and the growing use of collaborative tools that allow instant communication are driving help desks to revisit support assumptions. To address these trends effectively, help desks must analyze their business processes and ensure that their processes and the skills of their people are designed to make the most of available tools. They must also address issues such as security and available bandwidth, and look for automation opportunities that benefit both the customers and the support organization.

More is expected of us as the support industry matures. People working in this industry need to step up and face the challenges. Economic conditions have changed, our customers have changed, business demands are changing, and we need to change, too. Sixty percent of our lives are spent at work, and we all want to do meaningful work. In the support industry, we know our work is meaningful. That's why we do it. That's why we love it!

COMPONENTS OF A SUCCESSFUL HELP DESK

Companies that attain high levels of customer satisfaction have learned that many factors influence how customers perceive their experiences with the help desk. These companies have also learned that they must constantly monitor and manage customer expectations, because the level of service customers require is like a moveable bar that is constantly being raised. What's most important, companies have learned that there is no quick fix or "magic pill." They must pay attention to each of the components illustrated in Figure 1–5.

People, processes, technology, and information are the four critical components that determine a help desk's success.

People

The first and most important component of the help desk is people. The **people** component consists of the staff and structure put in place within a company or department to support its customers by performing business processes. The support services delivered by a company or department are often represented as a multi-level structure through which customer problems and requests may pass prior to being resolved.

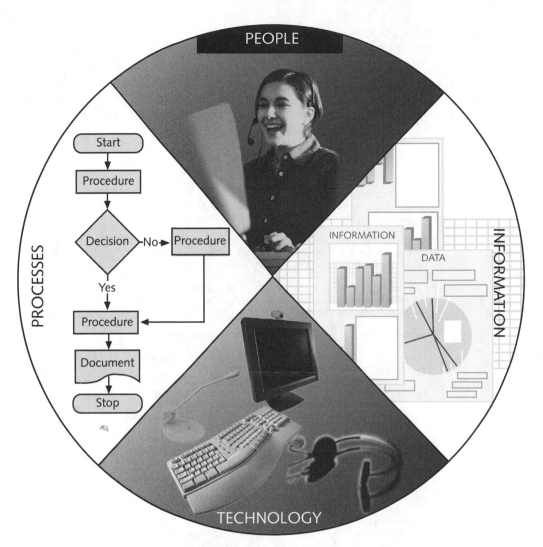

Figure 1-5   The integrated components of a successful help desk

The help desk, level one or tier one, is the initial point of contact for customers when they have a problem, request, or question. People at this level attempt to handle as many customer incidents as possible. If they cannot solve an incident, they pass it up the structure to the level two or level three group that has the experience, authority, or physical proximity needed to resolve the incident. Having level one people handle as many incidents as possible ensures economical use of level two and level three resources. This approach also promotes customer satisfaction because customers receive solutions more quickly and are not passed from one support person to another.

The different types of customer transactions—that is, problems, requests, and questions—are often called **incidents** or issues.

As a primary point of contact, members of the help desk team must also promote and enforce their company's or department's computer usage policies. Figure 1-6 shows a sample computer usage policy. These policies may cover topics such as abiding by software licensing agreements, protecting the company's data assets by using only authorized IDs and passwords, and using e-mail and Web-based systems appropriately and only for business reasons. As overseers of these policies, members of the help desk team must conduct themselves at all times in a professional and ethical manner.

ABC COMPANY
COMPUTER USAGE POLICY

I understand and agree to the following conditions governing the use and care of computer hardware and software assigned to me.

1. I agree to abide by the license agreement between the proprietor of the software and the ABC Company and I understand that the improper reproduction of proprietary software by any means is prohibited.

2. I will not use proprietary software that is NOT the property of the ABC Company on any computing devices of the ABC Company unless I have specific authorization to do so.

3. I understand that safeguarding the software is my responsibility.

4. I have read the policies and procedures in the computer usage policies memorandum and agree to abide by them.

5. I will access the ABC Company's local area network only with my user ID and password. I will not use unauthorized codes or passwords to gain access to other employees' files.

6. I understand that Internet and World Wide Web access should be used only for work-related purposes.

7. I understand that the e-mail system is designed to facilitate business communication among employees and other business contacts. In addition, I understand the following about the e-mail system:
   • E-mail communications may be considered ABC Company documents and may be subject to review.
   • The e-mail system is not to be used for personal gain or to solicit outside business ventures or political or religious causes.
   • The ABC Company reserves the right to review the contents of employees' e-mail when necessary for business purposes.
   • Foul, inappropriate, or offensive messages are prohibited.
   • E-mail messages are capable of being forwarded without the express permission of the original author. Accordingly, due caution should be exercised when sending e-mail messages.

I understand that ABC Company personnel who violate any of these guidelines are subject to disciplinary actions or dismissal.

Signed:_____   Dated:_____

Figure 1-6 Sample computer usage policy

Recent financial scandals in the business world and dilemmas such as the ease with which Internet sources can be plagiarized have prompted an increased awareness of the need for ethics. Ethics are the rules and standards that govern the conduct of a person or group of people. Such rules and standards dictate, or provide guidance, about what is considered right and wrong behavior. Ethical behavior is behavior that conforms to generally accepted or stated principles of right and wrong. The policies of a department or company dictate what is right and wrong behavior; these policies may vary from one department or company to the next. For example, some companies permit limited personal use of the company's e-mail system, whereas others restrict the use of e-mail to work-related correspondences.

The support industry must continuously change in an effort to gain and keep customer loyalty. In this dynamic environment, companies have difficulty finding and keeping people who possess the mix of skills needed to take on the expanding responsibilities of the help desk. The principal skills required to work successfully at a help desk include:

- **Business skills**—The skills people need to work successfully in the business world, such as the ability to understand and speak the language of business and the ability to analyze and solve business problems. Business skills also include the skills people need that are unique to the profession their help desk supports, such as accounting skills or banking skills, and the skills that are unique to the service industry, such as understanding the importance of meeting customers' needs and managing their expectations.

- **Technical skills**—The skills people need to use and support the specific products and technologies the help desk supports. Technical skills also include basic computer and software literacy.

- **Soft skills**—The skills people need to deliver great service, such as listening skills, verbal communication skills, customer service skills, problem-solving skills, writing skills, and the ability to be a team player.

- **Self-management skills**—The skills, such as stress and time management, people need to complete their work effectively, feel job satisfaction, and avoid frustration or burnout. Self-management skills also include the ability to get and stay organized and to learn new skills continuously and quickly.

Although clearly defined business processes and technology enable people to be more efficient and effective at the help desk, sometimes only human qualities such as empathy, patience, and persistence will do. Successful help desks hire and train people who have good soft skills, who sincerely enjoy working with customers, and who like helping others solve problems. The most service–oriented companies try to ensure employee satisfaction as well as customer satisfaction.

Chapter 3 explores in detail the people component of a successful help desk.

MEG FRANTZ
VICE PRESIDENT, ENTERPRISE HELP DESK
COMPUCOM SYSTEMS, INC. (SERVICES PROVIDER)
DALLAS, TEXAS
www.compucom.com

The Enterprise Help Desk at CompuCom is part of the Workplace Outsourcing Services division, and provides application, desktop, mobile, and network support for over 75 clients nationwide.

Organization. We have approximately 300 people in our Enterprise Help Desk between Dallas and Phoenix and another 200 analysts and technicians who are located at client sites. We have a number of different job positions that offer a great deal of opportunity to our employees. Our Customer Support Specialists are generalists and support a wide range of desktop products. Our Product Support Specialists provide first- and second-level support for specific software and hardware products or for a suite of products. Our Field Services Specialists troubleshoot, order parts, and dispatch Field Engineers to customer sites. We also have Client Advocates who serve as account managers for specific clients, as well as operational Team Leaders and Managers.

In addition, we have a Technical Services group that supports the call management (telephone), problem management, knowledge management, call forecasting, and agent scheduling systems used by the analysts, as well as other tools used for e-support. This team is also responsible for client satisfaction reporting, training, team and individual performance reporting, and reporting performance to clients.

At the heart of our success as an organization is a commitment to continuous improvement. For example, in 2002 we achieved the prestigious Support Center Practices (SCP) certification for the fifth consecutive year. This program requires comprehensive on-site audits and examines the major criteria required to operate a successful help desk. Additionally, all of our analysts are required to be A+ certified within three months of being hired, and over 90 percent of our analysts are vendor-certified. We also have an internal certification program that focuses on our analysts' customer service and technical troubleshooting skills. Analysts are required to renew this training and achieve a score of 95 percent or better every six months.

Tasks. Depending on the Service Level Agreement we have with a client, our analysts provide first- and second-level hardware, software, and network support. We try to resolve problems over the phone, or we can dispatch an on-site engineer. Most of our customers contact us over the telephone; however, we do have customers contact us over fax, e-mail, the Web, and directly through links from their own request-tracking systems. Our analysts log every customer request we receive, and we make every effort to ensure resolutions are thoroughly documented in our knowledge base so other analysts can use them in the future. Because of the number of different customers we support, it is important to be consistent using our knowledge base because that is where we house standard technical knowledge as well as client-specific knowledge.

Philosophy. Our commitment to continuous improvement and our "easy to work with" approach has led to a strong reputation for quality and an extremely loyal customer base. We know that our people are the key to that success. We like to hire competent people who apply their knowledge and experience to their work and who keep the customer's perspective in mind as they do so. To keep employee retention high, we focus on a "Total Agent Package" for our employees: offering a good work environment, a team building atmosphere, additional pay on performance, a good working relationship with others, and recognition for jobs done well.

Processes

The processes that people perform are the next important component of a successful help desk. Processes determine the procedures people follow relative to their specific area of the business. People often confuse the terms *process* and *procedure*. A **process** is a collection of interrelated work activities that take a set of specific *inputs* and produce a set of specific *outputs* that are of value to a customer. For example, problem management is the process of tracking and resolving problems. Problem management takes evidence that a problem has occurred (input) and produces a solution (output). A **procedure** is a step-by-step, detailed set of instructions that describes how to perform the tasks in a process. The directions that show how to record information about a problem or how to determine the source of a problem are examples of procedures. In other words, processes define the tasks to be performed, and procedures describe how to perform the tasks.

Some processes found in a help desk environment include:

- **Problem management**—The process of tracking and resolving problems, for example, a jammed printer or an illegal operation error message when using software. The goal is to minimize the impact of problems that affect a company's systems, networks, and products.

- **Request management**—The process of collecting and maintaining information about customer requests for new products or services and enhancements to existing products or services, for example, a request for new software or a laptop computer. The goal is to identify and document the tasks required to satisfy requests and ensure that appropriate resources are assigned.

- **Service level management**—The process of negotiating and managing customer expectations, with regard to, for example, how and when customers contact the help desk, the help desk's hours of operation, target response and resolution times, and so forth. The goal is to promote a common (two-way) level of expectation about the services to be delivered and provide measurable performance objectives.

The rigorous, consistent use of processes leads to customer confidence, employee satisfaction, and, ultimately, process improvement. Companies find that in today's competitive business climate it is not enough to do things right; rather, they must do the *right* things right. In other words, companies must perform the correct processes and they must perform them well. Processes must be continuously fine-tuned and occasionally redesigned to ensure that customers' ever-rising expectations are met.

Chapter 4 explores in detail the processes component of a successful help desk.

Technology

The third integrated component of a successful help desk is technology. **Technology** is the tools and systems people use to do their work. Help desk technology includes the data collection systems, monitoring systems, and reporting mechanisms that employees and managers use to perform processes. Successful help desks use technology to capture, store, and deliver the information that satisfies the needs of both the customers and the company.

Some tools found in a typical help desk include:

- **Incident tracking and problem management systems**—The technology used to log and track customer problems and requests.

- **Knowledge management systems**—The technology used to capture and distribute known solutions to problems and answers to frequently asked questions (FAQs).

- **Self-service systems**—The technologies such as self-help and self-healing systems that enable customers to, for example, reset their own password or restore the configuration of their desktop in the event of a crash.

- **Telephone systems**—The technology used to manage incoming and outgoing telephone calls.

- **Web-based systems**—The technology used to enable customers to submit problems and requests or solve incidents on their own through the World Wide Web without calling the help desk.

Companies that were designated the Ten Best Web Support Sites of 2002 by The Association of Support Processionals (ASP) are listed in the table.

Open Division	
Company	**URL**
Cisco Systems	**www.cisco.com/public/Support_root.shtml**
National Instruments	**www.ni.com/support**
Cognos	**support.cognos.com**
Crystal Decisions	**support.crystaldecisions.com**
Microsoft Great Plains	**www.greatplains.com/services/support.asp**
Network Associates	**www.nai.common/services/default.asp**
Small Company Division	
Company	**URL**
eHelp Corporation	**www.ehelp.com/support**
Lexign	**www.lexign.com/support_services/default.asp**
Made2Manage	**www.m2mexpert.com/m2mexpert**
Pervasive Software	**www.pervasive.com/support**

Because help desk technology is increasingly sophisticated, many companies require that help desk candidates meet predefined computer literacy standards. Then after the people are hired, their training can focus on the specific tools the company uses, not on the basics of telephony and computers. The most successful people in a help desk combine those all-important business skills and soft skills with proficiency at using the company's tools.

 Chapter 5 explores in detail the technology component of a successful help desk.

Information

The final component of a successful help desk is **information**, data that are organized in a meaningful way. People need information to do their work. Similarly, management needs information to control, measure, and standardize business processes. In today's global economy, information is a company's most precious resource.

It is difficult to find a book or an article about help desks that does not describe the tools and technologies that enable help desk analysts and managers to do their work. Such tools and technologies are useless, however, if they do not provide and produce meaningful information. For example, it is a waste of time for help desk analysts to log every problem in an incident-tracking system if they cannot search the system in the future and retrieve historical information about the problems they logged. Similarly, managers must be able to use the incident-tracking system to run reports and produce charts that show problem trends.

People working in a help desk must understand clearly that the data they collect on a daily basis becomes information. This information is not used just to track outstanding problems and requests. It is also used to measure their personal performance, the overall performance of the help desk, and, more important, customer satisfaction with the department or company. Failing to record events and activities accurately and completely can have very negative results for the department or company, the help desk, and the help desk employee. Figure 1-7 shows a sampling of the types of data and information collected and used by help desks.

Forward-thinking companies use the data they capture at the help desk to spot trends and discover the causes of problems. By getting a good grasp of problem trends and causes, companies can increase customer satisfaction, enhance productivity, improve the quality of products and services, increase the efficiency and effectiveness with which services are delivered, and create new products and services. Because people working in a help desk have daily contact with customers, they enjoy a unique opportunity to capture an enormous amount of information about customers' wants and needs. Successful help desks seize this opportunity by designing and implementing processes and technologies that enable them to capture and use customer information efficiently. People interested in a service-industry career must learn how to interpret data and share and add value to information.

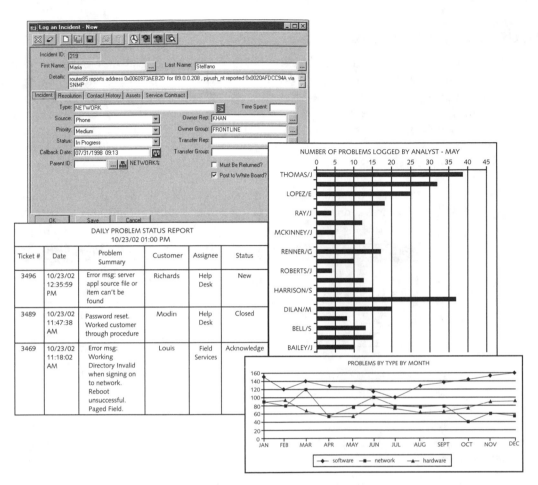

Figure 1-7   Types of data and information collected and used by help desks

Chapter 6 explores in detail the information component of a successful help desk.

Of the four help desk components, people are by far the most important and expensive component. This is because when customers—living, breathing human beings with feelings and expectations—contact the help desk for support, they expect to be assisted by competent, friendly, and efficient people. Finding qualified people to deliver excellent customer service is one of the greatest challenges the support industry faces.

CUSTOMER SERVICE—THE BOTTOM LINE

High-quality customer service is the goal of every customer-oriented company or department. **Customer service** involves ensuring that customers receive maximum value for the products or services they purchase. **Value** is the perceived worth, usefulness, or importance of a product or service to the customer. Each customer's definition of value is influenced by every customer service encounter he or she experiences, which is why every contact a customer has with a help desk is an opportunity for the company to enhance its customer service image.

 A number of membership organizations and associations provide information, guidance, and networking opportunities to support professionals. The most recognized are:Organization URL

Organization	URL
The Association of Support Professionals	**www.asponline.com**
The Help Desk Institute	**www.helpdeskinst.com**
Service & Support Professionals Association	**www.thesspa.com**
STI Knowledge (Help Desk 2000)	**www.stiknowledge.com**

Young, leading-edge companies once were able to get by with mediocre service because they were delivering a phenomenal new product. However, as they grew and competition increased, they needed to quickly rethink their customer service strategy. Some internal IT departments have historically taken a "We'll give you what we think is best" attitude, but they, too, have had to adopt a more customer-driven approach. Otherwise, their companies may replace them with a service agency that focuses on customer needs.

Customer service does not mean giving customers everything they ask for, whenever they ask for it. This misinterpretation of customer service can cripple the most well-meaning company or cause it to fail completely. For example, sending a technician to a customer site without attempting to resolve the problem over the telephone is very costly and quickly overworks the company's pool of technicians. Likewise, failing to define what products the help desk supports causes them to receive calls about products for which they are not trained and have difficulty supporting. Instead, a help desk must manage customer expectations. Managing expectations involves clearly communicating to customers what the help desk can and cannot do to meet their needs, given available resources.

 By definition, **customer satisfaction** reflects the difference between how a customer perceives he or she was treated and how the customer expects to be treated.

1

Managing expectations is a challenge because expectations can vary from one person to another, one situation to another, and even one day to another. Left unmanaged, customer expectations quickly exceed the resources and capabilities of even the most successful help desk. Failing to recognize the importance of managing customer expectations can cause a help desk to fall into one of four traps:

- Promising more than it can deliver
- Delivering more than it promises, which raises the bar on customer expectations
- Promising one thing and delivering something else
- Not promising anything specific, leaving the customer to set expectations

Any of these scenarios will, in the end, lead to customer dissatisfaction. Companies that provide world class customer service work diligently to determine what services are important to their customers and how customers expect services to be delivered. These companies are gaining market share and increasing the size of their client base by delivering superior customer service and support before and after the customer purchases or uses a product. Customers increasingly use customer service to differentiate companies and products, leading to an ever-increasing demand for quality service. Establishing a responsive, competent help desk is no longer an option; it is a critical factor for success.

CHAPTER SUMMARY

- A vastly increased dependence on computing technology has created a tremendous demand for technical support. Technical support services enable individuals and corporations to continuously use the computing technology they have acquired or developed.

- A well-thought-out and properly implemented help desk provides a company with a primary mechanism for measuring and managing the delivery of technical support services to the customer community. The role of the help desk has evolved from that of a reactive dispatch function to a proactive provider of solution-oriented, customer-driven services.

- People, processes, technology, and information are the tightly integrated components that contribute to the success of a help desk. By far, people are the most important and expensive component. Tremendous opportunity exists for people who have the mix of business, technical, soft, and self-management skills needed to work in the support industry and who sincerely enjoy working with customers and helping others solve problems.

▢ High-quality customer service is the goal of every customer-oriented company or department. To deliver high-quality customer service, a help desk must manage customer expectations. Managing expectations involves clearly communicating to customers what the help desk can and cannot do given available resources. Because customers are increasingly using customer service to evaluate companies and products, establishing a responsive, competent help desk is no longer an option for companies; it is a critical success factor.

KEY TERMS

best-in-class — A company that is the finest in its relative industry peer group. For example, a best-in-class manufacturing company is considered excellent by its customers when compared only to other manufacturing companies.

channels — Routes of communication to and from the help desk, such as the telephone, voice mail, e-mail, and the Web.

customer — A person who buys products or services.

customer satisfaction — The difference between how a customer perceives he or she was treated and how the customer expects to be treated.

customer service — Services that ensure customers receive maximum value for the products or services they purchase.

customer support — Services that help a customer understand and benefit from a product's capabilities by answering questions, solving problems, and providing training.

development — The construction of new systems.

dispatch — To send or route.

ethics — The rules and standards that govern the conduct of a person or group of people.

external customer — A person or company that buys another company's products and services.

help desk — A single point of contact within a company for managing customer problems and requests and for providing solution-oriented support services.

incident — The term for different types of customer transactions—that is, problems, requests, and questions; also called issues.

information — Data that are organized in a meaningful way.

information center — A forerunner of the help desk; a place within a company where employees could receive training and help using personal computers.

internal customer — A person who works at a company and at times relies on other employees at that company to perform his or her job.

Internet — A global collection of computer networks that are linked to provide worldwide access to information.

metrics — Performance measures.

off-the-shelf — Personal computer software products that are developed and distributed commercially.

outsource — To have services provided by an outside supplier instead of providing them in-house.

peer-to-peer support — A practice in which users bypass the formal support structure and seek assistance from their coworkers or someone in another department whom they believe can help.

people — The help desk component that consists of the staff and structure put in place within a company or department to support its customers by performing business processes.

procedure — A step-by-step, detailed set of instructions that describes how to perform the tasks in a process.

process — A collection of interrelated work activities that take a set of specific inputs and produce a set of specific outputs that are of value to a customer.

support — Services that enable the continued use of a system once it is released for distribution.

support center — A help desk with a broader scope of responsibility and the goal of providing faster service and improving customer satisfaction.

technical support — A wide range of services that enable people and companies to continuously use the computing technology they acquired or developed.

technology — The tools and systems people use to do their work.

total cost of ownership (**TCO**) — The total amount that a company or person spends on computer technology over its lifetime. A considerable portion of the TCO is technical support.

value — The perceived worth, usefulness, or importance of a product or service to the customer.

world class — A company that has achieved and is able to sustain high levels of customer satisfaction. For example, a world class manufacturing company is considered excellent by its customers when compared to other service companies, regardless of what industry they are in.

World Wide Web (**WWW** or **Web**) — A collection of documents on the Internet with point-and-click access to information that is posted by government agencies, businesses, educational institutions, nonprofit organizations, and individuals around the world.

REVIEW QUESTIONS

1. What two factors create the need to provide help to a growing number of technology users?

2. What is a help desk?

3. What is the purpose of technical support?

4. Describe how technical support was viewed in the early 1970s.

5. What are four negative consequences experienced by companies that failed to recognize the need to distinguish between development and support?

6. What action on the part of vendors began the move toward help desks?

7. What concept about customers did the quality movement introduce?

8. How is the focus of customer support different from that of technical support?

9. In the 1990s, what two factors led to an explosion in the number of people using computers on a daily basis?

10. What are the three factors that influence the technical support services a company delivers?

11. Why do some companies take a more formal approach to technical support?

12. When a person bypasses the formal support structure and directs a computer-related question or problem to a coworker, it is called _____.

13. Why do many companies consider the help desk a strategic corporate resource?

14. Describe the difference between a world class company and a best-in-class company.

15. Describe the characteristics of a world class help desk.

16. What are the benefits of having the support center performance tasks that various other support groups performed historically?

17. List the four components of a successful help desk, and briefly describe each one.

18. In addition to technical skills, list and briefly describe the three other types of skills people need to work successfully at a help desk.

19. What are three characteristics that successful help desks look for in people they hire and train?

20. A(n) _____ is a collection of interrelated work activities that take inputs and produce outputs that are of value to the customer.

21. What must help desks do to ensure that processes meet their customers' ever-rising expectations?

22. How do successful help desks use technology?

23. List four ways that information is used at a help desk.

24. What must people interested in a career in the service industry learn to do with data and information?

25. _____ involves ensuring customers receive maximum value for the products and services they purchase.

26. What influences a customer's definition of value?

27. Customer service means giving customers everything they ask for, whenever they ask for it. True or False?

28. What are the consequences of leaving customer expectations unmanaged?

29. What are four traps companies can fall into if they do not manage customer expectations?

30. Why is establishing a help desk a critical success factor in business today?

HANDS-ON PROJECTS

Project 1-1

Evaluate technical support experiences. The quality of technical support varies greatly from company to company. Talk to at least three friends or classmates about their experiences with technical support. Ask each person the following questions:

❑ What kind of technical support did they need?

❑ When and how did they contact the company?

❑ Did the company they contacted have a help desk?

❑ What expectations did they have before they contacted the company for support?

❑ Why did they have those expectations?

❑ Did the company meet their expectations?

❑ Could the company have done anything better? If so, what?

Write a report that summarizes each experience and presents your conclusions about each experience.

Project 1-2

Determine how to obtain technical support. Be prepared by knowing what company or department to contact when you need technical support. Perform an inventory of all the hardware and software you use on a regular basis. Determine how you would obtain help if you had a problem or a question. Make a list for future reference that includes the names of the products and the telephone numbers or Web site addresses you would use to obtain support.

Project 1-3

Perform proactive technical support services. Technical support includes reactive activities such as repairing problems; however, it also includes proactive activities such as having a regular PC maintenance schedule. Complete the following steps:

1. Search the Web for articles about PC maintenance.

2. Prepare a list of the 10 most frequently suggested PC maintenance tips.

3. If you have a PC, perform each of the suggested maintenance activities on your PC.

4. If you do not have a PC, offer to perform each of the suggested maintenance activities on the PC of a classmate, friend, or family member. Provide him or her with a copy of your tip list for future reference.

5. Share your tips with your classmates and add to your list any new tips that your classmates identified.

6. As a class, prepare a list of three to five benefits that are derived from having a regular PC maintenance schedule.

Project 1-4

Explore perceptions about customer support. Customer support services include answering questions and providing training, in addition to solving problems. Portable Internet-enabled devices such as two-way pagers, personal digital assistants (PDAs), and cellular telephones are becoming extremely popular. These devices are perceived to be fairly easy to use. Do they need to be supported? Talk to three friends or classmates that regularly use one of these devices. If you use one of these devices regularly, you can count yourself as an interviewee. Ask each person the following questions:

❐ How did you learn to use this device?

❐ If you had questions, how did you get answers?

❐ Are you using all of the features and functionality this device provides? If not, please explain why.

❐ Have you had any problems using this device? If so, how were they resolved?

Determine each person's *expectations* about how they would obtain user information and support for the device. Compare their expectations to their *perceptions* about any support services they actually received from a help desk (such as the help desk where they work) or from the product's manufacturer. Conclude whether the support services each person received failed to meet, met, or exceeded his or her expectations. Summarize your friends' or classmates' responses by briefly describing how customer expectations influence their perceptions and ultimately their satisfaction with customer support services.

Project 1-5

Compare reactive and proactive employees and companies. The term *fire fighting* is often used to describe the reactive way in which employees and companies approach their work. For example, it is not uncommon to hear an executive exclaim that he or she spent most of the day "fighting fires." Assemble a team of at least three of your classmates and discuss the challenges and drawbacks of fire fighting at work. Brainstorm and prepare a list of ways that real fire fighters are proactive. For example, fire fighters promote fire safety in an effort to prevent fires. See how many analogies you can draw between the way fire fighters work and the way a help desk works. When you are done, share your list with the rest of the class.

1

Project 1-6

Uncover processes and procedures. Many activities you are involved in follow specific processes and procedures. Think about a hobby or sport that you enjoy. Determine the "process" your hobby or sport requires and the "procedures" that make up that process. For example, if your hobby is flying model airplanes, flying the plane to its target destination is a process. Procedures include selecting a destination, preparing the plane for flight, taking off, avoiding obstacles, landing, and so on. Briefly describe the process your hobby or sport involves and list its associated procedures.

Project 1-7

Evaluate a company's technical support services. Visit the Web site for a hardware or software company that you do business with now or are considering doing business with in the future. For example, you could contact the company that manufactured your computer or published your favorite software package. Or visit one of the Web sites selected for The Association of Support Professionals' Ten Best Web Support Sites award. From the Web site you choose, do the following:

❐ Determine all the ways the company delivers technical support. Does it have a help desk?

❐ Find out what commitments, if any, the company makes about how it delivers customer support. For example, does it promise to respond to all inquiries within a certain time? Does it make any promises about how it handles telephone calls? Does it promise to provide access to knowledgeable analysts?

Critique the company's technical support services based on the information you found. Was it easy to locate this information about the company's support services? Do its technical support services encourage or discourage you from using the company's products? Write a report that summarizes your findings.

Project 1-8

Understand your customers' expectations. Customers have expectations, and you satisfy customers by meeting their expectations. Customers are anyone to whom you have delivered a product or service in a professional or personal setting. For example, a customer could be a family member for whom you cooked dinner, a neighbor whose lawn you mowed, a friend to whom you sold candy or greeting cards, parents whose children you babysat, or strangers whose car you washed at a fund raiser. Think about one customer you have had, and then answer the following questions:

❐ What product or service were you responsible for supplying to your customer?

❐ How did you determine your customer's expectations?

❐ Did you meet your customer's expectations?

❐ How did you know your customer was satisfied?

Write a report that summarizes and analyzes your experience.

Project 1-9

Compare your positive and negative customer experiences. Think about situations, within the past week or two, in which you were a customer. For example, you may have been a customer while dining at a restaurant or shopping in a local store. Select one positive experience and one negative experience. For each experience, do the following:

❑ Briefly describe the situation.

❑ Explain what made the customer service experience positive or negative.

❑ Suggest how the service encounter could have been handled better.

❑ Determine if your recommendation is feasible. For example, would you be willing to pay more or wait longer for service if that was a byproduct of implementing your suggestion?

Summarize what you learned from these experiences in a report.

Project 1-10

Determine the value of a product. Recall that value is the perceived worth, usefulness, or importance of a product or service to a customer. Assemble a team of at least three of your classmates. Select a product that everyone is familiar with and has purchased at some point. It does not have to be a hardware or software product (for example, you could select a clothing item or a medicine such as aspirin). Brainstorm and document the value of the selected item to you and your classmates.

CASE PROJECTS

1. Mama Mia Pizzeria Company

The Mama Mia Pizzeria Company hired you to set up a help desk for external customers who have questions about Mama's frozen pizzas. One of the things you must do is prepare a profile of the skills the help desk should possess. Prepare an outline that lists all the business, soft, technical, and self-management skills you recommend that management looks for in a potential help desk employee. Indicate which skills the potential employee should already have and which the employee could acquire through training.

2. Help Desk Resources

Your manager wants to improve the efficiency and effectiveness of the help desk. She asks you to locate potential help desk resources. Search the Web to locate any organizations your help desk can join or magazines your help desk can buy to learn more about the help desk industry and how other companies run their help desks. Prepare a report of your findings that includes the name and brief description of each organization and magazine you found, along with the URL of its associated Web site.

1

3. Secret Shopper

You have been hired as a "secret shopper" for a local restaurant or retail store. This means that, without telling the employees of the establishment, you will evaluate the service you receive the next time you visit, and report back to the owner. Select a restaurant or store you visit regularly. Before entering the restaurant or store, prepare a checklist of your expectations. For example, you expect to be greeted cheerfully upon entering the restaurant; you expect to be seated quickly and given a menu; and so forth. Visit the restaurant or store. After receiving service, indicate on the checklist how well the company met your expectations. Prepare a brief overview about the service you received.

2

HELP DESK OPERATIONS

Help desks, like any customer service and support organization, serve as a point of contact for customers and exist to ensure their satisfaction. Although this underlying purpose is the same from one organization to the next, the specific services the help desk offers and its operating characteristics (such as type, size, and structure) vary, depending on the needs of its customers. Customer needs determine the mission of both the larger corporation and the help desk. For example, if a company is highly committed to customer satisfaction, then the help desk's mission reflects this. The amount of resources (such as staffing and equipment) the company gives the help desk also reflects the company's mission and the priority it places on customer satisfaction.

To work in a help desk, you must understand the different types and sizes of help desks that exist, how they are structured, and the daily activities that employees perform in these different help desks. Also, it is important to know that your individual performance as a help desk employee will be measured against how well you contribute to the help desk's mission and to the company's mission.

Types of Customer Service and Support Organizations

Customer service and support organizations come in all shapes and sizes and deliver a wide range of services. These organizations can be either a company or a department within a company devoted to customer service and support. One type of customer service and support organization is a **call center**, which is a place where telephone calls are made, or received, in high volume. An **inbound call center** receives telephone calls from customers and may answer questions, take orders, respond to billing inquiries, and provide customer support. An **outbound call center** makes telephone calls to customers, primarily for telemarketing. **Telemarketing** is the selling of products and services over the telephone. Some call centers are **blended call centers**, which means that they receive incoming calls and make outgoing calls. The term **contact center** is being used increasingly to refer to a call center that uses technologies such as e-mail and the Web in addition to the telephone to communicate with its customers. Examples of call centers and contact centers include airline reservation centers, catalog ordering centers, and home shopping centers.

The help desk is another common type of customer service and support organization. Recall that a help desk is a single point of contact within a company for managing customer problems and requests and for providing solution-oriented support services. Help desks are often structured in a series of levels, an approach commonly known as a **multi-level support model**. In a multi-level support model, customers contact the help desk when they are unable to solve problems on their own. The help desk refers problems it cannot resolve to the appropriate internal group, external vendor, or subject matter expert. A **subject matter expert** (**SME**) is a person who has a high level of experience or knowledge about a particular subject.

 In the context of a multi-level support model, customers solving problems on their own using self-services is known as level zero. Self-services such as a help desk Web site that contains answers to frequently asked questions (FAQs) and a knowledge base of solutions to known problems empower customers to support themselves. Chapter 5 explores in detail how help desks use the Internet to provide self-services.

Level one is the help desk because it is the first point of contact for customers. If the level one help desk cannot resolve an incident, it hands off the incident to the next highest level, level two. Level two might consist of a development group for a particular software application, a network support group, or an expert in a particular application. If level two cannot resolve the problem, then it hands off the problem to level three, which is usually a software vendor, a hardware vendor, or a subject matter expert. The help desk's ultimate goal is to resolve a high percentage of problems at level one and to escalate a very low percentage of problems to level three. Figure 2-1 shows a multi-level support model. The goal of the multi-level support model is to resolve problems in the most efficient and cost-effective manner possible.

Not all help desks require three levels of support. For example, it is not uncommon for smaller help desks to have only two levels of support. This is particularly true in organizations that support primarily off-the-shelf computer software products. In those organizations, if a level one analyst cannot resolve a problem, he or she contacts the appropriate software vendor.

 Chapter 4 explores in detail the responsibilities of groups within a multi-level support model.

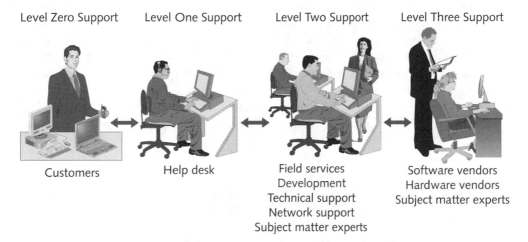

Level Zero Support   Level One Support   Level Two Support   Level Three Support

Customers   Help desk   Field services   Software vendors
Development   Hardware vendors
Technical support   Subject matter experts
Network support
Subject matter experts

Figure 2-1   Multi-level support model

An emerging type of customer service and support organization is the support center, which is a help desk with a broader scope of responsibility and the goal of providing faster service and improving customer satisfaction. New technologies have enabled this enhanced help desk to absorb many of the activities that relate directly to the customer from other support groups, such as network support, field support, and system administration. These other groups then can focus on tasks such as projects, operations activities, and maintenance activities. Thus, support centers handle problems and requests with greater efficiency because they hand off fewer incidents to other groups. This increases the value of their services to customers and the company because customers receive faster service, the other support groups can focus on their primary missions, and the company achieves a maximum return on its investment in the support center. Using the same multi-level support model as the help desk, the support center refers problems it cannot resolve to other groups or subject matter experts.

This book focuses on the help desk and the support center. Unlike call centers and contact centers, help desks and support centers are very similar in that customers can contact them using a number of methods, or channels, including the telephone, fax, e-mail, or the Web.

In some companies, customers can even walk in to the help desk or the support center for support. Another similarity is that help desks and support centers typically handle technology-oriented problems and questions, whereas a call center handles a wide range of problems and questions that may or may not be technology oriented.

HELP DESK MISSION

Without a clearly defined mission that is determined by its customers' needs, a help desk can fall prey to the "all things to all people" syndrome. A help desk's **mission** is a written statement that describes the customers the help desk serves, the types of services the help desk provides, and how the help desk delivers those services. In other words, a mission defines who the help desk supports, what it supports, and how it provides that support. These things determine the type, size, and structure of the help desk. The mission is like a roadmap the help desk can use to determine how it operates. A help desk's mission reflects the values expressed in the company's mission. A clearly defined mission also provides help desk management, staff, and customers with an overall objective against which they can measure performance. The essence of the mission is often captured in a mission statement. Figure 2-2 shows an example of a mission statement for a help desk.

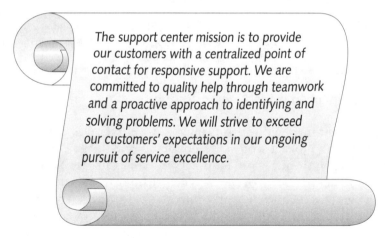

The support center mission is to provide our customers with a centralized point of contact for responsive support. We are committed to quality help through teamwork and a proactive approach to identifying and solving problems. We will strive to exceed our customers' expectations in our ongoing pursuit of service excellence.

Figure 2-2   Sample help desk mission statement

It is important that every help desk employee understand the help desk's mission—and how it fits into the company's mission—and his or her role in that mission. Companies whose employees understand both the company mission and their department mission attain considerably higher customer satisfaction rates than companies whose employees do not. These companies tend to experience high employee satisfaction rates as well because employees understand their purpose and know how to contribute to the department's mission and the company's mission.

When a department's mission reflects the company's mission, employees perform activities that support the mission and customers are satisfied. For example, if a company's mission is to be a low-cost provider of quality products, the help desk's mission may be to enhance product quality by delivering efficient, effective, and low-cost services. The mission of a help desk determines the type of help desk and how it operates.

There are two principal types of help desks: internal help desks and external help desks. An internal help desk supports internal customers, or the employees who work at its company, whereas an external help desk supports external customers, the people who buy a company's products and services. Some help desks support both internal customers and external customers, although that is somewhat uncommon. Regardless of whether the help desk has internal or external customers, it is still a customer service organization and, as such, must strive to meet its customers' needs.

INTERNAL HELP DESKS

An **internal help desk** responds to questions, distributes information, and handles problems and service requests for its company's employees. A company can have several types of internal help desks that employees contact for support. For example, employees usually go to the human resources (HR) department for questions about medical insurance or to receive directories of health-care providers. They contact the facilities department to have office fixtures installed or repaired. Similarly, they contact the company's information technology (IT) department about the hardware and software they use to accomplish their work. These departments all function as internal help desks because they serve internal customers and are responsible for satisfying those customers. This section focuses on the IT help desk, which may also be known as an IT service desk, customer support center, or support services.

Internal IT Help Desk's Role

Historically, IT departments focused solely on the technology for which they were responsible, such as hardware, software, and networks, and concentrated on ensuring that the systems were "up and running." They did not always focus on the technology users, nor did they always emphasize doing things as efficiently and cost-effectively as possible. Although IT departments provided a necessary function in the company, their role was limited.

IT departments are now being challenged to function as internal vendors. An **internal vendor** is a department or a person within a company that supplies information, products, or services to another department or person within the same company. For example, the HR department is an internal vendor of employment and company policy information and of paychecks to company employees. Like an external vendor, an internal vendor must supply a high-quality product on an agreed-upon schedule at an agreed-upon price. As an internal vendor, the IT department must supply competitively priced services that help the company's employees use technology to improve productivity and increase corporate profitability. To do this, the IT department must acknowledge that it is a customer service organization and provide a high level of service to its customers. It is no longer enough for the IT department to simply keep the company's computer systems in good working order. As a customer service organization, it must also ensure that customers receive maximum value for those computer systems. In other words, the IT department must ensure that customers perceive that the computer systems are useful. To do this, many IT departments are establishing help desks or enhancing their existing help desks. The IT help desk provides company employees a single point of contact within the IT department. The help desk acts as a customer advocate and ensures that quality services are being provided.

In an effort to satisfy their customers, most IT help desks strive to resolve 70 percent to 80 percent of reported problems and service requests. They also take ownership of all incidents, whether or not they can resolve them. **Taking ownership** of an incident means tracking the incident to ensure that the customer is kept informed about the status of the incident, that the incident is resolved within the expected time frame, and that the customer is satisfied with the final resolution.

Chapter 4 explores in detail the concept of ownership.

An internal help desk often participates in other activities besides assisting internal customers with problems. Especially in smaller organizations, the help desk can serve as a jack-of-all-trades and be actively involved in performing other functions, such as those listed in Figure 2-3.

- Training
- Network and system administration
- Asset management

Figure 2-3   Additional help desk functions

In larger organizations, separate groups and, possibly, even external vendors may perform some or all of these functions.

Training   Training involves preparing and delivering programs that provide people the knowledge and skills they need to use technology effectively. The help desk may also provide ad-hoc, or informal, and one-on-one training in the course of responding to users' questions and problems. Training is often a significant expense. Companies must spend a lot of time and money to develop and deliver the training, and users must leave their regular duties to attend the training. Not giving formal training to users and help desk staff can, however, be just as costly. The cost comes in the form of lost productivity as employees and help desk staff waste time trying to informally learn how to use systems, fix problems, and correct mistakes made because of lack of training.

Training might take place in a classroom setting with an instructor, on a one-on-one basis in a user's office, through media such as audio, video, computer-based training, or Internet-based training. **Computer-based training** (**CBT**) uses computer software packages to train and test people on a wide range of subjects. **Internet-based training** (**IBT**) uses training systems that people access from any personal computer that has an Internet connection and a browser. People benefit most when training programs deliver the appropriate content at the appropriate level. A training program should include basic or introductory classes for new users and advanced classes for those who have already mastered the basics. An effective training program reduces support costs and increases employee productivity and satisfaction. In other words, proper training means fewer calls to the help desk.

Network and System Administration Network and system administration activities include day-to-day tasks such as setting up and maintaining user accounts, ensuring that the data the company collects is secure, and performing e-mail and database management. Administrators protect the company's data by performing regular backup and restore procedures and by ensuring that backup and restore processes are in place and working. Other activities include file management, printer and server management, monitoring server and network performance, performance tuning, and capacity and disaster recovery planning.

Asset Management Asset management activities include moving equipment, installing and configuring new systems, and upgrading existing systems. These activities are often referred to as **moves**, **adds**, **and changes** (**MACs**). Most companies prefer to have experienced staff perform these tasks because they can complete them more quickly than an inexperienced user, and they know about and can avoid many of the problems that may occur during the installation process. Other asset management activities include ensuring that the hardware and software required to connect to the company's network are installed and operating properly, and distributing software. Asset management also includes keeping track of the location, condition, and status of all the company's technology assets. These activities often are referred to as asset tracking. Asset tracking also includes maintaining the legal and financial details associated with technology assets, such as licensing agreements and the terms of any lease, warranty, or support contracts that exist. Asset management activities are important because companies usually have a large investment in their technology and, understandably, want to protect that investment. Companies also want to maximize their return on investment by ensuring that the technology is utilized fully.

As the internal help desk's role has expanded, so has the variety of skills needed to keep it functioning smoothly. These skills vary considerably from one help desk to the next because the help desk must support the specific hardware, software, network, and application components a particular company uses. For example, supporting Microsoft

Windows is very similar from one company to the next, whereas supporting internally developed, or "home-grown," applications changes from company to company. The people who support these home-grown applications usually receive specialized training. The internal help desk can also expose analysts to and prepare them for opportunities that exist in other parts of the company. What better way to learn about the company than to interact regularly with people who work in different areas of the business?

Some internal help desks operate very informally. Others have very formal processes and require users to follow clearly defined procedures to obtain services. For example, some organizations have established Service Level Agreements with their internal clients. A **Service Level Agreement (SLA)** is a written document that spells out the services the help desk will provide to the customer, the customer's responsibilities, and how service performance is measured. Examples of customer responsibilities include:

- Customers must call the help desk (not someone else in the company) when they have a problem.

- Customers must maintain their systems.

- Customers must attend training.

An SLA helps to set customer expectations so customers don't have an unrealistic view of what support they should be getting. It also enables the help desk to know its limits for supporting internal customers and what it must do to satisfy them. SLAs are becoming increasingly necessary as organizations struggle to balance the need to satisfy ever-increasing internal customer demands with the costs associated with meeting those demands.

 Chapter 6 explores in detail how SLAs are used to manage customer expectations and measure help desk performance.

Internal Help Desk's Position in the Organization

Establishing and maintaining a help desk can be costly. One ongoing challenge that internal help desks face is proving their worth to the company. Although computers, tracking systems, and people are expensive, they are investments that help the company avoid lost productivity and lost opportunity, which are also costly but harder to quantify. Because productivity and opportunity cannot be purchased, there are no invoices for them. Yet the loss of them has a very real cost, even if it does not seem that "real" dollars are being spent. An efficient, effective help desk can help lower those costs by increasing the effectiveness with which employees can use technology. The help desk can also lower those costs by reducing the time employees cannot use technology because of problems or lack of information.

2

The technologies that internal help desks use to do their work usually reflect the company's willingness to invest in the help desk. Some companies have rudimentary systems, such as simple databases the help desk has developed in-house, whereas other companies have commercially developed, state-of-the-art problem management and resolution systems that were customized to meet the company's needs. Because people are the most expensive component of a help desk, companies are increasingly willing to invest in technology in an effort to maximize their human resources.

Few companies have the human resources required to provide unlimited customer service, and this is particularly true for an internal help desk. IT departments are notoriously understaffed, and because internal help desks have not historically charged for their services, they also tend to be underfunded. This situation is compounded by the fact that some internal help desks try to be all things to all people; in other words, they have a hard time saying no. In these cases, an underfunded help desk may ineffectively use its resources by stretching them too thin.

The best help desks strive to provide high-quality service within the limits of their funding. For example, an internal help desk may limit the products it supports in an effort to work within its limited resources. In other words, it prefers to provide quality service for fewer products rather than mediocre service for all products. Or, instead of rejecting requests that are beyond their capabilities (sometimes called **out-of-scope requests**), underfunded help desks provide the best possible alternative by directing the customer to another source that can help. These help desks are aware of their limitations and work diligently to balance customer needs with available resources.

EXTERNAL HELP DESKS

External help desks support customers who buy their company's products and services. In other words, the customers they support are not employees of the company. Most hardware and software companies have external help desks to support their customers. The services that external help desks provide vary by industry. For example, the external help desk of an equipment manufacturer may be responsible primarily for ensuring that field service representatives are dispatched to a customer site when a problem occurs. In this environment, a help desk usually resolves a fairly low percentage—10 percent to 15 percent—of the problems reported; the dispatched field service representatives solve the rest. The external help desk of a software publisher, on the other hand, may handle a majority of questions by telephone or through the Web and strive to resolve a very high percentage—80 percent to 90 percent—of the problems reported.

External Help Desk's Role

External help desks can provide a variety of services to customers. Some external help desks provide **pre-sales support**, meaning that they answer questions for people who have not yet purchased the company's products or services and may take orders and respond to billing inquiries. Most external help desks provide traditional **post-sales support**, which involves helping people who have purchased a company's product or service. Post-sales support activities include answering questions, helping the customer learn to use the product, explaining the advanced features that the product offers, and resolving problems.

The role of the external help desk is evolving as companies start to fully appreciate the fact that positive customer experiences help sell products and services. These companies recognize the enormous contribution the help desk makes by capturing and sharing customer feedback with the appropriate groups in the company. The company can then use this information to develop new and more desirable products and services. External help desks are continuously being challenged to build customer relationships and contribute to corporate growth and profitability. Many companies are implementing customer relationship management programs in an effort to serve their customers better. **Customer relationship management** (**CRM**) involves using customer contact and relationship information to generate additional sales and increase levels of customer service and retention. A CRM initiative involves implementing software products and processes that enable the help desk to collect, maintain, and share information about the company's customers with other authorized company employees.

External Help Desk's Position in the Organization

In much the same way that an internal help desk shares information with other groups, such as development and network support, an external help desk exchanges information with its company's sales, marketing, field services, development, and research and development (R&D) departments. By collecting and disseminating information about the company's customers, how those customers are using the company's products, and how customers would like those products enhanced, the external help desk provides an invaluable service to the company. Figure 2-4 illustrates how the external help desk collects information about the company's customers and shares that information with other departments.

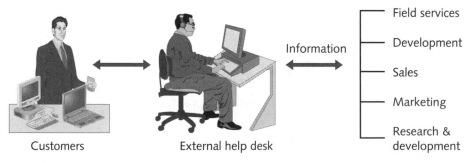

Figure 2-4   External help desk sharing information

External help desks have become a major focal point for customer interactions. They are responsible for creating a **customer memory**, a record that includes all the information and transactions relevant to a given customer. A sales representative who is planning to call a customer and suggest a new product can refer to the customer memory to find out if that customer recently had a problem with any existing product. A help desk analyst who is working with a customer to resolve a problem can use this integration of customer data to suggest that the customer upgrade to the next release of a product, or note the benefits the customer might receive from training provided by the company.

External help desks do not always face the same budget and staffing constraints as do internal help desks. Some external help desks cover their own costs by either (1) charging for their services or (2) including the support costs with the cost of the product. However, other external help desks experience the same underinvestment and understaffing problems as internal help desks. This occurs because some companies place a higher priority on selling and shipping products than on supporting products they have already sold. External help desks may also be challenged by an excessive and perhaps underfunded workload when the engineering department, in response to an extremely competitive situation, distributes a product before it has been fully tested, thus overwhelming the help desk for a while.

As with internal help desks, the resources available to an external help desk reflect the company's commitment to customer satisfaction and willingness to invest in the help desk. For example, some external help desks invest heavily in technologies that enable them to deliver exceptional services, such as highly sophisticated telephone systems and Web-based systems. These companies may, however, become so highly automated that customers feel alienated and view the help desk as an impenetrable point of entry to the company. Other companies invest heavily in training their help desk analysts and providing opportunities for them to specialize and attain a high level of knowledge and experience. Companies that become too highly automated do not invest in their staff fail to understand that the help desk is the "front door" into the company.

The best companies realize they must deliver high-quality products *and* superior customer support to retain today's savvy customers, who have increasingly high expectations. These companies value the help desk as a nucleus for customer service and as a primary means to capture and disseminate customer information. Also, they appreciate and reward people who understand the company's goals and actively contribute to them.

The Help Desk Institute (HDI) annually presents the *Team Excellence Award* to the team that most enhances the image of the help desk profession by setting and achieving the highest standards of excellence in customer support. HDI also presents individual awards such as their *All STAR Award* and *HDI Hero Award*. To learn more, go to **www.thinkhdi.com/community/ awardsexplained.asp**. The Service & Support Professionals Association (SSPA) presents an annual *STAR Award* to recognize excellence in nine categories of software and technical support. The SSPA also presents a *Webstar Service Award*, a *STAR Awards Hall of Fame*, a *Life Time Achievement Award*, and an individual award called the *SSPA ROSE Award*. To learn more, go to **www.thesspa.com** and click "Awards" (free visitor registration is required).

SIZES OF HELP DESKS

Help desks range in size from small to large. Although it may seem logical for small companies to have small help desks and large companies to have large help desks, that is not always the case. The size of a help desk is determined by its mission and the scope of its responsibilities. For example, the more customers and products a help desk supports, the larger it tends to be—in terms of staffing, budget, and so forth. The number of additional activities the help desk performs such as training, network and system administration, and so forth also influences its size.

Small Help Desks

Small help desks have anywhere from one to 10 people on staff. Companies may have small help desks for a number of reasons. For example, the help desk may be new and just getting started, or the company has limited its initial scope of responsibility to give it a chance to get off to a good start. Some help desks remain small simply because they do not receive a high volume of requests, they support products that are fairly stable and easy to use, or customers have other ways to obtain support, such as from a Web site. Figure 2-5 illustrates a small help desk setting.

Some companies have a single-person help desk, although most will grow to have more people in time, if only to provide backup for the primary analyst. Efficiently and effectively operating one-person help desks are rare, but they do occur. It takes a very organized and very easygoing person to manage the stress that often comes from being the only person available to answer calls.

Some large companies prefer to have a number of small help desks, rather than one large help desk. For example, a company might place a small help desk in each district office. Specialized departments, such as engineering or product testing, also might have separate help desks if they use highly specialized and sophisticated equipment.

Courtesy of Utility Partners, Inc.

Figure 2-5   Small help desk setting

Some smaller companies set up their help desks as a one-stop shop, which means that the help desk is fully responsible for resolving all problems and service requests, even if the solution requires extensive research or even coding changes. They don't hand off incidents to other groups or vendors, as in the multi-level support model. Although this may sound like a good way to provide support, it works well only if customers have simpler problems or are willing to occasionally wait for a solution. This is because complex or high priority problems that require a quick resolution can quickly consume the help desk's limited resources. As a result, customers with simpler problems can end up waiting a long time for service.

Small help desks can be world class, but they also face challenges. For example, small help desks tend to be people-dependent, which means that individual analysts specialize in a particular area, such as a customer community, vendor, product, or suite of products. As a result, they can be severely affected when someone leaves the company or is out because of illness or vacation. Small help desks may find it difficult to provide adequate training for their staff because every available person is needed to serve customers, and small help desks may not have the tools that enable them to capture knowledge and the information required to justify additional resources. Small help desks tend to be more informal, which is good for people who don't enjoy a highly structured environment or doing paperwork, but this can result in a highly reactive and stressful environment. All these challenges can be overcome by effectively using people, processes, technology, and information.

Working in small help desks can be gratifying to people who are highly motivated and capable of staying organized and managing stress. People working in smaller help desks can get to know their customers, tend to relate well to them, and fully understand their customers' needs. Small help desks usually offer people the opportunity to perform a diversity of tasks and assemble a broad base of skills.

Medium help desks have between 10 and 25 people on staff and can take on the characteristics of both small and large help desks.

Large Help Desks

Large help desks vary in size, depending on whether they are internal or external. Large internal help desks have more than 25 people on staff, whereas large external help desks can have as many as several hundred people. Large help desks evolved in several ways. Many grew from small help desks over the years as the company produced more products. Some large help desks were consolidated from several smaller help desks, an initiative that many companies undertook in the 1980s to reduce redundant support efforts and maximize their return on investment in people, processes, technology, and information. A large help desk can also occur as a result of a corporate merger or acquisition. Figure 2-6 shows a large help desk setting.

Courtesy of CompuCom Systems, Inc.

Figure 2-6   Large help desk setting

2

It is common for large help desks to be subdivided into specialty teams. Specialty teams can be product-oriented—one team supports a particular product or category of products—or customer-oriented—that is, one team supports a particular segment of the customer community or a specific customer account.

The challenges that large help desks face are different than those for small help desks. For example, large help desks, particularly those that have evolved over time, may lack the discipline that a larger work force needs. They sometimes retain their informal ways far longer than they should. As a result, in such organizations, many people make independent decisions about how to handle problems, which can cause inconsistent service. On the other hand, some large help desks are extremely performance oriented. For example, they place an excessive emphasis on efficiency (such as answering the phone quickly) and forsake effectiveness and quality. Either of these characteristics can lead to high stress levels that companies must work hard to manage.

Large help desks enable people to work in a team setting and usually offer many opportunities for advancement. People working in a large help desk can choose to specialize in a particular product or customer set, or they can decide to rotate through a number of different areas and experience a variety of customers and products.

Help desk size is a critical issue for companies, because it determines how much they invest in the help desk, which, in turn, determines the quality of service the help desk can deliver. Another factor that influences help desk size is its structure.

HELP DESK STRUCTURES

Some companies have a single **centralized help desk** that supports all of the technologies used by its customers. Others have multiple **decentralized help desks** that support specific products or customer communities. More often, companies use a combination of centralized and decentralized help desks.

Centralized Help Desks

A centralized help desk provides customers with a single point of contact for support services. Customers appreciate this approach because they do not have to determine whom to call within the company. Their problems and requests are more likely to be remembered and solved because a centralized help desk ensures that incidents are logged, solutions are delivered, and customers are satisfied. Because incidents are logged, the centralized help desk can identify trends easily and proactively take steps to prevent problems and questions.

Let's look at this approach in action. A common practice is for companies to have a level one help desk at a centralized location, such as the corporate office, and keep level two resources at remote offices. This practice uses the multi-level support model discussed earlier. Customers contact the level one help desk, which contacts the level two resources at the remote site *only* when the level one help desk cannot resolve an incident. However, some customers at remote offices search out these on-site resources by going directly to level two staff or stopping the level two staff in the hall, rather than first calling the level one help desk. Customers often perceive that they are receiving a very high level of service when they can call or visit an on-site resource. In reality, customers who directly contact level two resources quickly become dissatisfied if these limited local resources are not available because they are already working on a problem, attending training, or taking vacation. Also, because on-site resources are constantly being pulled in different directions, they may not log customer problems, which might then be lost or forgotten. In addition, because problems are not logged, their solutions typically are not logged either. As a result, the level one help desk and the on-site resources at all of the company's sites may solve the same problem multiple times because a solution identified at one site is not available to the others. A trend is to provide on-site analysts with personal digital assistants (PDAs) that can be used to capture information about customer problems and requests when they cannot readily access the company's call tracking system. A **personal digital assistant** (**PDA**) is a small mobile hand-held device that provides computing and information storage and retrieval capabilities for personal or business use.

A centralized help desk receives a wide diversity of calls on any given day. Because of this, effective tools and adequate training are key. Without them, analysts can find the centralized help desk a frustrating place to work. However, a clear management vision, an effective training program, and a desire to continuously learn new skills make the centralized help desk an exciting and dynamic place to work.

Decentralized Help Desks

Some companies establish multiple decentralized help desks in an effort to provide a high level of service to customers with specific needs. When help desk services are decentralized, procedures or technology must direct customers to the appropriate help desk, based on their questions or problems. A decentralized help desk can provide fast resolutions for incidents because customers receive expert assistance immediately from someone familiar with their needs and who may be on-site as well. However, if customers contact the wrong help desk for a problem, resolution can take longer.

Help desks can be decentralized in several ways. Some companies establish internal help desks at each of their corporate offices. This approach provides customers with on-site assistance but can duplicate the same services from office to office. Other companies have specialized help desks that customers contact based on their needs. For example, PC users call one number, mainframe users call another, and customers experiencing a network problem call another. Although the goal is to match customers with the help desk best able to assist them, customers can find it difficult to determine which help desk to call. PC users accessing the mainframe through a local area network (LAN) or from a remote PC, for instance, might call either the PC help desk *or* the mainframe help desk *or* the network help desk. Some companies establish regional help desks to make their

2

customers feel more comfortable. For example, global companies commonly establish one help desk in the Americas to support customers there and, possibly, in Canada, another in Europe to support customers there, and still another in Asia to support customers in the Pacific Rim. These companies have found that factors such as language, culture, legal issues, and time-zone considerations warrant a decentralized approach.

Decentralized help desks face challenges in providing quality support and service. For example, they sometimes have difficulty justifying the resources that a centralized help desk can justify. As a result, resource limitations can cause the help desk to become overwhelmed. Another challenge that decentralized help desks must overcome is communicating to customers what they should do—what help desk they should call—when problem symptoms are unclear. Also, they must define procedures for handling those times when the customer has contacted the "wrong" help desk. Without clearly defined procedures for handling these situations, customers may be referred continually from one part of the company to another without getting their questions answered. Ultimately, the customer will become dissatisfied.

CLOSE UP

CALVIN HASTINGS
MANAGING DIRECTOR
MOUSE
NEW YORK, NEW YORK
www.mouse.org

MOUSE (Making Opportunities for Upgrading Schools and Education) is a nonprofit organization funded by the local business community, private foundations, and government agencies, which works with high schools and middle schools in New York City to set up student-run help desks called MOUSE Squads. Founded in 1997, MOUSE launched its MOUSE Squad program in early 2001 with squads in three high schools in Brooklyn, Manhattan, and Queens. Currently in 32 schools citywide, MOUSE hopes to establish squads in 40 schools by 2003 and expand further by 2004.

Organization. MOUSE Squads (MSs) are elite teams of high school and middle school students recruited to set up and run a technology help desk in their schools. The MSs operate during the school day and after school to provide teachers, administrators, and students with a trained support staff to troubleshoot and solve technical problems. On average, MSs provide their schools with over 20 hours of Level 1 technical support each week, up to 1,000 hours throughout the school year. Each squad has an average of seven students per squad per year.

Using help desk industry best practices as a guide, MOUSE has developed the MOUSE Squad program that includes a training program for both squad Faculty Advisors and student participants, operating processes and procedures, a Microsoft Access–based Ticket Filing System, and MOUSE Squad materials such as a Guide

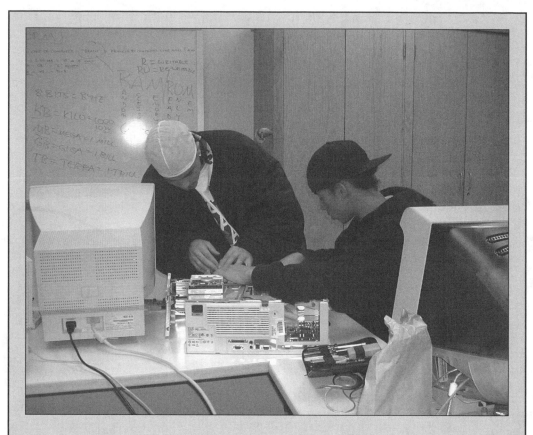

to MS for Teachers, an MS Help Desk Operations Manual, and an MS Technical Support Manual.

MOUSE has also created a number of incentives in order to promote individual and team excellence in MOUSE Squad. Individual incentives include a Technician of the Year Award, an Information Manager of the Year Award, the opportunity to participate in advanced training workshops, the opportunity to qualify for a tuition-free summer technical certification course (A+), and eligibility for technical certification exam scholarships. Students are also given the opportunity to participate in IT School-to-Career Workshops that enable them to explore careers in Information Technology. Team incentives include a MOUSE Squad School Service Award and an annual Management Information System Contest that is held to promote the use of Help Desk data to develop and implement strategies that improve the capacity of the school community to use technology.

Each MS has a Faculty Advisor who has direct responsibility for his or her school's squad. The Faculty Advisor also functions as a point person for communication between MOUSE and the school's squad. At the start of each school year, MOUSE trains the Faculty Advisors, who in turn recruit the students who will make up the current year's squads. Students from throughout the city come together (most recently at Columbia University) and engage in a series of hands-on workshops where they learn how to run a technical support help desk. In addition to learning basic troubleshooting skills, students learn customer-relations skills and the role that data plays in developing a technical support solution.

Back at their schools, squads establish a Base of Operations where students can meet with their Faculty Advisor and store MOUSE-related equipment. Each squad conducts an inventory of their school's technology and ensures the MS is aligned with the school's technology plan. Squads set up ticket collection sites that teachers and students use to report technology problems. To ensure their resources are used effectively, squads adopt a strict "No Ticket, No Service" policy that is published at the start of and throughout the school year. This policy also ensures that data is collected that can then be used to prioritize problems, refer problems to Level 2 when necessary, and measure the success of the Help Desk.

Tasks. Students participating in the MS program can assume one or more of three roles: Technician, Team Leader, or Information Manager. All members of the squad serve as Technicians, which means they provide an average of at least five hours of weekly service on the Help Desk and must log those hours in the Hours Log. Technicians respond to ticket requests to the best of their ability, complete scheduled maintenance projects, log ticket requests on a daily basis, and participate in weekly team meetings and required training sessions.

Ticket requests and projects may include activities such as fixing a computer that is frozen, installing, upgrading, and configuring operating systems, configuring Web browsers, resolving malfunctions with internal hardware components (such as CD-ROM drives and NICs) and hardware peripherals (such as keyboards and printers), loading and configuring software applications, and troubleshooting software problems.

In keeping with their commitment to provide polite, prompt, and skilled technical support, squads develop and hand out Customer Satisfaction Surveys once per semester that measure not only how quickly and how well squads handle requests, but also how well they serve their school community in general.

Problems that cannot be resolved by the Level 1 Help Desk are referred out to Level 2. The Level 2 resources that are available vary from one school to the next. For example, some schools have a Technology Coordinator, while other schools hire consultants to address higher-level issues.

The Team Leader is the student manager of the MS Help Desk. In addition to his or her duties as a Technician, it is the Team Leader's responsibility to coordinate the weekly schedule to ensure maximum Help Desk coverage, oversee responses to ticket requests, ensure maintenance activities are being completed, ensure that Help Desk data is being properly logged, and facilitate communication among squad members. The Team Leader also provides the Faculty Advisor with periodic updates and oversees the Help Desk's Base of Operations.

The Information Manager (IM) manages data and information related to the MS Help Desk, in addition to his or her duties as a Technician. In keeping with the program's focus on data collection and analysis, the IM compiles regular reports for MS members and the Faculty Advisor and coordinates efforts to use Help Desk data to support and modify services and to identify MS training needs. Most importantly, the IM catalogs completed ticket requests and hour logs in the MS database and sends database updates to MOUSE via e-mail on a weekly basis. MOUSE aggregates the data each semester and sends it to the District's Information Technology Director and to the Principals and Faculty Advisors at the individual schools. This continuous feedback loop promotes awareness of MS activities and ensures the goals of the program are being met.

Philosophy. MOUSE maintains three specific goals for the successful implementation of MOUSE Squads in schools: (1) To improve the educational and career opportunities of youth by providing a hands-on, standards-based information technology school-to-career program for public school students; (2) To provide a student-powered solution to the technical support crisis facing urban middle and high schools; and (3) To support the effective use of technology in teaching and learning in public schools by helping to create a more reliable technology infrastructure. This program is not just about establishing help desks in schools. More importantly, MOUSE Squad creates an opportunity for students to be of service to their schools while learning hands-on technical, teamwork, problem-solving, and other job readiness skills by running a school-based technology help desk. Students who participate in the MOUSE Squad program are given the chance to learn about and prepare for careers in the information technology field in a real-world setting.

Centrally Decentralized Help Desks

Some companies, particularly large companies, take a "centrally decentralized" approach to delivering help desk services. This approach combines a single, central help desk with multiple, specialized help desks. Customers contact the central help desk first. If it is unable to assist them, the central help desk uses common tools and processes to seamlessly transfer the customer to the appropriate help desk within the company. This approach eliminates the need for customers to determine what help desk to call and yet enables the individual help desks to focus on their specific scope of responsibility. The process of determining a customer's need and routing him or her to the appropriate support group is known as **triage**. If it is determined that the customer has an immediate need, his or her problem may be expedited more quickly or given a higher priority.

HELP DESKS AS COST CENTERS OR PROFIT CENTERS

Help desk services can cost companies a considerable amount of money. Whether internal or external, small or large, centralized or decentralized, help desks need many resources—tangible and intangible—to run. Figure 2-7 shows some common help desk expenses.

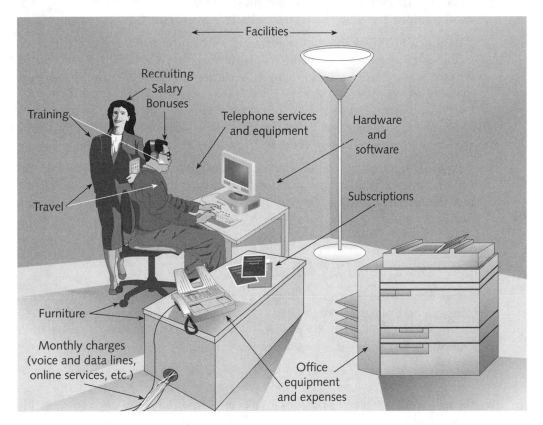

Figure 2-7   Help desk expenses

To pay for these expenses, help desks are run either as cost centers or as profit centers.

Help Desks as Cost Centers

Historically, help desks have been **cost centers**, in which the budget items required to run the help desk are considered a cost (or expense) to the company. When a help desk is run as a cost center, management's main objective is to minimize and eliminate expenses so that profits will be as high as possible. In the past, some help desks tried to recover some of their expenses by charging customers for each call. This approach was not always successful because customers were instructed by their managers, who also wanted to contain costs, not to call the help desk. They would then waste precious time trying to resolve problems themselves or with coworkers. Managers couldn't always see that this approach incurred "hidden" costs in the form of lost productivity and peer-to-peer support. The cost of peer-to-peer support often equals or even exceeds the cost of formal help desk support. For example, imagine the cost to a company if a lawyer or an engineer spends a portion of his or her day assisting coworkers with their computer problems. If managers understood these hidden costs, perhaps they would be more willing to pay "real" dollars to the help desk for support.

Running a help desk as a cost center can reduce the need to track expenses and effort in the detailed manner the help desk would have to if it were a profit center. Also, help desks run as cost centers can focus on existing customers because they do not have to market their services and generate new customers the way a profit center does. On the other hand, help desks run as a cost center may not be given the resources and management support they need, despite the fact that they often support millions of dollars worth of technology investments and customer relationships.

To remedy this, many help desks define standards that limit help desk services in some way. For example, help desks may support only certain products or they may limit the hours that the help desk is open. By defining standard services, the help desk can ensure that it is staffed properly and has the resources it needs (such as hardware, software, training, and so on) to deliver high-quality support.

Help Desks as Profit Centers

Some help desks are run as **profit centers**, in which the help desk must cover its expenses and, perhaps, make a profit by charging a fee for support services. Rather than charge for each call, as in the past, many help desks base the fee for their services on the company's actual cost to provide the services, plus a reasonable profit margin.

Some organizations, particularly internal help desks, establish the help desk as an overhead expense; each department in the company is assessed a fee based on how great its need is for help desk services. For example, a department might be assessed a fee based on the number of desktop computers it has. This fee might cover standard help desk services during normal business hours. Departments can then opt to obtain premium services—such as after-hours support or holiday support—at an additional fee.

Other organizations, particularly external help desks, establish detailed pricing structures that allow customers to choose free services (self-help services such as Web-based and fax-back systems), fee-based standard services, or premium services. In charging for help desk services, organizations recognize the increased cost of delivering nonstandard services.

Help desks run as profit centers can often justify expenses and acquire needed resources by demonstrating their benefit in the form of increased revenue. This is a positive benefit of profit centers because lack of resources, such as tools, training, and procedures, contributes to the stress and frustration of analysts. One drawback to the help desk as a profit center is that the staff must account for every activity they perform throughout the day.

Whether run as a cost center or profit center, help desks are under increasing pressure to analyze and control their costs, market the value of their services, and—without alienating customers—charge a premium for "customized" services. This approach requires that each and every person appreciate the fact that his or her actions contribute to the company's bottom line.

GROWTH OF OUTSOURCING

In the 1980s, organizations began to **outsource** their help desk services—that is, to have services provided by an outside supplier instead of providing them in-house. Companies that provide help desk outsourcing services are often called **service agencies**. Service level agreements (SLAs) are typically used to determine the services that a service agency will provide. Many managers thought outsourcing would be more cost-effective, but in many cases, this strategy didn't save the companies any money. The reason was that few companies understood what it cost to deliver services internally, so they could not make an accurate cost comparison. For example, companies whose internal staff were not logging all the calls they were handling did not know their actual call volume and were shocked when the service agency began billing them for a higher number of calls than expected.

Some companies naively hired an outsourcer in the mistaken notion that they could wash their hands of service problems. They found, however, that outsourcing support did not make service problems go away. Instead, it added another layer of complexity to the problem. For example, the issue of who retains ownership of outstanding problems, the service agency or the company, is a hotly debated topic when SLAs are being negotiated. Companies "assume" the service agency will retain ownership, while service agencies try to make it clear that companies must be willing to pay for that service. As a result, many early outsourcing engagements failed and companies reestablished their internal help desks.

Despite these early misconceptions and failings, help desk outsourcing is a rapidly growing industry for a number of reasons. First, many companies realize that although the help desk is a critical service for their customers, they lack either the ability or the desire to build and manage this function internally. These companies do not consider the help desk their company's primary purpose—or core competency—and choose to hire a company that does. Second, some companies are unwilling to make the capital investments required to deliver competitive help desk services. Third, some companies want to accommodate after-hours or peak volumes that may arise as a result of seasonal or project-driven business fluctuations—such as a new release of software—without increasing staffing levels.

A better understanding of how to negotiate SLAs and monitor those agreements has led to more successful outsourcing engagements. For example, many service agencies now monitor call volumes and proactively notify companies if the call volume is higher than normal or approaching a predefined threshold. Also, many service agencies are moving beyond traditional reactive help desk services and offering incident prevention services. For example, a service agency may produce and analyze trend reports and recommend ways the company can reduce or prevent certain types of help desk incidents.

Help desk service agencies offer a variety of technical support services. Outsourcers can act as an external help desk, such as when they provide support for original equipment manufacturers (OEMs); or they can act as an internal help desk, such as when they provide support for the employees of a company. A service agency can take over all or part of a company's support services. Some companies outsource specific activities, such as training, network and system administration, and asset management.

 Some of the largest providers of help desk outsourcing services include CompuCom Systems, Inc., Electronic Data Systems Corporation (EDS), International Business Machines Corporation (IBM), SafeHarbor Technology Corporation, STI Knowledge, Inc., and Sykes Enterprises, Inc.

Service agencies' charges to customers vary. For example, some service agencies pay their employees an hourly rate and then charge customers that rate plus a reasonable profit. Some service agencies charge customers a fee for each call; this fee may increase during certain times, such as after-hours or on weekends. Still other service agencies offer a "menu" of standard and optional services, such as the one shown in Table 2-1, that enable customers to determine the level of service they want. Increasingly, service agencies are being paid for performance, based on measurable indicators spelled out in their service contracts. Measurable indicators include how quickly service agencies respond to customers, the percentage of incidents they resolve, how well they keep customers informed, and overall customer satisfaction.

Table 2-1   Sample pricing "menu" for help desk services

Fee	Service	Cost per Call
Standard	Standard support hours (HH:MM – HH:MM, x days per week)	$
Optional	Extended support hours (24 hours per day, 7 days per week)	$
Optional	Holiday support (standard support hours)	$
Optional	Holiday support (extended support hours)	$
Standard	Toll-free service	$
Standard	Online (or Web-based) service	$
Optional	E-mail service	$
Optional	Customized interfaces (for example, to a customer's problem management system)	$
Standard	Entitlement Verification • To help desk services • To level two/level three services (such as on-site support)	$
Optional	Incident ownership	$
Standard	Incident logging and tracking	$
Standard	Problem diagnosis	$

Table 2-1   Sample pricing "menu" for help desk services (continued)

Fee	Service	Cost per Call
Optional	Remote diagnosis (utilizing remote control software)	$
Standard	Problem resolution	$
Standard	Dispatching or escalating to level two or level three support	$
Optional	Multi-vendor management	$
Optional	Weekly performance reporting	$
Standard	Monthly performance reporting	$
Optional	Customized reports	$
Optional	Trend and root cause analysis	$
Standard	Customer satisfaction verification and follow-up prior to incident closure	$
Optional	Independent survey services (such as to measure customer satisfaction)	$
Total Cost per Call		

Service agency employees must keep careful records of their time and effort. The agencies use these records to create customer invoices and to measure employee performance. Because the success and profitability of the service agency is based on the quality of the services their staff delivers, many service agencies carefully screen applicants, offer extensive training for new hires, and provide ongoing training. These companies expect to see a return on their training investment in the form of satisfied customers.

Companies now realize that when they outsource they are establishing a complex partnership in an effort to focus on their mission, expand their services, or contain costs. These companies recognize that when they outsource certain services, they do not outsource their customers. Therefore, companies that outsource services must show that they remain deeply committed to their customers' satisfaction by rigorously measuring and managing their service agency's performance.

THE SUPPORT CENTER MODEL

As the support industry has evolved, there has been an important shift toward consolidating support services. First, many companies consolidated multiple decentralized help desks into fewer help desks or a single, centralized help desk. Now, companies are further consolidating their support services into support centers. As discussed earlier, support centers deliver services that historically were provided by other support functions, such as network support, field support, and system administration. The support center model enables the help desk to deliver more services directly to their customers. This trend is challenging managers throughout the company to move customer-related transactions into the support center. Companies develop support centers because of customer demand, the desire to streamline business processes, and a need to reduce costs. By expanding their services beyond those traditionally offered by the help desk, the support center can avoid engaging groups unnecessarily, thus delivering services more efficiently and cost-effectively to customers. Figure 2-8 shows the expanded services being offered by support centers.

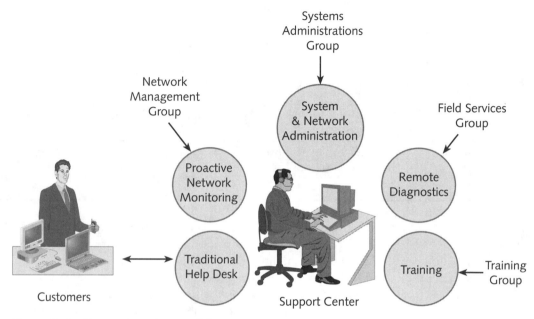

Figure 2-8   Support center model

Technology is enabling this further consolidation of support services. For example, network management tools are making it possible for the support center to perform proactive network monitoring rather than waiting to hear about a problem from the network management group. Because the support center now has the ability to do proactive network monitoring, it can detect problems more quickly, contact the network management group, and then inform customers that the company is aware of a network problem and that it is being resolved.

Another area in which technology is consolidating support services is remote support. In the past, the help desk dispatched a field service technician to investigate problems it could not properly diagnose, or required customers to ship their equipment to the help desk, resulting in a delay of hours or even days. With remote support technologies, the help desk can take control of networked devices to resolve problems, distribute software, and deliver informal training on the spot. This leaves field service technicians free to work on complex problems or projects, such as installing new systems.

A third example of consolidation is in the area of system administration. Rather than hand off a service request to the system administration group, many support centers are setting up and maintaining user accounts and performing some security functions. Taking over this function has reduced the time required to satisfy these requests.

 Chapter 5 explores in detail the technologies used by help desks.

Under the support center model, companies can deliver services more efficiently and effectively, increasing customer satisfaction. Some organizations further enhance this model by rotating subject matter experts (such as application developers and customer representatives) through the support center so they can share their knowledge with the permanent staff and enhance communications between coworkers. Many companies that have adopted the support center model see an increase in employee satisfaction because help desk analysts have expanded responsibilities and are given the tools and skills needed to resolve incidents quickly and correctly.

The help desk industry is growing and changing, and clearly, one size does *not* fit all. Because there are so many different types and sizes of help desks, people who want to enter the help desk industry can choose from a range of opportunities. The dramatic rise in the number of help desk classes in colleges and technical schools is evidence that the help desk industry is becoming increasingly important and that the available opportunities are growing. Companies are actively recruiting candidates for the thousands of new help desk positions opening up around the world.

CHAPTER SUMMARY

- ☐ Although the underlying purpose of the help desk is the same from one organization to the next, the services it offers and its operating characteristics such as type, size, and structure vary, depending on the needs of the company and its customers. A company's commitment to satisfying its customers determines its help desk's mission as well as its investment in the help desk.

- ☐ Call centers, contact centers, help desks, and support centers are all examples of customer service and support organizations. Call centers make or receive telephone calls in high volume and handle a wide range of problems and questions. Contact centers are call centers that use technologies such as e-mail and the Web in addition to the telephone. Help desks and supports centers tend to handle technology-oriented problems and questions. Customers can contact them using a number of methods, including the telephone, fax, e-mail, or the Web.

❑ The two principal help desk types are internal help desks and external help desks. An internal help desk supports the employees of its company, whereas an external help desk supports the people who buy its company's products or services. Within these two categories, some organizations are small and others are large, some are centralized and others are decentralized, some are run as cost centers and others as profit centers. All have strengths and all have challenges.

❑ The skills required to work in these different organizations vary. People who consider the strengths and challenges of the different help desk types can determine the type of help desk opportunities they choose to pursue.

❑ Help desk outsourcing is a rapidly growing industry. The relationship between a company and a service agency is a complex partnership aimed at enabling the company to focus on its mission, expand its services, and contain costs. The success and profitability of a service agency is based on the quality of the services the help desk delivers to its customers.

❑ The consolidation of support services continues to be a primary theme in the support industry. The support center model challenges managers throughout the company to move transactions that directly involve customers into the support center. Technology is enabling a further consolidation of support services, which is resulting in more efficiently and effectively delivered services.

KEY TERMS

blended call centers — Call centers that receive incoming calls *and* make outgoing calls.

call center — A place where telephone calls are made, or received, in high volume.

centralized help desk — A single help desk that supports all of the technologies used by its customers.

computer-based training (CBT) — Computer software packages used to train and test people on a wide range of subjects.

contact center — A call center that uses technologies such as e-mail and the Web in addition to the telephone.

cost centers — A help desk in which the budget items required to run the help desk are considered a cost (expense) to the company.

customer memory — A record that includes all the information and transactions relevant to a given customer.

customer relationship management (CRM) — A program that involves using customer contact and relationship information to generate additional sales and increase levels of customer service and retention.

decentralized help desks — Multiple help desks, each of which supports specific products or customer communities.

external help desks — Help desks that support customers who buy their company's products and services (external customers).

2

inbound call center — A call center that receives telephone calls from customers and may answer questions, take orders, respond to billing inquiries, and provide customer support.

internal help desk — A help desk that responds to questions, distributes information, and handles problems and service requests for its company's employees (internal customers).

internal vendor — A department or a person within a company that supplies information, products, or services to another department or person within the same company.

Internet-based training (IBT) — Training systems that people access from any personal computer that has an Internet connection and a browser.

large help desks — Internal help desks that have more than 25 people on staff, or external help desks that have as many as several hundred people on staff.

medium help desks — Help desks that have between 10 and 25 people on staff; can take on the characteristics of both small and large help desks.

mission — A written statement that describes the customers the help desk serves, the types of services the help desk provides, and how the help desk delivers those services.

moves, adds, and changes (MACs) — Activities that include moving equipment, installing and configuring new systems, and upgrading existing systems.

multi-level support model — A common structure of help desks, where the help desk refers problems it cannot resolve to the appropriate internal group, external vendor, or subject matter expert.

one-stop shop — A help desk that is fully responsible for resolving all problems and service requests, even if the solution requires extensive research or even coding changes.

outbound call center — A call center that makes telephone calls to customers, primarily for telemarketing.

out-of-scope requests — Requests that are beyond the capabilities of the help desk.

outsource — To have services provided by an outside supplier instead of providing them in-house.

personal digital assistant (PDA) — A small mobile hand-held device that provides computing and information-storage and retrieval capabilities for personal or business use.

post-sales support — Helping people who have purchased a company's product or service.

pre-sales support — Answering questions for people who have not yet purchased a company's products or services.

profit centers — A help desk that must cover its expenses and, perhaps, make a profit by charging a fee for support services.

service agencies — Companies that provide help desk outsourcing services.

Service Level Agreement (SLA) — A written document that spells out the services the help desk will provide to the customer, the customer's responsibilities, and how service performance is measured.

small help desks — Help desks that have anywhere from one to 10 people on staff.

subject matter expert (SME) — A person who has a high level of experience or knowledge about a particular subject.

taking ownership — Tracking an incident to ensure that the customer is kept informed about the status of the incident, that the incident is resolved within the expected time frame, and that the customer is satisfied with the final resolution.

telemarketing — The selling of products and services over the telephone.

triage — The process of determining a customer's need and routing him or her to the appropriate support group.

REVIEW QUESTIONS

1. List and briefly describe the four types of customer service and support organizations described in this chapter.

2. When incidents that cannot be resolved at the help desk are referred to another group, an external vendor, or a subject matter expert, they are being referred to the next _____ of support.

3. List the three components of a help desk mission.

4. Why do companies experience higher customer and employee satisfaction when employees understand the company's mission and their department's mission?

5. A help desk that supports a company's employees is a(n) _____ help desk.

6. A help desk that supports the customers that buy a company's products and services is a(n) _____ help desk.

7. How can an IT department function as an internal vendor?

8. Define the concept of ownership in a help desk setting.

9. List and briefly describe three activities an internal help desk may perform in addition to assisting customers with problems.

10. Describe two ways that an efficient, effective internal help desk can help reduce costs.

11. Why are internal support organizations increasingly willing to devote funds to technology investments?

12. Describe two ways an external help desk helps its company sell products and services.

13. What does CRM involve and what are its goals?

14. A(n) _____ includes all the information and transactions relevant to a given customer.

15. What must companies do to retain today's savvy customers?

16. What are three reasons some help desks remain small?

17. What challenges are faced by help desks that are people-dependent?

18. List at least three benefits of working in a small help desk.

19. What are two ways specialty teams in a large help desk can be oriented?

20. List four benefits of working in a large help desk.

21. What are three benefits of a centralized help desk?

22. Why do some companies establish multiple decentralized help desks?

23. List four factors that may prompt global companies to establish multiple help desks.

24. What are the benefits of combining a single centralized help desk with multiple decentralized help desks?

25. Describe the triage process.

26. What does it mean when a help desk is run as a cost center?

27. Describe how internal and external help desks that run as profit centers determine their service fees?

28. List the three primary reasons that help desk outsourcing is a rapidly growing industry.

29. Why must people who work for service agencies keep careful records?

30. How do companies that have outsourced their support services ensure their customers' satisfaction?

31. List three ways that new technologies are enabling the support center to deliver help desk services more efficiently and effectively.

HANDS-ON PROJECTS

Project 2-1

Consider your options (Part 1). Think about the two primary help desk types discussed in this chapter: internal help desks and external help desks. What type of help desk would you like to work at? Why? Explain your choice in one or two paragraphs.

Project 2-2

Consider your options (Part 2). Think about the two primary help desk sizes discussed in this chapter: small help desks and large help desks. What size of help desk would you like to work at? Why? Explain the reasons for your choice in a paragraph or two.

Project 2-3

Discuss help desk types. Assemble a team of at least three of your classmates. Discuss the following types of help desk operations:

- Centralized versus decentralized

- Cost center versus profit center

Prepare a list of the advantages and disadvantages that people may experience working at these different types of help desks.

Project 2-4

Determine a company's mission. Visit the Web site for a hardware or software company you do business with or are considering doing business with in the future. For example, you could contact the company that manufactured your computer or published your favorite software package. From the Web site, determine the following:

- Does the company have a help desk mission statement? If so, what is its mission?

- Describe the support services offered:

  - Free

  - For a standard fee

  - At an optional (premium) rate

- Does the help desk provide pre-sales support as well as post-sales support?

- How does the help desk say it delivers services (for example, professionally, courteously, etc.)?

- What you have learned about external help desks in this chapter, what else can you learn about this company's help desk from its Web site?

Critique the company's mission based on the information you found. Write a report that summarizes your findings.

Project 2-5

Learn about help desk industry awards. Visit the Web site of either the Help Desk Institute (**www.thinkhdi.com/community/awardsexplained.asp**) or the Service & Support Professionals Association (**www.thesspa.com** and click "Awards"). Review the awards that the organization presents. Prepare a brief paper that answers the following questions:

- What criteria do these organizations use to select recipients of their "team" excellence awards?

- What criteria do these organizations use to select recipients of their "individual" excellence awards?

Briefly describe the benefits you believe that companies and individuals derive from being award winners.

Project 2-6

Assist a small help desk. A single-person help desk is a challenging place to work, and its inherent stresses can lead to burnout. Assemble a team of at least three of your classmates. Discuss and list the factors that most likely contribute to burnout in this situation. For each factor you identify, explore ways that the burnout can be avoided.

Project 2-7

Analyze your school help desk. Assemble a team of at least three of your classmates. Identify all the ways that help desk services are delivered at your school, perhaps by visiting the help desk's Web site. If your school doesn't have a help desk, use the help desk at a company where one of your teammates works. Are the services centralized? Are there multiple decentralized help desks? If there are multiple help desks, how do customers determine which one to call? Having discovered how services are delivered, discuss ways the services could be refined to make it easier for customers to obtain support. If you feel the services are being delivered well as they are, explain why. Prepare and present a brief report.

Project 2-8

Learn about help desk outsourcing. Visit the Web sites of three of the help desk outsourcing companies mentioned in this chapter. For each company, write a paragraph that describes the following:

- ❑ What services do they deliver?
- ❑ What do they consider standard services, and what do they offer as optional services?
- ❑ How do they distinguish themselves from their competition?
- ❑ What do they say about their staff?
- ❑ What do they say about their hiring practices?
- ❑ What do they say about satisfying their customers?

CASE PROJECTS

1. School Help Desk

You've been assigned the task of preparing a first draft of a mission for the new school help desk to be set up in your school's computer lab. In addition to supporting students attending classes on campus, this help desk must also accommodate distance learners (that is, students who are taking correspondence courses or Web-based classes). Based on your knowledge of your school (review its Web site if you need additional information) and your own need for support as a student, draft a mission for the new help desk. Document your answers to the following questions:

- ❑ Who needs support?
- ❑ What kind of support do they need?
- ❑ How should the support be delivered?

To view the Web sites of other colleges and universities, search the Web for topics such as "academic computing" and "university help desk."

2. Sticks & Stuff

You were recently hired as the internal help desk manager for Sticks & Stuff, a hockey equipment manufacturer that uses several off-the-shelf software packages as well as a number of home-grown applications. After only two weeks with this small help desk, you realize that the help desk is trying to be "all things to all people" and that the staff is getting burned out. There are no defined standards of what the help desk should support, and the company's employees call about anything and everything from technology questions to burned-out lightbulbs in their offices. Draft a brief presentation for management outlining the pitfalls of the current situation and suggest three to five ways to remedy the situation.

3. Julian's Gourmet Recipes

You've been hired as a consultant by Julian's Gourmet Recipes to help it turn the help desk that supports its external customers into a profit center. Julian sells a software package that comes with hundreds of recipes and to which users can add their own recipes. Julian's customers call a toll-free number when they have questions or problems, but have never been charged a fee. Now Julian would like to cover his company's cost for delivering help desk services and make a reasonable profit if possible. He asks you to prepare a brief report that outlines what he needs to consider to turn his help desk into a profit center without alienating his customers. He also wants you to recommend two ways he could expand his help desk services.

3

THE PEOPLE COMPONENT: HELP DESK ROLES AND RESPONSIBILITIES

In this chapter you will learn:

♦ The principal help desk job categories

♦ The responsibilities associated with each job category

♦ The skills required to be a successful front-line service provider

♦ The management opportunities within the help desk

♦ The supporting roles within the help desk

♦ The characteristics of a successful team

The people who work in a help desk play a variety of roles. The principal roles include the front-line service providers and help desk management personnel who directly support customers and ensure their satisfaction. Additional supporting roles support the front-line staff and provide more indirect customer support. Each of these roles is important, and each requires a specific set of skills. People in both these primary and supporting roles must work together as a team to provide quality customer service.

The roles and responsibilities of help desk staff and the advancement opportunities within and beyond the help desk are typically a reflection of the help desk's size and structure. A company's commitment to customer satisfaction and its willingness to invest in the help desk further influence the roles and opportunities that exist. This diversity makes the help desk a rewarding and exciting place for people who want to pursue a career in customer service and support.

To have a successful career in the help desk, you must continuously assess your current skills and develop new ones. Also, it is important that you contribute to the help desk team and that you value other team members' contributions. A sincere desire to satisfy customers and contribute to the help desk's goals will bring you success and enable you to create and pursue a wealth of opportunities.

PRINCIPAL JOB CATEGORIES

Although titles and job descriptions vary from one help desk to the next, two principal job categories are common throughout the support industry. These principal categories, or roles, are the front-line service providers and the management personnel who work in the help desk. The front-line service provider category consists of dispatchers, level one analysts, and level one specialists. Depending on the size of the help desk, management personnel include team leaders, supervisors, and other levels of management. Figure 3-1 shows a sample help desk organization chart.

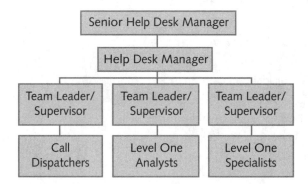

Figure 3-1   Sample help desk organization chart

Front-line service providers and help desk management perform specific roles in the help desk. Each has certain responsibilities and required skills.

 Help desk salaries vary based on factors such as job category, job responsibilities, industry, geographic region, company size, an individual's experience and ability, and so forth. *The Robert Half Technology 2003 Salary Guide* contains salary information for North America and can be obtained at **www.rhii.com/resources/index.html**. International salary information can be obtained by visiting one of the Help Desk Institute's international sites; links to HDI's international sites can be found at **www.thinkhdi.com/community/international.asp**.

Front-Line Service Providers

Front-line service providers are the help desk staff who interact directly with customers. In other words, they serve on the front line between a company or department and its customers. This role is crucial to the success of the help desk. Customers form opinions of the entire company or department the help desk represents based on their interactions with front-line service providers. Figure 3-2 lists the various types of front-line service providers you may find in a help desk.

- Dispatcher
- Level one analyst
- Level one specialist

Figure 3-2 Types of front-line service providers

Each of these roles has a particular function in the help desk.

Dispatcher

Some help desks rely on dispatchers as the first contact with customers. A **dispatcher** is the person who initially handles customer problems, requests, or inquiries. The dispatcher logs customer incidents and then routes them to the appropriate level one analyst or specialist or level two group. This first point of contact may also be called help desk agent, customer care agent, customer service representative, or call screener. Generally, dispatchers resolve a low percentage of the incidents they handle. Instead, their primary job is to log a customer's incident accurately, ensure the customer that the incident will be handled in a timely fashion, and then dispatch it to the correct group. Whether or not the dispatcher retains ownership of incidents once they have been dispatched varies from one company to the next. For example, in some companies, if the dispatcher routes an incident to a level one analyst, the analyst assumes ownership of the incident. In other companies, if the dispatcher routes an incident to a level two group (such as field services), the dispatcher may retain ownership, in keeping with the help desk's role as customer advocate.

Dispatchers are common in companies such as equipment manufacturers or resellers that primarily provide hardware support. Customers who experience hardware problems contact the help desk. The dispatcher logs the call, diagnoses the problem, and, if he or she determines that a hardware failure has occurred, dispatches a field service representative to the customer site. If the dispatcher thinks some other type of problem exists, such as a software problem, he or she may route the problem to a level one analyst or specialist.

Dispatchers are also common in help desks whose customers prefer to have an analyst answer the phone, rather than navigate a complicated phone menu. For example, if the phone system requires a large number of options that may potentially be confusing to customers (such as press 1 for software-related problems, press 2 for hardware-related problems, and so on), the help desk may opt to use dispatchers. The dispatcher answering the call listens and asks questions to determine the nature of the customer's incident. Then the dispatcher logs the incident and routes it to the appropriate level one analyst or specialist.

When hiring dispatchers, employers look for people with excellent interpersonal skills and an exceptional customer service orientation. On the job, dispatchers are typically measured by their ability to efficiently follow clearly defined procedures and ensure customer satisfaction. People who enjoy helping other people find this role very rewarding. This role can also serve as an excellent training ground for people interested in pursuing a level one analyst position.

Level One Analyst

Because today's demanding customer is less willing to wait for a solution, most help desks strive to resolve a high percentage of problems at the first point of customer contact. Thus, not all companies have dispatchers; sometimes, companies have level one analysts who initially handle customer problems and requests. In these companies, a **level one analyst** takes calls (e-mails, faxes, and so forth), logs customer incidents, and resolves incidents when possible. These people often have titles such as help desk analyst, customer support analyst, or help desk technician. When level one analysts cannot resolve a problem, they hand it off to the appropriate level two group along with a clear explanation of the problem and, when possible, the information the level two group needs to resolve it quickly.

When hiring level one analysts, employers look for good technical and analytical skills, as well as excellent customer service skills. The required technical skills vary, based on customer needs. For example, help desks that support off-the-shelf software usually hire analysts who have experience running and supporting the software packages used by the company. Help desks that support home-grown systems may focus more on a candidate's customer service skills, knowing they will have to train the person on their unique systems. In most cases, the ideal candidate for a level one analyst position has a broad base of technical knowledge, as opposed to extensive knowledge in a single subject area. People who enjoy solving problems, and, of course, enjoy helping other people solve problems, find the level one analyst role rewarding and challenging. The level one analyst role also serves as a great training ground for individuals interested in pursuing a level one specialist position or a help desk management position.

JAMES PULLEN
CUSTOMER SUPPORT GROUP MANAGER
STEPHANIE JONES
FORMER SYKES REGIONAL CALL CENTER DIRECTOR
SYKES ENTERPRISES, INC. (SERVICES PROVIDER)
TAMPA, FLORIDA
WWW.SYKES.COM

SYKES is a global leader in providing customer management solutions and services to external and internal customers of companies primarily in the technology, communications and financial services markets. Services offered by the Customer Support Services division include third-party hardware and software technical support and corporate help desk services. Headquartered in Tampa, Florida, SYKES operates 43 customer support centers and four fulfillment centers with operations throughout the United States,

3

Canada, Europe, Latin America, Asia, and Africa. These centers handle over 90,000 incoming calls per day, and many operate 24 hours per day, 7 days per week.

In 1999, SYKES was awarded the prestigious STAR (Software Technical Assistance Recognition) Award for the fifth consecutive year by the Service and Support Professionals Association (SSPA). SYKES's fifth consecutive STAR Award earned the company a place in the SSPA's STAR Hall of Fame.

Tasks.   On any given day we have roughly 4,000 people on the phones providing first- and second-level customer support. Our technicians begin by supporting hardware and operating systems and may be part of a shared agent pool that supports dozens of customers on various products. Or, they may be part of a team that supports a suite of products for a single client. Technicians "advance" in our company and can increase their compensation by acquiring additional skills. Our training efforts are aimed at enabling technicians to acquire first a "breadth" of experience, and then a "depth" of experience. For example, technicians may first acquire a broad-based understanding of word processing, and then acquire more in-depth knowledge of specific word processing packages such as Word and WordPerfect. We also make every effort to ensure that technicians know how their performance is being measured and what they must do to succeed. We develop a profile for each technician that illustrates the characteristics of a "good day." Measurable performance indicators include average call duration, after call work, number of calls per day, and resolution percentage. We believe this approach enables our technicians to feel a sense of accomplishment and that it also enables SYKES to reward and retain good people.

Organization.   Our typical Support Center houses 432 seats on a single shift basis. Each center has a management team that includes a Human Resources Manager, an Accounting Manager, a Training Manager, supervisors, and technicians. We try to maintain a ratio of one supervisor for every 20 technicians. This ratio enables us to continuously monitor the technicians' calls and provide immediate feedback aimed

at improving the quality of our services. We also have an Account Manager assigned to each of our clients and a Product Knowledge Information Manager (PKIM), which is, essentially, a technical account manager. The PKIM organizes training, oversees new product rollouts, and develops training for the technical staff. This position enables us to promote and retain good people who choose to stay focused on the technical aspects of our relationship with a client. It also enables the Account Managers to focus on the business aspects of our relationship with a client.

Philosophy.   SYKES' strength lies in its people. We recruit well-rounded, versatile individuals with strong customer support skills. Our employees are dedicated professionals who work in a challenging atmosphere. Ideas are exchanged freely and all our people are empowered to be problem solvers. Through extensive training, our technicians come to understand that the #1 priority is customer satisfaction. Customers don't interrupt the work you do each day; they *are* your day.

Level One Specialist

In some companies, level one analysts refer incidents they cannot resolve within a pre-defined period of time to level one specialists. A **level one specialist** researches complex incidents and develops solutions that require more skill—or in some cases, more time—than a level one analyst typically can devote to a single incident. These people often have titles such as help desk specialist, technical support specialist, or customer support specialist. The use of both level one analysts and level one specialists enables a company to strike the right balance between the need to respond quickly to customer requests and the need to resolve incidents correctly and permanently.

In companies that do not have a level one specialist position, level one analysts hand off incidents they cannot resolve directly to the appropriate level two person or group.

When hiring level one specialists, employers value expertise in a specific subject matter, as well as excellent analytical skills and an exceptional customer service orientation. As with the level one analyst, the specific required technical skills vary based on the customers' needs. The ideal candidate for a level one specialist position is able and willing to continuously update his or her skills and share his or her knowledge and experience with other members of the help desk team. This role can serve as an excellent training ground for individuals interested in pursuing a help desk management position, a supporting role, or a technical role in another part of the company.

Job Responsibilities

In a fast-paced customer service and support environment, every member of the help desk must understand his or her purpose, job responsibilities, and professional responsibilities. Customer confidence can dissolve into mistrust as a result of one perceived bad experience. Although that confidence can be regained if the help desk resolves the problem quickly and demonstrates a desire to satisfy the customer, a customer will be loyal to the help desk only if it consistently delivers a high level of service.

The primary responsibilities of a help desk are to provide a single point of contact for all support services, deliver value to customers, and capture and distribute information. The job

3

responsibilities of help desk staff correspond to those responsibilities. Typically, a help desk front-line service provider:

- Receives customer problems, requests, and inquiries (that is, incidents) reported over the telephone, e-mail, fax, the Web, and so on.

- Logs each incident by gathering pertinent information about the customer and a description of the incident. This electronic "ticket" is updated continuously until the customer's incident is resolved.

- Determines the nature of the customer's incident.

- Delivers a solution, when possible, using available tools (such as remote control systems) and procedures (such as troubleshooting procedures).

- Documents the resolution thoroughly so that the help desk can reuse it.

- If unable to solve the incident, determines how quickly the customer needs the incident resolved.

- Communicates to the customer how often he or she will receive status updates or how he or she can obtain status updates, for example, by going to the help desk's Web site and retrieving the ticket.

- Records the incident's severity in the ticket, all steps taken by both the help desk and the customer to try to resolve the incident, and any additional information the customer provides (such as directions to their site).

- Hands off the incident to the correct level one specialist or level two group, external vendor, or subject matter expert (SME).

- Retains ownership of incidents that have been handed off to a level two person or group.

- Periodically reports the incident's status to the customer (such as when the customer can expect a field service engineer to arrive or when ordered parts should arrive).

- Reviews the incident's resolution once it is identified to learn how the incident was solved or to determine what caused the incident to occur.

- Follows up with the customer to ensure that he or she is satisfied with the resolution.

- Closes the ticket.

The term *ticket* is actually a throwback to the days when incidents were recorded on paper forms. Today, of course, incidents are logged electronically, but the term *ticket* is still widely used. Tickets also may be called records, cases, incidents, and logs.

Job descriptions outline the specific tasks assigned to a person and provide managers and their employees a clear understanding of the work to be done. The amount of detail included in job descriptions varies from company to company, ranging from highly specific to quite generic. Although some companies work without job descriptions, this practice is risky and often results in employees performing unnecessary work or failing to do necessary work. In addition, the lack of a job description may cause an employee and a manager to have mismatched expectations about the nature of a help desk job. A well-defined job description provides employees with a clear understanding of work expectations and increasingly spells out employees' professional responsibilities.

Sample job descriptions for the primary help desk roles are provided in Appendix A.

Professional Responsibilities

As a focal point for their company or department, members of the help desk team must conduct themselves at all times in a professional and ethical manner. In their dealings with customers, management, and coworkers, they must promote and ensure the highest standards of professional and ethical conduct by:

- Giving customers an honest and accurate estimate of the time it will take to resolve their incident.

- Building confidence and good will with customers by keeping commitments and promptly advising customers when commitments cannot be met.

- Communicating in the language of the customer and avoiding the use of confusing terminology and technical jargon.

- Avoiding and discouraging the use of profanity.

- Encouraging good security practices, such as not sharing user IDs and passwords, frequent changing of passwords, and using unique passwords.

- Discouraging unethical, illegal, and potentially disruptive computing practices (such as those illustrated by the next three responsibilities) by enforcing security procedures and reporting violations to management.

  - Preventing unauthorized access to proprietary and sensitive company data by following procedures and requiring proper authorization prior to granting access.

  - Discouraging and reporting software piracy. **Software piracy** is the unauthorized use or reproduction of copyrighted or patented software.

  - Discouraging and reporting inappropriate and wasteful use of computing resources such as sending objectionable or harassing e-mails, printing large unnecessary listings, downloading and playing computer games, and unnecessary Web browsing.

- Communicating ways to detect, prevent, and cure computer viruses. A **computer virus** is a software program that can "infect" a computer by storing itself in the computer's memory or attaching itself to program or data files.

- Maintaining current technical skills and using all available knowledge resources, thus avoiding unnecessary escalations to other technical staff.

Trust is an integral part of the help desk's relationships with customers, management, and coworkers. Trust is earned when members of the help desk team consistently behave in an honest and ethical manner. There may be times when help desk analysts are tempted to violate the law or company policies. For example, the help desk may be aware that a customer is using an unauthorized, unlicensed software package and they fail to report the violation. Or, a customer appeals to a help desk analyst to reset his or her password without proper authorization as he or she is late completing an assignment. In these and all instances of illegal and unethical behavior, it is the help desk's duty to strictly follow and enforce the company's computing policies.

 Widespread use of e-mail and the Internet has led to a dramatic increase in the number of computer viruses affecting home and business computer users. Although some viruses won't harm an infected system, others are destructive and can damage or destroy data. Some viruses that are attached to files execute, or run, when the infected file is opened or modified. Other viruses sit in a computer's memory and infect files as the computer opens, modifies, or creates them. One of the best ways to prevent viruses is to use anti-virus software that can be purchased from vendors such as McAfee Security (**www.mcafee.com**) and Symantec (**www.symantec.com**). For additional virus detection and prevention tips, go to **www.mcafee.com/anti-virus/virus_tips.asp**.

Required Skills

Finding people for front-line positions who have the right mix of skills is one of the most difficult challenges facing help desk managers today. Strong technicians may lack the empathy skills or the patience required for the service industry. People-oriented individuals may lack the technical skills required to work in a complex computing environment. Some people prefer a hands-on approach to technical support and become dissatisfied when their position requires them to spend a lot of time on the telephone. The employee and the company benefit when the right skills are matched with the right position.

In general, when hiring people for front-line positions, companies look for people who genuinely enjoy helping other people and who work well with others. Many companies believe that technical skills can be developed more easily than interpersonal skills; therefore, they are willing to hire people with good interpersonal skills and a customer service orientation and then provide the necessary technical training. This is not to say that technical skills are unimportant. Some companies—particularly those that support highly sophisticated technology—at times hire people with strong technical skills and provide extensive customer service training. The bottom line is that in the current, highly competitive marketplace, customer service skills take center stage. In fact, a Fortune magazine article referred to technical workers with interpersonal skills as "The Worker Elite."

The specific skills a company requires are determined by the company's job description. These skills typically fall into four main categories: business skills, technical skills, soft skills, and self-management skills.

Business Skills

Business skills, such as the ability to understand and speak the language of business and the ability to analyze and solve business problems, are the skills people need to be successful in the business world. These skills are called business knowledge. When working in a help desk, business skills also include the skills that are unique to the industry or profession the help desk supports, such as accounting skills or banking skills. These skills are called industry knowledge. Business skills also include skills that are specific to the customer service and support industry, such as understanding the importance of meeting customers' needs and knowing how to manage their expectations. These skills are called service industry knowledge.

Business Knowledge People throughout the support industry are learning that it is no longer enough to have just strong technical skills. Technical professionals are being challenged to do more than support technology; they are being challenged to ensure that a company's technology enables its employees and customers to achieve their business goals. In other words, they are being challenged to ensure that technology is useful and that it enables people to be productive.

Some business knowledge is useful regardless of the profession you enter. Furthermore, your business knowledge will grow as you acquire education and experience, and through simply observing the activities that occur where you work. The term business encompasses a broad range of topics and disciplines. Some basic skills needed to acquire business knowledge include:

- Understanding and speaking the language of business.
- Analyzing and solving business problems.
- Using data, such as help desk data, to analyze trends and quantify improvement opportunities.
- Understanding the importance of developing cost-effective solutions that clearly benefit your company's business goals, not just solutions that take advantage of the latest technology trend.
- Learning to develop and make presentations in order to market your ideas; Figure 3-3 shows a professional making a presentation.
- Communicating the benefits of your ideas in financial terms.

Most employers will not expect technical professionals to have fully developed business knowledge skills when they first join the workforce. It is important, however, to assimilate the role technology plays in a business venture and why these skills are important. For example, even a company that manufactures computer games, a seemingly fun use of technology, is in business to make a profit. Technical professionals should know that and understand the role they play in achieving that goal.

Figure 3-3   Professional making a presentation

Managers are increasingly requiring senior technical professionals to hone and use business skills. For example, senior technical professionals may be required to quantify their proposed projects using techniques such as cost benefit analysis. **Cost benefit analysis** compares the costs and benefits of two or more potential solutions to determine an optimum solution. Another commonly accepted financial measure used when assessing projects is return on investment (ROI). **Return on investment (ROI)** measures the total financial benefit derived from an investment—such as a new technology project—and then compares it with the total cost of the project.

The absence of business knowledge skills may not hinder a technical professional as he or she pursues a career. The presence of business knowledge skills will, however, increase the opportunities available to a technical professional and increase his or her speed of advancement.

Hundreds of books, ranging from basic to advanced, have been written about business. Furthermore, these books span a broad range of topics. To learn more about business skills, go to your local library or bookstore and search for topics such as "business," "workplace skills," "business jargon," "finance for non-financial professionals," "making presentations," and "project management." Books, tapes, and videos can also be purchased at Web sites such as **www.bizhotline.com**, **www.amanet.org**, and **www.careertrack.com**. You may want to begin with a business primer and then take a more in-depth look at a topic you find interesting or important.

Industry Knowledge   Some help desks seek to hire people who understand the specific industry in which the company is engaged, such as manufacturing, retail, or financial. This knowledge makes it easier for an employee to understand the company's goals and contribute accordingly. Many help desks recruit from within the company to find candidates who are already familiar with the company and its goals. Help desks also often value candidates who have skills and knowledge that pertain to the product or service being sold. For example, a company that sells accounting software may seek help desk personnel who have an accounting background. Such knowledge enables the help desk analyst to understand the customer's needs and appreciate the impact on the customer's business when a product fails to perform properly.

Service Industry Knowledge   When hiring analysts or specialists, many help desks require knowledge of the customer service and support industry. Those that don't require this kind of experience at least consider it highly desirable. Many employers scan candidates' résumés for previous service experience or job experience that involves helping people. Relevant fields include teaching, sales, social work, and healthcare. People in these fields must be able to recognize that they are delivering a service and that their "customers" look to them for help.

The business skills and knowledge required for a help desk job vary, depending on the company's market niche and the job category (such as level one analyst or level one specialist). People applying for entry-level positions are expected to have little to no business experience. Some basic knowledge and a willingness to learn, however, is viewed as a positive. On the other hand, people applying for management positions are expected to have a great deal of business experience.

Technical Skills

The technical skills required for a help desk position vary depending on the customers' technical needs. **Technical skills** are the skills people need to use and support the specific products and technologies the help desk supports. At the very least, companies expect people applying for entry-level positions to be computer literate. In other words, they must have experience using computers and know how to use Microsoft Windows as well as popular software packages such as Microsoft Word or Corel WordPerfect. Many companies now use the Web for recruiting purposes. This enables them to find job seekers who are comfortable using the Internet—a technology that an increasing number of help desks use and are required to support.

3

People applying for level one specialist positions are expected to have skill and experience in a specific area or with a specific product. For example, a company that provides software support values software literacy. A position in an internal help desk that supports a complex computing environment may require a broader base of skills, including experience with network environments, operating systems, applications, and hardware systems.

 The ability to type—or keyboard—well is an important asset in the help desk. Someone with good keyboarding skills can enter data easily and accurately into a computer; this frees the analyst or specialist to focus on listening to the customer. Because listening to the customer is vital in a help desk setting, some companies test the keyboarding skills of job candidates and even offer keyboarding classes in an effort to improve performance.

Help desks that want to hire people with past support industry experience consider an applicant's knowledge of support technologies—such as telephone systems, problem management and resolution systems, and knowledge management systems. Although these skills are not usually required, candidates who demonstrate a level of comfort using support technologies may have the upper hand. Most companies, however, provide training on their specific systems.

When interviewing a potential help desk analyst or specialist, an employer may assess technical skills in a number of ways, including:

- **Asking questions**—Some companies have experts prepare a list of questions that assess a candidate's knowledge about a particular subject.

- **Testing**—Some employers prefer to administer a standardized exam to evaluate a candidate's abilities.

- **Problem solving**—Many employers present candidates with a problem (such as a disabled or incorrectly configured system) and evaluate the person's ability to isolate and fix the problem. Some give candidates a puzzle to solve or ask candidates to write down the steps that they would use to solve a sample problem. As candidates' technical abilities can vary, employers may ask candidates to solve a non-technical problem, such as why a car won't start, in an effort to evaluate the person's ability to approach problems in a logical manner.

- **Certification**—Some companies look for candidates who have completed relevant certification program(s), such as those offered by vendors like Cisco, Microsoft, and Novell. An increasing number of vendor-neutral organizations, such as the Help Desk Institute, Service and Support Professionals Association, and STI Knowledge, also offer certification programs geared to help desk professionals.

 Chapter 8 explores in detail the role of certification in the help desk industry.

Soft Skills

Soft skills are the qualities that people need to deliver great service, such as listening skills, verbal skills, customer service skills, problem-solving skills, writing skills, and the ability to be a team player. What's most important, soft skills enable people to enjoy working in the customer service and support industry. These skills are recognized as the most basic and important skills that analysts must possess because all the technical skills in the world cannot overcome a lack of soft skills. This is illustrated in Figure 3-4, which shows the qualities the members of the Help Desk Institute, a networking forum for help desk professionals, rated as important in a support representative.

Some of the most important soft skills include:

- **Listening**—In the survey conducted by the Help Desk Institute in 2002, 99 percent of respondents cited listening as the most important quality for a support person. Listening has been ranked the most important quality since the Help Desk Institute began surveying its members in 1990. **Active listening** is when the listener participates in a conversation and gives the speaker a sense of confidence that he or she is being heard. Active listening is particularly important when interacting with customers over the telephone because they cannot see you nodding your head or making eye contact. Two non-visual ways to demonstrate listening are to (1) ask questions and (2) respond to the customer using a verbal nod of the head through phrases such as "Uh-huh," "I see," and "I understand."

- **Verbal skills**—Because many interactions between a help desk analyst and the customer occur over the telephone, the analyst's ability to communicate verbally is critical. The analyst must be able not only to solve problems, but also to tell others how to solve problems at a level appropriate to each customer. For example, a help desk analyst must use much simpler terminology when talking to a first-time computer user than when talking to an experienced power user.

- **Customer service skills**—Often referred to as "people" skills, customer service skills include the ability to handle difficult customer situations, such as calming irate or extremely demanding customers or saying "no" to customers without antagonizing them. A person with good customer service skills can gain customer confidence and maintain goodwill, even when the customer's needs cannot be fully met. The art of customer service can be learned through practice, as explained in the numerous books, tapes, and training programs devoted to the topic.

- **Problem-solving skills**—Solving a problem involves more than randomly trying things to find an answer or simply searching a database of solutions. Problem solving involves logical thinking and requires a methodical approach through which the analyst first determines the probable source of a problem and then decides on a solution. A good problem solver has effective questioning skills. Persistence is also important, as proficient problem solving requires going beyond the "quick fix."

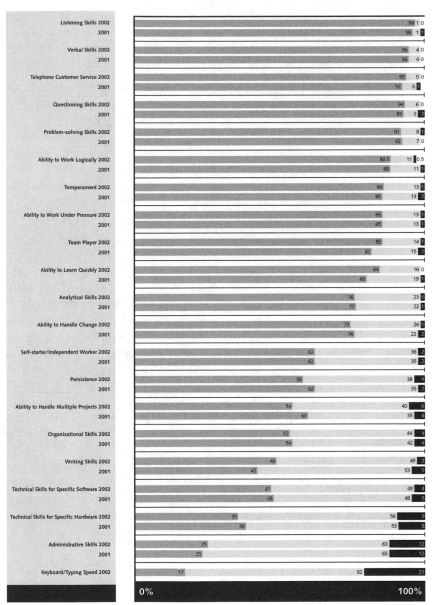

"Help Desk Institute Practices Survey," July 2002 survey results, [54].

Figure 3-4   Important qualities in a support person

- **Temperament**—The term temperament refers to the way a person thinks, behaves, or reacts to situations on a daily basis. Temperament is largely a matter of attitude. In the support industry, a positive attitude—the ability to seek out the good in any situation—is essential. It is also a key to being able to see the good in people and to understand that extraordinary situations sometimes cause even the most reasonable customers to lose patience or become angry. (It happens to the best of us.) In addition, a person temperamentally suited to work at a help desk should be able to handle pressure and resist becoming defensive or hostile in difficult situations.

- **Ability to be a team player**—Support is an ideal environment for working in teams due to the complexity of the work and the diversity of skills required. Simply working on a team does not, however, make an individual a team player. Rather, a team player is someone who works well with others and will share information with others, receive information and feedback from others, and focus on the goals of the help desk. Being a team player is a way of life that stems from a desire to accomplish more than you can on your own. Team players understand how they personally contribute to the team and respect and appreciate others' contributions.

- **Writing skills**—Although writing has not figured largely in help desk job descriptions in the past, the ability to write well is increasing in importance. This is because help desk analysts have to write well to log calls, document resolutions, develop procedures, and correspond with customers and coworkers using technologies such as e-mail, chat, and instant messaging. Also, many companies now allow customers to directly access the help desk's incident tracking system to check the status of outstanding tickets. Other companies use the Internet or their internal company **intranet**—a secured, privately maintained Web site that serves employees and that can be accessed only by authorized personnel—to publish the answers to frequently asked questions (FAQs) and allow customers to search online databases for possible solutions. In these situations, a customer's perception of the company is greatly influenced by the clarity and professionalism of the help desk's writing skills.

The Help Desk Institute's member practices survey illustrates how writing skills are increasing in importance. In 1997, 34.2 percent of members considered writing skills a very important quality in a support person. By 2001, 42.2 percent of members considered writing skills very important, and that number jumped to 49 percent in 2002.

The essential skills just described are difficult to assess during an interview. To get a better understanding of a job candidate's soft skills, an employer may use one or more of the following techniques:

- **Role playing**—Some help desks have employees (or even customers) conduct the first interview with candidates over the phone to simulate a real help desk situation and assess applicants' verbal communication skills. Candidates may face a demanding caller or one who continuously interrupts them and questions their skills. The interviewer uses this role playing to determine how candidates handle pressure.

- **Sample documentation**—Some help desks ask candidates to bring samples of documents they have prepared, such as procedures, flowcharts, or technical solutions. Alternately, candidates may be asked to solve a problem and then document the solution at the interview.

- **Past experience**—Some help desks encourage candidates to describe specific situations they have handled in the past. Candidates may be asked, for example, how they have handled a situation in which a caller was unwilling to answer questions. Alternately, candidates may be asked to describe how they handled a stressful situation at work.

- **Testing**—Some help desks rely on personality tests, such as the Myers–Briggs Type Indicator (MBTI) and the Motivational Appraisal of Personal Potential (MAPP) to learn more about a job candidate. These tests measure qualities such as motivation, temperament, learning style, and people skills.

- **Certification**—Several help desk organizations such as the Help Desk Institute, Service and Support Professionals Association, and STI Knowledge now offer certification programs that focus on or at least include soft skills training for help desk professionals, in much the same way the vendor certification programs discussed earlier focus on a candidate's technical skills. These programs are becoming more widely used, and companies are beginning to use them to indicate peoples' skills.

Soft skills affect which help desk job people are most suited for. Some people prefer working alone or find the front line stressful. If that is the case for you, you may want to pursue a job away from the front line. On the other hand, people who enjoy working with customers and helping others solve problems will enjoy working as a help desk dispatcher, level one analyst, or level one specialist.

Continuously step back and objectively assess your soft skills throughout your help desk career. Good soft skills will serve you well throughout any career and your life.

Self-Management Skills

In addition to business skills, technical skills, and soft skills, help desk personnel need good self-management skills. **Self-management skills**, such as stress and time management are the skills people need to complete their work effectively, feel job satisfaction, and avoid frustration or burnout. Self-management skills are particularly important in the customer service and support industry because customer service is ranked in the United States as one of the most stressful occupations. Analysts and specialists who can manage their own time and organize their work enjoy greater job satisfaction. Some of the most important self-management skills include:

- **Stress-management skills**—The term stress refers to the adaptation of our bodies and minds to change. Given that change is a constant in the support industry, it is no wonder that people in this industry experience high levels of stress. With stress-management skills, people can minimize stress as much as possible and respond effectively when stressful situations occur. In other words, stress-management skills enable people to work well under pressure. Every person handles change differently and must develop a personal way of coping with stressful events.

- **Time-management skills**—The computer industry and its related support industry are constantly and dramatically changing, leading people to feel they are constantly behind. Help desk analysts and specialists must effectively manage their limited time to minimize stress and frustration and promote high self-esteem. Time-management techniques, such as establishing priorities and avoiding procrastination, enable individuals to gain control over their day and focus on their work. The first step toward managing time effectively is to identify and eliminate the ways you waste time. Next, focus on activities that contribute to your personal goals and the goals of the help desk.

- **Organizational skills**—Slow, quiet days on a help desk are rare. People who work in the support industry must continually develop the skills needed to handle new technologies, multiple projects, changing policies and procedures, and a somewhat chaotic physical environment. Organization is the key to handling those busy days. Getting and staying organized requires setting up effective paper- and computer-based filing systems and having the personal discipline to maintain those systems on a daily basis.

- **Learning and information-retrieval skills**—Learning is the labor of the information age. When discussing learning skills, it is important to distinguish between knowledge and information retrieval. Knowledge implies understanding, whereas information refers to data organized in a meaningful way. Retrieving information is the easy part. You can obtain the information you need through textbooks and class notes, expert systems, Web sites, online help, manuals and procedure guides, and so on. Good analysts don't try to store all the information they need between their ears. Instead, they determine where to find the information and learn how to get it quickly when they need it. Then, they focus on acquiring knowledge—an understanding of what information means and why information is important. Acquiring knowledge requires study, analysis, reflection, and a focus on the bigger picture. Getting ahead in the support industry requires both the ability to retrieve information and the ability to acquire knowledge—that is, understanding. Both require an inherent curiosity and willingness to learn.

Like soft skills, self-management skills are difficult to assess during an interview. To get a feel for candidates' self-management skills, employers often use some of the same techniques described earlier for assessing soft skills. Self-management skills also warrant ongoing self-assessment. The support industry is particularly fast-paced, and things are never "normal." People who enjoy a variety of responsibilities and who feel comfortable, and even motivated, when they are faced with challenging problems and situations make perfect candidates for a front-line role.

Continuously step back and objectively assess your self-management skills throughout your help desk career. Like soft skills, good management skills will serve you well throughout any career and your life.

PETE MCGARAHAN
CHAIRMAN
STI KNOWLEDGE 2000
YORBA LINDA, CALIFORNIA
www.stiknowledge.com

In today's rapidly changing business environment, career paths are no longer as predetermined as they used to be. I believe that the roles people play within an organization are becoming very dynamic, and the one thing people can expect is change. The help desk employee has the opportunity to have contact with all of the people in the organization, and that can lead you into any direction you choose to go. The world is an oyster for people in IT support who have a great customer service attitude, technical skills, and business acumen.

It really starts with a great attitude. People like a can-do attitude, an empowered attitude. I can help you! Managers today want employees who have a solid work ethic. That means it's up to you to be self-motivated and self-disciplined. Constantly be on the lookout for ways that you can add value. Don't be content to answer the same boring questions day-in and day-out. Be in the problem-prevention business. Recommend ways to eliminate low value-add activities, for example, through automation, and to minimize business impact when technology changes occur. In today's business world, it's not enough to just have great technical skills. It's what you do with your skills. It's all about results.

Help Desk Management Personnel

The size of a help desk determines how many layers of management it requires. Some help desks have front-line staff report directly to a manager. Others have team leaders, and perhaps supervisors, handle day-to-day operations, so that the help desk manager can focus on more strategic activities such as planning, preparing budgets, and improving service. Larger help desks may assign one or more people to each manager position. In smaller help desks, a single person may take over the duties associated with several management positions. Whether performed by one person or a hierarchy of people, help desk management is critical to the success of the help desk. Figure 3-5 lists the common help desk management roles, although these titles may vary from help desk to help desk.

- Senior help desk manager
- Help desk manager
- Help desk supervisor or team leader

Figure 3-5   Common help desk management roles

Senior Help Desk Manager

Typically, a **senior help desk manager** establishes the help desk mission and focuses on the help desk's strategic or long-term goals. He or she approves the help desk budget and acquires (from the larger corporation) the funding needed to make improvements such as hiring additional staff, implementing new processes, acquiring new technologies, and so forth. The senior help desk manager actively promotes the value of the help desk to upper management and the entire company, thus gaining support for the efforts of the help desk and its improvement plans.

Help Desk Manager

The **help desk manager** works closely with the senior help desk manager to prepare the help desk's budget and plan its activities for the coming year. He or she is involved with activities such as preparing reports and analyzing statistics, establishing Service Level Agreements (SLAs), and working with other managers (such as level two managers) to ensure that the help desk's processes and technologies are meeting the company's needs. Working in the help desk manager position can prepare a person for the senior help desk manager role. These management positions also can lead to management opportunities in another part of the company.

Help Desk Supervisor or Team Leader

A **help desk supervisor** (also called a team leader) oversees the day-to-day operation of the help desk, which includes making sure the help desk is meeting its SLA commitments, monitoring and evaluating the performance of help desk staff, and ensuring that the staff is properly trained. The help desk supervisor and team leader also work closely with help desk managers to hire help desk staff and evaluate their performance.

Many companies turn to their front-line service providers when they need to fill help desk supervisor and team leader roles because these people have in-depth knowledge about the company, the products it uses or sells, and the needs of the help desk. The help desk supervisor or team leader role can also serve as a training ground for people interested in pursuing a position as a help desk manager.

3

Required Skills

When hiring help desk managers, employers look for skills related to the particular management position. For example, companies interviewing candidates for a senior help desk manager position usually want someone with a strong background in customer service and support, along with long-range planning experience and the ability to manage a budget. Companies interviewing candidates for a help desk manager position often look for people who know how to prepare budgets and plan help desk activities. Experience hiring people, evaluating performance, and coaching and counseling people to maximize their performance is also important. When hiring a help desk supervisor or team leader, companies focus on the candidate's leadership skills and team-building experience. Smaller companies with few layers of management look for people who have all of these skills or the combination of skills needed at that particular company.

Help desk management personnel need excellent communication skills and the ability to present information and ideas in a manner appropriate for each audience. For example, when communicating with upper levels of management, help desk managers must be able to succinctly present briefings and recommendations using appropriate business terms and supporting statistics. When communicating with their peers—other managers—help desk managers must be able to promote a spirit of cooperation and build the rapport needed to work together toward shared goals. When communicating with staff, help desk managers must be able to inspire and motivate while providing clear, firm direction. When communicating with customers, help desk managers must relay empathy and understanding and must excel at managing expectations.

Help desk management personnel need technical skills, but they are typically not expected to maintain their skills at the same detailed level as help desk analysts and specialists. Help desk managers need a higher-level understanding of the particular products and systems supported by the help desk. In other words, they don't have to know everything. Rather, they must have sufficient knowledge to inform the company about the overall performance of the products and systems the help desk supports. They must also be able to prepare the help desk when new products and systems are being implemented or provide direction when critical problem situations occur. They use this technical knowledge to plan training and evaluate the technical ability of the help desk team and individual analysts within the team.

People leaving front-line positions for management roles often find it difficult to "give up" their technical skills. They are used to being the experts and may enjoy having others look up to them and seek them out for assistance. In time, however, managers must move from knowing how to *fix* technology to how to *use* technology to achieve business goals. The best managers hire and train good analysts to do the fixing.

SUPPORTING ROLES

Front-line service providers and management often rely on others within the help desk department for the tools, processes, and information they need to perform their tasks. In smaller help desks, one person may perform a number of the supporting roles listed in Figure 3-6. Or, a number of people may share these responsibilities. In larger help desks, teams may perform these different roles.

As companies strive to make the most of the tools and procedures available to the help desk, supporting roles are growing more important and are becoming much more commonplace. Figure 3-7 shows one example of an organization chart for a larger help desk that includes these supporting roles.

- Knowledge base administration
- Network monitoring
- Resource desk
- Service management and improvement
- Technical support
- Training

Figure 3-6   Common supporting roles in a help desk

Supporting roles are also important because they create a diversity of opportunity in the help desk. Some help desks dedicate people to these positions, whereas other help desks rotate analysts and specialists through these supporting roles. This gives people the opportunity to broaden their base of skills and occasionally step away from the front line. The way help desks handle this rotation varies considerably from one company to the next. Whether people are dedicated to these positions or rotate through them, these roles help to retain valued people in the help desk.

Figure 3-7   Sample help desk organization chart with supporting roles

Knowledge Base Administration

Many companies maintain sophisticated knowledge management systems which allow them to consolidate all of their information sources into a single knowledge base. A **knowledge base** is a collection of information sources such as customer information, documents, policies and procedures, and incident resolutions. To maintain these systems, many companies designate a knowledge base administrator (KBA), or knowledge engineer. A **knowledge engineer** develops and oversees the knowledge management process and ensures that the information contained in the help desk's knowledge base is accurate, complete, and current. Knowledge management is a critical process because the rapid pace of change makes it difficult for companies to provide help desk analysts with as much training as the companies or the analysts would like. As a result, companies must supplement their analysts' skills by providing them with access to effectively managed and maintained knowledge bases.

Chapter 4 explores the knowledge management process in more detail. Chapter 5 looks at knowledge management systems in more detail.

A knowledge engineer's responsibilities may include:

- Researching and gathering information sources to be included in the knowledge base.

- Developing and distributing resolution documentation standards, such as the format and writing style to be used when preparing resolutions.

- Reviewing incident resolutions submitted by help desk analysts and level two service providers.

- Ensuring that information sources (1) are technically valid, (2) are reusable—for example, details relating to a single specific incident, such as names and dates, are removed so other analysts can reuse the source to solve the same problem for a different customer or at a future date, (3) are presented in a clear, consistent, and logical manner, (4) conform to knowledge management standards, and (5) do not duplicate existing information sources.

- Conferring, when necessary, with the author of a resolution or information source to clarify the information and determine where the information should be stored in the knowledge base.

- Approving or rejecting resolutions and information sources as appropriate.

- Ensuring that analysts can quickly and easily retrieve information added to the knowledge base.

- Ensuring that the data used to log problems is consistent with the data used to store information in the knowledge base so analysts can easily match problems to resolutions.

- Providing help desk and level two staff with the training they need to create quality information and improve their ability to retrieve information from the knowledge base.

In smaller companies, a help desk analyst may perform this role on a part-time basis, whereas larger companies may have one or more full-time knowledge engineers. For example, each level two group in larger companies may have an individual who maintains the information sources relative to his or her group's area of expertise. This position is increasing in importance as companies strive to ensure that the information contained in their knowledge bases is accessible, current, accurate, and complete.

Network Monitoring

Network monitoring involves activities that use tools to observe and control network performance in an effort to prevent or minimize the impact of problems. Network monitoring tools include remote monitoring and network management systems. At some companies, level one analysts and specialists use these tools in the course of their daily work; other companies establish a separate function and dedicate people solely to the role of network monitoring. They may be called network analysts or network management specialists. The support center model—discussed in Chapter 2—is prompting help desks to transition network monitoring from the network management group into the help desk. This transfer of responsibilities enables the help desk to proactively identify and prevent problems and resolve problems more quickly. Network monitoring involves:

- Monitoring the network for signs of degradation.

- Analyzing network-related information to forecast trends.

- Recommending actions to prevent network problems and optimize network performance.

- Locating and correcting network-related problems.

- Notifying level one analysts and specialists and level two specialists (such as the network management group) when the network is down or likely to be unavailable.

Network monitoring is a logical activity for help desks because it enables them to be proactive. Available network management technologies are making it possible for help desks to extend their reach and increase their ability to quickly solve and prevent problems.

Resource Desk

Some help desks establish a **resource desk**, which is a reference desk where level one analysts can get help with difficult incidents and training to handle similar incidents in the future. Resource desk specialists work at the resource desk. **Resource desk specialists** are senior level one analysts or specialists who are dedicated to the resource desk or who rotate between the resource desk and the front line. Senior level one analysts or specialists are those people who have the most seniority within the help desk or who have the greatest depth of experience. The resource desk specialist's responsibilities may include:

- Maintaining a high level of knowledge about the products and systems the help desk supports.

- Staffing the resource desk during scheduled shifts and assisting analysts with difficult calls.

- Ensuring that the resource desk's library, tools, and so on are up-to-date.

- Taking over difficult problems from analysts when time constraints (such as a period of high call volume) keep them from researching the problem, and then communicating the resolution or course of action back to the analysts.

- Training analysts on the use of knowledge resources, such as knowledge bases, remote support technologies, reference guides, technical documents, and manuals.

- Identifying and recommending knowledge resources to help desk management and the knowledge engineer.

- Keeping team leaders and supervisors informed about the types of problems analysts are bringing to the resource desk.

- Helping to identify training needs for help desk analysts.

- Helping to identify repetitive problem areas.

The goal is that resource desk specialists are always accessible and that they compensate for when the analyst's supervisor or coworkers cannot provide assistance or do not have the most current information.

 In a help desk, ongoing training is a way of life, and it's expected that everyone participate. Even the new person on the team might teach somebody something.

Service Management and Improvement

Some larger help desks assign one or more people to proactive tasks designed to ensure that the help desk meets its service commitments and continuously improves. In smaller help desks, these tasks are performed by help desk management or by help desk staff on a part-time basis. **Service management and improvement** includes activities such as monitoring help desk performance and identifying and overseeing improvements to the help desk. Service management and improvement responsibilities include:

- Developing and distributing management reports that are used by customers, help desk staff and management, and level two staff and managers to monitor metrics, measure performance, analyze trends, and so forth.

- Looking for trends (such as an increase in the number of problems with a particular product) and root cause analysis. **Root cause** is the most basic reason for an undesirable condition or problem, and which, if eliminated or corrected, would have prevented it from existing or occurring. **Root cause analysis** involves determining why problems occur and identifying ways to prevent them.

- Developing and monitoring help desk performance reports.

- Negotiating SLAs and monitoring performance to ensure that the help desk is meeting its commitments.

- Developing, monitoring, and refining business processes.

- Soliciting customer feedback and measuring customer satisfaction.

- Identifying ways the help desk can improve and facilitating the implementation of improvements.

- Performing benchmarking activities. **Benchmarking** is the process of comparing the help desk's services, standardized metrics, and practices to those of a rival or world class company in an effort to identify ways it can improve.

Service management and improvement are the hallmark of a world class customer service and support organization. These companies understand the adage "you can't manage what you aren't measuring," and work diligently to ensure that their services are aligned with their customers' needs.

Technical Support

Technical support involves maintaining the hardware and software systems used by the help desk. In larger help desks, one or more people provide technical support. In smaller help desks, help desk management and staff may perform these tasks on an as-needed basis. In some organizations, level two staff may perform some of these tasks or work jointly with the help desk's technical support staff to perform these tasks. The technical support function includes activities such as routine maintenance, enhancing and upgrading systems, and providing training. Technical support may also involve evaluating and selecting new systems, identifying and developing the training needed to implement new systems, and managing the implementation of new systems. Technical support responsibilities may include:

- Evaluating and selecting support technology.

- Developing and delivering training for support technology.

- Creating and maintaining project plans for implementing new technology and associated processes.

- Monitoring the performance of and maintaining support systems, such as ensuring that systems are backed up, archiving data when needed, performing database tuning, and so forth.

- Resolving problems related to the technologies used by the help desk.

- Evaluating requests to customize help desk technologies.

- Managing the help desk's asset and configuration management database and ensuring that the licenses, warranties, and service contracts for all help desk technologies are up-to-date.

Technology loses its effectiveness if it is not properly maintained and continuously upgraded to keep pace with its users' needs. Help desk technology is no different. Companies that devote resources to supporting their help desk systems realize this and are willing to do what is required to get the most out of their technology investment.

Training

Although some help desks rely on their company's training department, other help desks have a dedicated person or team that oversees the training needs of the help desk team. This is in addition to the cross-training and mentoring that is a daily part of help desk life. This person or team focuses on the special needs of the help desk team and ensures that they receive training that addresses the business, technical, soft, and self-management skills that help desk analysts need. The responsibilities of a help desk trainer or training group may include:

- Developing and delivering training programs.

- Providing one-on-one training when needed.

- Evaluating and implementing commercially developed training programs (such as computer-based or Internet-based training).

- Working with help desk management personnel to determine training needs.

- Observing help desk operations and soliciting feedback from help desk staff to determine training needs.

The one sure thing in a help desk setting is that things will change. Because of this, training is essential for a help desk team, and the people that deliver training provide an invaluable service.

How help desks organize themselves to incorporate these supporting roles varies considerably from one company to the next. Larger help desks have no choice but to dedicate full-time resources to these functions. Smaller help desks may have front-line service providers handle these functions along with their customer support responsibilities. Some help desks have people or teams performing some functions full-time and help desk analysts and specialists perform other functions part-time. Regardless of how these functions are handled, they all add up to customer and employee satisfaction.

CHARACTERISTICS OF A SUCCESSFUL HELP DESK TEAM

You might be tempted to define a team as a group of people doing the same thing, but that's not really true. In a baseball team, for instance, the members of the team all perform different tasks. One plays first base, another specializes in pitching, and so on. Each player has an area of expertise and actually may perform poorly in areas other than his or her specialty. (Pitchers, for example, are notoriously poor batters.) Each player must also at times be a leader and at other times follow the leader. What makes these people with varying talents a team? The answer is their desire to play together to win the game.

In the modern business world, no single person can know all there is to know about a company's products and systems and provide all the support customers need. The demands are too great. Instead, the members of the help desk need to work together as a team. Each help desk analyst must maintain a high level of knowledge about the products and systems for which he or she is recognized as an expert, and at the same time show respect and support for the other team members. In other words, a member of the help desk team who is highly skilled in one particular product cannot discount the efforts of another team member who is unfamiliar with that product. That other team member may be highly experienced in another product or may also have business skills, soft skills, or self-management skills that contribute to the team's goals.

The characteristics of a successful team, and of successful team players, include:

- **Ability to collaborate**—When people identify with a team, they want to work well together. Members of a team support each other and do what is best for the team.

- **Effective communication**—When team members interact, information flows freely. People support and trust each other and willingly share information and knowledge.

- **Enhanced capability**—In a team setting, the team performs better than the individual team members alone. The team benefits when it recognizes and uses the talents of each team member. Successful teams capitalize on team members' strengths and compensate for each other's weaknesses.

- **Consensus sought and reached**—Consensus means that all team members work together to make decisions and solve problems that affect the help desk's performance. In the course of reaching consensus, team members are able to come up with more ideas and options than any one person could develop alone.

- **Sense of commitment**—People feel a responsibility to the team and its members and don't want to let them down.

Most people who work on a help desk value the fact that they are part of a team. They rely on others for their knowledge, experience, and support and want their coworkers to appreciate and respect them in turn. The most successful teams rise up and meet the most demanding performance challenges. In fact, a common performance goal is more important to a team than a great leader or special incentives. In the support industry, the performance goal is clear: Satisfy the customer.

CHAPTER SUMMARY

- ❒ The help desk is a rewarding and exciting place for people who want to pursue a career in customer service and support. A variety of roles fill the help desk with opportunity. These roles include the front-line service providers (such as dispatchers, level one analysts, and level one specialists) and help desk management personnel (such as managers, supervisors, and team leaders) who directly support customers and ensure their satisfaction. Additional people in supporting roles support the front-line staff and provide more indirect customer support.

- ❒ The primary responsibilities of a help desk are to provide a single point of contact for all support services, deliver value to customers, and capture and distribute information. The job responsibilities of help desk dispatchers, analysts, and specialists correspond to those responsibilities. The professional responsibilities of help desk staff involve conducting themselves at all times in a professional and ethical manner. In instances of illegal and unethical behavior, it is the help desk's duty to strictly follow and enforce the company's computing policies.

- ❒ Each of the help desk roles requires a specific set of skills. Front-line service providers need the right mix of business skills (business, industry, and service industry knowledge), technical skills (expertise with the products and technologies the help desk supports), soft skills (such as listening, communication, customer service, and problem-solving skills), and self-management skills (such as stress and time management). Soft skills are the most important because people need them to deliver great service and to enjoy working in the customer service and support industry.

- ❒ The size of a help desk determines how many layers of management it requires. Management roles may include senior help desk manager, help desk manager, and help desk supervisor or team leader. Whether performed by one person or a hierarchy of people, help desk management is critical to the organization's success. Management activities such as strategic planning, preparing budgets, and monitoring and evaluating performance enable the help desk to continuously improve.

- ❒ Front-line service providers and help desk managers often rely on others within the help desk for the tools, processes, and information they need to perform their tasks. As a result, supporting roles such as knowledge base administration, service management and improvement, and technical support are growing in importance. These roles enable companies to make the most of the tools and procedures available to the help desk, create diverse opportunities in the help desk, and enable the help desk to retain valued people.

- ❒ Members of a help desk need to work together as a team because no single person can know it all or do it all. Most people who work on a help desk value being part of a team. They know they can rely on their coworkers for their knowledge, experience, and support and that their teammates appreciate and respect them in turn. The most successful teams rise up and meet the most demanding performance challenges. In the support industry, the primary performance goal is clear: Satisfy the customer.

KEY TERMS

active listening — When the listener participates in a conversation and gives the speaker a sense of confidence that he or she is being heard.

benchmarking — The process of comparing the help desk's services, standardized metrics, and practices to those of a rival or world class company in an effort to identify ways it can improve.

business skills — The skills people need to work successfully in the business world, such as the ability to understand and speak the language of business (business knowledge); the skills that are unique to the industry or profession the help desk supports, such as accounting skills or banking skills (industry knowledge); and also the skills that are specific to the customer service and support industry, such as understanding the importance of meeting customers' needs and knowing how to manage their expectations (service industry knowledge).

computer virus — A software program that can "infect" a computer by storing itself in the computer's memory or attaching itself to program or data files. Some viruses won't harm an infected system, whereas others are destructive and can damage or destroy data.

cost benefit analysis — A business calculation that compares the costs and benefits of two or more potential solutions in order to determine an optimum solution.

dispatcher — The person who initially handles customer problems, requests, or inquiries; also called a help desk agent, customer care agent, customer service representative, or call screener.

front-line service providers — Help desk staff who interact directly with customers.

help desk manager — A person who works closely with the senior help desk manager to prepare the help desk's budget and plan its activities for the coming year.

help desk supervisor — A person who oversees the day-to-day operation of the help desk, which includes making sure the help desk is meeting its SLA commitments, monitoring and evaluating the performance of help desk staff, and ensuring that the staff is properly trained; also called team leader.

intranet — A secured, privately maintained Web site that serves employees and that can be accessed only by authorized personnel.

knowledge base — A collection of information sources such as customer information, documents, policies and procedures, and incident resolutions.

knowledge engineer — A person who develops and oversees the knowledge management process and ensures that the information contained in the help desk's knowledge base is accurate, complete, and current; also called knowledge base administrator (KBA).

3

level one analyst — A person who takes calls (e-mails, faxes, and so forth), logs customer incidents, and resolves incidents when possible; also called help desk analyst, customer support analyst, or help desk technician.

level one specialist — A person who researches complex incidents and develops solutions that require more skill—or, in some cases, more time—than a level one analyst typically can devote to a single incident; also called help desk specialist, technical support specialist, or customer support specialist.

network monitoring — Activities that use tools to observe and control network performance in an effort to prevent or minimize the impact of problems.

resource desk — A reference desk where level one analysts can get help with difficult incidents and training to handle similar incidents in the future.

resource desk specialists — Senior level one analysts or specialists who are dedicated to the resource desk or who rotate between the resource desk and the front line.

return on investment (ROI) — A business calculation that measures the total financial benefit derived from an investment—such as a new technology project—and then compares it with the total cost of the project.

root cause — The most basic reason for an undesirable condition or problem, and which, if eliminated or corrected, would have prevented it from existing or occurring.

root cause analysis — A methodical way of determining why problems occur and identifying ways to prevent them.

self-management skills — The skills, such as stress and time management, that people need to complete their work effectively, feel job satisfaction, and avoid frustration or burnout.

senior help desk manager — A person who typically establishes the help desk mission and focuses on the help desk's strategic or long-term goals.

service management and improvement — Activities such as monitoring help desk performance and identifying and overseeing improvements to the help desk.

soft skills — The qualities that people need to deliver great service, such as listening skills, verbal skills, customer service skills, problem-solving skills, writing skills, and the ability to be a team player.

software piracy — The unauthorized use or reproduction of copyrighted or patented software.

technical skills — The skills people need to use and support the specific products and technologies the help desk supports.

REVIEW QUESTIONS

1. What two principal roles exist within a typical help desk?

2. What factor determines the levels of management found in a help desk?

3. What role do front-line service providers play in a help desk?

4. Why is the role of front-line service provider crucial?

5. Describe the primary difference between the dispatcher role and the level one analyst role.

6. What do dispatchers and level one analysts have in common?

7. Briefly list the skills that companies look for when hiring people for the following front-line roles:

   ❑ Dispatcher

   ❑ Level one analyst

   ❑ Level one specialist

8. What are the three primary responsibilities of a typical help desk?

9. List two specific tasks performed at the help desk that correlate to the help desk's three primary job responsibilities.

10. How are members of the help desk team expected to conduct themselves?

11. List three ways that help desk team members can exhibit professional and ethical behavior.

12. When hiring people for front-line positions, what kind of people do companies look for?

13. List the four main skill categories necessary for working in a help desk.

14. What are the three types of business skills that may be required to work in a help desk?

15. Define the term *cost benefit analysis* and describe how it is used.

16. What determines the technical skills required for a help desk position?

17. What are the minimum technical skills that most companies require in a help desk analyst?

18. Describe two ways that companies assess a job candidate's technical skills.

19. Can technical skills overcome a lack of soft skills?

20. What is the most important soft skill that analysts must possess?

21. What are two ways an analyst can let a customer know he or she is listening over the telephone?

22. Describe the characteristics of problem solving.

23. What soft skill is increasing in importance? Why?

24. Describe two ways that companies assess a job candidate's soft skills.

25. Why are self-management skills important?

26. What two skill categories warrant self assessment? Why?

27. List one responsibility for each of the three help desk management categories discussed in this chapter.

28. How do managers need to present information and ideas? Explain your answer with two examples.

3

29. How must people learn to use their technical skills when moving into a management position?

30. What supporting role is increasing in importantance? Why?

31. Why is training essential in a help desk setting?

32. Why does it make sense to manage the help desk as a team?

33. What single factor is more important to a help desk team than any other?

HANDS-ON PROJECTS

Project 3-1

Investigate help desk job opportunities and salaries. Look at the Sunday newspaper or search the Internet for help desk want ads. On the Web, search for topics such as "help desk jobs" or visit one or more of the following sites: **www.justhelpdeskjobs.com**, **www.monster.com**, or **www.hotjobs.com**. Also obtain salary information at these sites, or by going to **www.rhii.com/resources/ index.html** and downloading their salary guide, or by going to one of the Help Desk Institute's international sites. Links to HDI's international sites can be found at **www.thinkhdi.com/community/international.asp**. Locate want ads for each of the primary job categories described in this chapter. Prepare a spreadsheet or report that contains your answers to the following questions:

❑ What business skills are required for each job category?

❑ What technical skills are required for each job category?

❑ What soft skills are required for each job category?

❑ What self-management skills are required for each job category?

❑ What is an average salary for each job category?

Summarize your findings by answering the following questions:

❑ Generally speaking, what do these want ads tell you about the help desk profession?

❑ Generally speaking, what do these want ads tell you about the skills required in the help desk profession?

Project 3-2

Assess your business knowledge skills. Prepare a list of the business knowledge skills discussed in this chapter. Then assess your own business knowledge skills by answering the following questions:

❑ In what areas are your business knowledge skills strong?

❑ In what areas can you improve your business knowledge skills?

❑ Given what you have learned in this chapter, what conclusions can you draw about your business knowledge skills?

Project 3-3

Perform a cost benefit analysis. Many people who perform cost benefit analyses on a regular basis tend to call it "shopping around." Think of an acquisition you have been considering. For example, you may be thinking about acquiring a digital camera, a PDA, or a fairly expensive gift for a friend or family member. Complete the following steps:

❑ Document the goal you are trying to achieve.

❑ Produce a table that shows all of the costs (purchase price, monthly service fee, time to set-up, and so forth) and benefits of two or more of the products you want to purchase.

❑ Analyze the costs and benefits and select a product.

❑ Document the reason for your decision.

Project 3-4

Assess your soft skills. Prepare a list of the soft skills discussed in this chapter. Then assess your own soft skills by answering the following questions:

❑ In what areas are your soft skills strong?

❑ In what areas can you improve your soft skills?

❑ Given what you have learned in this chapter, what conclusions can you draw about your soft skills?

Project 3-5

Test your classmates' problem-solving skills. Check out a book from the library that contains exercises or "brain teasers" designed to improve your problem-solving skills. Take two brain teasers and their solutions to class and test the problem-solving abilities of your classmates. You may want to give your classmates a time limit before you reveal the solutions. Discuss as a class what you learn from these exercises.

Project 3-6

Assess your self-management skills. Prepare a list of the self-management skills discussed in this chapter. Then assess your own self-management skills by answering the following questions:

❑ In what areas are your self-management skills strong?

❑ In what areas can you improve your self-management skills?

❑ Given what you have learned in this chapter, what conclusions can you draw about your self-management skills?

Project 3-7

Become a better listener. Assemble a team of three to five classmates. As a team, discuss the obstacles of being a good listener. In other words, what gets in the way of being a good listener? Identify at least five obstacles to good listening. Determine whether each of those obstacles is self-imposed or caused by what is happening around us. Next, identify ways to remove each of these obstacles. Present your findings to the class.

3

Project 3-8

Learn about balancing technical and management skills. Interview an acquaintance, family member, or coworker who manages a team of people who perform technical jobs. For example, the person might manage people who provide technical support, develop computer programs, or install or repair technology or equipment. Write a short paper that answers the following questions:

❑ What level of technical skill does this person feel he or she must maintain to be an effective manager?

❑ How does this person balance the need to maintain his or her technical skills while at the same time developing managerial skills?

❑ What satisfaction does this person derive by being a manager as opposed to a technician?

Project 3-9

Learn about working in a team. Talk to at least three people (friends, family members, or classmates) who work in a team setting or play on a sports team. Write your answers to the following questions:

❑ What is the common goal of their teams?

❑ How do they personally benefit from being a member of a team?

❑ In what ways do they feel they contribute to their team?

❑ Given what you have learned in this chapter, what conclusions can you draw about each of their experiences?

Project 3-10

Discuss what it means to be a team leader. Go to the library and research the subject of leadership and what it takes to be a team leader. List the three qualities you think are most important and explain why. Assemble a team of at least three of your classmates. Have each member describe the three qualities he or she believes are most important and explain why. As a team, prepare a list of the top three qualities identified.

CASE PROJECTS

1. Ethical Dilemma

You work for the help desk at a growing law office. A young lawyer who is always pleasant when he contacts the help desk has asked you to provide him a copy of the firm's standard word processing software so that he can install it on his home computer. He has a big case coming up and he wants to put in some extra hours. Your company's software licensing agreement with the vendor is machine specific, and home computers are not covered in the agreement. Also, due to the confidential nature of client information, it is against the firm's computing policy for associates to store client information on computers that are not hooked up to the firm's network. You really like this guy and want to help him out. Write a short paper describing the possible ramifications of providing the software and explain what you would do. Would you provide him a copy of the software? Would you notify management? What other steps could you take to address this situation?

2. Consulting Engagement: Personality Testing

A company that wants to begin testing help desk job candidates to assess qualities such as their temperament and people skills has hired you as a consultant. The help desk manager asks you to research the two most common personality tests: Myers-Briggs Type Indicator (MBTI) and Motivational Appraisal of Personal Potential (MAPP). Prepare a brief report that describes the purpose of each test, how the tests are delivered, and what the tests are designed to show.

3. Operation "Netiquette"

As help desk team leader, you've noticed that your staff tends to be very informal when it comes to sending e-mails, whether they are sending them to coworkers or customers. You want the team to present a more professional image with their written correspondences. Prepare a memo that describes your "10 Tips for E-mail Etiquette." Search the Web or visit the library for ideas.

4

THE PROCESS COMPONENT: HELP DESK PROCESSES AND PROCEDURES

In this chapter you will learn:

- ♦ The evolution of business processes
- ♦ The leading quality improvement programs and their maturity lifecycle
- ♦ The benefits of a process-oriented approach
- ♦ The goals of the five most common help desk processes
- ♦ Processes that support the help desk and enable quality improvement
- ♦ Why processes are important

Processes enable people to know the expected results of their efforts. By understanding an overall process—all of the tasks that must be performed to produce a result—people can better understand the importance of completing a single task. Procedures describe how to do a single task. When processes are understood, people know the work they are doing is necessary and valued. In other words, they know *why* they are doing that work. Processes and procedures also help to produce consistent results because people know *what* needs to be done and *how* to do it.

An integral component of every help desk, processes and procedures represent the work to be done and how to do that work, for example, solving problems and handling customer requests. These seemingly simple processes can involve numerous steps or procedures. Clearly defined procedures ensure that problems are solved and that requests are handled quickly and correctly. When multiple groups are involved in solving a problem or request, processes and procedures provide the framework that enables each group to understand its role and responsibilities.

This chapter explores some of the most common processes used at help desks. Be aware that the terminology and exact procedures for each process differ from company to company. The degree of formality with which the processes are defined and executed also varies. Regardless of the terminology and formality, if you understand the goals of these processes, you can produce the intended results at any help desk. This way, you will satisfy your customers and management and thus promote your career. You will also have the personal satisfaction that comes from helping and working with others.

EVOLUTION OF BUSINESS PROCESSES

Processes and procedures exist in every help desk and in every business. A **process** is a collection of interrelated work activities, or tasks, that take a set of specific inputs and produce a set of specific outputs that are of value to the customer. A **procedure** is a step-by-step, detailed set of instructions that describes how to perform the tasks in a process. Each task in a process has a procedure that describes how to do that task. In other words, processes define *what* tasks to do, whereas procedures describe *how* to do the tasks.

Every worker is responsible for a process at some level. Furthermore, every worker is simultaneously a supplier (or creator) of input and a customer (or recipient) of output. Figure 4-1 illustrates how workers follow procedures to take input and create the output needed to complete a process.

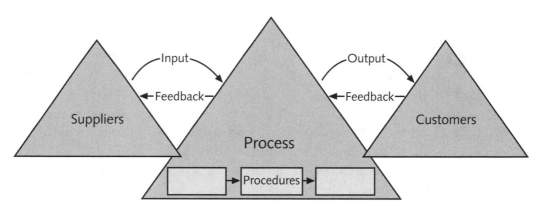

Figure 4-1   Components of a process

The concept of processes and procedures used by help desks, and by business in general, originated in 1776 when philosopher and economist Adam Smith introduced his principle of the division of labor. Smith believed that the same number of workers is more efficient and productive when each performs one simple, specialized task rather than all the tasks in a process. Because each person performed only a single task, businesses needed complex processes to pull together and integrate these specialized tasks and achieve the expected output or result. As a result, workers knew only the procedures required to complete their portion of a process and did not understand the entire process. It was the supervisor's responsibility to ensure that every person performed his or her tasks properly and in the appropriate time frame and then handed off the results to the next person in the process.

Given the lack of education and training most workers received at the time, Smith's principle was embraced widely. Many companies still operate on this division of labor principle today. Think about going to the movies: one person sells you a ticket, a different person collects your ticket, another person takes your snack order, someone else gets your popcorn, and still another gets your drink. Although some division of labor makes sense, we can all think of frustrating situations where one person is doing nothing while another—the one you're waiting for—is overloaded with work.

Today's workers are far more educated and self-motivated than those Adam Smith observed in the 1700s. To accommodate this change in workers, companies are assigning people greater responsibilities and empowering them to make decisions about how to do their work. Rather than completing one simple task and handing off the result to another worker, today's workers complete all or most of the procedures required to perform a process. At a minimum, they understand what procedures are required to perform a process.

When employees understand an entire process and clearly understand the expected result, they see where their jobs fit into the process and how their contributions work with others to produce that result. Because they understand the expected result, employees can eliminate bottlenecks and unnecessary tasks that may stand in their way or slow them down. Also, because employees are continuously identifying new customer requirements, employees who understand an entire process can respond quickly to changing customer needs. They can see that if they change one procedure, which, in turn, can change the input for the next procedure in the process, the next procedure will have to change as well. When a single procedure changes, the effect on the entire process must be analyzed, and employees can do that only if they understand the entire process.

 Anyone in a company—whether in the help desk, sales, marketing, accounting, or another department—can identify a new customer requirement. For example, someone in the accounting office might identify the fact that customers would prefer their invoices in a different format that includes additional information that the help desk must supply.

Because today's workers have a better understanding of processes, companies can use simpler processes. Simpler processes are more efficient, less prone to error, and less costly. Simpler processes also enable companies to eliminate management layers by allowing workers or teams of workers to make their own decisions, instead of waiting for management approval or direction. Companies that have few layers of management are often called "flat" organizations.

Whether simple or complex, processes must be continuously refined, or improved, to remain effective. This is because customer expectations about the products and services that companies deliver are constantly changing, just as customer expectations about the services that the help desk delivers are constantly changing. Companies that are committed to consistently providing products and services that meet or exceed their customers' expectations often establish a quality improvement program.

QUALITY IMPROVEMENT PROGRAMS

Quality improvement programs, or quality programs, represent a company's commitment to consistently providing products and services that meet customer expectations, or requirements. A **requirement** is something that is essential. New requirements are constantly surfacing. As a result, companies must continually assess the quality of their products and services, just as help desks must continually assess the quality of their services. **Quality** is a characteristic that measures how well products or services meet customer requirements.

Companies that have a quality program in place typically dedicate resources to activities such as developing, documenting, and improving processes. Some companies that establish quality programs are simply striving to use processes to continuously improve. Other companies are striving to improve their business opportunities or to receive awards. Figure 4-2 lists the most common quality improvement programs you may encounter in the business world:

- Total Quality Management (TQM)
- Malcolm Baldrige National Quality Award
- ISO 9000
- Capability Maturity Model (CMM)
- Information Technology Infrastructure Library (ITIL)

Figure 4-2   Quality improvement programs

Total Quality Management (TQM)

In the 1950s Japan developed a system known as **Total Quality Control** (**TQC**) to implement *Kaizen* in the workplace. *Kaizen* means continuing improvement that involves everyone—managers and workers alike. TQC is based on the teachings of Dr. W. Edwards Deming, an American consultant who specialized in statistical studies. Dr. Deming was invited to Japan by the Union of Japanese Scientists and Engineers (JUSE) to present a series of lectures on the basic principles of statistical quality control. His teachings made a deep impression on the participants—executives, managers, and engineers of Japanese industries—and led to the development of TQC in Japan.

Although its roots are in TQC, today the term Total Quality Management is used more commonly. **Total Quality Management (TQM)** is a management approach to long-term success through customer satisfaction. The term TQM was initially coined by the United States Naval Air Systems Command to describe its Japanese-style management approach to quality improvement. Since then, TQM has taken on many meanings. For the most part, however, total quality management relies on a single fundamental principle, which in today's competitive business climate very often serves as the core mission of any business: *Maximize productivity while minimizing costs.*

Productivity is an efficiency measure that relates output (goods and services produced) to input (the number of hours worked.) Companies and departments that produce information and services sometimes have a hard time quantifying output because their results are less obvious than, for example, a manufacturing company that produces products that can be easily counted. **Costs** are the amounts paid to produce a product, such as worker's wages, salaries, and benefits; the facilities and equipment that workers use; any materials and supplies they consume; and so on. When companies are able to maximize productivity while minimizing costs, they can increase the wages, salaries, and benefits they pay to workers without raising the prices they charge to their customers.

Malcolm Baldrige National Quality Award

Many American companies show their commitment to TQM by striving to receive the Malcolm Baldrige National Quality Award. Malcolm Baldrige was the U.S. Secretary of Commerce from 1981 until his death in July 1987. He felt strongly that continuous quality improvement was a key to the Unites States' prosperity and long-term strength, and he helped draft an early version of the quality improvement act that was eventually named after him. In recognition of his contributions, the U.S. Congress established the **Malcolm Baldrige National Quality Award** in 1987 to recognize U.S. organizations for their achievements in quality and business performance and to raise awareness about the importance of quality as a performance indicator. The award is not given for specific products or services. Rather, it is given to companies that are committed to delivering ever-improving value to customers and improving overall organizational performance. Five awards may be awarded annually, one in each of the following categories: manufacturing, service, small business, education, and healthcare.

Organizations that are headquartered in the United States may apply for the award. An independent Board of Examiners evaluates applications, looking for achievements and improvements in all of the following seven categories: leadership, strategic planning, customer and market focus, information and analysis, human resource focus, process management, and business results. Whether or not they apply for the award, thousands of organizations of all kinds use these seven categories, known as the Baldrige performance excellence criteria, for self-assessment and training and as a model for performance excellence.

ISO 9000

ISO 9000 is a set of universal standards for a quality assurance system that is accepted around the world. The standards were formulated and are maintained by the International Organization for Standardization, which is a worldwide federation of national standards bodies from some 100 countries, one from each country.

The first standard, ISO 9000, establishes a starting point for understanding the set of standards and defines the fundamental terms and definitions used in the ISO 9000 family. The second standard, ISO 9001, is the most comprehensive of the standards. It applies to industries involved in the design and development, manufacturing, installation, and servicing of products or services, and it is the standard that companies use to assess their ability to meet customer and applicable regulatory requirements. The remaining standards provide guidance that companies can use to manage their quality program.

ISO 9000 registration has become a must for any company that does business in Europe. Furthermore, many companies require their suppliers to become registered because a company's compliance with, in particular, ISO 9001 ensures that it has a commitment to continuously improve.

To become registered, companies must document and distribute their processes in a manner that conforms to the ISO standards. Companies must train their employees in the documented processes, and must be able to demonstrate through a series of quality audits that they are performing the processes as documented.

Although becoming registered is hard work, ISO 9000 registered companies have had dramatic reductions in customer complaints, significant reductions in operating costs, and increased demand for their products and services.

ISO is not an acronym for International Organization for Standardization, but a Greek word that means equal. ISO was selected because it is valid in English, French, and Russian, the three official languages of ISO.

Capability Maturity Model (CMM)

A set of quality-oriented management practices that are becoming more familiar to IT organizations are the Software Engineering Institute's Capability Maturity Models. The **Capability Maturity Models** (**CMMs**) assist organizations in maturing their people, process, and technology assets to improve long-term business performance. The Software Engineering Institute (SEI) has developed CMMs for software, people, and software acquisition, and assisted in the development of CMMs for systems engineering and integrated product development.

The CMMs are basically organized into five maturity levels: (1) initial, (2) repeatable, (3) defined, (4) managed, and (5) optimizing. Processes at the initial maturity level are characterized as ad-hoc and occasionally even chaotic. As organizations use TQM practices to develop and document processes, they move through the levels to the optimizing level where continuous process improvement has become a way of life.

Information Technology Infrastructure Library (ITIL)

The **Information Technology Infrastructure Library** (**ITIL**) is a set of best practices for IT service management. A **best practice** is an innovative process or concept that moves a company or department to a position of improved performance. ITIL was created in the mid-1980s by the United Kingdom's Central Computer and Telecommunications Agency (CCTA) in recognition of the fact that businesses worldwide were becoming increasingly dependent on information technology.

The ITIL consists of a series of books that give guidance on IT service management topics. Two of the main topics covered are service support and service delivery. Together, the service support and service delivery topics cover 10 disciplines or processes that are responsible for the provision and management of effective IT services. The service support books describe the operational processes required to provide efficient and cost-effective IT services on a daily basis. Service support processes include change management, configuration management, help desk, problem management, and software control and distribution. The service delivery books describe the tactical processes required to plan the delivery of IT services in anticipation of changing business requirements and technology advancements. Service delivery processes include availability management, capacity management, contingency planning, cost management, and service level management.

Today, ITIL is the most widely accepted approach to IT service management in the world. Like ISO 9000, ITIL certification is rapidly becoming a must for any company that does business in Europe. ITIL is used by companies such as Microsoft and Hewlett-Packard; many vendors that publish help desk call tracking and problem management systems have also been working hard in recent years to make their products ITIL compliant. As a result, its philosophy and vocabulary are quickly becoming familiar to help desk management and staff.

Although the quality improvement programs previously discussed are aimed at different audiences and may have slightly different vocabularies, the process maturity lifecycle represented by each is essentially the same. Processes must be:

- **Defined**—The processes' purpose and goals must be clearly stated.

- **Documented**—The processes' associated procedures and vocabulary must be published.

- **Managed via performance metrics**—The processes must be monitored and measured to ensure conformance to requirements.

- **Continuously improved**—The processes must be continuously refined to meet new and changing requirements.

Understanding how these programs are similar and how they are all aimed at enabling companies to produce quality products and services enables employees to be successful whether they work for a company that has formally adopted one of these programs or is "simply" trying to implement efficient and effective processes and procedures.

HELP DESK PROCESSES

Processes and procedures are particularly important in a fast-paced help desk setting, where the bottom line is always to meet or exceed customer expectations. A successful help desk must manage several tightly interconnected or integrated processes to achieve customer satisfaction. These processes are interconnected because the output produced by one process might be used as input to another process. Figure 4-3 shows the five most important help desk processes. These processes are needed to manage and support technology.

- **Problem management**—The process of tracking and resolving problems. A **problem** is an event that disrupts service or prevents access to products.

- **Request management**—The process of collecting and maintaining information about customer requests. A **request** is a customer order or request to obtain a new product or service, or an enhancement to an existing product or service.

- **Knowledge management**—The process of gathering and maintaining a company's information assets (knowledge) in a knowledge base.

- **Change management**—The process of controlling changes to the production environment while minimizing service disruptions.

- **Asset and configuration management**—The process of collecting and maintaining information about IT assets and showing the relationships that exist among those assets.

Figure 4-3   Important help desk processes

These five help desk processes are vital to the success of the help desk. Problem management, request management, and, increasingly, knowledge management are essential to achieving customer satisfaction—the main goal of a help desk. Change management and asset and configuration management are just as important. Change management allows change to occur as quickly as possible with the least amount of risk and impact (and the fewest number of problems). Asset and configuration management facilitates the capture and maintenance of information about the products and systems that the company supports. The help desk and others involved in support use this information to diagnose problems more quickly and to determine the potential impact of change. For example, analysts who perform the problem management process often use the information collected through the asset and configuration management process to determine where a failing hardware device is located or what software is installed on a customer's PC.

While important, these processes may not exist in some companies, or they may be defined differently from one company to the next. For example, some companies do not treat problem and request management as separate processes. Some companies adopt the philosophy that any time a customer cannot do something he or she wants to do, it is a problem. Other companies view any customer contact as a request for service, even when that request for service involves fixing a problem. Knowledge management may not exist because it is difficult to implement and some companies lack the technology needed to maintain this process successfully. The change management and asset and configuration management processes, although necessary, may not exist in some companies because either they do not have the resources to perform these processes or they simply do not recognize the importance of these processes.

 A clearly defined process ensures that people focus their efforts on tasks that produce the intended result. In a help desk setting, this means satisfying customers.

Flow charts are often used in business to outline processes. The flow charts in this chapter present overviews of the most common help desk processes. A **flow chart** is a diagram that shows the sequence of tasks that occur in a process. Table 4-1 describes the purpose of each symbol used in flow charts. Flow charts are a good way to show how all the procedures involved in a process are interconnected.

Table 4-1   Flow chart symbols

Symbol	Name	Purpose
(A)	**On Page Connector**	Represents an exit to, or entry from, another part of the same flowchart.
Task	**Task**	Shows a single task or operation.
Predefined Process	**Predefined process**	Represents another process that provides input or receives output from the current process.
Decision	**Decision**	Represents a decision point and typically has a "yes" branch and a "no" branch.
—No→	**No result**	Used in conjunction with a decision to show the next task or decision following a "no" result.
Yes	**Yes result**	Used in conjunction with a decision to show the next task or decision following a "yes" result.
Terminator	**Terminator**	Shows the end or stopping point of a process.

Problem Management Process

Problem management is the process of tracking and resolving problems. A **problem** is an event that disrupts service or prevents access to products. Common problems include a broken device, an error message, and a system outage. The goal of problem management is to minimize the impact of problems that affect a company's systems, networks, and products. Sometimes called **incident management**, problem management also includes answering customers' questions and inquiries. **Questions**, such as "How do I...?," are customer requests for instruction on how to use a product. Questions occur when a product is not broken, but the customer simply needs help using it. **Inquiries**, such as "When will the part for my equipment arrive?," are customer requests for information. Inquiries, like questions, typically occur when the product is not broken, but the customer wants a current status report. Most companies distinguish between problems, questions, and inquiries because they represent varying degrees of impact and speak differently to product and company performance. For example, a customer calling to inquire about the date for the next release of a software package may not be dissatisfied with the existing product and is just looking forward to the new version. On the other hand, a customer who gets error messages or loses data when trying to use a software package clearly is dissatisfied, and the company must try to resolve the problem quickly or risk losing that customer.

Some help desks distinguish between problems, questions, inquiries, and "requests" when categorizing the types of incidents they manage via their problem management process. This is because some companies do not have a separate request management process. In time, however, most help desks distinguish between problems—events that disrupt installed products or existing services—and requests—requests for new products or services.

Problem management includes a series of activities that can occur consecutively, simultaneously, or not at all. These tasks include:

- **Problem recognition**—Detecting and identifying problems or potential problems through monitoring, trend analysis, and observation.

- **Reporting and logging**—Notifying a central point such as the help desk about a problem and logging information about the problem, typically in an incident tracking system.

- **Problem determination**—Identifying the source of a problem; also called problem isolation.

- **Bypass and recovery**—Circumventing a problem either partially or completely, usually before implementing the final resolution; also called **workaround**. Bypass and recovery procedures can make the failing product or system usable again.

- **Resolution**—Performing the final and permanent corrective action that repairs, replaces, or modifies the source of a problem to the customer's satisfaction. The fix to a problem is generally applied under the control of change management.

- **Management Review**—Evaluating the efficiency and effectiveness of the problem management process and associated reporting system.

The management review task differentiates problem "tracking" from problem "management." **Problem tracking** follows *one* problem from recognition to resolution. The problem management process reviews *all* problems to help ensure that they have been permanently resolved in a timely fashion and that steps have been taken to prevent similar problems in the future. Tracking a single problem through to resolution is important because it ensures the customer's satisfaction. Looking at all problems that have occurred allows the help desk to identify related or recurring problems, trends, and problem-prevention opportunities.

Help desks resolve a high percentage of reported problems—around 70 percent—when effective processes and procedures are in place. In addition, analysts must have the technical skills needed to support the products that customers are using. They also need the tools that enable them to diagnose and resolve problems quickly.

The flow chart in Figure 4-4 shows how responsibility for specific tasks changes as a problem moves from recognition to resolution in the problem management process. Note that each level tries to resolve the customer's problem before handing it off to the next level and that after the problem is resolved and a change implemented, the owner contacts the customer to make sure the customer is satisfied with the solution before closing the problem record.

This flow chart is a fairly simple representation of how the problem management process may work within a company. This process varies from one company to the next and is refined continuously. Once the overall process is defined or refined, a company develops procedures so that everyone involved in the process of solving problems understands exactly who needs to do what to satisfy customers. These procedures, along with the company's policies with regard to issues such as customer entitlement, problem severity and priority, problem escalation, problem ownership, and problem notification, clearly define how to perform each step in the process.

Customer Entitlement

Before the help desk tries to resolve a customer's problem, it must check **customer entitlement**, which is the determination of whether the customer is authorized to receive support and, if so, the level of support the customer should receive. Some companies don't determine entitlement. For example, internal help desks that provide "free" support to the company's employees rarely determine entitlement. Companies that charge for all or some

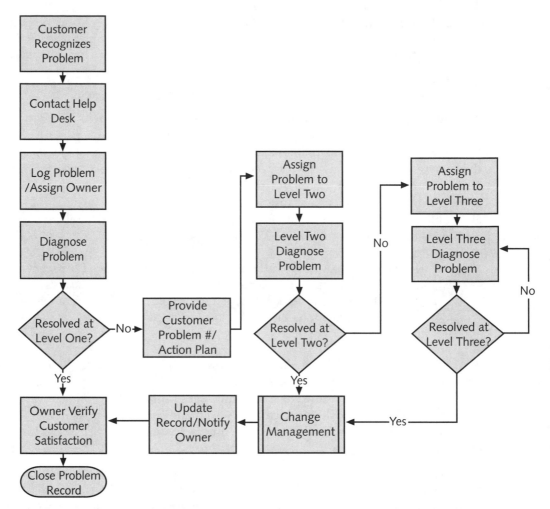

Figure 4-4   Problem management process

help desk services (such as after-hours support, premium support, and so forth) verify that a customer's service contract is current or that the customer is entitled to the level of support being requested. In many companies, entitlement consists simply of asking the customer for a contract number, customer ID number, or personal identification number (PIN).

Problem Severity and Priority

Once entitlement is verified, the help desk must establish how severe the problem is and then determine when and how to solve it. Although first-come, first-served may sound fair, it is ultimately not in the best interest of the business. Severe problems that have a greater impact on the customer's ability to do his or her work must be resolved more quickly than minor or inconvenient problems. The help desk uses severity and problem priority codes to categorize reported problems.

Severity is the category that defines how critical a problem is based on the nature of the failure and the available alternatives or workarounds. For example, problems that affect a high number of customers are typically considered more critical than a problem that affects a single customer. Typically, the help desk and customer work together to determine a problem's severity. As shown in Table 4-2, each severity level has a **target resolution time**, the time frame within which the support organization is expected to resolve the problem. Most companies establish guidelines for target resolution times that consider the problem severity and the combined efforts of service providers in level one, level two, and level three that may be called upon to resolve the problem. However, there tend to be provisions for adjusting the target resolution time after all resources involved in resolving the problem have diagnosed the problem and can more accurately estimate how long it will take to resolve. Also, some companies establish guidelines for **target response time**, the time frame within which the help desk or level two acknowledges the problem, diagnoses the problem, and estimates the target resolution time.

Table 4-2   Sample Severity Definitions

Severity	Definition	Example
1	System or device down, critical business impact, no workaround available, begin resolution activities immediately, bypass/recover within four hours, resolve within 24 hours.	A network device is not working and many customers are affected. The only printer that can print checks or special forms is malfunctioning. A real-time critical application, such as payroll or the company's Web site, is down.
2	System or component down or level of service degraded, potential business impact, alternative or workaround available, resolve within 48 hours.	A slow response time on the network is severely affecting a large number of customers. The network is down but customers can dial in to do their work. A product is usable; however, its use is restricted due to memory constraints.
3	Not critical, customer can wait, a workaround is possible, resolve within 72 hours.	A printer is down, but customers can route their output to a similar printer down the hall. One of many registers in a retail store is down at a slow time of the month.
4	Not critical, customer can wait, a workaround is possible with no operational impact, time to resolve negotiated with customer.	A "how to" question or a request for one-on-one help using a product. Intermittent errors that the customer can work around. One of two speakers attached to a PC is not working.

Determining problem severity is one of the most difficult challenges for help desk analysts. Customers often insist their problem is critical when it may be relatively minor compared to other problems. To combat this, many companies publish definitions with specific examples of each problem severity so that their customers and the help desk define severity in the same way.

Make sure you understand the problem severity definitions for any company where you work. What is more important, make sure you understand the target resolution time associated with each severity so that you can be specific when telling a customer when he or she can expect a resolution or a status update. Promising a swift resolution may make a customer happy in the short term; however, he or she will become dissatisfied and distrusting if the support organization cannot deliver a swift resolution.

Problem severity typically remains the same throughout the life of a problem. This ensures that a problem is resolved in the proper time frame and that it is not forgotten or neglected, even if a workaround is possible. In other words, a workaround is only temporary and does not reduce the problem's severity. The problem still exists and can happen again until it is permanently resolved. Using a single severity rating also ensures that ad-hoc, daily, weekly, and month-end reports accurately reflect the severity of outstanding problems.

A common misconception is that the terms *problem severity* and *problem priority* (discussed below) are interchangeable. For example, some companies use only problem severity to manage their workload. Other companies use only problem priority. Furthermore, the definitions of these terms vary from one company to the next. These terms are not, however, interchangeable. By definition, problem severity is used to communicate the impact that problems are having on the business. Problem priority is used to manage workload. Severity rules. However, in the absence of higher-severity problems, problem priority determines the order in which problems are addressed.

After the help desk determines a problem's severity, a problem priority is assigned by the help desk or by the level two or level three group designated to work on the problem. **Problem priority** identifies the order for working on problems with the same severity. Table 4-3 shows some sample problem priority definitions.

Table 4-3   Sample Problem Priority Definitions

Priority	Definition
1	Target resolution time exceeded by 100 percent; problem recurs more than five times; as directed by management.
2	Target resolution time exceeded by 50 percent; problem recurs more than two times; as directed by management.
3	Initial priority setting for all problems.

Note that the problem priority increases if a problem is not resolved within its target resolution time, the customer's down time is excessive, the problem recurs, or management directs it. Management may increase the priority of a problem when, for example, the customer affected is a company executive, the customer has had a similar problem before that was not resolved to the customer's satisfaction, or management simply makes a judgment call and prioritizes one problem over another. Increasing the priority of a problem when it is not being resolved in a timely manner is called **priority aging**. Priority aging eliminates any confusion that the help desk, the customer, or other involved parties may have when determining the order in which to work on problems. Figure 4-5 shows how the priority of a problem might change as it ages.

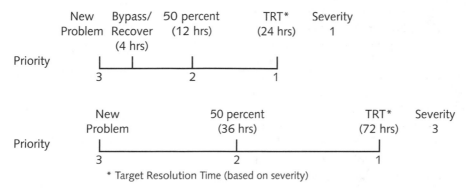

Figure 4-5   Sample priority aging matrix

Notice in the case of the severity 1 problem that even though a bypass (workaround) is required within four hours, the priority continues to age until a *permanent* resolution that satisfies the customer is identified and implemented.

 Figure 4-5 shows the priority aging based on the percentage of time that has elapsed relative to the target resolution time. Some companies, however, escalate problems based simply on time elapsed. For example, some companies escalate high-severity problems every hour or every two hours. The priority of lower-severity problems might escalate every 24 hours, or every 48 hours, and so forth.

Problem Escalation

Sometimes, the help desk is unable to figure out a problem's cause or find a permanent resolution. For those cases, the help desk needs clearly defined escalation procedures for each type of potential problem. **Escalation** (or escalate) means to raise a problem from one level to another, such as from level one to level two, to dedicate new or additional resources to the problem. The severity and priority of the problem influence how quickly the help desk escalates problems from one level to the next. For example, typically the help desk escalates high-severity problems quickly to level two and, if necessary, to level

three. Escalation ensures that the support organization resolves problems in the most efficient and cost-effective manner possible whether the help desk or a level two group or
a level three group resolves them, and that appropriate problem notification activities
occur until the problem is resolved.

 Many companies use the term *escalation* differently, which can be confusing.
Some use escalation interchangeably with the term *priority aging*. For example, a company might "escalate" the priority of a problem to give it more
importance. Others use escalation to indicate that management should be
involved or notified. For example, a company might "escalate" a problem to
management when the help desk has insufficient resources to resolve the
problem; or, a company might establish "escalation" procedures that describe
who to notify during a system outage. Make sure you understand how the
company where you work defines this term.

Customers sometimes perceive that the help desk escalates a problem because it does
not have the knowledge or ability to solve the problem. Although this is true in some
cases, the help desk often escalates problems based on a **target escalation time**, a time
constraint placed on each level that ensures that problem resolution activities are proceeding at an appropriate pace. For example, a company might establish the guideline
that if level one doesn't find a solution within 30 minutes, it escalates the problem to
level two. The help desk might also escalate a problem because of a security consideration or to involve a resource that is closer to the problem (such as an on-site service
representative). Figure 4-6 shows how a PC hardware problem might be escalated.

Figure 4-6   Sample escalation sequence for a PC hardware problem

The ultimate goal is to resolve most problems at level one and to escalate only a few
problems to level three. Escalating a problem from level one does not indicate lack of
skill at the help desk. For example, the help desk may have to hand off the problem to
field services simply because it doesn't have the tools needed to diagnose the problem
remotely and must send someone to the site. As problems escalate, each level must document its efforts to resolve the problem and pass along as much information as possible
to the next level. This enables analysts at each level to know the current status of the
problem and to learn how they can handle similar problems in the future.

Each level has specific responsibilities and activities. Recall that **level one** is the initial
point of contact for customers when they have a problem, question, inquiry, or request.
For example, a customer experiencing an error message while using a software application

contacts the help desk to report the problem. The customer reaches a level one analyst, who then performs the following activities:

- Gathers data about the problem from the customer and creates a problem ticket.

- Provides the customer a problem number.

- Determines the probable source of the problem.

- Resolves the problem, if possible, using available tools and procedures.

- Records (or documents) the resolution in the problem ticket.

- Negotiates problem severity with the customer when necessary.

- Documents the problem's current status and the resolution steps attempted or completed.

- Escalates the problem to level two as necessary.

- Retains ownership of escalated problems in an effort to ensure timely resolution (discussed below).

- Ensures that the customer has an up-to-date status.

- Ensures that the customer is satisfied once the problem is resolved.

- Closes the problem ticket.

If the level one analyst cannot resolve the customer's problem, then the problem escalates to level two. **Level two** is the person or group that resolves problems which are beyond the scope or authority (such as system access rights or permissions) of level one. Level two might be a software development group, a network support group, or a subject matter expert. Continuing the earlier example, the level one analyst contacts the development group responsible for the software application that is generating the error message. The person or group at level two performs the following activities:

- Acknowledges assignments from level one.

- Reviews data provided by level one and gathers additional data as needed.

- Resolves problems related to their area of expertise within the time frame required by the problem's severity.

- Documents the resolution of all problems assigned to them.

- Regularly documents the status of problems that require an extended period of time to resolve.

- Provides the customer and other interested parties, such as management, with ongoing communication regarding the status of problems that require an extended period of time to resolve. Communication is direct or through the help desk.

- Reassigns problems when appropriate (for example, to other level two service providers if the problem was assigned to the wrong group).

- Documents the current status of problems and the resolution steps attempted or completed.

- Escalates problems to level three when necessary.

If level two cannot resolve the customer's problem, the problem then escalates to level three. **Level three** is the person or group that resolves complex problems that are beyond the scope of level two. This level might involve multiple technical areas (for example, the network group and the application group may work together to solve a problem), hardware or software vendors, consultants, or a subject matter expert. Continuing the example, the development group supporting the application may find it is necessary to contact the software publisher that originally developed the product that is producing the error. The person or group at level three performs the following activities:

- Acknowledges assignments from level two.

- Reviews data provided by level one and level two, and gathers additional data as needed.

- Regularly documents the status of problems that require an extended period of time to resolve.

- Regularly communicates the status of problems that require an extended period of time to resolve to the customer—directly or through the help desk—and other interested parties, such as management.

- Resolves problems related to their area of expertise within the time frame required by the problem's severity.

- Oversees resolution activities that require multiple technical areas, a third-party vendor, or a consultant.

- Documents the current status of problems and the resolution steps attempted or completed.

- Documents the resolution.

After a problem is escalated to level three, any and all resources needed to solve the problem are engaged and work together until the problem is resolved. Occasionally, problems cannot be resolved. For example, the solution to a problem may require that the software publisher change the software in a way it is not willing to do. In that type of situation, the vendor's response is communicated to the customer—the person or group who relays the information to the customer varies from one situation to the next—and efforts are made to provide the customer an acceptable workaround. Most problems can, however, be solved to the customer's satisfaction at level one, and only the most complex problems escalate through level two to level three. The goal is to solve as many problems as possible at level one.

4

MALCOLM FRY
PRESIDENT
FRY-CONSULTANTS
UNITED KINGDOM
WWW.MALCOLMFRY.COM

In the past ten years, help desks have gotten very good at first level problem resolution. They've had to in some respects because service and support is being looked at in a different way. Once considered a back office role, the help desk is now part of the front office and the impact of problem management is hugely magnified. Consider a retailer with an online store. If the company's Web site is down, the CEO may now have a direct line to the help desk to ask, "Why is our biggest store down?"

People entering the help desk field today are joining an industry that is increasingly important and the level of professional opportunity is proportional. You could say that in the last ten years the help desk has gone from being simply a job to a profession with career prospects, qualifications, and recognition. Working in a help desk will enable you to hone your problem-solving skills and, more importantly in the coming years, your problem-elimination skills. Going into the future, help desks must get better at problem elimination, which can be accelerated by adopting a best practice such as the Information Technology Infrastructure Library (ITIL). They must integrate their processes, use good processes to expose bad processes, and get better at harnessing technology, all in an effort to prevent problems, rather than simply fixing them quickly. If people want to be exposed to how a business works and how they can impact a company's bottom line, there is no better place to start than the help desk.

Problem Ownership

The concept of **problem ownership**, also known as total contact ownership, ensures that when the help desk analyst cannot resolve a problem during the first call or escalates the problem to a person or group outside of the help desk, a problem owner is designated. The **problem owner** is an employee of the support organization who acts as a customer advocate and proactively ensures that a problem is resolved to the customer's satisfaction. When a problem owner is designated, the customer shouldn't have to initiate another call. Nor should the customer have to call around to the different groups involved in solving the problem to find out the problem's status or progress. The problem owner does that for them. In addition, the problem owner:

- Tracks the current status of the problem, including who is working on the problem and where the problem is in the process.

- When possible, identifies related problems.

- Ensures that problems are assigned correctly and not passed along from level to level or group to group without any effort being made to identify a resolution.

- Ensures that appropriate notification activities occur when a problem is reported, escalated, and resolved.

- Before closing a problem, ensures that all problem-solving activities are documented and that the customer is satisfied with the resolution.

- Closes the problem ticket.

In many companies, the person who logs the problem initially is the owner. In other words, the level one analyst who initially handles a problem continues to follow up, even when problems are escalated to level two or level three. Often, the level one analyst (problem owner) is the only person who can close the problem and does so only after verifying that the customer is satisfied. Figure 4-7 shows a sample escalation sequence where the level one analyst and the problem owner are the same person.

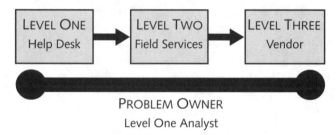

Figure 4-7   Sample escalation sequence with problem owner

In other companies, the problem owner changes as problems are escalated from one level to the next. The person designated to work on the problem must accept responsibility for the problem and agree to assume ownership before the previous problem owner transfers responsibility for the problem (ownership) to the new owner.

 Problem management is often known as a "closed loop process" because the customer who reports a problem must accept the solution before the problem can be closed.

Ownership is critical to the problem management process. Without it, customer dissatisfaction invariably occurs. Ownership forces everyone involved in the problem management process to stay focused on the customer's need to have the problem solved in a timely fashion and to be informed when the problem requires more than the expected time to resolve.

Problem Notification

An extremely important part of problem management is promoting awareness that a problem has occurred and regularly communicating the status of problem resolution activities. These activities are known as problem notification. **Notification** informs all of the stakeholders in the problem management process (including management, the customer, help desk analysts, and so forth) about the status of outstanding problems. Notification can occur when a problem is reported or escalated, when a problem has exceeded a predefined threshold (such as its target resolution time), or when a problem is resolved.

Notification to each of the stakeholders occurs at different points and has different goals. For example, *management* notification is appropriate when:

- The problem is extremely severe.
- The problem priority has changed.
- The target resolution time has been or is about to be reached.
- Required resources are not available to determine or implement a solution.
- The customer expresses dissatisfaction.

In each of these cases, notification keeps management aware of problems that might require management intervention. The goals of management notification are to ensure that:

- Management knows the current status of problems that are in an exception state, meaning that the problems have exceeded a predefined threshold. For example, the target resolution time has been exceeded, or a level two group is not acknowledging a problem that has been assigned to them.

- Management has sufficient information to make decisions (such as add more resources, determine what group a problem should be assigned to, or reassign responsibilities), follow up with the customer, or call in other management.

- Management actions are recorded in the problem record so that everyone affected by or involved in solving the problem knows what decisions management has made or what steps they have taken to follow up with the customer or involve other management.

These goals make sure that the customer's problem is being addressed and responded to in an appropriate time and way. Like management notification, customer notification is appropriate in specific situations, such as when:

- The problem priority has changed.
- The target resolution time will not be met.
- Customer resources are required to implement a solution.
- The problem is a high severity and justifies frequent status updates.

- The customer has been promised status updates at certain times.

- The customer was dissatisfied with earlier solutions.

Customer notification keeps the customer informed about the progress of problem resolution activities. The goals of customer notification are to ensure that:

- The customer knows the current status of the problem.

- Customer comments or concerns are recorded in the problem record and addressed.

These goals make sure that the customer knows that the problem is being addressed and responded to in an appropriate time and way.

Three ways that help desks deliver value are by: (1) making it easy for customers to report problems; (2) delivering solutions; and (3) ensuring that problems which cannot be resolved immediately are addressed in the required time frame. One of the most common complaints that help desks hear from customers is that they were not kept informed. It is important to remember that even bad news is better than no news at all. Calling the customer to let them know that the target resolution time cannot be met and perhaps explaining the reason for any delays (such as having to order parts) is far better than having the customer hear nothing.

Keep the customer informed.... Keep the customer!

The help desk can notify management, customers, and others verbally by telephone or in person, with an e-mail message, through a paging device, or automatically by the problem management system. How notification occurs and who is notified varies based on conditions such as the severity of the problem, who is affected by the problem, and when the problem occurs. Many companies have documented procedures that spell out who to notify and how to notify them. Figure 4-8 shows a sample problem notification procedure.

To see how this procedure works, consider a severity 1 problem (such as a server going down). The help desk staff follows the documented procedures and immediately notifies affected customers, management, and the appropriate level two group (in case they are unaware). Customers are notified verbally. Level two automatically receives notification through the problem management system when the problem ticket is assigned to them. The problem owner determines whether or not to notify management and senior management immediately. Once the problem has exceeded 50 percent of its target resolution time, the problem owner receives an alert from the problem management system, which prompts them to follow up and provide a status to management. Management is informed about the problem status through a page.

	Problem Identification	Based on Severity												Problem Resolution
		1			2			3			4			
		50	75	100	50	75	100	50	75	100	50	75	100	
Customer	V		V	V	V	V			D	D		D	D	D
Problem Owner	V	A	A	A	A	A	A		A	A		A	A	A
Level Two	A		A	A	A	A	A		A	A			A	D
Management	D	P	P	P		P	P	E	E				E	D
Senior Management	D		P	P	P									D

Legend:

A – Automatic notification (via the problem management system)
D – Notification requirements are determined by the problem owner
E – E-mail notification
P – Pager notification
V – Verbal notification

50 – 50% of the target resolution time has passed
75 – 75% of the target resolution time has passed
100 – 100% of the target resolution time has passed

Figure 4-8   Sample problem notification procedure

Now consider a severity 4 problem, such as a customer calling to say a printer needs to be cleaned. In this case, management would not be notified about this problem until it had exceeded its target resolution time, and then they would receive that notification by e-mail, a media that is used for less urgent notifications because there is no guarantee management checks their e-mail regularly.

Problem notification procedures are designed to ensure that all involved parties are kept fully informed when highly severe problems occur and are informed only when non-critical problems exceed predefined thresholds. The ultimate goal is to ensure that notification occurs *before* the target resolution time is exceeded so that the support organization can meet the customer's expectation.

The help desk cannot be held solely responsible for effective problem management. The company must commit the resources necessary to design, implement, and maintain a problem management process that ensures timely notification and permanent problem resolution in a time frame in keeping with the severity of the problem. The company also must capture resolution information and procedures, a process known as knowledge management (discussed later), so that information can be reused and the time required to resolve problems reduced.

ELAINE FROST
DIRECTOR OF PRODUCT SERVICES
ISLAND PACIFIC SYSTEMS (SOFTWARE PUBLISHER)
IRVINE, CALIFORNIA
WWW.ISLANDPACIFIC.COM

Island Pacific Systems is a software development company specializing in retail management systems. Our corporate headquarters is located in Irvine, California, and we have an office in the United Kingdom that serves our European and Asian user community. The company consists of approximately 125 employees and its primary departments are Development, Quality Assurance, Services, Product Management, Sales, Marketing, and Administration. The success of each department is highly dependent upon the performance of the others.

The Support Center is located within Services and the customer Helpdesk is located within The Support Center. The Helpdesk is composed of Application, Technical, and Customer Relations personnel. The Application team is unique in that it is composed of retailers who have extensive work experience in the industry versus individuals who have had prior call center or computer support experience. Unlike most help desks, we use no automated call handling. Each caller is immediately greeted in person.

Tasks. The majority of incoming customer calls (90 percent) are routed through the Helpdesk. The remaining 10 percent represents calls to our Customer Relations Managers, whose role is to provide account management, project management, consultation, and training services to customers. The mission of the Helpdesk is to assist customers with procedure execution questions and to validate and correct suspected program defects.

Only customers enrolled in our maintenance program are eligible to receive assistance through the Helpdesk. The Helpdesk receives an average of 100 calls per week. Each call is electronically tracked from inception through resolution in our System Support Request (SSR) system. This allows us to monitor the current status of the request, the flow of incoming calls, the types of requests, and, most significantly, all activity taken to effect the resolution of the support request. It also serves as our knowledge base. Customers also have the option of e-mailing their questions directly to the Helpdesk. The response time for these e-mails is as quick as a phone call. An SSR is immediately assigned and the customer is called back promptly.

The tracking system also allows us to monitor the quality of our products and services and determine staffing requirements as well as provides a historical record of activity taken on behalf of the customer and on the development and maintenance activity of the product. Our SSR system links to our change management system and provides the supporting detail from which all programming activity begins. The SSR system is the "heart" of the company, and all employees access the system daily for entry, research, and follow-up purposes.

Organization. The Support Center is process-driven and follows a three-tiered model: Levels 1, 2, and 3, respectively.

Level 1: This level represents support requests handled by the Application team. These are typically questions related to the execution of the application. When problems are encountered, the Application team gathers as much information as possible and attempts to duplicate the problem in a test environment to determine if a program defect exists or if the customer's understanding of how to use the application is unclear. If technical or analytical business skills are required to advance toward resolution, the Application team will advance the issue to Level 2 support.

Level 2: This level is composed of a technical team (Technical) and an analytical business team (Client Relations). The technical team consists of programmers. The analytical business team consists of retail business analysts who are expert level in product knowledge. The technical team's primary responsibility is to provide technical consultation to the Application team and to correct program defects. Design-related issues or those of a larger scope requiring special consideration and resources are escalated to Level 3.

Level 3: This level is composed of senior programmers (Development) who have either authored the application program or have "ownership" responsibility for enhancing the program. These highly skilled technicians are always available to work with The Support Center on critical customer issues when requested. The Project Management team is responsible for maintaining the design and consistency of the product.

The Support Center processes serve us well by providing a fundamental baseline from which all support begins and ends. The three-tiered model ensures an escalation path is available to customers through The Support Center for complex requests. Additionally, to ensure we close the loop on all requests, the Application team member who entered the original customer request is responsible for following the request through our processes to successful resolution and distribution to the customer. Tracking reports are available to assist the Application team in this effort. Ultimately, the customer is given the opportunity to rate the performance of The Support Center.

Customer satisfaction also influences our hiring and individual performance management practices. Because we exclusively service the retail industry, we hire individuals who have extensive work experience in that industry. Individuals must be outgoing, friendly, organized, able to multi-task, and willing to be challenged on a daily basis.

Once someone has been hired, there are three levels of advancement. Each individual is rated by skill and placed into the appropriate grade of novice, intermediate, or expert. Each individual's Performance and Salary Evaluation is updated biannually and goals are established at that time as well. Compensation is tied to performance, skill, and customer satisfaction.

Philosophy. Our philosophy is to work internally as a team and to build partnerships and long-term relationships with our customers. Extremely complex issues often require multiple and varied skill levels to effect resolution. Each individual's role in the company is valued, from the receptionist who welcomes the caller to the Application team who interprets requests for help, from the technical and analytical business team who creatively solve complex problems to the developers who build the applications. No one individual can succeed without help from their teammates.

Request Management Process

Request management is the process of collecting and maintaining information about customer requests. A **request** is a customer order or request to obtain a new product or service or an enhancement to an existing product or service. Common requests include moves, adds, and changes, such as moving a printer, installing a new PC or new software, and enhancing an application or upgrading software. The goal of request management is to identify and document the tasks required to satisfy requests and ensure that appropriate resources are assigned. This includes maintaining information about the status of requests and knowing what requests are outstanding, how much effort those requests represent, and when the requests must be completed.

Request management is just as important as problem management because it ensures that customers have access to the systems, products, and networks they need to do their work. The difference between problem management and request management is that when customers have a request, they are asking for access they have never had. However, when customers contact the help desk with a problem, that problem is preventing them from gaining access to a system, product, or network that they were previously able to use.

Like problem management, request management includes a series of activities that can occur consecutively, simultaneously, or not at all. Request management activities include:

- **Request entry**—Submitting to a central point such as the help desk the initial request for service and logging information about the request, typically in an incident tracking system.

- **Assessment**—Evaluating the practicality and urgency of the request and recommending an action.

- **Management approval**—Evaluating the recommendations made during the assessment phase, followed by management accepting, rejecting, or deferring the request.

- **Implementation**—Performing the installation steps required to satisfy the request. These installation activities generally are applied under the control of change management.

- **Management review**—Evaluating the efficiency and effectiveness of the request management process and associated reporting system.

Like problem management, the management review activity of the request management process differentiates request "tracking" from request "management." Whereas tracking a single request through to implementation is important, analyzing request trends also is important because it enables the support organization to be proactive. For example, if a large number of customers are requesting the installation of a new software product, the support organization may want to develop a schedule and inform customers that they will be receiving the software in accordance with that schedule.

The flow chart in Figure 4-9 shows how responsibility for a specific task changes as a request moves from request entry to implementation.

Requests can vary considerably in complexity. The resolution of a simple request, such as setting up a new user account, might occur within hours of the request. A more complex request, such as developing a new program, can take months to complete. Some requests are never filled if, after analysis, the company or the customer determines that the cost associated with completing the request is greater than the benefit the customer or the company will gain from fulfilling the request.

The role of the help desk in the request management process can vary from one company to the next and even within a company based on the type of request. For example, the help desk may be involved actively with a request to set up a new employee by coordinating the efforts of groups such as facilities (who readies the person's cubicle), field services (who sets up the PC), and so forth; or, the help desk may simply log and hand off to the development group a request to enhance a software application. Because it may take months of development time to satisfy an application enhancement request,

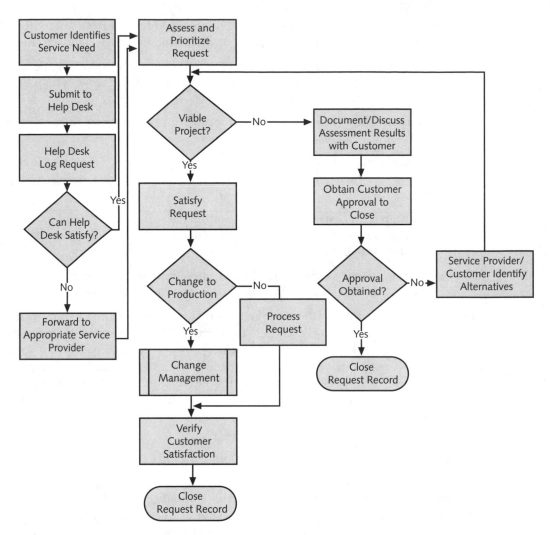

Figure 4-9 Request management process

the help desk may have little involvement until the software is nearing the point where it is ready to be released. Typically, the help desk performs the following activities in the request management process:

- Gathers data and creates a request ticket.
- Provides the customer a request number.
- Satisfies the requests when possible.
- Documents the resolution.
- Forwards requests to the appropriate service provider when necessary.

- Retains ownership when appropriate.

- Ensures that the customer has an up-to-date status when appropriate.

- Confirms that the customer is satisfied once a request is resolved.

- Closes the request ticket.

Like problems, requests are prioritized to ensure that they are resolved in a timely manner and in an order that meets the needs of the business. Also, it is important that each request has a designated owner and that appropriate notification activities occur.

Request Priority

Although the help desk fulfills some requests (such as setting up new user accounts and electronically distributing software), other service providers such as level two groups handle many of the service requests submitted to the help desk. Typically, the service provider works with the customer to establish the request priority. **Request priority** identifies the order for working on submitted requests. Some requests, such as requests to install new software or set up new user accounts, are handled on a first-in, first-out basis. Other requests receive a higher priority because the company or the customer will benefit by implementing the request or because the change is mandated. For example, a change in the law requires a change to the company's accounting package. Table 4-4 shows sample request priority definitions.

Few companies have the resources to satisfy every customer request immediately. Prioritizing ensures that requests that most benefit the business are handled first, followed by other requests, which then are handled on a first-in, first-out basis. Designating a request owner ensures that requests are not lost or forgotten and that appropriate notification activities occur.

Table 4-4   Sample Request Priority Definitions

Priority	Definition
1	Immediate attention. Request must be implemented because there is a legal, audit, regulatory, or business (mandatory) requirement. Pull resources from other projects and assign resources as needed to complete projects by deadlines.
2	Mandated requirement (such as legal, audit, regulatory, business, and so on) or business justified projects. Schedule on a first-in, first-out basis consistent with other projects of the same priority. Priority 2 requests have sufficient lead time, so there is no need to pull resources from other projects.
3	Low-priority projects that could increase customer productivity but lack the significant cost justification of priority 1 or 2 requests. Schedule on a first-in, first-out basis as fill-in work or between projects.
4	Very low priority. Projects for which the customer asked that the request remain open and is aware that no resources will be assigned to the request.

Request Ownership and Notification

Whether the help desk "owns" requests the way they own problems varies from one company to the next. In some companies, the help desk assumes ownership of all or certain types of requests. For example, the help desk may own requests that require multiple groups to complete so that it can coordinate the efforts of those groups and serve as a single point of contact for customers. In other cases, the help desk may transfer ownership to the assigned service provider. For example, the development group may take ownership of requests for enhancements to a software program. The **request owner** is an employee of the support organization who keeps the customer informed and is involved in scheduling any installation activities needed to complete the request. Typically, new hardware, application programs, off-the-shelf software products, and so forth are first installed and tested in a "development" environment that customers cannot access. This way, any problems that occur do not affect customers. Once companies feel that the programs or products have been tested fully and as many problems as possible have been eliminated, the programs or products are scheduled for installation in the "production" environment, where customers can access them. Requests that change the production environment usually flow through the change management process (discussed below).

Distinguishing Problem and Request Management

Although it may seem that the help desk could use the same process to manage problems and requests, most companies find sufficient differences to warrant separate processes. For example:

- Management approval is typically not needed to resolve problems, whereas management approval is almost always needed before work begins on a request.

- Problems are typically worked on until they are resolved, whereas requests may be rejected. For example, if a customer requests a piece of equipment that does not conform to the company's standard, his request will typically be rejected unless the purchase can be justified.

- Problems are often prioritized differently from requests because customers typically view restoring service as more important than adding new service.

- A single group typically solves problems, whereas requests often require the efforts of multiple groups. For example, the help desk can reset a customer's password without involving any other groups, but setting up a new office requires the facilities group, the network group, the field service group, and so forth.

- Companies want to be able to accurately report their performance and the impact of their actions to customers. For example, an unscheduled outage that occurs as a result of a problem often has a greater impact than a scheduled outage that occurs so that a new system can be implemented. In the case of the scheduled outage, customers are able to prepare for the impact, whereas with unscheduled problems they are not.

Both the problem and request management process provide input to and receive output from the knowledge management process.

Knowledge Management Process

A majority of today's technology problems and requests are recurring, meaning that they happen over and over. Because of this, many companies continuously enter the information needed to resolve known problems and requests into knowledge bases. Recall that a knowledge base is a collection of information sources such as customer information, documents, policies and procedures, and incident resolutions. Anyone who needs the information, such as help desk staff, level two and level three staff, and even customers, can use or reference these knowledge bases. **Knowledge management** is the process of gathering and maintaining a company's information assets (knowledge) in a knowledge base. The goal of knowledge management is to enable the support organization and customers to share and reuse previously acquired knowledge. Knowledge management activities include:

- **Knowledge capture**—Submitting to a central point, such as the knowledge engineer, reusable information and logging that information, typically in a knowledge base.

- **Knowledge review**—Evaluating the information to make sure it is accurate and conforms to predefined standards.

- **Knowledge revision**—Refining the information as needed to improve its accuracy and ensure that it conforms to standards.

- **Knowledge approval**—Evaluating the refinements made during the knowledge revision phase followed by the knowledge engineer's acceptance or rejection of the information.

- **Management review**—Evaluating the efficiency and effectiveness of the knowledge management process and associated reporting system.

As these activities indicate, the knowledge management process is becoming increasingly more important and formalized. This is because the rapid pace of change is making it very difficult for people to maintain their skill through training alone. They must be able to learn quickly and avoid rediagnosing and solving problems that have been solved before. To avoid "reinventing the wheel," any person who solves a problem or request must document the resolution and submit it to the knowledge engineer for inclusion in the knowledge base. Recall that a knowledge engineer is the person who develops and oversees the knowledge management process and ensures that the information contained in the help desk's knowledge base is accurate, complete, and current.

The flow chart in Figure 4-10 shows how information flows through the knowledge management process and the responsibilities of people involved in the process.

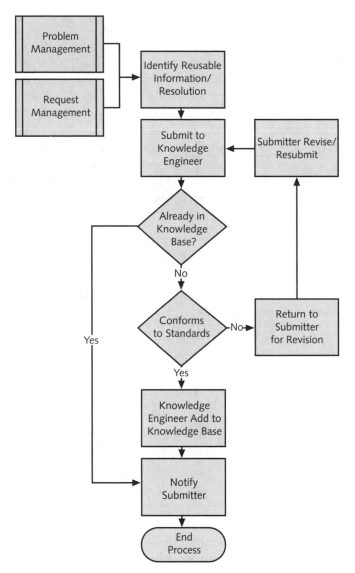

Figure 4-10 Knowledge management process

The knowledge engineer approves or rejects information as appropriate and ensures that analysts can quickly and easily retrieve information and resolutions from the knowledge base. An effective knowledge management process enables help desk analysts to solve a greater number of problems and requests quickly and accurately.

A **resolution** is a definitive, permanent solution to either a problem or a request, *or* it is a proven workaround.

The help desk is an important part of the knowledge management process. Not only does it use the information collected, it also helps compile the information and encourages use of the knowledge base. Specifically, the help desk:

- Uses the knowledge base to resolve problems and requests.

- Documents resolutions, procedures, and so forth and submits them to the knowledge engineer for review and approval.

- Makes suggestions to the knowledge engineer about information to add to the knowledge base.

- Promotes awareness of the knowledge base to others who may benefit from using it, such as customers, level two and level three staff, and so forth.

The widescale proliferation of Web-based technology has dramatically changed the way companies view the knowledge management process. Because Web-based technology makes it so easy for users to access information 24 hours a day, 7 days a week, companies have realized that they must diligently capture knowledge and make it available for re-use. However, companies recognize that no matter how easily users can access information, they will value the information only if it is accurate, current, and presented clearly. Companies that are serious about capturing and leveraging knowledge reward people who willingly share what they know and understand how important knowledge management is to the company's growth and success.

Change Management Process

Change management is the process of controlling changes to the production environment while minimizing service disruptions. As mentioned earlier, new hardware, software, network and application components, and upgrades to existing components typically are installed or developed and tested in a development environment before they are moved into the production environment, where customers can access and use them. This is so that any problems with, for example, a version of the Windows operating system can be identified and resolved before the software is distributed to customers, thereby minimizing service disruptions. Programmers, technicians such as network technicians, vendors, and occasionally help desk analysts may develop or test these new or upgraded components. They must then complete the activities specified by the change management process in order to install the component in the production environment. In other words, change management is the "gate" through which new or upgraded hardware, software, network, and application components pass on their way from the development environment to the production environment. The goal of change management is to ensure that changes made to information technology resources balance risk, resource effectiveness, and potential disruption to customer service.

Change management activities include:

- **Change entry**—Submitting to a central point such as a change committee all plans to change the production technology environment and logging information about those plans, typically in an incident tracking system or enterprise solution.

- **Technical assessment**—Evaluating the technical practicality, technical completeness, impact, and risk of the change.

- **Business assessment**—Evaluating the business impact and risk of the change based on timing and compatibility with business plans and goals.

- **Management approval**—Evaluating the technical and business recommendations made during the technical and business assessment phases, followed by management accepting, rejecting, or deferring the change.

- **Monitor test**—Ensuring that trials of proposed changes produce nondisruptive results, identifying problems or concerns (prior to change installation), and communicating the results.

- **Monitor installation**—Ensuring that the change is complete and notifying all concerned or involved parties of installation activity results.

- **Management review**—Evaluating the efficiency and effectiveness of the change management process and associated reporting system.

These activities work together to provide an effective way to manage changes. The flow chart in Figure 4-11 provides an overview of the activities in the change management process.

Some companies have a very formal change management process. For example, some companies have a separate group or a committee that is responsible for assessing the readiness of proposed changes to the production environment. Many companies hold regular change assessment meetings to discuss changes scheduled for the coming week, month, and so on, along with high-impact changes scheduled for the longer-term future. All affected stakeholders, including representatives from the help desk, involved level two and level three groups, and the customer community, attend these meetings. In an effort to prevent problems, the attendees discuss each change to determine its technical readiness for the proposed scheduled time. Also, some companies designate certain days of the week for changes. For example, a company may state that unless it is an emergency, changes can only be made on Saturdays and Wednesdays, assuming they have been approved by the change committee. The day or days of week selected would correspond to the needs of the business. For example, companies that experience heavy workloads on Mondays and Fridays tend not to make changes on Sundays and Thursdays in an effort to avoid service disruptions on their busiest days.

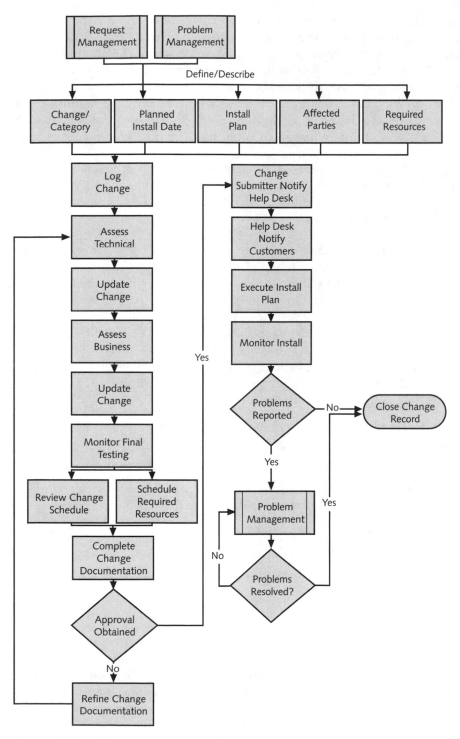

Figure 4-11   Change management process

In companies that have a formal change management process, the help desk typically plays an important role. For example, help desk employees may chair the change assessment meetings or they may post the change schedule for the coming week on the help desk's Web site. In companies that do not have a formalized change management process, the help desk simply has to do its best to stay on top of changes that developers, technicians, vendors, and so forth may make with little advance communication. One of the best ways they can do this is to log all problems so that problems caused by change can be tracked and ultimately prevented when similar changes are made in the future.

 Change causes an estimated 80 percent of the problems that occur in a typical technology environment. For example, installing new software on a PC can result in a memory shortage that causes other software on the PC to have problems or run slowly.

Change management enables the help desk to be proactive because it knows what changes are coming and can do all it can to get ready for them. For example, the help desk can determine what staff training is required to support the new systems, networks, or products being released. Or, the help desk can hire people with specialized knowledge to cross-train existing staff. The help desk also may need to adjust its incident handling procedures. For example, the help desk may need to extend its hours of operation or provide Web-based support after hours. Some changes may prompt the help desk to install new support systems, such as more advanced remote diagnostic equipment. The help desk also tracks and analyzes problems that result from change to determine how to perform changes better in the future.

The help desk's role in the change management process includes the following activities:

- Participates in change management meetings—and often serves as the customer advocate.

- Determines if help desk staffing levels, skills, processes, or technologies need to be refined in order to accommodate the scheduled change.

- Participates in change approval activities.

- Ensures that all affected parties are notified prior to a scheduled change.

- Follows up with affected parties to ensure satisfaction with the change when appropriate.

- Tracks problems caused by change.

The change management process is very important because it enables the help desk to prepare for upcoming changes. However, the help desk's involvement in change management may not be limited to simply getting prepared. The help desk also may act as a testing site for new products and systems, help develop the installation procedures, prepare answers to questions it believes customers may ask frequently, and may even perform the actual change, such as electronically distributing new software. The more actively the help desk is involved in the change management process, the more value it adds to its company and customers.

Change Categories

Not all changes are equal. Some are very simple and have little impact if problems occur; others are very complex and could seriously disrupt service if problems occur. **Change categories** provide a consistent way to communicate the potential risk and impact of a change. Table 4-5 lists sample change categories.

Table 4-5   Sample Change Categories

Category	Description
1	These changes are the most critical. They combine several factors that will make a major impact on the delivery of services if problems occur during change implementation.
2	These changes provide a greater degree of exposure and increased impact on the delivery of services if problems occur.
3	These changes have a minor impact on customer services if problems occur.
4	These changes are least significant and will cause little or no impact if problems occur during or after installation.
Emergency	These changes fall into any of the above categories under ordinary circumstances, but for any of several reasons, they are not classified as normal changes. For example, the change may be initiated on an emergency basis to correct problems affecting the delivery of service.

People or groups that are implementing change must consider many factors when categorizing changes. These factors include complexity, dependencies (activities that must occur before the change is made, such as backing up data), the estimated duration of the change, ease of recovery when problems occur, and the potential impact and the potential risk associated with making the change at the proposed time.

Each category has an associated lead time requirement. **Lead time** is the amount of time needed to adequately plan and implement a categorized change. Some companies determine a minimum lead time (the standard time frame) and an emergency lead time (the time frame required under emergency change conditions). Table 4-6 shows sample minimum and emergency lead times.

Table 4-6   Sample Lead Times by Category

Category	Minimum Lead Time	Emergency Lead Time
1	45 working days	5 working days
2	14 working days	1 working day
3	3 working days	Same day
4	1 working day	Same day

Some companies do not have a formal change management process. In those cases, help desk management and staff must find communication channels (formal and informal, verbal and written) they can use to learn about upcoming changes. When the help desk staff knows about potential changes, it can prepare for the changes and positively influence the ultimate outcome.

Asset and Configuration Management Process

Problems can be diagnosed more quickly, the impact of changes assessed more accurately, and a company's financial investment managed more effectively when the entire support organization has access to information about the company's IT assets. An **IT asset** is any product or service that represents a cost or adds value to an IT organization. For example, hardware, software, network, and communication components, cell phone services, and so forth are all IT assets. **Asset and configuration management** is the process of collecting and maintaining information about IT assets and showing the relationships that exist among those assets. This process actually consists of two processes, each of which serves a specific purpose. *Asset management* is focused on capturing financial information, such as license and warranty information. *Configuration management* is focused on capturing nonfinancial information about IT assets along with how the assets are related or configured. For example, information collected and maintained may include a record of all hardware devices installed, where they are installed, their model and serial numbers, and how they are, or can be, connected to other devices on the company's network.

 Configuration management may also be called inventory management; however, *inventory management* typically encompasses only the activities involved in collecting and maintaining information about IT assets, not the relationships that exist among those assets.

The asset and configuration management process provides a central database for IT asset information that is typically called the **configuration management database (CMDB)**. In many companies, the CMDB is a logical entity, rather than a physical entity. In other words, the information that composes the CMDB may actually reside in a number of physical databases, rather than one large physical database. For example, network-related information may be housed in one database, data center hardware and software information in another, and so forth. The individual records that are stored in an organization's CMDB are typically known as **configuration items (CIs)**. In addition to the IT assets already discussed, other examples of CIs include Service Level Agreements (SLAs) and knowledge assets such as those housed in knowledge bases.

Asset and configuration management activities include:

- **Purchase request processing**—Creating a purchase request and recording information about the order in the CMDB.

- **Change request processing**—Entering into the CMDB all changes to the CMDB.

- **Management review**—Evaluating the efficiency and effectiveness of the asset and configuration management process and associated reporting system.

The flow chart in Figure 4-12 shows how these activities progress in the asset and configuration management process.

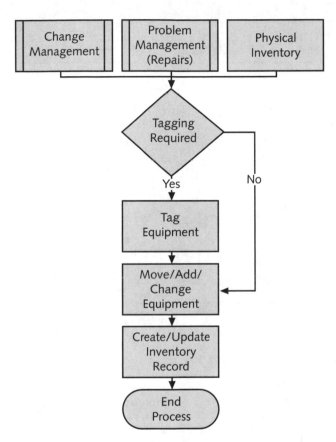

Figure 4-12   Asset and configuration management process

The help desk does not usually have primary responsibility for this process, although it may in a support center environment or in a smaller company. In larger support organizations, the groups responsible for setting up and installing new products and systems usually maintain the asset and configuration management database, and the help desk uses the database. Table 4-7 lists the groups that typically oversee the day-to-day maintenance of the CMDB. The information these groups keep about assets includes a physical description of each item, location information, financial information including licensing information, and any warranty and service contract details.

Table 4-7   Sample List of Groups that Maintain Asset and Configuration Management Data

Group	Data Area Maintained
Field Services	PC-related components (within the confines of a workstation)
Network Management	Non-PC-related components/network components (voice and data)
Computer Operations	Data center hardware and software
Purchasing	Contracts or service and license agreements

The CMDB provides essential information to a number of processes including problem, request, knowledge, and change management. In turn, these processes provide information that ensures that the information stored in the CMDB remains accurate and complete. Figure 4-13 shows how these processes are integrated via the CMDB.

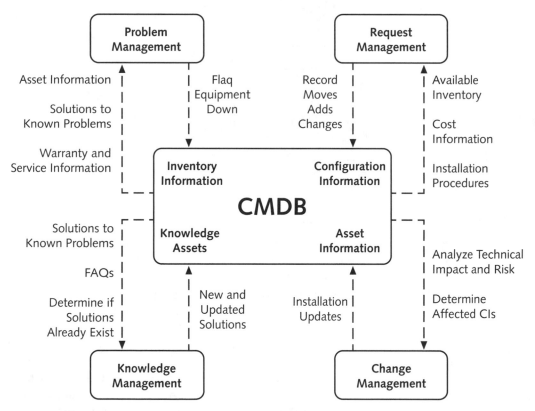

Figure 4-13   Process integration via the CMDB

Having access to information housed in the CMDB increases the efficiency and effectiveness of the help desk considerably. For example, when a customer calls to say "it" broke, a level one analyst can search the CMDB to determine what "it" the customer is using. In addition, some companies link the CMDB to their problem management system so the help desk staff has less data to enter. For example, if the help desk analyst types a serial number into a problem record, related information such as device type, version, and so forth, may appear. In that case, the customer also benefits because the help desk can create problem records more quickly. The help desk can also use the contract data stored in the CMDB to determine a product's warranty and service status prior to contacting a vendor.

Integrating the Help Desk Processes

As discussed earlier, the problem, request, knowledge, change, and asset and configuration management processes are key to the success of the help desk. These processes are all important and they are very tightly integrated. Figure 4-14 illustrates how these processes interconnect.

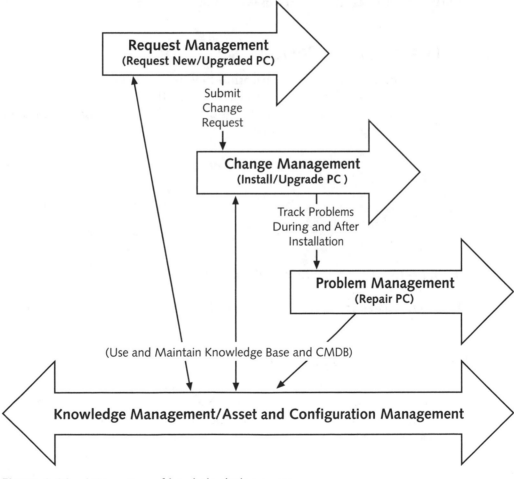

Figure 4-14   Integration of key help desk processes

This illustration begins with a request to purchase a new PC. The request is made and the purchase of the PC is authorized (assuming it is justified) via the request management process. When the PC is ready to be installed—that is, when it is ready to be introduced to the production environment—a change request is submitted, assessed for readiness, and scheduled for installation via the change management process. Once the PC is installed, any problems will be handled via the problem management process until the PC is removed from the production environment. Requests to upgrade the PC will, however, be made via the request management process and installed via the change management process. The request, change, and problem management processes all use information that is housed in the company's knowledge bases and CMDB. The request, change, and problem management processes also contribute information to those databases via the knowledge management and asset and configuration management processes.

Quality improvement processes use the information produced by all of these processes.

QUALITY IMPROVEMENT PROCESSES

Several processes analyze the information captured by help desk analysts and help maximize customer satisfaction, improve help desk efficiency and effectiveness, and contribute value to the company and its customers. Figure 4-15 lists the most common of these quality improvement processes.

- Service level management
- Account management
- Trend and root cause analysis

Figure 4-15   Quality improvement processes

Front-line analysts typically do not perform these processes, although they may in some help desks.

Service Level Management

Service level management is the process of negotiating and managing customer expectations by establishing Service Level Agreements (SLAs). Recall that an SLA is a written document that spells out the services the help desk will provide to the customer, the customer's responsibilities, and how service performance is measured. SLAs help ensure that both the service provider and customer have the same level of expectation about the services the provider will deliver.

SLAs are explored in detail in Chapter 6.

4

SLAs also provide performance objectives and identify reports to create regularly that monitor how well the help desk is achieving its targeted objectives. A help desk manager, supervisor, or team leader uses these SLA performance reports to perform trend and root cause analysis as well as to develop and execute action plans that improve performance. In addition, analysis of SLA performance reports may reveal changes in the service environment that signal the need to adjust or renegotiate the SLA. Some companies assign analysis of SLA performance reports to dedicated account managers.

Account Management

Customer relationships are complex and must be constantly monitored and maintained. One of the reasons most frequently cited by customers who stopped doing business with a company is that they felt an attitude of indifference. To combat this problem, some companies establish an account management function to ensure that customers' needs are being met. **Account management** is a process that dedicates an account manager to each business unit within a company or to large or important clients who receive external support. An **account manager** is an employee who has in-depth knowledge of a specific customer community and serves as the primary contact for the customer and the help desk staff supporting the customer. Account managers take the lead when a customer's problems or requests require special attention. Also, account managers review reports, measure customer satisfaction, and ensure that negotiated service levels are being met. In some companies, a help desk team leader or senior staff member serves as account manager.

Trend and Root Cause Analysis

Trend analysis is a methodical way of determining and, when possible, forecasting service trends. Trends can be positive, such as a reduction in the number of "how to" questions the help desk receives after an improved training program. Or, trends can be negative, such as a dramatic increase in call volume after a new product is introduced into the market.

Root cause analysis is a methodical way of determining the root cause of problems. **Root cause** is the most basic reason for an undesirable condition or problem, which, if eliminated or corrected, would prevent the problem from existing or occurring. Root cause is captured when incidents are closed and typically is supplied by the person who identified the resolution. For example, if the help desk resolves an incident, an analyst will enter the root cause. If level two resolves an incident, it will enter the root cause. The goal is to determine and document *why* the incident occurred so the company can take steps to prevent similar incidents from occurring in the future.

Trend and root cause analysis work hand-in-hand. They can be used together reactively to solve problems or proactively to identify improvement areas. Root cause analysis is the more difficult of the two disciplines, and so not all companies determine and document root cause. These companies fail to take the extra time needed to determine *why* the problem occurred once they have "fixed" it. Unfortunately, by not capturing and then eliminating root cause, these companies put themselves at risk that the incident will happen again.

Although some help desks have highly skilled statisticians perform trend and root cause analysis, any or all members of the help desk team can perform the analysis. Very often, the front-line staff can identify trends simply by considering the calls they are receiving. For example, the help desk might notice that it is receiving a lot of calls about a certain system or product and bring that fact to management's attention. A trend report can then be created to validate statistically the help desk's "hunch."

Without the data captured by the help desk, trend and root cause analysis is impossible. Trend analysis and root cause analysis enable a help desk to avoid problems and, as a result, enhance its productivity, its customers' productivity, and its customers' satisfaction.

WHY PROCESSES ARE IMPORTANT

All of the processes discussed in this chapter are designed to define clearly the work to be done, clarify roles and responsibilities, ensure that data is captured, and generate information. The most successful companies understand that processes are not static. Instead, they must be treated as living, breathing organisms that need care and feeding. Because customer requirements are changing constantly, processes must be continuously improved and occasionally redesigned or they will cease to be effective.

Companies in today's competitive business climate cannot afford to waste resources. They have to maximize their resources, especially their precious human resources, and accomplish more with them than was ever possible. With processes, roles and responsibilities are clearly defined and people understand what they are expected to do. People who understand the expected result can determine the most efficient and effective way to achieve it. What's most important, with processes, required information is captured in a meaningful and useful way. Through analysis and understanding, this information becomes knowledge. Knowledge enables help desk staff to be proactive because they can foresee potential problems, identify preventative measures, and, ultimately, enhance customer satisfaction as well as their own job satisfaction.

CHAPTER SUMMARY

- ❐ Processes and procedures are an integral component of every help desk because they represent the work to be done and how to do work such as solving problems and handling customer requests. Processes define *what* tasks to do, whereas procedures describe *how* to do the tasks. When processes are understood, people know *why* they are doing the tasks. When multiple groups are involved in solving a problem or satisfying a request, processes and procedures provide the framework that enables each group to understand its role, responsibilities, and the expected results of its efforts.

❐ Many companies have a quality improvement program, or quality program, in place that represents a commitment to consistently providing products and services that meet customer expectations, or requirements. Companies that have a quality program typically dedicate resources to activities such as developing, documenting, and improving processes. You may encounter a number of quality programs in the business world. The most common programs found in IT organizations are CMM and ITIL.

❐ A successful help desk must manage several tightly interconnected or integrated processes to achieve customer satisfaction. Two processes that are vital to the success of a help desk include problem management and request management. Problem management is the process of tracking and resolving problems, which are events that disrupt service or prevent access to products. Problem management involves determining how severe a problem is, and then when and how to solve it. Request management is the process of collecting and maintaining information about customer requests, such as requests for new products or services and enhancements to existing products or services. Request management involves identifying and documenting the tasks required to satisfy requests and ensuring that appropriate resources are assigned.

❐ Because the help desk cannot always resolve problems and requests (incidents) during the first call, incidents that are assigned to groups outside of the help desk must have a designated owner. Typically, the owner is the help desk analyst who handled the customer's problem or request initially, although this may vary based on the type of incident. The owner is the customer advocate and ensures that the incident is resolved to the customer's satisfaction. The owner also sees that appropriate notification activities occur (such as management and customer notification) when incidents are reported, escalated, and resolved.

❐ Three increasingly important processes include knowledge management, change management, and asset and configuration management. Knowledge management is the process of gathering and maintaining a company's information assets (knowledge) in a knowledge base. The knowledge management process is becoming increasingly important and formalized because the rapid pace of change is making it very difficult for people to maintain their skill through training along. Change management and asset and configuration management are just as important. Change management allows change to occur as quickly as possible with the least amount of risk and impact (and the fewest number of problems). Asset and configuration management facilitates the capture and maintenance of information about the products and systems that the company supports. The help desk and others involved in support use this information to diagnose problems more quickly and to determine the potential impact of change.

❑ Quality improvement processes such as service level management, account management, and trend and root cause analysis use the information produced by all of these processes. Quality improvement processes analyze the data captured by help desk analysts and help maximize customer satisfaction, improve help desk efficiency and effectiveness, and contribute value to the company and its customers.

❑ The most successful companies understand that processes and procedures are not static. They must be treated as living, breathing organisms that need care and feeding. Because customer requirements are constantly changing, processes and procedures must be continuously improved and occasionally redesigned or they will cease to be effective. Processes and procedures enable people to understand what they are expected to do. People who understand the expected result can determine the most efficient and effective way to achieve it.

KEY TERMS

account management — A process that dedicates an account manager to each business unit within a company or to large or important clients who receive external support.

account manager — An employee who has in-depth knowledge of a specific customer community and serves as the primary contact for the customer and the help desk staff supporting the customer.

asset and configuration management — The process of collecting and maintaining information about IT assets (such as hardware, software, network, and communication components) and showing the relationships that exist among those assets; it also captures financial information, such as license and warranty information.

best practice — An innovative process or concept that moves a company or department to a position of improved performance.

Capability Maturity Models (CMMs) — A set of quality-oriented management practices that assist organizations in maturing their people, process, and technology assets to improve long-term business performance.

change categories — A consistent way to communicate the potential risk and impact of a change.

change management — The process of controlling changes to the production environment while minimizing service disruptions.

configuration items (CIs) — The individual records that are stored in an organization's configuration management database, such as IT assets, Service Level Agreements (SLAs), and knowledge assets.

configuration management database (CMDB) — A central database for IT asset information.

costs — The amounts paid to produce a product, such as workers' wages, salaries and benefits; the facilities and equipment workers use; any materials and supplies they consume; and so on.

customer entitlement — The determination of whether the customer is authorized to receive support and, if so, the level of support the customer should receive.

escalation (or escalate) — To raise a problem from one level to another, such as from level one to level two, to dedicate new or additional resources to the problem.

flow chart — A diagram that shows the sequence of tasks that occur in a process.

incident management — *See* problem management.

Information Technology Infrastructure Library (ITIL) — A set of best practices for IT service management.

4

inquiries — Customer requests for information, such as "When will the part for my equipment arrive?"

inventory management — A process that encompasses only the activities involved in collecting and maintaining information about IT assets, not the relationships that exist among those assets. *See* configuration management.

ISO 9000 — A set of universal standards for a quality assurance system that is accepted around the world.

IT asset — Any product or service that represents a cost or adds value to an IT organization.

Kaizen — A Japanese term that when applied to the workplace means continuing improvement involving everyone—managers and workers alike.

knowledge management — The process of gathering and maintaining a company's information assets (knowledge) in a knowledge base.

lead time — The amount of time needed to adequately plan and implement a categorized change.

level one — The initial point of contact for customers when they have a problem, question, inquiry, or request.

level three — The person or group that resolves complex problems which are beyond the scope of level two.

level two — The person or group that resolves problems that are beyond the scope or authority (such as system access rights or permissions) of level one.

Malcolm Baldrige National Quality Award — Established by the U.S. Congress in 1987 to recognize U.S. organizations for their achievements in quality and business performance and to raise awareness about the importance of quality as a performance indicator.

notification — The activities that inform all of the stakeholders in the problem or request management process (including management, the customer, help desk analysts, and so forth) about the status of outstanding problems or requests.

priority aging — Increasing the priority of a problem.

problem — An event that disrupts service or prevents access to products.

problem management — The process of tracking and resolving problems; also called incident management.

problem owner — An employee of the support organization who acts as a customer advocate and proactively ensures that a problem is resolved to the customer's satisfaction.

problem ownership — A practice that ensures that when the help desk analyst cannot resolve a problem during the first call or escalates the problem to a person or group outside of the help desk, a problem owner is designated; also known as total contact ownership.

problem priority — Identifies the order for working on problems with the same severity.

problem tracking — Follows *one* problem from recognition to resolution.

procedure — A step-by-step, detailed set of instructions that describes how to perform the tasks in a process.

process — A collection of interrelated work activities, or tasks, that take a set of specific inputs and produce a set of specific outputs that are of value to the customer.

productivity — An efficiency measure that relates output (goods and services produced) to input (the number of hours worked).

quality — A characteristic that measures how well products or services meet customer requirements.

questions — Customer requests for instruction on how to use a product, such as "How do I...?"

request — A customer order or request to obtain a new product or service or an enhancement to an existing product or service.

request management — The process of collecting and maintaining information about customer requests.

request owner — An employee of the support organization who keeps the customer informed and is involved in scheduling any installation activities needed to complete the request.

request priority — Identifies the order for working on submitted requests.

requirement — Something that is essential.

resolution — A definitive, permanent solution to either a problem *or* a request, or it is a proven workaround.

root cause — The most basic reason for an undesirable condition or problem, which, if eliminated or corrected, would prevent the problem from existing or occurring.

root cause analysis — A methodical way of determining the root cause of problems.

service level management — The process of negotiating and managing customer expectations by establishing Service Level Agreements (SLAs).

severity — The category that defines how critical a problem is based on the nature of the failure and the available alternatives or workarounds.

target escalation time — A time constraint placed on each level that ensures that problem resolution activities are proceeding at an appropriate pace.

target resolution time — The time frame within which the support organization is expected to resolve the problem.

target response time — The time frame within which the help desk or level two acknowledges the problem, diagnoses the problem, and estimates the target resolution time.

Total Quality Control (TQC) — The system that Japan developed to implement *Kaizen* or continuing improvement.

Total Quality Management (TQM) — A management approach to long-term success through customer satisfaction.

trend analysis — A methodical way of determining and, when possible, forecasting service trends.

workaround — Circumventing a problem either partially or completely, usually before implementing the final resolution; also called bypass and recovery.

4

REVIEW QUESTIONS

1. Define the terms *process* and *procedure*.

2. Explain the relationship between processes and procedures.

3. Why have companies begun to assign workers greater responsibilities than called for in Adam Smith's principle of the division of labor?

4. Describe the benefits of establishing simpler business processes.

5. Companies that have a quality program in place typically dedicate resources to what activities?

6. Describe the two main topics covered by ITIL.

7. What four things do all quality improvement programs have in common?

8. Name and define the two processes you will find in most help desks.

9. Draw the symbol that represents a task in a flow chart.

10. Draw the symbol that represents a decision point in a flow chart.

11. What is a problem?

12. What is the goal of the problem management process?

13. What are questions and inquiries?

14. Describe the difference between problem tracking and problem management.

15. What determines a problem's severity?

16. Why does problem severity remain the same throughout the life of a problem?

17. What three conditions cause a problem's priority to increase?

18. Define the term *escalation*.

19. List three reasons why problems might be escalated from level one to level two.

20. People at level one, level two, and level three are all responsible for _____ a problem's current status and the resolution steps attempted or completed.

21. Describe the responsibilities of a problem owner.

22. Why is problem management often referred to as a "closed loop process"?

23. What is the purpose of problem notification?

24. What is the goal of the request management process?

25. Describe two techniques that may be used to determine the priority of requests.

26. List at least two reasons why companies differentiate between problems and requests.

27. Define the term *knowledge management*.

28. What is the goal of the knowledge management process?

29. Why is knowledge management becoming increasingly important?

30. What is a resolution?

31. Why is it important to test new hardware, software, network, and application components, and upgrades to existing components before they are moved into the production environment?

32. What are two ways the help desk may participate in the change management process?

33. How does the change management process enable the help desk to be proactive?

34. List five factors that change implementers must consider when categorizing changes.

35. What can help desk management and staff do if there is not a formal change management process in place in the company?

36. What is the difference between inventory and configuration management?

37. Describe a scenario wherein the CMDB integrates with the problem management process.

38. Describe a scenario wherein the CMDB integrates with the request management process.

39. What three items are described in a Service Level Agreement?

40. How do SLAs influence help desk and customer expectations?

41. Describe three tasks that an account manager performs.

42. Define the term *root cause*.

43. Why is it important to determine the root cause of problems?

44. What makes it possible for the help desk to perform trend and root cause analysis?

HANDS-ON PROJECTS

Project 4-1

Discuss Adam Smith's principle. Assemble a team of at least three of your classmates and discuss Adam Smith's principle of the division of labor. Think of business examples in which you still see this principle in action, and then select one example that everyone has experienced. Write a brief description of the example you have selected, and then document your answers to the following questions:

❑ What are the pros and cons of assigning specialized tasks to the workers at this business?

❑ How could this business potentially streamline its business process?

❑ How would customers benefit from a streamlined business process?

❑ What factors may hinder the business's ability to implement this streamlined business process?

Project 4-2

Develop a process flow chart. Assemble a team of three to five classmates. Develop a flow chart that shows all the steps for having a pizza delivered that contains the toppings the entire team agrees upon. Begin the process with the decision to order a pizza, and end the process by throwing the pizza box in the recycling bin. If you have access to flow charting software, use it to construct and print your flow chart. The most popular flow charting software is Microsoft Visio (**www.microsoft.com/office/visio**). Smartdraw.com (**www.smartdraw.com**) also offers flow charting software that you can download free of charge.

Project 4-3

Determine the severity of a problem. Working with a group of two or three classmates, discuss the following problem scenarios and document the severity the team would assign to each problem and why. You must make some assumptions in order to determine the severity; document your assumptions.

1. The company president calls with a question about how to use an advanced spreadsheet feature.

2. An administrative assistant calls to report that one of the five computers in her area is not working.

3. An angry customer calls and insists that someone come to his department immediately to change the toner in his printer.

4. A customer calls to indicate that neither she nor her coworkers can log on to the system through the network. She can, however, use a software package installed on her PC.

4

Project 4-4

Identify and prevent root causes. Get together with one or two of your classmates. Brainstorm and prepare a list of root causes for hardware problems. For each root cause listed, identify at least one proactive way to prevent the problem from recurring. Compare your list to the lists developed by other teams in your class.

Project 4-5

Learn about knowledge management. Knowledge management is increasingly being recognized as a very important help desk process. A few excellent magazines and portal sites that focus on knowledge management include **www.kmworld.com**, **www.kmresource. com/exp.htm**, and **www.kmtool.net**. Visit these sites and then write a brief report describing the content of these sites and any other sources of knowledge management information you are linked to by these sites.

Project 4-6

Identify the tasks required to complete a request. Either alone or with a small group of classmates, consider all of the tasks that are required to log a work request for setting up an office for a new employee. Prepare a list of all the tasks that must be completed to provide the new employee with the office setup you would expect to have when starting work at a new company.

Project 4-7

Categorize a change. Imagine yourself in outer space aboard the space shuttle "Columbia." The head development engineer calls to indicate he would like to make a small change to one of the programs that controls the reentry program for the shuttle. He indicates that he has tested the change on his system and it worked fine. Write a report to your boss explaining what category you would assign to this change and why.

Project 4-8

Learn about asset and configuration management. Interview an acquaintance, family member, or coworker who works in an IT department. Write a short paper that answers the following questions:

❑ Does this person have access to a CMDB (even if it is called something different)?

❑ If so, what information can he or she derive from this CMDB? How often does he or she use the CMDB? Does he or she consider the CMDB a useful tool? Please explain.

❑ If not, would he or she benefit if a CMDB were established? Please explain.

CASE PROJECTS

1. Internal Help Desk Incident Examples

An internal help desk has hired you to help it develop documentation for its problem management process. As your first assignment, the help desk manager asks you to prepare examples for the three types of incidents it handles: problems, questions, and inquiries. The help desk supports a standard PC environment and uses Microsoft software products. List three examples for each incident type.

2. Minimize Customer Dissatisfaction

A level two service provider has just informed you that because another problem he is working on is taking longer than expected he will not meet the target resolution time for a problem that you own. The only other person who could work on the problem is on vacation this week. Briefly describe who you would notify and how you would minimize customer dissatisfaction in this situation.

3. Customer Responsibilities in Service Level Agreements

You have been chosen to work on a committee that is drafting a Service Level Agreement to be used during negotiations with help desk customers. For the first meeting, each attendee has been asked to prepare a list of suggested customer responsibilities. Prepare for the meeting by listing your recommendations. Think through any service encounters you have been involved in (such as calling a software publisher or hardware vendor) when preparing your list and determine what you feel was reasonable for vendors to ask you to do.

5

THE TECHNOLOGY COMPONENT: HELP DESK TOOLS AND TECHNOLOGIES

In this chapter you will learn:

- ♦ How technology benefits the help desk
- ♦ The primary help desk technologies
- ♦ How help desks use remote support technologies
- ♦ How help desks use help desk communications tools
- ♦ The tools used by help desk managers
- ♦ The relationship between business processes and technology
- ♦ The steps involved in selecting help desk technology

The help desk uses a wide array of tools and technologies—collectively referred to as technology—to do its work. A **tool** is a product or device that automates or facilitates a person's work. **Technologies** enable the creation and enhancement of tools. For example, advances in microchip technology have made it possible to develop smaller, faster PCs. Help desk tools and technologies give the help desk the ability to handle customer contacts such as telephone calls and e-mails, log and resolve problems and requests, and generally manage information. Help desk tools range from simple e-mail and voice mail to more complex and sophisticated telephone systems and incident tracking systems. With these tools, help desk staff can work more quickly than if they had to rely on manual methods. As a result, the help desk can reduce or maintain costs while increasing productivity.

Help desks often combine or integrate tools and technologies to more easily and quickly transfer data between systems and automate routine tasks. The tools and technologies a help desk uses depends on the number and complexity of the processes being supported—such as problem, request, knowledge, change, and asset and configuration management—and the funding it has available. Very small or new help desks often rely on the telephone and paper forms or a simple PC-based tracking system. Larger help desks tend to use a wide variety of tools in an effort to address incidents more efficiently and effectively.

Whether you work in a small, growing help desk or a large, established one, tools and technologies will be a part of your job. In fact, technology is becoming increasingly more prevalent in a help desk setting. Although the variety of technologies and the actual tools used vary from one company to the next, the intent and benefits of them typically do not. Understanding the advantages of these tools and technologies will help enrich your job because you will be able to adapt quickly when new technologies are introduced and use tools to be more self-sufficient and productive.

How Technology Benefits the Help Desk

The number of incidents that help desks handle, the number of customers that help desks support, and the number of hardware, software, network, and application components that help desks support all are on the rise. In fact, according to META Group, call volumes are doubling from 1.75 calls per user per month to 5 calls per user per month ("IT Service Automation Trends," META Group, Inc., 2002). This increase, coupled with management pressure to do more with less, is prompting many companies to use technology.

A help desk can use technology to:

- Gather, organize, and use information about its customers, which, in turn, improves decision making and reduces the number of recurring problems.

- Eliminate manual, repetitive functions such as password resets, which frees help desk staff to work on complex problems and special projects.

- Empower customers to identify and potentially solve routine problems, which frees help desk staff to develop and provide even more self-services.

- Manage its costs, optimize its staffing levels, and, most important, provide excellent customer service, which leads to management and customer satisfaction.

Technology enables a help desk to handle more incidents, resolve incidents more quickly, provide additional services, offer more ways for customers to request services, and optimize the efficiency and effectiveness of its staff. Technology also enables help desk staff to focus on more complex and challenging incidents and projects that offer the opportunity to learn new skills.

Primary Help Desk Technologies

Each help desk chooses its tools based on its size, company goals, the nature of the business it is in, and customer expectations. For example, with regard to help desk size, very small help desks tend to use a small set of fairly simple tools. As help desks grow, they rely on increasingly more sophisticated and complex technology. With regard to company goals, some companies are committed to maximizing their use of technology (such as companies in the banking and airline industries), whereas the goal of other companies is to offer more personalized service.

All help desks, regardless of size, can benefit from technology. Small help desks, however, sometimes make the mistake of thinking they don't need technology, or they don't have time to implement or use technology. Unfortunately, as a help desk grows and becomes busier, it becomes increasingly difficult to implement technology, and so the help desk becomes overwhelmed. A better approach is to implement technology—even if only simple technology—while the help desk is small, and then migrate to more sophisticated technology as the help desk grows. This approach enables analysts to become familiar with using technology to do their jobs, and reduces the time it takes to adopt new technologies.

5

The nature of the company's business and customer expectations also influence a help desk's tool selection. For example, customers expect companies in high-technology industries to use state-of-the-art support technology. Customers would be surprised if companies that market Web browsers, such as Microsoft and Netscape, didn't have Web sites that offered, at a minimum, answers to frequently asked questions (FAQs). On the other hand, customers do not expect industries and companies that are less technology-oriented to use sophisticated systems.

However, there are some tools and technologies you find in most help desks. For example, most companies have a telephone number that customers can call to report problems and requests. Telephone technologies range from simple voice mail boxes to highly complex, automated systems. Some companies also provide customers with the ability to report incidents through e-mail, fax, and Web-based systems.

Help desks must carefully manage customer expectations regarding the help desk's target response times for contact channels such as the telephone, voice mail, and e-mail. Unless help desks inform them otherwise, customers will expect to receive an immediate—real-time—response to all of these contact channels. Many companies are now specifying target response times for all contact channels in their SLAs or when communicating their services to customers. For example, a help desk may indicate that telephone calls will be answered within 60 seconds, voice mail messages will be answered within 15 minutes, and e-mail messages will be answered within 30 minutes. This target response time reflects the time it will take the help desk to acknowledge the customer's contact, not the time it will take to resolve the customer's technical problem.

Most companies also use tools to record their customers' problems and requests in some way. Some companies use paper forms to record incidents. However, pressure from customers and management to deliver services faster, cheaper, and better is prompting even very small help desks to implement an incident tracking and problem management system. In fact, a 2002 Help Desk Institute (HDI) survey found that 84 percent of companies have implemented a system to enable their help desks to log and manage problems and requests. An additional 7 percent of the companies surveyed plan to add an incident management system within 12 months. Increasingly, companies are integrating their incident tracking and problem management systems with expert and knowledge management systems that provide the ability to capture and reuse known solutions to problems and requests.

Telephone Technologies and Services

The telephone is the primary way that most help desks communicate with their customers. According to the Help Desk Institute's 2002 Practices Survey, 69 percent of its members indicated that customers request services via the telephone. Another 10 percent have customers leave a voice mail and then return their calls. Although many companies are increasingly using technologies such as e-mail and the Web to deliver support services, the telephone will always play a role in customer service. This is because some customers do not have access to e-mail or the Web. Also, some customers simply prefer to interact with a living, breathing human being, particularly when they are having a problem. During a typical telephone call, a help desk analyst talks to a customer, asks questions, enters responses into a computer, and assists the customer, often while using information from a computer system. Telephone technology automates many of these functions.

Telephone Technologies

An increasing number of help desks depend on a number of telephone technologies. Figure 5-1 lists the telephone technologies most commonly used in help desks and those that most benefit help desk analysts.

Voice mail	Automatic call distributor
Fax	Voice response unit
Fax-on-demand	Computer telephony integration
Announcement systems	Recording systems

Figure 5-1   Telephone technologies commonly used at help desks

Because telephone technologies tend to be tightly integrated, it can be difficult to tell where one technology ends and another begins.

Voice Mail Voice mail is an automated form of taking messages from callers. Companies often combine voice mail with automatic call distributors and voice response units, enabling customers to choose between waiting in a queue or leaving a message. Customers can perceive voice mail negatively if, for example, they have left a voice mail message in the past that was not returned or if they are not given an idea of when their call will be returned. The best companies set and manage voice mail response times and promptly return all customer calls, even if only to let the customer know their call was received and logged and is being handled.

Fax A **fax** is an electronic device that sends or receives printed matter or computer images. Some companies allow their customers to fill out forms or write letters requesting service and then fax the form or letter to the help desk. Some help desks ask customers to fax reports that contain error messages, for example, so the analyst can see the report and better diagnose the problem. Faxed requests typically are logged the same way as a telephone call.

Fax-on-demand   With **fax-on-demand**, customers use their touch-tone telephone to request that answers to FAQs, procedures, forms, or sales literature be delivered to the fax machine at the number they provide. Help desks encourage analysts, when appropriate, to inform customers that this type of system is available. Then, analysts are free to work on more complex issues, while customers can quickly receive the desired information at their convenience, even if it is after hours and the help desk is closed.

Announcement Systems   An **announcement system** greets callers when all help desk analysts are busy and can provide valuable information when customers are asked to wait on hold. For example, companies often use an announcement system to let customers know about a problem such as a computer virus that is affecting a high number of customers. Or companies may use an announcement system to announce the release of a new product. Customers then can obtain additional information by pressing numbers on their telephone keypad to select a certain menu option or by visiting the company's Web site. Often, announcement systems are integrated with automatic call distributors and voice response units.

Automatic Call Distributor   An **automatic call distributor** (**ACD**) answers a call and routes, or distributes, it to the next available analyst. If all analysts are busy, the ACD places the call in a queue and plays a recorded message, such as "We're sorry, all of our service representatives are currently assisting other customers; your call will be answered in the order it has been received." ACDs are very common in medium and large help desks that handle a high volume of calls and, increasingly, are found in small help desks that are experiencing a growing call volume. According to the Help Desk Institute's 2002 Practices survey, 65 percent of its members use automatic call distributors, up from 51 percent in 2001. Another 9 percent plan to add ACDs within 12 months.

 A **queue** is, quite simply, a line. In terms of an automatic call distributor, the term *queue* refers to a line of calls waiting to be processed. The term *queue* can also be used to refer to a list of tickets waiting to be processed in an incident tracking system or a list of e-mail messages waiting to be processed in an e-mail response management system.

ACD software determines what calls an analyst receives and how quickly the analyst receives those calls. Analysts use an ACD console to perform ACD functions. Figure 5-2 shows a sample ACD console. An ACD console, like the one shown in Figure 5-2, enables analysts at their desks to:

- Log on at the start of a scheduled shift each day and place the telephone in an available state. An **available state** means the analyst is ready to take calls.

Figure 5-2   Sample ACD console

- Log off anytime they leave their desk for an extended period of time and log on when they return.

- Log off at the end of a scheduled shift each day.

- Answer each call routed to them within a certain number of rings, as specified by help desk policy, to avoid an idle state. An **idle state** means the analyst did not answer a call routed to his or her telephone within the specified number of rings. When an idle state occurs, the ACD transfers the call to the next available analyst.

- Correctly use **wrap-up mode**, a feature that prevents the ACD from routing a new inbound call to an analyst's extension. Help desk analysts use this wrap-up time to finish documenting the customer's request after they have hung up, to escalate a call, and to prepare for the next call. Many companies establish guidelines for how long analysts can stay in wrap-up mode before making themselves available to take the next call.

The terminology used to describe these ACD functions and states varies slightly from one ACD system to the next.

 ACDs provide a wealth of statistical information that the help desk can use to measure its performance. For example, ACDs can track information such as the number of calls received by the help desk, when calls are received, how quickly the help desk answers calls, and the duration of calls. Chapter 6 discusses these performance measures in detail.

5

ACDs can integrate with and use other technologies to deliver information to analysts and customers. For example, when integrated with an announcement system, an ACD can inform customers about the status of a system that is down. Or, the ACD can use caller ID data to provide the help desk analyst with the name of the caller. ACDs also can use the caller's telephone number or information collected from the caller to route the call. This information can be captured in a number of different ways, such as an automated attendant, automatic number identification, dialed number identification service, or a voice response unit (all of which are discussed later).

ACDs also may come with advanced features. Two common ACD advanced features are automated attendant and skills-based routing.

An **automated attendant** is an ACD feature that routes calls based on input provided by the caller through a touch-tone telephone. Systems that have speech-recognition capability allow customers to speak their input, rather than key it in through their telephone keypad. A basic automated attendant prompts the caller to select from a list of options or enter information, such as the extension of the party the caller wants to reach, and then routes the call based on the caller's input. Automated attendants can be much more sophisticated. They can also be integrated with other technologies to enhance functionality. For example, automated attendants can use caller ID or automatic number identification data to identify the customer and then route the caller to an appropriate analyst or group of analysts.

Skills-based routing (**SBR**) is an ACD feature that matches the requirements of an incoming call to the skill sets of available analysts or analyst groups. The ACD then distributes the call to the next available, most qualified analyst. Skills-based routing determines the call requirements from the customer's telephone number or information collected from the customer or from a database. This information is obtained from services such as automatic number identification and dialed number identification services, or from a voice response unit. Companies that use SBR require analysts to create and maintain a skills inventory that correlates the products, systems, and services supported by the help desk to each analyst's level of skill. Then, calls can be routed to an analyst who has the skill needed to handle the customer's problem or request. For example, with SBR, a call concerning a spreadsheet application can be routed to an analyst who has a depth of experience supporting spreadsheets.

Chapter 6 discusses creating a skills inventory in more detail.

Voice Response Unit Also called an interactive voice response unit (IVRU), a **voice response unit** (**VRU**) integrates with another technology, such as a database or a network management system, to obtain information or to perform a function. Like an automated attendant, a VRU obtains information by having the caller use the keys on their touch-tone telephone or, when speech recognition is available, speak their input into the telephone. For example, a VRU can collect a customer's personal identification number (PIN) and then use it to handle the customer's request or verify that the customer is entitled to service. Companies also use a VRU to automate routine tasks such as changing a password or checking the status of an order, or to communicate information such as the help desk's hours of operation or directions to the company's computer lab or training rooms. Other companies use a VRU to provide access to a predefined, typically reduced set of help desk services during non–business hours. For example, customers may be able to obtain system status information, reset their passwords, or request emergency service.

When poorly implemented, voice response technology can lead to customer frustration and may be perceived negatively. For example, some companies offer long menus with a number of confusing options. To make matters worse, there may not be any way to reach a human being who can help callers determine which option to choose. In that situation, customers select the option they think most closely matches their need. As a result, help desk analysts occasionally receive calls that they are not qualified to handle because a customer inadvertently selected the wrong option. Most companies have procedures that describe how to transfer the caller to the correct analyst or analyst group when this occurs.

Many of us have experienced the frustration of reaching a company and being prompted to select an option from a long list of choices. To increase customer acceptance, the optimum number of choices for a VRU menu is four options that lead to no more than four additional options. Optimally, one of the options enables customers to speak with an analyst. To avoid confusion and frustration, VRUs should also be programmed to provide callers with the ability to repeat the menu options, return to the main menu, and cancel input by, for example, using the asterisk key. A well-designed VRU enables callers to feel that they are in control of calls and that they have options, rather than feeling the company is simply trying to avoid human interaction.

Computer Telephony Integration **Computer telephony integration** (**CTI**) links computing technology with telephone technology to exchange information and increase productivity. Companies use CTI at the help desk to perform functions such as screen pops and simultaneous screen transfers. CTI also can facilitate fax server transmissions and outgoing calls. For example, people can send faxes or dial outgoing calls from their computer.

A **screen pop** refers to a CTI function that enables information about the caller to appear, or "pop" up, on the analyst's monitor, and is based on caller information captured by the telephone system and passed to a computer system. Figure 5-3 illustrates how the telephone system can use caller ID to determine the caller's telephone number and the computer system can look up the telephone number in the company's customer database to find additional information about the caller, such as the caller's name and address. The computer can add this information to the telephone number and create a new ticket that pops up on the screen of the analyst taking the call. The analyst can quickly verify the customer information and then ask questions and add details of the customer's incident to the ticket.

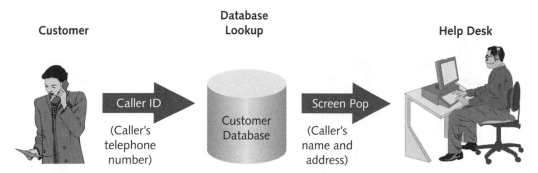

Figure 5-3   Computer telephony integration

If the help desk analyst realizes that the customer should be transferred to another support group, they can perform a **simultaneous screen transfer**, a function that transfers the call as well as all the information collected in the ticket up to that point. The ticket pops up on the screen of the analyst receiving the transferred call as the customer comes on the line. Customers greatly appreciate this function because they do not have to repeat details they already provided to the first analyst.

Recording Systems   **Recording systems** record and play back telephone calls. These systems enable a company to monitor calls and evaluate analyst performance or record calls for security purposes. Companies that use this technology often inform customers about the recording system by playing a message such as, "Please be advised that for quality purposes this call may be monitored or recorded."

Telephone Services

Telephone technologies are even more effective when combined with certain services provided by many local and long distance carriers. These telephone services deliver information that the telephone technologies use to process calls. This information can considerably increase the efficiency with which analysts handle calls. Customer satisfaction increases as well because customers may not have to provide as much preliminary information such as their name and address when their call is answered or transferred to another analyst; rather, they can focus on describing their incident. Figure 5-4 lists the most common telephone services used in conjunction with telephone technologies at help desks.

- Automatic number identification
- Caller identification
- Dialed number identification service
- Information indicator digits

Figure 5-4   Common telephone services

Automatic Number Identification **Automatic number identification** (**ANI**) is a service provided by a *long distance* service provider that delivers the telephone number of the person calling.

Caller Identification **Caller identification** (**caller ID**) is a service provided by a *local* telephone company that delivers the telephone number of the person calling.

Dialed Number Identification Service **Dialed number identification service** (**DNIS**) provides the number the person called when they call using a toll-free number or a 1–900 service. A popular use of DNIS is to direct customers to specialized support groups without requiring the caller to select from a telephone menu. For example, a catalog company may assign different toll-free numbers to its clothing, furniture, and other catalogs. With DNIS, the company can determine which toll-free number the customer dialed. As a result, it knows what catalog the customer is calling about and can route the call to analysts familiar with that catalog.

Information Indicator Digits **Information indicator digits** (**IID**) identify the origin of a call from the type or location of the telephone being used to place the call, such as a pay phone, cellular phone, hotel phone, and so forth. Some help desks that support a remote work force recently have begun using this service so they can adjust their call handling procedures based on where the customer is calling from. For example, if a customer calls from the corporate office, their telephone number, automatically obtained with caller ID, can be used to do a CTI lookup. If that same customer calls from a pay phone, they may be prompted to key in his or her PIN so the CTI lookup can be performed.

Other basic telephone services that local service providers may deliver include call waiting, which allows a person to get a second call while he or she is on the phone; three-way calling, which allows three people at different telephone numbers to talk at the same time; and call forwarding, which allows a person to forward a call to another telephone number. These features are typically used in residential, or home, settings. In a business setting, however, a company's telephone system typically provides similar features such as the ability to place calls on hold, establish conference calls with multiple people, and transfer calls to other telephone numbers or extensions. Help desks typically have policies regarding the use of these features because these features can be very frustrating to customers when they are not used properly. For example, have you ever experienced the frustration of being placed on hold before you are able to speak a word or of being transferred repeatedly? If so, you understand the importance of using these features sparingly and with the customer's consent.

Customers are unaware that these services are being used if the telephone technologies are implemented properly. They just know their call is being routed efficiently to the analyst who has the skills needed to provide assistance. Or, they are being given alternate ways to request support such as voice mail, e-mail, or the Web. Analysts also benefit from these technologies in that calls suited to their skills are routed to them in an orderly manner and arrive with information that analysts can use to immediately begin supporting the customer.

E-Mail at the Help Desk

Most help desks—93 percent according to the Help Desk Institute—use e-mail in some way to communicate internally, with other support groups, and with their customers. For example, e-mail can be used within the help desk to communicate schedule changes, promote awareness of process or procedure changes, and notify staff of upcoming system changes. Help desk analysts and managers may use e-mail to communicate with other support groups about the status of projects or about changes to existing procedures. A growing number of companies use e-mail to communicate with customers.

Using E-Mail to Communicate with Customers

E-mail is an easy way to communicate with customers. For example, some companies use e-mail to distribute the help desk's newsletter or to announce an upcoming change that might affect customers. Help desks have been slow to view e-mail as a primary way of communicating with customers, however, for a number of reasons. First, e-mail can be perceived as impersonal and typically doesn't provide the immediate, interactive feedback that customers desire, particularly when they are confused or upset. Second, e-mail does not provide many of the capabilities that an incident tracking system provides. For example, e-mail cannot be used to automatically create trend reports and it cannot be used as a knowledge base. As a result, help desk analysts are usually required to log all e-mail requests from customers in their company's incident tracking system. Analysts are then able to record all status updates related to a customer's problem or request in the incident tracking system, not in e-mail messages that may be lost or forgotten. Third, analysts sometimes find that using e-mail elongates the problem-solving process. For example, if the help desk receives an e-mail that does not contain sufficient information, the analyst must either try to contact the customer by telephone, or send an e-mail message back to the customer requesting the needed details. The analyst must then wait for a response before being able to solve the problem.

Despite these downsides, many customers find e-mail to be a convenient form of communication, and so a small but growing number of help desks—17 percent according to the Help Desk Institute—provide customers with the ability to use e-mail to submit problems and requests. Companies that engage in e-commerce—that is, do business online—are working particularly hard to make the most effective use of this tool.

Help desks are using a number of techniques to ensure that e-mail communications are handled efficiently and effectively. These techniques include:

- Providing help desk analysts with e-mail etiquette training and guidance.
- Integrating e-mail and incident tracking packages.
- Using forms and templates.
- Using e-mail response management systems.

Let's explore each of these techniques in more detail.

Providing Help Desk Analysts with E-Mail Etiquette Training and Guidance

A growing number of help desks provide analysts with training and guidance to ensure that they use common sense, courtesy, and e-mail best practices when using e-mail to communicate with customers. E-mail best practices include making sure all of a customer's questions and concerns are addressed, avoiding lengthy discussions and debates, and using correct grammar, punctuation, and spelling, to name just a few. Some companies recommend that analysts have a coworker or a supervisor review important or complicated e-mails before they are sent to customers.

 To learn more, search the Web for sites about "e-mail etiquette" or go to sites such as **www.iwillfollow.com/email.htm**, **www.emailaddresses.com/ guide_etiquette.htm**, and **www.emailreplies.com**.

Integrating E-Mail and Incident Tracking Systems

Many incident tracking and problem management systems (discussed later) integrate with standard e-mail packages such as Microsoft Outlook and IBM's Lotus Notes to allow, for example, e-mail messages from customers to be logged as tickets automatically. The incident tracking system then can automatically send a return e-mail message to inform customers that their incident was logged and provide a ticket number. Some companies send e-mail messages to customers whenever the status of their incident changes in the incident tracking system. Other companies send e-mail messages with a detailed description of the final resolution when the ticket is closed. This integration makes it possible for companies to provide customers with the convenience of using e-mail, while still having the ability to use their incident tracking systems to collect and maintain incident-related data. Companies are also then able to combine data about incidents submitted via e-mail with data about incidents submitted via other channels such as the telephone and the Web.

Many help desks use e-mail to conduct customer satisfaction surveys. Customers are sent a form to complete and return, or they are sent a link to a form on the help desk's Web site that they can fill out and submit. The responses are typically stored in a database that help desk managers can then use to run reports and analyze help desk performance.

Using Forms and Templates   Help desks are increasingly using forms and templates to customize their e-mail messages and to distribute and collect information electronically. A **form** is a predefined document that contains text or graphics users cannot change and areas in which users enter information. Forms can be designed to use elements such as text-entry boxes, check boxes, buttons, and pull-down menus to collect information. Forms can also be designed to require responses to any of these elements before the user can submit the form. The data entered in a form can be saved in a file or in a database. Companies that integrate their e-mail and incident tracking systems typically design their forms to correspond to the entry screen of the incident tracking system so that incidents can be logged automatically. Customers may choose forms from a forms library or a location within their e-mail system or from a Web site. Figure 5-5 shows a sample of a Web form used to send an e-mail to the company that hosts the Web site.

Forms save time for both customers and analysts. Customers save time because they know what information they must provide to submit an incident. Analysts save time because they get the information they need to begin working on the incident.

A **template** is a predefined item that can be used to quickly create a standard document or e-mail message. For example, help desks can prepare standard openings and closings for e-mails being sent to customers. Templates save analysts time because they can save text and items such as links to Web sites or pages on the help desk's Web site and quickly reuse those items to create documents and e-mail messages.

Using E-Mail Response Management Systems   **E-mail response management systems** such as Kana (**www.kana.com**) and RightNow (**www.rightnow.com**) enable help desks to manage high volume chat, e-mail, and Web form messages in much the same way that ACDs enable help desks to handle telephone calls. For example, these systems enable help desks to route messages to queues; run real-time reports to determine such statistics as how many e-mails are received per hour, per day, and so forth; prioritize messages; and categorize messages so help desks can report on the types of messages being received. These systems also provide analysts with the ability to search and review customer messages and view a history of a customer's activities on the support Web site. In other words, help desk analysts can see the different Web pages, FAQs, and so forth that a customer examined prior to submitting his or her message. Although these systems typically lack the ability to manage other forms of customer contacts such as telephone calls, they are an excellent option for help desks that use e-mail as their primary communication channel with customers.

Figure 5-5 Sample Web form

Regardless of how a help desk uses e-mail to communicate internally, with other support groups, and with its customers, always remember that when you send or receive e-mail, you are conversing with another person. Think about and acknowledge that person, just as you would if you were interacting in person or over the telephone. Include only those things you would say if that person were standing in front of you.

 Thanks to e-mail, communicating with coworkers and customers is easier and faster. Common sense, good judgment, and good writing skills will enable you to make the most of this powerful communication tool.

The Internet and Help Desks

One of the hottest technology topics in recent years has been the Internet. Recall that the Internet is a global collection of computer networks that are linked to provide worldwide access to information. Much of the Internet's explosive growth can be attributed to the Web.

Recall that the Web is a collection of documents on the Internet with point-and-click access to information that is posted by government agencies, businesses, educational institutions, nonprofit organizations, and individuals around the world. The proliferation of Web sites and the ease with which information can be delivered through these sites has prompted the support industry to embrace the Web and use it to support customers.

The Web is having a profound impact on the support industry for a number of reasons, including:

- It provides the help desk with an invaluable source of information about the products and systems the help desk supports and about the help desk industry in general.

- It provides an excellent vehicle for communicating with coworkers, vendors, and customers.

- It has brought many companies new customers, many of whom have very little computing experience and may require a great deal of support.

- It gives the help desk an alternative and less expensive way to provide customers with support.

- It enables the help desk to empower customers to support themselves, a concept that is often called self-service. Recall that in the context of a multi-level support model, customers solving problems using self-services is known as level zero.

Think about how accustomed we have become to using self-services, such as vending machines, voice mail, automatic teller machines (ATMs), and banking by phone. Self-service through the Internet for customer support is no different. We are an impatient society and, given proof that a new way of obtaining service works, customers will embrace and then demand services that free up their most valued commodity—time. According to a survey conducted by supportindustry.com, 76 percent of respondents said that customer demand for Web-based services increased within the past year (Trends in Web-Based Support, September 2002). Soon, companies that fail to embrace the Internet by establishing Web sites will appear inefficient and out of touch. Conversely, companies that offer ineffective Web sites and that fail to provide customers with multiple ways to obtain support will be perceived as trying to avoid direct communication.

 A number of excellent portal sites provide the help desk industry with a source of information about help desk-related products and services. A **portal** is a Web "supersite" that provides a variety of services such as a site search where pertinent articles and white papers may be located, a product and services buyer's guide, a discussion center or forum, event calendars, publications, and so forth. Help desk portals include: **www.helpdesk.com**, **www.philverghis.com**, and **www.supportindustry.com**. One of the most popular IT portals is **www.techrepublic.com**. TechRepublic serves the needs of professionals representing all segments of the IT industry (including help desk), providing information and tools for IT decision support and professional advice by job function. Previously discussed organizations such as the Help Desk Institute, the Service & Support Professionals Association, and STI Knowledge also have excellent and useful sites.

Functionality and ease of use are the keys to a successful help desk Web site. Through their Web sites, some help desks are providing customers:

- Answers to FAQs.

- A "Call Back" button that customers can use to request that an analyst telephone them to discuss an incident.

- A "Chat" button that customers can use to correspond with help desk analysts online.

- A "Contact Us" button or tab that customers can use to learn other ways they can contact a company or department, such as the telephone or e-mail.

- A discussion center or forum for customers to submit questions and exchange ideas with other customers.

- A glossary that customers can use to learn the definition of terms they may encounter.

- A knowledge base of solutions that customers can use to solve incidents on their own.

- A place where customers can check the status of outstanding incidents by pulling up a previously submitted ticket.

- A place where customers can maintain a personal account that houses information such as the customers' telephone number, postal address, e-mail address, and so forth.

- Customer satisfaction surveys that customers can use to provide feedback.

- Information about new and planned products and services.

- Links to other useful Web sites.

- Products and product updates that authorized users can download.

- The ability to use remote control systems (discussed later) to aid problem solving.

- Tips, techniques, and helpful hints.

- Training schedules for company-sponsored training classes.

- Web forms that customers can use to submit problems and requests.

Like help desk technologies in general, the functionality that a help desk's Web site provides varies based on factors such as the help desk's size, company goals, the nature of the company's business, and customer expectations. Furthermore, not all help desks and companies have Web sites, although the number of help desks that do have Web sites is increasing rapidly. According to the Help Desk Institute, 68 percent of help desks had Web sites in 2001; that number increased to 88 percent in 2002, and an additional 3 percent plan to add a Web site within 12 months. Figure 5-6 shows a sample help desk Web site.

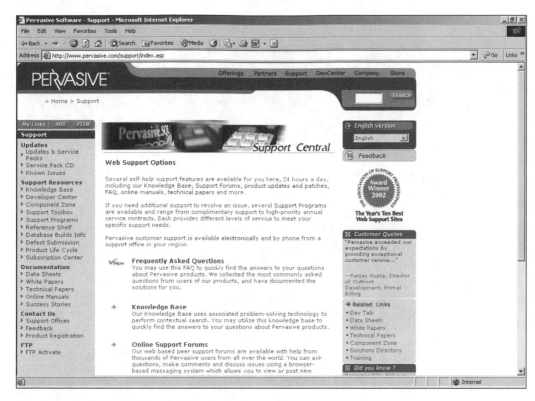

5

Figure 5-6   Sample help desk Web site

The Internet is quickly changing the way customers expect support services to be delivered. Web-based services will not, however, eliminate the telephone- and e-mail–based communication channels for a number of reasons. Some customers simply do not have access to the Web. Others may try to use the Web, become frustrated, and then pick up the telephone or send an e-mail message. Some customers simply prefer to speak with a human being. Web-based services do, however, offer a cost-effective alternate way to provide support services. Use of the Web will continue to grow as customers become more comfortable with this technology and more willing to do business through it.

Web sites typically reflect one of three stages of development—passive, interactive, or real-time. Passive Web sites are essentially online brochures or bulletin boards. They provide customers with access to basic information and direct customers to call the help desk for additional details. Interactive Web sites provide customers with more of a two-way experience. For example, customers can specify a problem and obtain a solution, or customers can post messages and view the responses of other customers. Real-time Web sites enable customers to have "live" contact with analysts or other customers. That contact may involve a chat, a demonstration using a white board system, or fixing a technical problem using remote control software. The state of development that a help desk's Web site reflects typically corresponds to its customers' needs and expectations.

MIKE LANDRETH
CUSTOMER SERVICE MANAGER
SHUTTERFLY, INC.
REDWOOD CITY, CALIFORNIA
WWW.SHUTTERFLY.COM

Shutterfly, Inc. (Shutterfly) is the leading provider of online photo services for digital and film cameras. Shutterfly's Help Center is part of the Operations & Customer Service division and provides answers to customers' technical, order, and billing questions.

Tasks. Shutterfly offers e-mail, telephone, and Web-based customer support. We try to provide as much information as possible on our Web site in an effort to anticipate and answer our customers' questions. We've developed an extensive series of FAQs, troubleshooting procedures, and tips & techniques that are organized by topic. We also offer a glossary, a getting started guide, a camera buyer's guide, and a monthly newsletter called "The Buzz." We monitor the number of page hits we get on our site and the types of contacts we receive, and we rotate our FAQs and our Top Ten Questions list based on the types of questions we're being asked.

When customers don't find the answers they need on our Web site, 90% contact us via e-mail. We receive on average 500 e-mails per day. To contact us via e-mail, customers use a pull-down menu to select the topic that best fits their question or concern. They then complete Web forms that are unique to each topic and click the Send Now button to e-mail the details of their inquiry to our Help Center. Our e-mail response management software enables us to place e-mails into queues, track and prioritize messages, and categorize e-mails so that we can track trends. Ten percent of our customers contact us by telephone, and we receive 60 to 70 telephone calls per day. We use an automatic call distributor to manage calls and to report on the types of calls we're receiving. We offer telephone support Monday through Friday from 8 a.m. to 5 p.m. (PST). We offer e-mail support 7 days per week from approximately 7 a.m. to 10 p.m., based on volume.

Organization. We have a fairly flat organization with 12 customer service representatives (reps) reporting to one customer service supervisor. All of our reps are trained to answer questions ranging from general customer service inquiries to questions that are more technical in nature. Some of our reps also specialize in areas that represent challenging and unique problems such as tricky browser issues (for example, firewalls), Internet security issues, corrupt files, and so forth. When unique problems arise, we encourage our reps to communicate and collaborate, and we empower our reps to do what's necessary to satisfy our customers.

New reps at Shutterfly receive three days of training on our tools, which are all browser based. We then have reps begin completing fairly routine tasks and handling predictable inquiries. New reps initially route their responses to customers to a peer rep for review. They then move on to handling more technical inquires on their own.

When hiring reps, we look for individuals who have a broad range of experience. For example, we look for individuals who are technically savvy and who understand browsers and e-commerce concepts and tools. We also look for good writing skills, problem solving skills, and a positive attitude. We have a close-knit team, so new reps must fit into that team. First and foremost, reps must have a genuine commitment to customer service and the desire and willingness to track things down and get to the root cause of problems.

All of our reps can write, and are encouraged to contribute content to our Web site. We have a customer service engineer (knowledge engineer) who administers our knowledge base and who develops content using customer inquiries and suggestions from our reps as input. We've developed a writing style and format that is fairly relaxed, so it is easy for our reps and our customers to follow.

Philosophy. We focus on educating our customers not only about the services we offer at Shutterfly, but about digital photography in general as well. Our customers include home computer users, small business users, amateur film and digital photographers, and professional photographers—all with different needs, expectations, and abilities. Some of our customers are new to the Internet. Some are new to digital photography. Regardless, we work hard to explain concepts clearly so that customers can get the most out of our services. At Shutterfly, we are so committed to customer satisfaction that we guarantee the quality of our products—and we guarantee the quality of our service and support.

Incident Tracking and Problem Management Systems

Incident tracking and problem management systems are the technology used to log and track customer problems and requests (incidents). By logging all customer incidents, the help desk prevents the most common customer complaint, which is that incidents are lost or forgotten. Figure 5-7 shows a sample problem entry screen that an analyst might use to log a customer incident.

Recall that in some companies customers can contact the help desk via multiple channels such as the telephone, e-mail, fax, or the Web. In an effort to consolidate data about incidents, many help desks require analysts to log all incidents in an incident tracking system, regardless of how they are reported. Furthermore, when analysts log incidents in an incident tracking system, they can use the many features these tools provide to track incidents from start to finish. For example, many incident tracking and problem

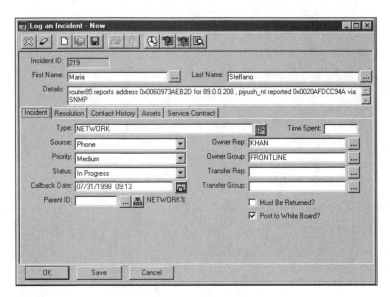

Figure 5-7   Sample problem entry screen

management systems generate alerts that remind analysts to periodically contact customers with status updates when incidents cannot be resolved immediately. Many incident tracking systems also allow analysts to access an asset and configuration management database and obtain information about the products and systems a customer is using or to access a knowledge base and obtain solutions to known problems.

Logging all incidents provides the help desk with the data needed to track, and when necessary, escalate outstanding incidents, and to perform trend and root cause analysis. When incidents must be escalated, the data documented in tickets is used by level two and level three groups to further diagnose and ultimately solve problems. This data is also used by management to create reports and analyze trends. When working in a help desk, analysts must work hard to ensure that the data they collect is accurate, complete, and timely. Many help desks encourage analysts to capture data real-time. For example, analysts are encouraged to log calls while they are talking to a customer on the telephone.

Many help desks provide analysts with telephone headsets that free their hands for typing, or keyboarding. Technologies such as CTI and the technologies that enable, for example, e-mails to be automatically logged have considerably reduced the amount of keyboarding done by analysts. Incident tracking system features such as check boxes, buttons, and pull-down menus also make it easier for analysts to quickly log incidents. In the future, speech recognition technology will further reduce the amount of typing needed to create and update tickets. **Speech recognition** is the conversion of spoken words into text or mouse emulation commands. All of these technologies make it increasingly easier for analysts to record data real-time.

5

Incident tracking and problem management systems fall into several distinct types, or categories. The first category breaks down into incident tracking and problem management systems used by companies that provide external support and those that provide internal support. Although external and internal help desks use many of the same types of tools, they have slightly different requirements. For example, external help desks often verify customer entitlement, whereas internal help desks do not. Also, companies that provide external support often must capture information needed to create customer invoices, whereas internal help desks typically do not. The tools external and internal help desks use must enable them to automate these varying procedures.

 Companies that provide external support may use Customer Relationship Management (CRM) systems to track problems and requests. Recall that CRM involves using customer contact and relationship information to generate additional sales and increase levels of customer service and retention. These systems and their associated processes provide companies with the ability to track *all* interactions with a customer, not just problems and requests. For example, a company's sales force may record their discussions with customers about the purchase of a new product or about upgrading an existing product in the CRM application.

The second category breakdown considers the processes the system will manage, the volume of requests being processed, and the number of system users. The number of system users includes level two and level three management and staff and, in some cases, customers, in addition to level one help desk management and staff. This second category breakdown divides incident tracking and problem management tools into incident tracking systems, problem management and resolution systems, and enterprise solutions.

Incident Tracking Systems **Incident tracking systems** typically support only the problem management process and offer basic trouble ticketing and management reporting capability. These systems often run on a standalone proprietary PC database (as opposed to an open, relational database) and may not be able to support a high number of users or a high volume of data. Smaller help desks or medium help desks that are looking for an interim system they can get up and running quickly often use incident tracking systems. Leading incident tracking systems include Clientele HelpDesk by Epicor (**www.clientele.com**), DKHelpDesk by DKSystems (**www.dksystems.com**), and HelpSTAR by HelpSTAR.com (**www.helpstar.com**).

 Small help desks sometimes develop their incident tracking system in-house using tools such as Microsoft Access and Microsoft SQL Server. Given a good design and ongoing support, these systems can provide a small help desk with a system that meets their needs. If nothing else, these systems enable help desks to collect the data they need to justify a commercially developed system. A downside is that in-house developed systems tend to be poorly documented so maintaining and enhancing the system can be difficult, especially if the individual who developed the system originally has moved to another department or company. In time, most companies acquire a commercially developed system so they can rely on the vendor to support and continuously improve the product.

Problem Management and Resolution Systems **Problem management and resolution systems** offer enhanced trouble ticketing and management reporting capability. For example, they often offer the ability to log quick calls with only a click or two and the ability to link related calls. They may also support and integrate the request management and asset and configuration management processes. For example, Figure 5-8 shows how the assets used by the requester can be viewed from a problem entry screen.

These systems work well in a multi-level support environment where problems and requests are handed off to other analysts or specialty groups because this environment needs automated escalation and notification capabilities, which are part of problem management and resolution systems. These systems also provide more advanced diagnostic capabilities and knowledge management systems. In addition, these systems offer some customization and integration capability, such as e-mail integration. Because these tools are based on relational or structured query language (SQL) database engines, they can support a higher number of users and a higher volume of data. Medium help desks, as well as smaller help desks that anticipate considerable growth, often use problem management and resolution systems. A larger help desk looking for an interim system also may use these tools. Leading problem management and resolution systems include HEAT by FrontRange Solutions (**www.frontrange.com**), Magic Service Desk by Network Associates (**www.networkassociates.com**), and Track-IT! by Blue Ocean Software (**www.blueocean.com**).

Enterprise Solutions **Enterprise solutions**, sometimes called integrated enterprise solutions, are a suite of systems that companies use to manage their problem, request, knowledge management, change, and asset and configuration management processes. In addition, enterprise solutions tightly integrate with network and systems management tools, asset management tools, and sophisticated expert and knowledge management systems. Enterprise solutions can be customized comprehensively and are very feature-rich. Typically, enterprise solutions are based on relational databases and a client-server architecture, which makes this tool able to support a high number of users and a high volume of data. Medium to large help desks that require—and see the value in implementing—an integrated tool suite often use enterprise solutions. Leading enterprise solutions include Action Request System by Remedy (**www.remedy.com**), ServiceCenter by Peregrine (**www.peregrine.com**), and Unicenter ServicePlus Service Desk by Computer Associates (**www.computerassociates.com**).

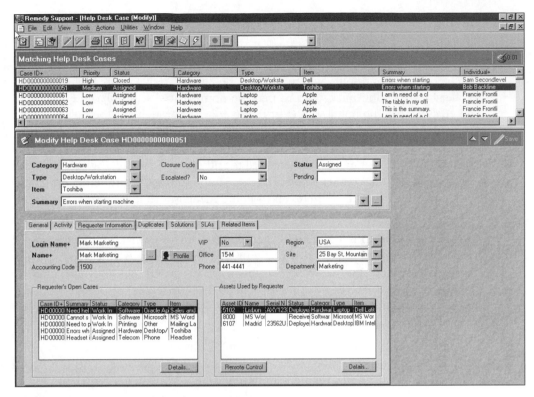

Figure 5-8   Sample asset details screen

 The incident tracking and problem management system market has been dramatically affected by the recent slow-down that has occurred in the software industry. Companies are frequently acquired and smaller companies may simply stop doing business. Help desks that are thinking of acquiring a new system must use great care when selecting technology.

Companies tend to change their incident tracking and problem management systems periodically. Either they outgrow their existing systems, indicated by slow response time and inadequate functionality, or they replace their systems as new technology becomes available. Experienced help desk analysts depend on up-to-date incident tracking and problem management systems to provide quality support to customers. Increasingly, companies are integrating their incident tracking and problem management systems with expert and knowledge management systems.

Expert and Knowledge Management Systems

As children, we learn to work with other people and to acquire skills from them. As adults, we bring this same approach to the workplace. However, the pace of change has accelerated to the point where we can no longer depend on learning only from our colleagues. As companies strive to find the optimal staff size, colleagues with the expertise an analyst needs do not always exist in the company, much less the help desk. If colleagues with expertise do exist, they often carry a heavy workload or are busy learning new skills themselves. As a result, many companies have installed expert and knowledge management systems, which capture human knowledge and make it readily available to others who are involved in solving problems and requests. Although initially implemented to aid help desk analysts, these systems are increasingly being made available to customers, for example, via the help desk's Web site.

An **expert system** is a computer program that stores human knowledge in a knowledge base and has the ability to reason about that knowledge. A **knowledge management system** combines the reasoning capability of an expert system with other information sources, such as databases, documents, policies, and procedures. Although a knowledge management system is in fact an expert system, the support industry more commonly uses the term *knowledge management system*.

Expert and knowledge management technology has advanced considerably in recent years, and its use has become more widespread in the support industry. This is primarily because most of the problem management and resolution systems and enterprise solutions discussed earlier can be purchased with embedded knowledge management systems. In other words, if a company acquires a leading problem management and resolution system or enterprise solution, that system either comes with a built-in knowledge base or a knowledge base can be purchased as an add-on product and integrated with the base product.

Some companies do, however, purchase and implement standalone knowledge management systems. Leading knowledge management systems include ASK.ME Pro by KnowledgeBroker (**www.kbi.com**), Knowledgebase.net by Knowledge Base Solutions (**www.knowledgebase.net**), and Primus Answer Engine by Primus (**www.primus.com**).

Help desks that support custom applications must use expert and knowledge management systems that they can develop to capture knowledge in-house. Help desks that support standard industry applications from Microsoft, Lotus, Novell, Netscape, and others can purchase commercially available knowledge bases. Help desks can purchase subscriptions to these knowledge bases so they receive regular updates. Commercial knowledge bases typically are delivered on CD-ROM. Leading commercial knowledge bases include KnowledgeBases by KnowledgeBroker (**www.kbi.com**), Knowledge-Paks by RightAnswers (**www.rightanswers.com**), and TechNet by Microsoft (**www.microsoft.com**).

Much of the information about standard industry applications can be obtained free of charge on the Web. For example, most hardware and software vendors post answers to FAQs and solutions to known problems on their Web sites. Many help desks add links to vendor Web sites to the help desk Web site, making it easier for analysts and customers to quickly access the vendor information they need.

Another reason that knowledge management technology is used more widely in the support industry is because early rule-based expert systems have been replaced by more sophisticated case-based systems that are easier to use and maintain.

A **rule-based system** is made up of (1) rules, (2) facts, and (3) a knowledge base or engine that combines rules and facts to reach a conclusion. Some companies tried, unsuccessfully in most cases, to implement rule-based expert systems in the mid-1980s. Rule-based systems are difficult to build and maintain because every rule added to the rule base can potentially interact with every other rule. Because of this complexity, these systems are rarely used in the support industry anymore.

Case-based systems have proven to be a much more viable way to manage knowledge in today's fast-paced support industry. A **case-based system** is made up of (1) cases and (2) a set of question and answer pairs that can be used to confirm the solution to the problem. A **case** is a unit of information, such as an online document, a database record, or the solution to a common problem, which is indexed so an analyst can easily locate it when needed. A case contains a problem description and a solution description as well as a frequency counter that indicates how many times the solution has been used to solve the problem, or a score that indicates the relevance of the solution to the search criteria. Figure 5-9 shows the scored results of a knowledge base search.

Case-based systems are much easier to implement than rule-based systems and offer the help desk far more flexibility and power.

Search Retrieval Techniques

Much of the flexibility and power in a case-based system comes from the many search-retrieval technologies now available. Figure 5-10 lists the most common of these technologies. These retrieval technologies allow users to specify search criteria, which is then used to retrieve similar cases. **Search criteria** are the questions or problem symptoms entered by a user. Some of these retrieval technologies do very simple data matching, whereas others use highly sophisticated artificial intelligence.

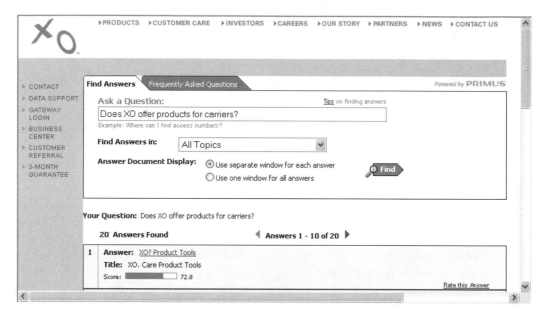

Figure 5-9   Sample knowledge base search results

- Case-based reasoning
- Decision trees
- Fuzzy logic
- Keyword searching
- Query by example

Figure 5-10   Common search retrieval techniques

Case-Based Reasoning   **Case-based reasoning (CBR)** is a searching technique that uses everyday language to ask users questions and interpret their answers. CBR prompts the user for any additional information it needs to identify a set of possible solutions. Not only does CBR find perfect matches based on user queries, but it also retrieves cases that are similar to the perfect match. Possible solutions are ranked in order of probability from most likely to least likely to solve the problem.

Decision Trees   A **decision tree** is a branching structure of questions and possible answers designed to lead an analyst to a solution. Decision trees work well for entry-level analysts and for help desk customers because they can walk through a methodical approach to solving problems. Senior analysts and "power users" often feel that decision trees take too long to identify a solution.

Fuzzy Logic **Fuzzy logic** is a searching technique that presents all possible solutions that are similar to the search criteria, even when conflicting information exists or no exact match is present. For example, fuzzy logic can get results when the exact spelling of a word is not known, or it can help users obtain information that is loosely related to a topic.

Keyword Searching **Keyword searching** is the technique of finding indexed information by specifying a descriptive word or phrase, called a keyword. Keywords must be indexed to be located, and an *exact* match must be found. For example, if a user specifies the keyword "computer," only records that contain the keyword "computer" are located; records that contain the keyword "PC" are not located. Some systems provide the ability to index synonyms as well as keywords to increase the number of matches found when a search is performed.

Query by Example **Query by example** (**QBE**) is a searching technique that uses queries, or questions, to find records that match the specified search criteria. Queries can include **search operators**, connecting words such as AND, OR, and NOT. Search operators may also be called Boolean operators. QBE also can find records that *do not* contain the search criteria or that contain a value less than, greater than, or equal to the specified search criteria.

Today's sophisticated search retrieval technologies have value only if the information stored in the knowledge base is current, complete, and accurate. The expression "garbage-in, garbage out" is appropriate: If out-of-date, inaccurate, or incomplete information (garbage) is stored in the knowledge base, then out-of-date, inaccurate, or incomplete information (garbage) will be delivered when a search is performed.

Storage Methods

Search-retrieval techniques are complemented by interactive storage methods, such as hypermedia and hypertext retrieval. **Hypermedia** stores information in a graphical form and **hypertext** stores information in a nongraphical form so users can access the information in a nonlinear fashion using hyperlinks. **Hyperlinks** are colored and underlined text or graphics in a hypertext or hypermedia document that allow readers to "jump" to a related idea, regardless of where that idea occurs in the document. Clicking a hyperlink might open a pop-up window with a definition, instructions, a still picture, or an animated picture. Hyperlinks can also run audio or video clips, or jump to Web pages. Readers can easily move to more detailed information and back to a higher level by clicking hyperlinks that are embedded in the document.

Expert and knowledge management systems are highly sophisticated systems that can be used to record newly found solutions and procedures and enable the quick retrieval of known solutions and procedures.

Expert and knowledge management systems benefit help desk analysts considerably because they do not have to wait until the resident "expert" returns from vacation or training to access that person's knowledge. With expert and knowledge management systems, the information is available online whenever it is needed. Storing knowledge online also enables help desks to make that knowledge available to customers via their Web sites.

These systems can also lead an analyst or a help desk customer through troubleshooting steps that help resolve problems, which in turn improve the analyst's and the customer's problem-solving skills.

Another way that expert and knowledge management systems benefit help desk analysts is that the resident expert may spend a great deal of time answering questions and handling difficult problems in one particular area. Sometimes, this occurs so much that the resident expert doesn't have the time, or the energy, to pursue new skills. Being the resident expert used to be considered "job security." Today, companies want people who share their knowledge with coworkers and customers, cross-train their coworkers, and continuously develop new skills. Storing knowledge online enables analysts to achieve all of these goals.

REMOTE SUPPORT TECHNOLOGIES

Few help desks have all of their customers in one building or in one location. In companies that do, help desk analysts often "jump and run" to the customer's desk to diagnose and potentially solve a problem or request. This approach is far too inefficient and costly for most companies, not to mention the fact that eventually no one is left at the help desk to answer calls. Many problems can be solved over the telephone or via e-mail or the Internet, and so a better approach is to offer remote support.

The need to provide remote support is compounded by the fact that an increasing number of help desk customers work remotely on a regular basis. For example, they work at home, in a hotel, or at a client site. Cahners In-Stat Group, a high-technology research group, estimates that roughly 24 percent of the U.S. work force, or 30 million workers, telecommuted at least one day a week in 2001. In-Stat expects this percentage to increase to 28 percent in 2004, growing to nearly 40 million telecommuters. Because the needs of remote workers can change daily as they move from one location to the next, supporting remote workers can be quite challenging.

Many help desks use remote support technologies to extend the help desk's reach and enhance their ability to resolve problems, particularly remote problems. Figure 5-11 lists the most common remote support technologies available to the help desk.

- Asset and configuration management systems
- Remote control systems
- Remote monitoring systems
- Self-healing systems
- Software distribution systems

Figure 5-11   Common remote support technologies

The availability of these technologies depends on factors such as need and available funding.

Asset and Configuration Management Systems

An **asset and configuration management system** is a technology that allows an analyst to "see" what hardware and software is installed on a computer or network along with financial information such as license and warranty information. Recall that the asset and configuration management processes provide a central database for IT asset information that is typically called the configuration management database (CMDB) and that in many companies the CMDB is a logical entity, rather than a physical entity.

A variety of systems may be used to collect and store information in the CMDB. For example, the problem management and resolution systems and enterprise solutions discussed earlier in this chapter typically provide applications that can be used to manually collect and store asset and configuration data. PC inventory software can automatically collect information about networked devices that can be loaded into the CMDB. Leading PC inventory products include BridgeAudit by Kemma Software (**www.kemma.com**), LANauditor by iInventory Ltd. (**www.lanauditor.com**), and systemhound by Software Innovations UK Limited (**www.systemhound.com**).

 Software packages that can automatically collect inventory information may also provide features such as software metering (knowing what software licenses have been purchased and where they are being used), remote control, remote monitoring, and software distribution systems.

Remote Control Systems

A **remote control system** is a technology that enables an analyst to take over a caller's keyboard, screen, mouse, or other connected devices to troubleshoot problems, transfer files, provide informal training, and even collaborate on documents. Leading remote control systems include LANDesk by LANDesk Software (**www.landesksoftware.com**), PCAnywhere by Symantec (**www.symantec.com**), and NetOp Remote Control by CrossTec Corporation (**www.crossteccorp.com**). Figure 5-12 shows how a remote control system can be used to access and support a remote PC.

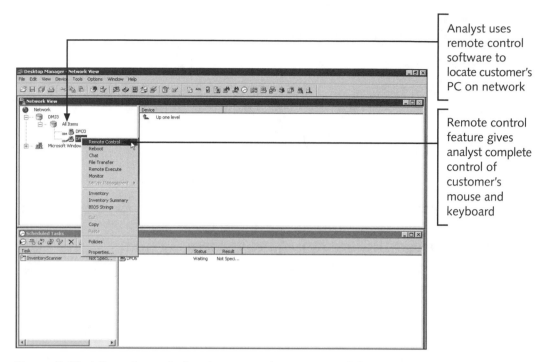

Analyst uses remote control software to locate customer's PC on network

Remote control feature gives analyst complete control of customer's mouse and keyboard

Figure 5-12   Remote control system accessing a remote PC

Although some help desks cannot use remote control systems because of security concerns, many help desks, small to large, are learning that problems can be solved more quickly when time is not lost traveling to a customer's location. Furthermore, most customers appreciate the immediacy with which their problem can be addressed when help desk analysts use a remote control system. As security can be a concern, many remote control systems provide security features such as "prompt to confirm connection," which allows a host computer user such as a help desk customer to permit or reject access to his or her system, and "view only mode," which allows an analyst to see but not control a host computer. These systems can control remote PCs over the Internet, networks, or modems.

Some help desks use Microsoft NetMeeting for remote support. NetMeeting can be downloaded free of charge from the Microsoft Web site. In addition to its chat capabilities, NetMeeting provides a help desk customer with the ability to tell NetMeeting to either share an application with the help desk or provide the help desk with the ability to remotely control the entire system. The NetMeeting file transfer feature also enables the help desk to transfer and install files such as service packs on the customer's PC. Also, beginning with Windows XP Professional, Microsoft is including Terminal Services technology in its workstation and server operating systems. Terminal Services technology provides remote control capabilities such as Remote Assistance and Remote Desktop.

Remote Monitoring Systems

A **remote monitoring system** is a technology that tracks and collects alerts generated by a network monitoring system and passes them to a central server, where they can be automatically picked up and logged in a problem management and resolution system or enterprise solution. This automation ensures that all network problems are logged, even those that may not cause a disruption that users notice. The help desk and network management group can then use this data to track trends and ultimately prevent network-related problems. This automation also ensures that network problems that may have gone undetected are addressed. Remote monitoring systems can also pass alerts to a special monitor or electronic white board system that the help desk and network management group can view easily. As network problems tend to affect many users, having a monitor that can be easily viewed makes it possible to keep all analysts informed about network problems, even those that may be on the telephone. Figure 5-13 shows a sample display that shows network, system, and application status information.

Self-Healing Systems

Increasingly, hardware devices and software applications have the ability to detect and correct problems on their own, a concept known as **self-healing**. Vendors such as McAfee and Microsoft are starting to deliver early examples of self-healing applications. For example, VirusScanOnline by McAfee (**www.mcafee.com**) can monitor a computer for viruses, automatically attempt to clean infected files when a virus is detected, and automatically check for virus updates and software upgrades. Windows XP by Microsoft (**www.microsoft.com**) can automatically detect and download software updates from the Internet.

Companies such as SupportSoft, Inc. (**www.supportsoft.com**) and SystemSoft Corporation (**www.systemsoft.com**) also offer products that are capable of detecting and automatically correcting PC hardware and software problems. These systems monitor, for example, software programs for errors. When errors are detected, these systems either find the source of the error and fix it or they notify the user that an error has occurred. These systems can also detect whether failing hardware devices or software applications have been changed and determine what changes could be causing an error. To correct a problem, self-healing systems may back out changes and restore the hardware or software back to its pre-change state.

The Information Week article *Computer, Heal Thyself* provides additional information about self-healing software. To view this article, go to **www.informationweek.com/story/IWK20020329S0005**.

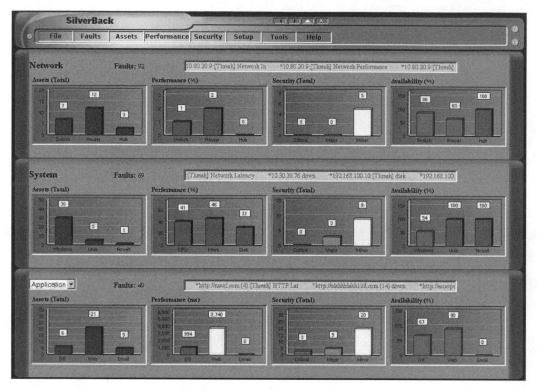

Figure 5-13   Sample network, system, and application status display

Software Distribution Systems

A **software distribution system** is a technology that allows an analyst to automatically distribute software to clients and servers on the same network. Software can be distributed to lists of people. For example, all of the users in a particular department can receive software upgrades at the same time. This technology also enables software to be distributed to remote workers.

Today's help desk supports a complex computing environment made up of PCs, servers, LANs, operating systems, application systems, databases, and so forth. Remote support technologies enable the help desk to centrally manage and support this complex environment, which results in reduced cost, increased productivity for the employees of the company and its customers, and increased customer satisfaction.

HELP DESK COMMUNICATION TOOLS

Help desk communication tools are manual, electronic, and computer technologies that display or share information within a help desk or between a help desk and other support groups and customers. Help desk communication tools promote awareness with customers and within the help desk when critical problems arise or when changes are scheduled to occur. These tools can display system status information obtained automatically from a network management system or queue activity obtained from an ACD. These tools, which include white boards, electronic reader boards, instant messaging systems, and push technology, enhance and complement the exchange of information that occurs with tools such as e-mail and voice mail.

White Boards

White boards are smooth, erasable white panels on which analysts write notes and communicate current and future events. This simple tool is a very effective way to share information and is often placed where all members of the help desk team can view it. The only downside to a white board is that it is a manual device. Team members must *neatly* write down important information in a timely fashion and remember to erase outdated information. **White board systems** allow two or more users on a network to view one or more user's drawing, or a document or application being projected on an onscreen white board. Some help desks use white board systems to project information on a large screen that is visible to all help desk analysts. This approach is particularly useful when there is a system-wide problem that analysts who may be on the telephone need to be made aware of, such as a virus alert or system outage.

Electronic Reader Boards

Electronic reader boards are bright displays that send out visual and, in some cases, audible messages to help desk staff and to customer sites that have reader boards installed. These tools can be combined with network management consoles to display real-time system and network status information. They can also be integrated with ACD management consoles, as shown in Figure 5-14, to display real-time statistics such as the number of calls in queue (CIQ), the average wait time per call, and the number of calls answered and abandoned.

Figure 5-14   Electronic reader board showing real-time ACD statistics

Electronic reader boards are particularly effective when used with color and sound to alert help desk staff that a situation is approaching a preset alarm threshold. For example, if company policy is for the help desk to answer all calls within 60 seconds, a board can display a yellow message accompanied by an audible alarm when a call is nearing the targeted time. The message changes to red after the targeted time is past. Red alarms notify management that standards have been exceeded and that management action is required.

Instant Messaging Systems

Instant message systems enable two or more people to communicate in real time (chat) over the Internet by typing on a keyboard. Instant messaging requires that all parties be online at the same time. Internet service providers (ISPs) such as America Online, Microsoft MSN, and Yahoo! all provide instant messaging services. Help desk analysts use instant messaging primarily to communicate with level two service providers about an ongoing problem. For example, a field service representative may use instant messaging to inform a help desk analyst that he or she has arrived at a customer site to begin work on a high severity problem. Or, a help desk analyst may use instant messaging to communicate with a member of the network support group about a network outage. Like e-mail, instant messaging does not provide the capabilities of an incident tracking system, so analysts are typically required to record any status updates obtained via instant messaging in the help desk's incident tracking system. Following this procedure ensures that all parties who access the incident tracking system have the latest information, not just the parties who are sending and receiving messages.

Communication tools such as e-mail, white board systems, and instant messaging systems are also called collaboration products. Generally, **collaboration products** are any products that enable multiple users to work together on related tasks. Another type of collaboration product is groupware software. **Groupware software** enables multiple users to coordinate and track ongoing projects. Groupware software uses a messaging system, such as e-mail, to notify team members about events and obtain responses. Other groupware applications include document sharing and document management, group calendaring and scheduling, group contact and task management, threaded discussions, text chat, data conferencing, and audio and video conferencing. **Workflow software**, which allows messages and documents to be routed to the appropriate users, is often part of a groupware system.

Push Technology

Push technology delivers information to Web-enabled PCs. The information is delivered in one of two ways: push or pull. In the push method, the server contacts the client when there is new information to send. In the pull method, the client contacts the server to determine whether new information is available. Push technology can deliver information through a screen saver, or through a floating ticker that can be moved to an out-of-the-way place on the computer desktop.

Help desks use push technology to notify customers about virus alerts, system outages, and scheduled changes. Some push technology can push software updates and install them on the recipient's computer—a capability the help desk can use to keep their remote customers up-to-date. Used properly, push technology is a proactive way to enhance communications. Rather than wait for customers and staff to browse the help desk's Web site or read their e-mail, information is delivered in an attention-getting way.

Push technology is just starting to gain wide-scale acceptance, and some people prefer not to have information pushed to their desktop out of concern that a virus or other inappropriate form of information will also be delivered. Because of this, help desks must offer customers the ability to simply view information through their Web site or to pull information or software updates from a server when they choose to do so.

HELP DESK MANAGEMENT TOOLS

A number of tools are designed to help supervisors and managers optimize staffing levels, prepare schedules, and monitor the performance of help desk staff. These tools are called **help desk management systems**. Larger help desks that handle a high volume of calls often use these systems because in larger organizations these tasks (determining staffing levels, preparing schedules, and so on) can be somewhat complex and time-consuming. In smaller help desks, managers tend to perform these tasks manually. Figure 5-15 lists some common help desk management systems.

- Staffing and scheduling systems
- ACD supervisor console
- Customer surveying systems

Figure 5-15   Help desk management systems

These are the most typical help desk management systems for larger help desks.

Staffing and Scheduling Systems

Staffing and scheduling systems work with ACD systems to collect, report, and forecast call volumes. This information about the volume of calls received by a help desk is then used to forecast future call patterns, schedule the optimal number of staff, track analyst productivity, and prepare budgets.

ACD Supervisor Console

An **ACD supervisor console** is a system that works with ACD systems and enables supervisors to monitor call volumes and the performance of individual help desk analysts or groups of analysts. As shown in Figure 5-16, the ACD supervisor console displays statistics that are constantly updated, such as the number of analysts logged in, how many calls are in queue, and the length of time calls have been waiting.

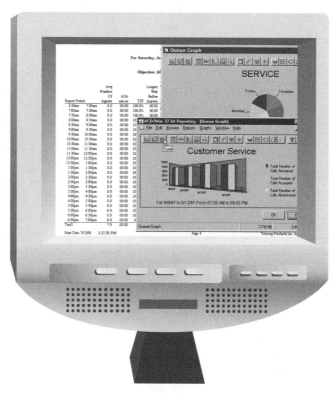

Figure 5-16   Sample ACD supervisor console

Customer Surveying Systems

Customer surveying systems are used to create and distribute questionnaires to customers and to collect and tabulate the results of their feedback. Some customer surveying systems can export the tabulated survey results to statistical-analysis packages, word processors, spreadsheets, and presentation packages.

These tools provide help desk managers with the ability to analyze help desk performance data and forecast help desk needs. As a result, help desk managers have the information they need to maximize the efficiency and effectiveness of the help desk team.

INTEGRATING BUSINESS PROCESSES AND TECHNOLOGY

The purpose of technology is to support and enhance business processes, but technology should not be added simply to automate existing processes and procedures. The reason is summed up in the adage, "If you're doing things wrong and you automate them, you'll only do them wrong faster."

Prior to selecting and implementing new technology, help desk management and staff must evaluate their existing processes and procedures to determine whether they really need new tools and technology or simply need to refine their business processes. If they decide to implement a new technology, then they must select the appropriate tool. Properly implemented, technology enables an organization to keep its help desk running efficiently and effectively and, ultimately, increases customer satisfaction. On the other hand, help desk management and staff may determine through analysis that they don't need new tools.

They simply need to more clearly define their processes and procedures. Technology is not a magic pill that can cure all evils. Processes and procedures must be well defined, and *then* tools and technology can enable people to execute the processes and procedures more quickly and effectively.

HARRIET CHAVEZ
INFORMATION SYSTEMS MANAGER
KASS, SHULER, SOLOMON, SPECTOR, FOYLE & SINGER, P.A.
TAMPA, FLORIDA
WWW.KASSLAW.COM

The help desk at the law firm of Kass, Shuler, Solomon, Spector, Foyle & Singer, P.A. provides technical support to the office staff of 65 attorneys, secretaries, paralegals, file room and bookkeeping personnel who work for the firm.

Tasks.   Our Computer Technician and I provide first level hardware, software, and network support and we handle on average 150 problems and requests each month. Our personnel contact our receptionist to report problems, which are logged as tasks in Microsoft Outlook. We can view and prioritize the tasks online and then work with our personnel over the telephone, or we can go to their office—all of our personnel are in the same building. We also use the Windows XP remote desktop feature to diagnose and resolve problems, particularly when we're away from the office.

Requests for new hardware or software are handled on a case-by-case basis. We typically try to first, determine if we already have a product that the personnel can use. If not, we perform a cost benefit analysis to justify a purchase. When the

Computer Technician (standing) provides support

cost is considerable, we obtain approval from the firm's partners prior to making that purchase. We maintain inventory information in a database that the Computer Technician developed using Microsoft Access. We use the database to track equipment, maintain warranty information, and so forth.

We also maintain the firm's network of servers by performing backups and completing network administration and security-related tasks. Security is very important to us and all of our data is password protected at the network level. To protect our client's confidentiality, some data, such as financial data, requires additional passwording. Password sharing is strictly discouraged.

Organization. Day to day, the Computer Technician and I do our best to stay on top of our workload with occasional backup from our Office Manager, who is the Legal Administrator for the firm. We resolve 81 percent of reported problems at level one. However, when we're unable to resolve problems or when we have a considerable backlog of problems, we work with a consulting firm called Network Business Solutions (NBS) that provides us with level two support. NBS also completes projects at our request such as file server updates and software upgrades.

NBS also uses Outlook, and so we're able to refer problems and requests to them and they are able to provide status updates in return. Although we occasionally need to contact a vendor such as Microsoft or the publishers of our various software packages about a problem, we typically consult with NBS first to obtain a solution for network, hardware, or system-related software.

Because NBS charges us an hourly fee for their services, we've established a fairly strict policy that requires personnel to contact our receptionist and have their problems and requests logged, rather than contacting NBS directly. This enables us to manage our costs and also ensures that we're aware internally of problems that are affecting our staff.

Philosophy. The firm has become increasingly dependent on technology. For example, we use case management software to maintain the massive amounts of documentation that a law firm is required to produce. Our personnel regularly use e-mail to communicate with our clients and the Internet to connect to the courthouse and conduct research. We also use fax servers to send and receive documents, and scanners and imaging software in our goal to become a paperless office. Because we are so dependent on our computer systems, our goal is to provide our personnel with a reliable computing environment. When problems do occur, we focus on getting our systems up and running as quickly as possible. When problems are critical, we do our best to remain calm and, in turn, calm our personnel so we can get the details we need to solve the problem. We've worked hard to build a good rapport with our personnel. This is particularly important because we're a small organization and so we occasionally have to draw the line in terms of what we can do and what we view as a priority. We do our best to stay organized, and take pride in the fact that anyone who needs to can look in Outlook and see what's going on at anytime.

STEPS FOR SELECTING TECHNOLOGY

With hundreds of products on the market, the process of selecting, acquiring, and implementing a support technology that will enhance the capabilities of a help desk can take six to nine months if the help desk follows all the steps required for successfully selecting a new technology. Many companies establish a committee that remains intact until a final decision is made. This committee includes representatives from all of the groups that will use the tool, such as the help desk, level two and three groups, customers, and so forth. Figure 5-17 lists the steps for selecting and implementing any technology for a support organization.

The next sections show how a help desk follows these steps to select a problem management and resolution system. These steps are not, however, unique to selecting a problem management system. The help desk can use this same approach, or methodology, to select and implement any new system.

Step 1. Define the goals.

Step 2. Define the requirements.

Step 3. Weight the requirements.

Step 4. Identify candidate vendors.

Step 5. Evaluate candidate vendors.

Step 6. Evaluate the finalists.

Step 7. Make a final decision.

Figure 5-17   Steps for selecting and implementing help desk technology

Step 1. Define the Goals   The first step in selecting a new technology is to determine what the help desk and the company want to achieve by acquiring and implementing the new system. They must be as specific as possible and clearly define how people will benefit from the technology.

 Effecting and managing organizational change is tough. Commitment climbs, however, when people can see the benefits of making a change, such as implementing a new system. They become even more committed when they see that the change benefits them personally. When implementing a new system, continuously communicate the goals of the system and how it will benefit the company, the help desk, and the people who will use it.

When defining goals, the help desk should ask for input from all of the groups and departments that will, or may, use the system to ensure that their needs are met. For example, possible goals for a problem management and resolution system are:

- Establish and maintain a central database of information on the status of all problems.

- Implement a system that enables customers to report problems easily and accurately.

- Increase the number of problems resolved by the help desk by X percent.

- Resolve problems within the time frame defined for each type of problem.

- Provide customers with timely and accurate problem status updates.

- Provide the information needed to anticipate and prevent the occurrence and recurrence of problems.

Notice that most of these goals are measurable, which means that the help desk will be able to statistically measure how well the implemented system attains these goals. These statistics also show management a return on investment (ROI).

Clearly defined goals enable a help desk to justify the cost of a new system and to tell vendors what the company is trying to achieve with the new system. In return, vendors can show specifically how their products help the company achieve its goals.

Step 2. Define the Requirements   A **requirement** is something that is essential. The selection committee should first define all the high-level requirements for a new system, and then focus on the specific feature and function requirements.

High-level requirements are the broad needs for a system. High-level requirements for a problem management and resolution system include operating platform, performance and growth needs, integration needs, and processes to be supported such as problem management and request management. High-level requirements provide a framework for the feature and functionality requirements.

Feature and functionality requirements are the specifics of how the selected tool must perform in order to support its associated business processes. Help desks often break these requirements into categories. Sample feature and functionality categories for a problem management and resolution system include:

- **Configuration and customization requirements**—To what extent do you want to be able to customize the product?

- **Data and reporting requirements**—What are your data-validation requirements? What kind of reports do you want to obtain (such as detail, summary, charts and graphs)?

- **Functionality requirements**—What are your requirements relative to problem logging, assignment, escalation and notification, solution capture and re-use, and so forth?

- **Miscellaneous requirements**—What are your vendor stability and support requirements? What about supporting documentation, utilities, training, and so forth?

- **Security requirements**—What are your security requirements? How do you want to prevent unauthorized users from accessing the system? What security mechanisms do you want within the system (that is, once an authorized user has logged on)?

- **Usability requirements**—What is your definition of user-friendly?

High-level requirements, along with feature and functionality requirements, enable the selection committee to narrow the field of candidate vendors for the new system. The committee should be as specific as possible when defining requirements. Too often, companies define requirements either at such a high level that the requirements add little value to the selection process or in specific detail without considering the bigger picture. Either approach hinders their ability to identify candidate vendors.

Step 3. Weight the Requirements   The next step is to weight, or prioritize, the requirements based on a scale of 1 to 5—not very important to extremely important, or nice to have to must have. Although, by definition, a requirement is a necessity, some necessities are more important than others. Listing every requirement as a "must have" requirement implies that the "perfect" system exists, which is rarely the case. When a company weights its requirements, it is more likely to find viable vendors and products early in the search. Table 5-1 shows a rating system for weighing requirements.

Table 5-1   Sample requirements rating system

Weight	Priority
1	Not very important
2	Somewhat important (nice to have)
3	Important
4	Very important
5	Extremely important (must have)

 Expect 80 percent of your requirements to be satisfied "out of the box," meaning that 80 percent of your requirements are satisfied without customizing the product.

Step 4. Identify Candidate Vendors   This is one of the most difficult steps in the technology selection process. Hundreds of vendors offer products, and many vendors offer multiple products, or a product suite. The selection committee must research vendors and products before determining its top candidates. Resources to research vendors and products include:

- Conferences, expositions, and technology showcases.

- Trade publications (remember that the articles that appear are not always unbiased).

- Buyers guides such as those found at *Call Center Magazine's* Web site (**www.callcentermagazine.com**) and the Help Desk Institute's Web site (**www.helpdeskinst.com**).

- Vendor Web sites and discussion forums on the Web.

- Product evaluation results from research firms such as Gartner, Inc. (**www.gartner.com**).

 Appendix B contains a list of Web sites for a number of these resources.

Step 5. Evaluate Candidate Vendors Step 4 often uncovers many possible vendors to assess. There are a number of ways to approach the candidate evaluation process. Some companies simply have all of the candidates send them product literature and demo packages and then use that information to determine if the product meets the defined requirements. Problems with this approach include:

- Vendors do not always provide the needed information in their literature.

- Not all vendors provide demo packages.

- Vendors receive hundreds of requests for literature and may not respond quickly.

- This process does not use the same criteria to evaluate each of the vendors.

To overcome these problems, some companies prepare and distribute a **request for information** (**RFI**), a form or letter that asks for specific product information relative to the company's requirements. Other companies prepare and distribute a **request for proposal** (**RFP**), a form or letter that requests financial information as well as product information. Although sometimes perceived as a time-consuming approach, an RFI or RFP is by far the most thorough and objective way to evaluate products. It can reduce the time it takes to select a product because all of the vendors are contacted at the same time, and they have the burden of documentation.

An RFI or RFP should include the following information:

- **Company introduction**—Provide information about the company, the goals, and a summary of the strategy for implementing a new system. Be specific!

- **Response guidelines**—Describe how, when, and to whom vendors are expected to respond.

- **Evaluation criteria**—Explain to vendors that the quality of their responses affects the company's decision and identify the criteria being using to select finalists, such as responses to your RFI; system features and functionality; system ease of use; system responsiveness; system architecture; quality of system and documentation; total implementation cost; vendor's qualifications, experience, and references; vendor's ability to consistently deliver quality service and support, both before and after purchase; vendor stability; and vendor's ability to provide training.

- **Vendor and product information**—Have the vendors spell out how their company and product satisfies the requirements. Ask specific questions that require a "yes" or "no" answer wherever possible to make it easier to score the products.

- **Solution costs**—Instruct the vendors to lay out all costs for the proposed solution. Require vendors to provide a cost breakdown so that you can see clearly where costs are incurred. For example, base or core product; adding additional users; add-on modules; annual maintenance; upgrade and support fees (if not included in annual maintenance); training services; consulting services that include implementation, database conversion, and system design and customization assistance.

- **Contractual agreements**—Require vendors to include a copy of the standard license agreement and product maintenance agreement for each proposed product.

- **References**—Require vendors to provide at least three references that are using the same version and release of the proposed product, as well as any proposed supporting products or add-on modules.

 Require all vendors to respond to an RFI or RFP based on the *currently available* production version and release of a product, not a future release. In a separate section, provide space for vendors to tell you about their next release. Also, inform vendors to clearly state when a supporting product or add-on module is needed to address your requirement. Finally, give vendors a deadline for returning their responses and let them know that missing the deadline may result in their being disqualified.

After vendors send in their responses to the RFI or RFP, the selection committee scores each response to determine how the products satisfy their requirements. Table 5-2 illustrates a rating system for scoring vendor responses.

Table 5-2   Sample vendor scoring system

Score	Rating
1	Poor—requirement is not satisfied
2	Fair—borderline implementation of requirement (for example, there is a workaround)
3	Good—requirement is satisfied through an add-on module or is partially satisfied
4	Very good—requirement is satisfied out-of-the-box
5	Excellent—requirement is fully satisfied out-of-the-box with added capability

An evaluation matrix makes it easy to collect and compare these vendor scores. Figure 5-18 shows a sample vendor evaluation matrix. The vendor's score equals its rating multiplied by the weight of the requirement.

Req #	Requirement	Weight	Vendor 1 Rate/ Score	Vendor 2 Rate/ Score	Vendor 3 Rate/ Score	Vendor 4 Rate/ Score	Vendor 5 Rate/ Score
			Operating Requirements				
1	Client platform	5	4 / 20	5 / 25	4 / 20	4 / 20	3 / 15
2	Server platform	5	5 / 25	5 / 25	3 / 15	4 / 20	4 / 20
3	Database	5	4 / 20	4 / 20	3 / 15	4 / 20	4 / 20
	Total Score		65	70	50	60	55

Figure 5-18 Sample vendor evaluation matrix

Step 6. Evaluate the Finalists If the committee selected vendor candidates carefully, the final vendor evaluation scores will usually be very close. Step 6 enables the selection committee to further narrow the field of candidate vendors. To help make a final determination of the best vendor, they take the two vendors that have the highest scores and perform the following additional steps:

- Have finalists come to the company and demonstrate their products. Have each person who attends a demo provide feedback in writing.

- Contact vendor references. Document the references, comments, and any issues or concerns they have with the product.

- If possible, visit other sites that are using the finalists' products. Document what was learned about each product and how it is being used at the site.

- Have representative(s) of your company install and conduct hands-on testing of evaluation copies of the finalists' products. Document the results.

- Conduct tests to ensure that each vendor's product will work with other products that may be installed on the help desk's desktop. For example, run other desktop applications at the same time as the product to ensure that they will work together. Document the results.

Step 7. Make a Final Decision When the selection committee has completed all of these steps, they then review the vendor scores compiled during Step 5 and the documented results of Step 6 activities. The committee considers the pros and cons of each product and of the vendor's performance in relation to the goals they defined for the system. All of this information and knowledge gained throughout the selection process helps the committee make a final decision. If they have taken their time, documented their efforts along the way, and worked diligently to protect the integrity of the selection process (meaning they required the same information from each and every vendor and subjected each product to the same tests), the committee's final decision should be easy.

Implementing a product goes much more smoothly when users are confident that the decision maker took care to select the best possible solution. The selection committee can encourage this confidence by preparing a report that describes the selection process and how the final decision was made. The report includes:

- **Introduction**—Describes the goals to be achieved by implementing the new system.

- **Summary of requirements**—Provides a brief overview of the requirements for the new system.

- **Evaluation methodology**—Describes the process for selecting candidates, evaluating candidates, and making a final decision.

- **Next steps**—Provides a high-level overview of the steps required to implement the selected product.

- **Appendices**—Includes all of the documentation, such as the evaluation matrix, completed questionnaires, and notes from meetings with references.

Selecting new technology is difficult and can be time-consuming, but the help desk gains nothing by cutting the selection process short. It is particularly important that all potential users of the system are involved in the selection process and that every effort is made to consider their needs.

The only constant in the computing industry is change. Without support tools and technologies, this constant and pervasive change would quickly overwhelm the help desk. With the right tools and technologies, the help desk can efficiently receive customer incidents, prioritize and manage those incidents, and deliver tested and proven solutions. Support tools and technologies also enable the help desk to help customers help themselves. Properly implemented technology enables the help desk to perform its processes quickly and correctly and to be more proactive. The end result is management, employee, and, most important, customer satisfaction.

CHAPTER SUMMARY

- ❏ There is a wide array of tools and technologies available to help desks. The availability of tools within an organization depends on the number and complexity of the processes being supported and the funding on hand. Very small or new help desks may use a telephone and paper forms or a simple PC-based tracking system. Larger help desks tend to use a wide variety of tools in an effort to address incidents more efficiently and effectively.

- ❏ The telephone is currently the primary way that customers contact the help desk. Telephone technologies commonly used at help desks include voice mail, fax, automatic call distributors (ACDs), voice response units (VRUs), and computer telephony integration (CTI). Telephone technologies are more effective when combined with telephone services such as automatic number identification (ANI) and caller identification (caller ID). When telephone technologies and services are implemented properly, customers are unaware that they are being used. They just know their call is being efficiently routed to the analyst who has the skills needed to provide assistance.

◻ Most help desks use e-mail in some way to communicate internally, with other support groups, and with their customers. Help desks are using a number of techniques to ensure that e-mail communications are handled efficiently and effectively, including providing help desk analysts with e-mail etiquette training and guidance, integrating e-mail and incident tracking packages, using forms and templates, and using e-mail response management systems. Common sense, good judgment, and good writing skills enable help desk analysts to make the most of the powerful communication tool.

◻ The Web is having a profound impact on the support industry and soon companies that fail to embrace the Internet by establishing Web sites will appear inefficient and out of touch. Conversely, companies that offer ineffective Web sites and that fail to provide customers with multiple ways to obtain support will be perceived as trying to avoid direct communication. Functionality and ease of use are the keys to a successful help desk Web site.

◻ Incident tracking and problem management systems are the technology used to log and track customer problems and requests (incidents). By logging all incidents and using tools to track the status of incidents, the help desk ensures that problems and requests are not lost or forgotten. Smaller help desks tend to use simple incident tracking systems that offer basic trouble ticketing and management reporting capability. Medium to large help desks tend to use more robust problem management and resolution systems or comprehensive enterprise solutions that provide enhanced capability. Companies may periodically change their incident tracking and problem management systems because either they outgrow their existing systems or they replace their systems as new technology becomes available.

◻ Expert and knowledge management systems are designed to capture human knowledge and make it readily available to people involved in solving problems and requests. Use of expert and knowledge management technology has become more widespread in the support industry because these systems are often embedded in problem management and resolution systems and enterprise solutions. However, they can be implemented as standalone systems. These systems are most effective when care is taken to ensure that the information captured in the knowledge base is current, complete, and accurate.

◻ Tools such as asset and configuration management systems, remote control systems, remote monitoring systems, self-healing systems, and software distribution systems extend the help desk's reach and enhance its ability to resolve problems, particularly remote ones. The availability of these technologies depends on factors such as need and available funding.

◻ Help desk communication tools such as white boards, white board systems, electronic reader boards, instant messaging systems, and push technology promote awareness with customers and within the help desk when critical problems arise or when

5

changes are scheduled to occur. These tools enhance and complement the information exchange that occurs with tools such as e-mail and voice mail.

❒ Help desk management tools such as staffing and scheduling systems, ACD supervisor consoles, and customer surveying systems enable help desk supervisors and managers to optimize staffing levels, prepare schedules, and monitor the performance of help desk staff. Larger help desks that handle a high volume of calls often use these systems because tasks such as determining staffing levels and so on can be somewhat complex and time-consuming. Smaller help desks tend to perform these tasks manually.

❒ The purpose of technology is to support and enhance business processes. However, technology is not a magic pill that can cure all evils. Processes and procedures must be well defined, *then* tools and technology can enable people to execute the processes and procedures more quickly and effectively.

❒ Selecting, acquiring, and implementing technology can be challenging because there are hundreds of help desk products on the market. Goals and requirements must be defined clearly before a selection committee begins evaluating products. Evaluating products takes time and a methodical approach. The implementation of a new product goes much more smoothly, however, when users are confident that care was taken to select the best possible solution. The end result of proper selection and implementation of support tools and technology is management, employee, and, most importantly, customer satisfaction.

Key Terms

ACD supervisor console — A system that works with ACD systems and enables supervisors to monitor call volumes and the performance of individual help desk analysts or groups of analysts.

announcement system — A technology that greets callers when all help desk analysts are busy and can provide answers to routine questions or promotional information.

asset and configuration management systems — Technology that allows an analyst to "see" what hardware and software is installed on a computer or network along with financial information such as license and warranty information.

automated attendant — An ACD feature that routes calls based on input provided by the caller through a touch-tone telephone.

automatic call distributor (ACD) — A technology that answers a call and routes, or distributes, it to the next available analyst. If all analysts are busy, the ACD places the call in a queue and plays a recorded message, such as "We're sorry, all of our service representatives are currently assisting other customers; your call will be answered in the order it has been received."

automatic number identification (ANI) — A service provided by a *long distance* service provider that delivers the telephone number of the person calling.

available state — An ACD state that occurs when an analyst is ready to take calls.

caller identification (caller ID) — A service provided by a *local* telephone company that delivers the telephone number of the person calling.

case — A unit of information, such as an online document, a database record, or the solution to a common problem, which is indexed so an analyst can easily locate it when needed.

case-based reasoning (CBR) — A searching technique that uses everyday language to ask users questions and interpret their answers.

case-based system — A system made up of (1) cases and (2) a set of question and answer pairs that can be used to confirm the solution to the problem.

collaboration products — Products that enable multiple users to work together on related tasks.

computer telephony integration (CTI) — The linking of computing technology with telephone technology to exchange information and increase productivity.

customer surveying systems — Systems that are used to create and distribute questionnaires to customers and to collect and tabulate the results of their feedback.

decision tree — A branching structure of questions and possible answers designed to lead an analyst to a solution.

dialed number identification service (DNIS) — A service that provides the number the person called when they call using a toll-free number or a 1-900 service.

e-mail response management systems — Systems that enable help desks to manage high volume chat, e-mail, and Web form messages.

electronic reader boards — Bright displays that send out visual and, in some cases, audible messages to help desk staff and to customer sites that have reader boards installed.

enterprise solutions — A suite of systems that companies use to manage their problem, request, knowledge management, change, and asset and configuration management processes; also called integrated enterprise solutions.

expert system — A computer program that stores human knowledge in a knowledge base and has the ability to reason about that knowledge.

fax — An electronic device that sends or receives printed matter or computer images.

fax-on-demand — Technology that enables customers to use their touch-tone telephone to request that answers to FAQs, procedures, forms, or sales literature be delivered to the fax machine at the number they provide.

feature and functionality requirements — The specifics of how the selected tool must perform in order to support its associated business processes.

form — A predefined document that contains text or graphics users cannot change and areas in which users enter information.

fuzzy logic — A searching technique that presents all possible solutions that are similar to the search criteria, even when conflicting information exists or no exact match is present.

groupware software — Software that enables multiple users to coordinate and keep track of ongoing projects.

high-level requirements — The broad needs for a system.

hyperlinks — Colored and underlined text or graphics in a hypertext or hypermedia document that allow readers to "jump" to a related idea, regardless of where that idea occurs in the document.

hypermedia — A storage method that stores information in a graphical form so users can access the information in a nonlinear fashion using hyperlinks.

hypertext — A storage method that stores information in a nongraphical form so users can access the information in a nonlinear fashion using hyperlinks.

idle state — An ACD state that occurs when an analyst did not answer a call routed to his or her telephone within the specified number of rings.

incident tracking systems — Technology that typically supports only the problem management process and offers basic trouble ticketing and management reporting capability.

information indicator digits (IID) — A service that identifies the origin of a call from the type or location of the telephone being used to place the call, such as a pay phone, cellular phone, hotel phone, and so forth.

instant message systems — Systems that enable two or more people to communicate in real time (chat) over the Internet by typing on a keyboard.

keyword searching — The technique of finding indexed information by specifying a descriptive word or phrase, called a keyword.

knowledge management system — Technology that combines the reasoning capability of an expert system with other information sources, such as databases, documents, policies, and procedures.

portal — A Web "supersite" that provides a variety of services such as a site search where pertinent articles and white papers may be located, a product and services buyer's guide, a discussion center or forum, event calendars, publications, and so forth.

problem management and resolution systems — Technology that offers enhanced trouble ticketing and management reporting capability; also may support the request management and asset and configuration management processes.

push technology — A way to deliver information to Web-enabled PCs. The information is delivered in one of two ways: push or pull. In the push method, the server contacts the client when there is new information to send. In the pull method, the client contacts the server to determine whether new information is available.

query by example (QBE) — A searching technique that uses queries, or questions, to find records that match the specified search criteria. Queries can include search operators.

queue — A line.

recording systems — Technology that records and plays back telephone calls.

remote control system — Technology that enables an analyst to take over a caller's keyboard, screen, mouse, or other connected devices in order to troubleshoot problems, transfer files, provide informal training, and even collaborate on documents.

5

remote monitoring system — Technology that tracks and collects alerts generated by a network monitoring system and passes them to a central server where they can be automatically picked up and logged in the problem management and resolution system or displayed on a special monitor or electronic white board.

request for information (RFI) — A form or letter that asks for specific product information relative to the company's requirements.

request for proposal (RFP) — A form or letter that requests financial information as well as product information.

requirement — Something that is essential.

rule-based system — A system made up of (1) rules, (2) facts, and (3) a knowledge base or engine that combines rules and facts to reach a conclusion.

screen pop — A CTI function that enables information about the caller to appear, or "pop" up, on the analyst's monitor based on caller information captured by the telephone system and passed to a computer system.

search criteria — The questions or problem symptoms entered by a user.

search operators — Connecting words such as AND, OR, and NOT sometimes used in queries; also called Boolean operators.

self-healing — Hardware devices and software applications that have the ability to detect and correct problems on their own.

simultaneous screen transfer — A function that transfers the call as well as all the information collected in the ticket up to that point.

skills-based routing (SBR) — An ACD feature that matches the requirements of an incoming call to the skill sets of available analysts or analyst groups. The ACD then distributes the call to the next available, most qualified analyst.

software distribution system — Technology that allows an analyst to automatically distribute software to clients and servers on the same network.

speech recognition — The conversion of spoken words into text or mouse emulation commands.

staffing and scheduling systems — Systems that work with ACD systems to collect, report, and forecast call volumes.

technologies — Enable the creation and enhancement of tools.

template — A predefined item that can be used to quickly create a standard document or e-mail message.

tool — A product or device that automates or facilitates a person's work.

voice mail — An automated form of taking messages from callers.

voice response unit (VRU) — A technology that integrates with another technology, such as a database or a network management system, to obtain information or to perform a function; also called interactive voice response unit (IVRU).

white board systems — Systems that allow two or more users on a network to view one or more user's drawing, or a document or application being projected, on an onscreen white board.

white boards — Smooth, erasable white panels on which analysts write notes and communicate current and future events.

workflow software — Software that allows messages and documents to be routed to the appropriate users; often part of a groupware system.

wrap-up mode — A feature that prevents the ACD from routing a new inbound call to an analyst's extension.

REVIEW QUESTIONS

1. List two benefits of combining or integrating tools and technologies.

2. What two factors are prompting companies to make use of technology?

3. List four factors that influence the availability of tools in a help desk.

4. What two things can be done to reduce customer resistance to voice mail?

5. From an analyst's perspective, what does ACD software do?

6. Describe four functions that an ACD console enables analysts to perform.

7. How is skills-based routing different than normal ACD routing?

8. A VRU integrates with another technology to do what? Provide one example.

9. What is a screen pop?

10. List the two most common reasons that companies implement recording systems.

11. ANI and caller ID services deliver the telephone number a customer is calling from. What does DNIS deliver?

12. List four benefits of integrating e-mail and incident tracking systems.

13. Why are analysts typically required to log all e-mail requests from customers in their company's incident tracking system?

14. List five of the most common services that support companies are delivering through their Web sites.

15. List three reasons why Web-based services will not eliminate the telephone and email-based communication channels?

16. What common customer complaint is prevented when all incidents are logged?

17. From the standpoint of managing processes, describe the difference between incident tracking systems, problem management and resolution systems, and enterprise solutions.

18. Enterprise solutions often offer tight integration with what other tools?

19. What symptoms might companies experience when they have outgrown their incident tracking and problem management systems?

20. How is a knowledge management system different from an expert system?

21. Describe three ways that help desks can establish or gain access to knowledge bases.

22. Name and define three types of search retrieval technologies.

23. What are two reasons that companies implement remote support technologies?

24. List and describe two of the remote support technologies available to the help desk.

25. List one very simple tool and one more sophisticated tool that help desks can use to communicate within the help desk.

26. Describe two systems that help desk supervisors and managers can use to optimize staffing levels and monitor the performance of help desk staff.

27. What is technology's purpose?

28. List the seven steps involved in a technology selection project.

29. What are the benefits of preparing and distributing an RFI or RFP?

30. Describe three ways to evaluate vendors after they have been selected as finalists.

5

HANDS-ON PROJECTS

Project 5-1

Discuss experiences using technology to obtain help. Talk to at least three of your friends, family members, or fellow students about their experiences with any of the technologies described in this chapter. For example, they might have been prompted to make a selection from a list of options (Press 1 for… Press 2 for…), waited in a telephone queue to speak with the next available analyst, used a Web form to submit an e-mail inquiry, or used a company's Web site to obtain support. Find out about their experiences, for example:

❑ How did they feel about interacting with support technology?

❑ What (if anything) was positive about their experience?

❑ What (if anything) was negative about their experience?

Prepare a brief summary of each of their experiences. Given what you have learned in this chapter, explain what could have been done to make their experiences more positive.

Project 5-2

Describe the benefits of self-service. Think about the different ways you use self-service technologies as you go about your day. For example, perhaps you use your credit card to pay for gas at the pump or you call your bank and use telephone technology to check your bank balance. Write a report that lists the self-service technologies you use and explains why you use them. What are the benefits? Also, describe ways you feel the self-service technologies you use could be made easier or more useful.

Project 5-3

Visit a help desk industry portal site. Visit one or more of the help desk industry portal sites described in this chapter. Join the site if necessary (membership is typically free). Prepare a brief report that answers the following questions:

❑ What functionality did the site provide?

❑ How was information on the site organized?

❑ Was the site easy to use? Please explain.

❑ What was one thing you learned, or learned more about, by visiting this Web site?

Project 5-4

Learn about Web-based support. Visit the Web site of an organization you do business with (such as the company that manufactured the computer you use or the publisher of a software package you use). Find out such information as:

❑ Does the company provide the ability for you to submit a problem or request? If so, how—simple e-mail, Web form, both?

❑ Can you check the status of an outstanding problem or request?

❑ Does the company provide answers to FAQs?

❑ What self-services does the company offer?

Prepare a brief report that describes your findings.

Project 5-5

Make it easy for customers to wait in a call queue. Recall that a queue is a line, in this instance, of calls waiting to be processed. Assemble a team of at least three classmates, and discuss ways that technology can be used to enhance the experience of customers waiting in a queue. For example, one way might be to offer customers the option of leaving a voice mail message. Prepare a list of at least five more ways to enhance customers' experiences.

Project 5-6

Learn about using support technology. Select a class representative who can arrange a site visit to a large help desk or call center in your area. Before the site visit, prepare a list of the technologies discussed in this chapter that you want to see in use. As a courtesy, have the class representative send this list to your tour guide in advance of your visit so that he or she knows that the goal of your visit is to see these technologies. While on-site, ask your tour guide to describe how the help desk or call center uses technology to support its customers. After the tour, prepare a short paper that answers the following questions:

- ❑ What technologies were being used?
- ❑ What technologies were not being used and why?
- ❑ Were you in any way surprised by what you saw? If yes, explain why.

Project 5-7

Learn about incident tracking and problem management systems. Go to the Web sites of the incident tracking, problem management and resolution, and enterprise solution vendors mentioned in this chapter. Download demonstration or trial versions of two of the systems. Complete the demonstration or explore the trial software. For example, log an incident and perform a search. Using what you can learn from the companies' Web sites and their demonstration software, prepare a table or spreadsheet that compares the features and benefits of the two products you've selected.

Project 5-8

Learn about remote control software. Go to the Web sites of at least three companies that publish remote control software. Use the companies mentioned in this chapter or search the Web for "remote control software." Prepare a table or spreadsheet that compares the features of the remote control products manufactured by the vendors you've selected. Also, briefly describe how each of these products addresses any security concerns that may arise from their use.

Project 5-9

Make effective use of a white board. Recall that a white board is a simple tool found in most help desks. Work alone or with another classmate and brainstorm ways to effectively use this simple tool to enhance communication within a help desk. Prepare a drawing of a white board that illustrates the type of information you would record and shows how the most important information can be displayed prominently.

Project 5-10

Prepare to check vendor references. Checking vendor references is an important part of any technology selection effort. Assemble a team of at least three classmates and develop a questionnaire that can be used to question vendor references. What questions would you ask about:

- ❑ The company's environment?
- ❑ How the company is using the vendor's product?
- ❑ How satisfied the company is with the vendor's product?

❏ How satisfied the company is with the support the vendor provides?

❏ How difficult or easy the product was to implement?

❏ How difficult or easy the product is to maintain?

Compare your questionnaire to the questionnaires developed by other teams in your class.

CASE PROJECTS

1. Supporting Telecommuters

The company where you work has decided recently that effective immediately, sales representatives will telecommute rather than work out of the corporate headquarters. These sales representatives will use laptops with high-speed modems that enable users to dial into the company's host systems.

Your internal customers currently contact extension 4357 (HELP) to obtain support. If all analysts are busy, the extension rolls over to voice mail, and customers are encouraged to leave a message. Your company has e-mail, but customers have never been encouraged to use it as a way to obtain support.

When the help desk is unable to solve a problem or request, level two technicians assigned to each floor are dispatched to the customer's office. Typically, technicians arrive within one to two hours if the customer is experiencing a problem. Requests are handled within 24 hours.

Because sales representatives could live many miles away from the office and dispatching a technician any time a problem occurs is not practical and could be quite costly, a new approach is needed. The help desk manager has asked you to recommend ways your help desk can use technology to support the sales representatives who are now working out of their homes. Limited funds are available. Prepare a short report that includes:

❏ Any considerations and concerns you have about how sales representatives will obtain support.

❏ Recommendations you have about how technology can be used to support the remote sales representatives.

❏ Suggestions you have concerning how the help desk can maintain communications with the remote sales representatives.

2. Get Fit with Michelle

You are a consultant to Michelle, a personal fitness trainer who has designed a software package that enables users to schedule their workouts and make journal entries of their results. Michelle wants to provide support for her package, but she has a limited budget and a busy schedule. She told you that in the future she may hire additional employees, but for now she's on her own and wants to keep it simple. Do the following:

❑ Prepare a list of questions you'll need to ask Michelle to understand her goals and requirements.

❑ Given your current understanding of Michelle's situation, prepare a report that describes how Michelle can use technology to support her product. Describe simple ways that Michelle can use technology to support her product now as well as more sophisticated ways that Michelle can use technology to support her product in the future.

5

3. Evaluating and Selecting Technology

The company you work for has decided to replace its simple incident tracking system with a state-of-the-art problem management system. Senior management envisions a system that can be customized to meet the unique needs of the entire organization. This tool also must provide the capability to manage the company's extensive configuration management database and the frequent changes to that database. You have been assigned to head up the project team that will be evaluating new products. Given what you have learned in this chapter, prepare a report that describes where you would begin and how you would proceed.

6

THE INFORMATION COMPONENT: HELP DESK PERFORMANCE MEASURES

> **In this chapter you will learn:**
> ♦ How information is a resource
> ♦ The most common data categories captured by the help desk
> ♦ The most common team performance metrics
> ♦ The most common individual performance metrics
> ♦ How individuals contribute to team goals

Customer expectations about service are rising, and businesses are making every effort to meet those expectations. In addition, companies must cut costs, optimize their staffing levels, and increase overall productivity. As a result, today's savvy customers have high expectations for the help desk, and business managers have high expectations for their employees. Every department, including the help desk, is expected to contribute to the goals of the business, and every employee is expected to contribute to the goals of his or her department. Information is used to determine how employees and departments are contributing to these goals. The most important goal for the entire company is customer satisfaction.

Customer satisfaction is essential for keeping current customers and attracting new ones. Companies focus on customer satisfaction by understanding their customers' needs and expectations in all areas of the business. They do this by analyzing data and creating information. Customers who contact the help desk need and expect prompt, courteous service. Their expectations—whether reasonable or not—set the standard for help desk performance. Companies use performance measures, or **metrics**, to evaluate the performance of their help desk and their employees against these standards. Information is used to create these metrics. The more clearly companies define how performance is measured, the more successfully the company, departments, and help desk analysts can meet their goals and customers' expectations.

When working in a help desk, you must understand its goals, the goals of your department, and the goals of your company as well as the metrics that your manager uses to measure your contribution to those goals. Also, you must understand that customers, managers, and your coworkers use the data you collect on a daily basis to create information. The accuracy and completeness of your work directly influence how customers and managers perceive your contribution to the goals of the help desk as well as to the goals of the department and company. When others perceive your work positively, you create and receive greater opportunity to advance your career.

INFORMATION AS A RESOURCE

Help desks can improve customer service and meet their goals by using many of the technologies discussed in Chapter 5. These technologies extend the help desk's ability to gather, organize, and use information. **Information** is data organized in a meaningful way. It takes time and effort to capture, or collect, the data needed to create accurate and meaningful information. **Data** are raw facts that are not organized in a meaningful way. Data and information are resources, in the same way that well-trained employees, well-defined processes, and well-implemented technology are resources.

Help desks that recognize information as a resource are more proactive than reactive. A **reactive help desk** simply reacts to events that occur each day, while a **proactive help desk** uses information to anticipate and prevent problems and prepare for the future. Some help desks are so overwhelmed with their responsibilities or so understaffed that they capture little or no data. Without data to analyze, these help desks cannot determine the underlying cause of problems or make strategic decisions, and so they remain reactive. Reactive help desks tend to:

- Capture little, if any, data.

- Perform little trend analysis. As a result, analysts identify problems when they happen but do not have the information to predict or prevent problems.

- Avoid activities such as logging, tracking, and providing status updates because analysts and perhaps supervisors see these activities as too time-consuming.

- Rediscover problems, which means that several analysts independently find solutions to the same problem rather than being able to look up the solution in a knowledge base.

- Fail to formally define business processes and, as a result, have unclear roles and responsibilities.

- Fail to clearly communicate who owns incidents (for example, level one, level two, and so forth). As a result, no one takes ownership of incidents, or many people take ownership of incidents, which can result in confusion and wasted effort.

- Handle problems and requests randomly rather than based on severity and priority categories.

- Work without clear individual, team, and department goals and performance measures.

- Use what little data is available to criticize or blame rather than to identify opportunities to improve.

- Experience high costs (due to inefficiencies) and lack the ability to forecast costs.

- Ignore customer needs, resulting in low customer satisfaction.

Because reactive help desks capture little data, they have trouble creating the information necessary to understand customer needs and expectations and measure customer satisfaction. As a result, they may waste precious time focusing on activities that are unimportant to customers. Without information, reactive help desks must rely primarily on their hardworking, sometimes–overutilized people because they cannot justify or implement other resources such as processes and technology, which would enable their people to be more efficient and effective. Companies must begin to capture information—if only basic information in an incident tracking system—if they want to break the cycle of having insufficient resources to capture the information needed to justify additional resources.

Successful companies realize that they can derive many positive benefits by viewing all pertinent information as a resource. Help desks in these companies tend to be more proactive in nature. Proactive help desks tend to:

- Capture all pertinent data.

- Perform trend and root cause analysis in an effort to predict and prevent problems.

- Automate activities such as logging, tracking, and providing status updates where possible.

- Minimize problem rediscovery by ensuring that all known solutions are stored in a knowledge base.

- Clearly define business processes, which leads to clear roles and responsibilities.

- Clearly define ownership. Owners manage by exception, which means owners are required to follow up only on incidents that are not being handled in a timely fashion.

- Handle problems and requests within predefined target resolution times that reflect the severity or priority of the incident.

- Meet clearly defined individual, team, and department goals.

- Use data to identify opportunities; continuous improvement is a way of life.

- Minimize costs; the entire support organization can accurately forecast costs.

- Meet customer needs and enhance customer self-sufficiency by providing the tools and information customers need to resolve problems and answer questions on their own, resulting in high customer satisfaction.

Proactive help desks rigorously analyze data and use the resulting information to justify other resources such as people, processes, and technology. They also use this information to increase customer satisfaction, enhance productivity, improve the quality of products and services, deliver services more efficiently and effectively, and create new products and services.

One of the most difficult things for help desks to demonstrate is that they are increasing customer productivity by proactively preventing problems or by providing self-services such as a Web site that enables customers to support themselves. A common technique is to capture a starting point, or **baseline**, metric. For example, prior to adding Microsoft Word-related FAQs to the help desk's Web site, the help desk's incident tracking system can be used to create a baseline metric that shows the number of Word-related "how to" questions the help desk receives on a monthly basis. Six months after the FAQs are implemented, the help desk can create a current metric. If the current metric indicates that the number of Word-related "how to" questions has gone down, it can be surmised that the FAQs are a success. The help desk could also show the number of **page hits**—Web page visits—the FAQs are receiving or use exit polls to show that the FAQs are being used and that customers consider them helpful. On the Internet, **exit polls** combine questions such as "Was this information helpful to you?" with Yes and No buttons that customers can use to provide feedback.

Help desks are not, however, *all* reactive or *all* proactive. Many help desks are highly reactive but demonstrate proactive tendencies. For example, they may do a good job of communicating information verbally within the help desk team and with other support groups. As a result, they can stay on top of things in the present, although in the long run they suffer because the information is not being captured for future reuse. On the other hand, proactive help desks can demonstrate reactive tendencies. For example, they may experience an exceptionally busy time during which they are unable to continuously improve and instead focus on dealing with daily demands.

Help desks cannot move from a reactive state to a proactive state overnight. They must follow a systematic plan to become more proactive over time. That plan involves recognizing that information is valuable, determining what categories of information to collect, setting up efficient processes to collect data, and gaining analysts' acceptance and enthusiasm for collecting and sharing information. These last two points are key. If the data is simple to capture, analysts will capture it completely and accurately, making the resulting information invaluable. If analysts understand the value of information, they will collect and share it willingly and openly. This enables the help desk to provide world-class customer service and meet its goals.

The amount of data a help desk captures is determined by (1) how much access to information management wants, and (2) what tools the help desk has. If senior management cares about and trusts the information produced by the help desk, they will encourage and direct the help desk to capture data. Help desk management may also encourage analysts to capture data to gain senior management's trust as well as their commitment to back the help desk's goals and provide needed resources. When the help desk has appropriate tools and technology, analysts perceive that capturing data takes little time. Analysts accustomed to logging calls and who understand the value of the captured information consider logging calls to be part of their job. In fact, help desk managers often include capturing data in the analyst's job description, use it as a criterion to measure job performance, and reward analysts who collect quality data.

6

DATA CATEGORIES CAPTURED BY HELP DESKS

Help desks that capture information divide that information into various data categories. These data categories tend to be similar from help desk to help desk because most help desks perform similar processes. Each help desk captures additional data categories specific to its business or industry. Figure 6–1 lists the most common data categories captured by help desks.

- Customer data
- Incident data
- Status data
- Resolution data

Figure 6-1   Common data categories

These data, typically captured through fields in the help desk's incident tracking or problem management system, enable help desks to track problems and requests; measure team, individual, and process performances; and perform trend analysis. Be aware that the actual field names used in the data categories vary from one help desk to the next.

Customer Data

Customer data are identifying details about a customer, including the customer's name, telephone number, department or company name, address or location, customer number, and employee number or user ID. These data are stored in fields. All of the fields that describe a single customer are stored in a **customer record** in the incident tracking or problem management database. Customer records are linked to incident records, which are also stored in the incident tracking or problem management system, by a unique *key* field such as customer name or customer number.

A **field** is a location in a database that stores a particular piece of data. A **record** is a collection of related fields.

Customer records may be housed in a database that is maintained by another department and then used by the help desk and other departments. For example, in internal help desks, the company's human resources department may maintain the customer records, because it is responsible for maintaining all employee-related data. In external help desks, the company's sales department may maintain the customer records, because it is responsible for maintaining all customer-related data. In some cases, the help desk's incident tracking system is linked directly to, for example, the human resources database. In other cases, such as in companies where security is a concern, only the data needed to log incidents is exported from the human resources database and imported into the help desk's incident tracking system. This data may be imported once, and then maintained by the help desk going forward. Or, a program may run periodically to keep the two databases in sync, in which case the human resources department continues to maintain the data.

Incident Data

Incident data are the details of a problem or request. They include incident type (such as a problem or request), channel used to submit (such as telephone or e-mail), category (such as hardware or software), affected component or system (such as a printer or monitor), symptom, date and time incident occurred, date and time incident was logged, analyst who logged incident, incident owner, description, and severity. These data are stored in fields, and all of the fields that describe a single incident are stored in an **incident record** in the incident tracking or problem management system. These fields can be used to research and track trends or to search the knowledge base for solutions. Figure 6-2 shows a sample trend report that uses the problem category field.

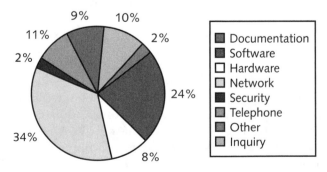

PROBLEMS BY CATEGORY - MAY

Figure 6-2 Sample trend report

Status Data

Status data are details about an incident that are used to track incidents not resolved at level one. Status data include incident status (such as assigned, awaiting parts, resolved, closed), the person or group assigned, date and time assigned, and priority. These data are stored in fields in the incident record in the incident tracking or problem management system. After an incident record is created, that record is continuously updated as new information—such as status information and resolution data—becomes available. These fields can be used to report on the status of outstanding incidents and to monitor SLA attainment. Figure 6-3 shows a sample problem aging report, which used to ensure that outstanding problems are being resolved within their target resolution time.

Assigned To	<1 Day	2-3 Days	4-5 Days	6-10 Days	>10 Days	% Within Target
Field Services	24	6	3	1	2	98
Network Support	54	23	15	9	13	94
Development	76	54	8	2	1	87
Vendor	93	27	3	4	12	75

Figure 6-3   Sample problem aging report

Resolution Data

Resolution data describe how an incident was resolved. They include the fields required to track service level compliance and perform root cause analysis, such as the person or group who resolved the incident, resolution description, date and time resolved, customer satisfaction indicator, date and time closed, and root cause. These data are stored in fields in the incident record in the incident tracking or problem management system. When resolution data becomes available, they are added to the incident record created when the incident was reported.

Most companies distinguish between resolving an incident and closing the incident. An incident is *resolved* when a level one or level two analyst delivers a solution. The incident is *closed* only after the incident owner verifies that the customer is satisfied with the resolution.

Help desk analysts and managers use these customer, incident, status, and resolution data fields to create detailed tracking and summary reports and to perform trend analysis. In addition, managers use these data fields to calculate many team and individual performance measures.

TEAM PERFORMANCE MEASURES

Help desk managers are under increasing pressure to demonstrate the value of help desk services and to justify the funds and resources the team needs to deliver those services. Managers use performance measures to prove the importance of the help desk team to the company. Team performance measures assess characteristics such as:

- **Efficiency**—How quickly services are delivered.

- **Effectiveness**—How completely and accurately services are delivered.

- **Quality**—How well services meet customer expectations.

The goal is to achieve a balance among efficiency, effectiveness, and quality—and not to overemphasize any one of these characteristics.

 Individual performance measures also measure the characteristics of efficiency, effectiveness, and quality.

Team performance metrics measure the combined efforts of the help desk team and show that not only is the help desk working hard but also that it is meeting its business goals and its customers' expectations. Furthermore, clearly defined performance measures enable the help desk management and team to objectively evaluate their performance, celebrate their achievements, and develop strategies for improvement. Figure 6-4 lists the most common ways that help desks define and measure team performance.

- Help desk goals

- Service Level Agreements (SLAs)

- Customer satisfaction surveys

- Benchmarking

Figure 6-4   Common team performance measures

Help desk goals provide the information that help desks need in order to know whether they are improving continuously. SLAs provide the information to understand customer expectations. Customer satisfaction surveys and benchmarking provide the information to identify areas for improvement. These measures enable the help desk management and team to satisfy customers at an appropriate cost to the organization. The best companies also consider job satisfaction of their employees in the team setting an important component of their overall performance.

Help Desk Goals

Help desk goals are measurable objectives that support the help desk's mission. Most organizations establish specific goals each year in an effort to clarify what analysts are supposed to focus on, eliminate conflicting goals, and encourage analysts to produce the desired results. Sample help desk goals include:

- Achieve an average four out of five rating on the annual customer satisfaction survey.

- Provide each analyst with eight hours of training each month.

- Resolve 80 percent of reported problems at level one.

- Reduce support costs by 5 percent by year's end.

- Maintain a cost per contact at or below the industry average, which is $15 to $30.

Cost per contact, historically called cost per call, is the total cost of operating a help desk for a given period (including salaries, benefits, facilities, equipment, and so on) divided by the total number of contacts (calls, e-mails, faxes, Web requests, and so on) received during that period. According to STI Knowledge, cost per contact increases dramatically when calls are escalated. They estimate the following average range of cost per contact at each level: level zero, $2 to $11; level one, $15 to $30; level two, $50 to $75; level three (on-site support), $100 ("The Enterprise Service Desk—A Roadmap to Success," STI Knowledge, Inc., 2002). Moving problems from level three to level one or level zero and eventually to elimination results in real cost savings to the organization. Some companies also calculate **cost per unit**, the total cost of operating a help desk for a given period (including salaries, benefits, facilities, equipment, and so on) divided by the total number of units (such as devices, systems, and so on) supported during that period.

Many companies distinguish between goals and operational performance metrics, such as those reflected in Service Level Agreements (SLAs). Goals represent what the help desk is *striving* to achieve. Operational metrics represent what the help desk is *expected* to achieve as determined by its SLAs with customers.

Service Level Agreements

Recall that a Service Level Agreement (SLA) is a written document that spells out the services the help desk will provide to the customer, the customer's responsibilities, and how service performance is measured. Senior management representatives from the help desk and from the customer community typically negotiate the terms of SLAs, which are designed to:

- Ensure that the help desk's services match their customers' needs.

- Ensure that the help desk and customers have the same expectations about the services the help desk will provide.

- Ensure that the help desk and customers clearly understand their respective responsibilities.

- Provide measurable performance metrics for the help desk.

- Provide a point of reference that can be used to discuss help desk and customer performance and to communicate the need to modify or enhance that performance.

- Ensure that all parties understand and are willing to follow the business processes managed by or through the help desk.

 According to the Help Desk Institute, 68 percent of its members have SLAs with some or all of their customers ("Help Desk Institute Practices Survey," Help Desk Institute, 2002). The reason most help desks have SLAs is that they are realizing that they can't keep pace with customers' rising expectations. SLA negotiations ensure that the help desk understands its responsibilities and that customers understand their responsibilities. While negotiating SLAs, the help desk and customer discuss the company's cost to meet the customer's expectations to ensure that it does not exceed the benefit that customers will obtain from a service. Consequently, help desks use SLAs as a tool for managing customer expectations and, when possible and appropriate, enhancing customer self-sufficiency.

SLAs are an excellent way to measure team performance because they show how well the team is meeting customer expectations. The help desk does not have to *guess* at what customers want and how they can satisfy their needs—they *know* what customers want and need because it is all clearly defined in the SLAs. Figure 6-5 shows a sample help desk SLA.

 SLAs can be quite complex, or they can be simple one-page documents such as the sample shown in Figure 6-5. For example, an SLA between a company and a service agency that provides help desk outsourcing will tend to be quite complex because it is typically viewed as a contract. On the other hand, an SLA between a help desk and a department in a company may be fairly simple, and used primarily to clarify expectations and responsibilities.

ABC HELP DESK
SERVICE LEVEL AGREEMENT

This document is an agreement between the ABC help desk and its customers. This service level agreement (SLA) has been designed to promote a common understanding about the services the help desk provides, and customer responsibilities relative to those services. This document also describes how service level performance is measured

Parties: The *help desk* provides a single point of contact for the ABC IT department. *Customers* are ABC employees who seek technical support services from the ABC IT department.

Responsibilities: The *help desk* provides first level support to customers using the processes and technology implemented by the ABC IT department. The help desk also facilitates second and third level support by engaging resources as needed to resolve problems beyond the scope and authority of the help desk. *Customers* obtain service using the processes and technology implemented by the ABC IT department and described in this document. Specifically, ABC employees must contact the help desk when support services are needed.

Hours of operation: The help desk is available to ABC employees 24 hours a day, 7 days a week.
* During *normal business hours*—Monday through Friday 7 a.m. to 8 p.m.—customers can
    contact the help desk and speak directly with an analyst
* *After-hours*—8 p.m. to 7 a.m. weekdays, weekends, and holidays—customers can access
    the help desk's Web site. For *severity 1* problems only, customers can contact the
    help desk and obtain support from on-call analysts who carry pagers.

Contact methods: Customers can use the following methods to obtain support:
* Telephone—Customers can contact the help desk by calling **(555) 555-4357**. Every effort will be made to answer all calls within one (1) minute. Following a brief introduction, customers may hear a system outage message. This message is broadcast only when a severity 1 problem exists. Customers are then prompted to:
    o   Press 1 to report a new problem or request
    o   Press 2 to obtain the status of an outstanding problem or request
* Voice mail—Voice mail is offered to customers who call the help desk during normal business hours after a two (2) minute delay. Customers can use this option in lieu of waiting in the queue. Voice mail messages will be answered within thirty (30) minutes during normal business hours.   **Note:** Customers calling with a severe problem are encouraged to wait in the queue. Voice mail messages left after hours will be answered the next business day.
* E-mail—E-mail messages sent to **helpdesk@abc.com** will be answered within one (1) hour during normal business hours. E-mails sent after-hours will be answered the next business day.
* Internet—The help desk's Web site at **helpdesk.com** provides forms that can be used to submit problems and requests. Problems and requests submitted via the help desk's Web site are automatically logged in the help desk's incident tracking system and are handled according to their severity. The Web site also provides self-services such as FAQs, a solution knowledgebase, a password reset utility, and access to remote diagnostic and control utilities.

Problem severity levels: Problem severity reflects the impact of a problem on the ABC business and as such, when and how the problem must be solved. Help desk analysts and customers will work together to determine problem severity using the following guidelines:

Severity	Business Impact	Target Resolution Time
1	System or device down, business halted.	2 hours
2	System or component down or level of service degraded, business impacted.	8 hours
3	Not critical, customer can wait.	48 hours

This agreement is effective through December 31st of the current year and will be evaluated and republished yearly or as needed.

Figure 6-5   Sample help desk SLA

A number of different help desk tools are used to create SLA metrics, including the automatic call distributor (ACD) as well as the incident tracking and problem management systems. Sample SLA metrics captured with an ACD include:

- **Abandon rate percent**—The percentage of abandoned calls compared to the total number of calls received. An **abandoned call** is a call where the caller hangs up before an analyst answers. For example, a caller may tire of waiting in a queue or become confused using a VRU and choose to hang up before an analyst answers.

- **Average Speed of Answer** (**ASA**)—The average time it takes an analyst to pick up an incoming call.

- **Average wait time**—Also known as average queue time—the average number of minutes a caller waits for an analyst after being placed in the queue by an ACD.

Help desks also use their incident tracking and problem management systems to capture SLA metrics. Sample SLA metrics captured with these systems include:

- **Response time**—The length of time a customer waits for a reply to a fax, e-mail, or Web-based request. Response time is comparable to the ASA metric used for telephone calls.

- **First call resolution rate percent**—The percentage of calls resolved during a customer's initial telephone call compared to the total number of calls received at the help desk for a given period of time.

- **Level one resolution rate percent**—The percentage of incidents resolved at level one, but not necessarily during the customer's initial telephone call.

- **Incidents resolved within target time percent**—The percentage of incidents resolved within a target resolution time. Help desks base the target resolution times on the severity of the problem or request.

- **Reopened percent**—The percentage of closed incidents that had to be opened back up within a given period of time. This usually occurs because the incident symptom recurs, which implies that the help desk or a level two or level three service provider delivered an incorrect or incomplete solution initially.

Help desks that have not established formal SLAs can still use metrics to measure their performance. They can set internal goals for the service levels they strive to achieve and measure their performance against those goals.

Companies often look for "industry standard" metrics that they can use as a starting point when negotiating SLAs or when establishing internal goals. Such metrics are difficult to find, however, because no one organization represents the support industry as a whole. Organizations such as the Help Desk Institute (**www.helpdeskinst.com**), META Group (**www.metagroup.com**), Service & Support Professionals Association (**www.thesspa.com**), and supportindustry.com (**www.supportindustry.com**) all provide, some for a fee, their version of these metrics. Typically they determine metrics by surveying their members or clients and by conducting surveys via the Internet. Metricnet (**www.metricnet.com**), a division of META Group, collects data from IT organizations around the world via the Internet. People fill out surveys on Metricnet's Web site and earn data credits. The data credits can then be used to access data reports about, for example, help desk metrics.

Customer satisfaction is another common SLA metric that is captured typically using satisfaction survey results. For example, an SLA may state that the help desk is expected to achieve an average four out of five rating on the annual overall customer-satisfaction survey. Customer satisfaction is an excellent quality metric that serves to balance out the efficiency and effectiveness metrics.

Customer Satisfaction Surveys

Customer satisfaction surveys are a series of questions that ask customers to provide their perception of the support services being offered. Whether conducted annually or on an ongoing basis, customer satisfaction surveys are an excellent way to measure the strengths and weaknesses of existing support services. Surveys provide insight as to whether customers *perceive* their needs are being met, unlike more quantifiable metrics, such as the number of calls answered per hour or the average time to resolve an incident. Surveys can be conducted during telephone calls, by sending out paper forms or e-mails, or by asking the customer to provide feedback through the Internet.

Studies show that a high percentage of unhappy customers never tell companies about their dissatisfaction so it is extremely important to *ask* customers for their feedback.

The two most common customer satisfaction surveys are event-driven surveys and overall satisfaction surveys. **Event-driven surveys** are a series of questions that ask customers for feedback on a single, recent service event. The results of these surveys give management the ability to measure the performance of the help desk team. These surveys can also be used to measure individual performance because they give feedback on the performance of the analyst who handled the event. Typically, the help desk conducts event-driven surveys within 48 to 72 hours of the service event. Figure 6-6 shows a sample event-driven survey.

Event-Driven Survey

Hello (customer's name), this is (analyst's name) from the help desk. On (date from problem ticket) you placed a call to us for assistance about (problem description from ticket). Would you mind answering a few brief questions for me regarding that call?

Thank you.

Rating Scale

1   Very dissatisfied
2   Dissatisfied
3   Neither satisfied or dissatisfied
4   Satisfied
5   Very satisfied

How satisfied are you with:

The speed with which your question was answered?

The courteous manner of the analyst who handled your call?

The knowledge of the analyst who handled your call?

The overall service you received?

Do you have any comments or suggestions regarding this call?

_____

_____

Thank you very much for your feedback. Please feel free to contact us whenever you need assistance.

Figure 6-6   Sample event-driven survey

Overall satisfaction surveys are a series of questions that ask customers for feedback about all calls they made to the help desk during a certain time period. Help desks use these responses to identify areas for improvement, and also to identify areas where the help desk is performing well. Some help desks also send these surveys to customers who *did not* contact the help desk in the previous 6 or 12 months to determine if they lack faith in the help desk's ability to satisfy their needs. Usually, the help desk conducts overall satisfaction surveys annually or semiannually. Figure 6-7 shows a sample overall satisfaction survey.

OVERALL SATISFACTION SURVEY

This survey has been designed to identify areas in which the help desk can improve the quality of service it provides to you, our customer. In addition, we would like to begin trending the performance of hardware, software, and office systems. Please take a moment to complete this brief survey and return it to the help desk.

Most used applications: (1) _____ (2) _____ (3) _____

1. How often do you call the help desk?

    ☐ Daily   ☐ Once a week   ☐ Never

    ☐ More than once a week   ☐ Once a month

2. When you call with a problem, is the problem resolution explained to you?

    ☐ Always   ☐ Usually   ☐ Sometimes   ☐ Never

3. Does the help desk notify you of system outages shortly after or prior to when they occur?

    ☐ Always   ☐ Usually   ☐ Sometimes   ☐ Never

4. Why do you usually call the help desk?

    ☐ System problems: terminal, printer, etc. not working

    ☐ Output problems: missing, late, misdelivered, etc.

    ☐ Other: Please Explain:

5. Have you received adequate training on how to effectively use your computer and/or printer? ☐ Yes ☐ No

6. Are you kept informed about the status of problems that cannot be solved immediately? ☐ Yes ☐ No

7. Do you currently receive the Help Desk Newsletter? ☐ Yes ☐ No

8. Please rate the competency and courtesy of the help desk staff:

    Most competent   4   3   2   1   Least competent
    Most courteous   4   3   2   1   Least courteous

OPTIONAL
NAME:
TITLE:
LOCATION:

Figure 6-7   Sample overall satisfaction survey

Overall satisfaction surveys are an excellent way to measure the quality of help desk services because customers are providing direct feedback. Management uses the feedback obtained from these surveys when defining the help desk's goals.

Benchmarking

Benchmarking is the process of comparing the help desk's performance metrics and practices to those of another help desk in an effort to identify improvement opportunities. Companies that provide benchmarking services require participants to complete comprehensive surveys that explore all aspects of their help desk and store the results in a database. This data can then be used to compare one company to others, for example companies for example companies that are similar in size or industry. Benchmarking services can be quite costly. Companies striving to be world class are often willing to pay for these services, however, because they know that they are comparing their metrics and practices to a true group of their peers. These services typically are also accompanied by consulting services that result in a clear roadmap that leads to specific improvement goals.

 Companies that provide help desk benchmarking services include the Help Desk Management Benchmarking Association (**www.hdmba.com**), Gartner, Inc. (**www.gartner.com**), and META Group (**www.metagroup.com**).

Companies benefit most from benchmarking when they identify opportunities for improvement rather than simply compare metrics. In other words, a help desk must not only determine whether its metrics are better than or worse than another company's; it must also thoroughly analyze benchmarking results to uncover practices in place at the other company that it can implement to improve. However, the help desk must also ensure that any changes it makes fit the needs of its customers. There is no guarantee that one company's practices will satisfy another company's customers or improve its performance.

Customers and management can use all of these techniques—help desk goals, SLAs, customer satisfaction surveys, and benchmarking—to measure help desk performance. Although not all companies use all of these techniques, successful ones understand that they can't manage or improve what they aren't measuring and, therefore, employ as many of these techniques as possible. No single technique can be used to measure help desk performance fully. They all work together to enable the help desk to meet its commitments to customers and to identify areas for improvement at the help desk. Also, many performance metrics influence each other. Placing too great an emphasis on any one metric can produce unintended results. For example, emphasizing efficiency can reduce the average queue time but could cause customer dissatisfaction because customers feel they are being rushed off the phone. On the other hand, emphasizing effectiveness by devoting an extensive number of analysts to research may produce high-quality solutions but might cause customer dissatisfaction because customers have a long average queue time.

The best companies strive to achieve a balance between efficiency, effectiveness, and quality when establishing performance measures. These companies rigorously collect the data required to measure performance and promote their performance achievements to customers and management.

DANNY L. MORSE
TECHNOLOGY SUPPORT MANAGER
SCHULTE ROTH & ZABEL LLP
NEW YORK, NEW YORK
WWW.SRZ.COM

6

The Help Desk at Schulte Roth & Zabel (SRZ) is part of the Technology Support group within the Information Technology department. The Help Desk supports the more than 330 attorneys, and 495 paralegals, managers, support personnel, secretaries, and so forth who are located in the firm's New York and London offices. We also support the firm's clients with both their onsite technology needs such as depositions, closings, presentations, and so forth, and offsite needs such as technical issues related to collaborating with our legal staff.

Tasks. The Help Desk serves as the firm's single point of contact for all of its technology needs and its primary service is user support. User support involves retaining knowledge about technology and the way the firm uses it, and translating that technical expertise into answers for our user community. We also provide services such as product evaluations, technology usage reports, wireless & remote technologies management, and so on.

To support both our New York and London offices, the Help Desk is available 24 hours per day, beginning Monday at 6:00 a.m. through Friday night at 11:30 p.m. Weekends are covered from 10 a.m. to 10 p.m. Our customers contact us by telephone, and e-mail as a backup in the event of a telephone outage. All calls are logged in eHelpDesk, our Web-based incident tracking system, which gives us accountability and also provides us the ability to create management reports and perform root cause analysis. We also use Proxy remote control software to reduce the time it takes to resolve problems.

While the firm has had a help desk for many years, we have worked hard since early 2002 to utilize processes and tools to formalize and improve our services. We now maintain a first call resolution rate of over 80 percent and a customer satisfaction rating of 4.9 out of 5. We've also worked hard to develop an escalation process, which gives us a methodical and disciplined structure to use when we need to engage level two or level three support.

Organization. The 17 member Technology Support group includes eight Help Desk Analysts who provide level one support, and one Help Desk Supervisor. Our Level Two Support Specialist provides second level support and the rest of the support team is made up of six Desktop Support Engineers (DSEs) and one DSE Supervisor. When problems cannot be resolved by the Help Desk, we use our escalation process to assign problems to other members of the Technology Support team, such as our Level Two Support Specialist, who handles complex or time-consuming problems, or our DSE group, who conducts site visits for a variety of support needs, such as troubleshooting desktops, laptops, wireless technologies, printers, offsite projects, conference room initiatives, and so forth. We also maintain a Master List of other groups within Information Technology who provide, when needed, level three support.

We have worked hard to develop a competent, team-oriented environment. Our analysts know their full capacity and so they demand technical proficiency and responsibility from themselves and from each and every other team member. We provide a "round table" atmosphere for discussing help desk issues so that everyone can participate in and contribute to our success. We succeed by setting short-term objectives and long-term goals that require personal growth and superlative performance by each member of the team. We acknowledge those who go above and beyond the call of duty, and we reward all who contribute to our goals.

We know our efforts are paying off. Every October, Amlaw Tech, the technology supplement to the monthly legal periodical The American Lawyer, surveys mid-level associates at nationwide law firms to rank their firm's technology. In 2001, we were ranked 103rd out of 177 firms. In 2002, we ranked 27th out of the 132 firms who participated. Among New York-based law firms we were ranked 4th. This is an incredible achievement for the entire department, particularly the Help Desk.

Philosophy. The legal industry provides a challenging, demanding, and dynamic environment with high technology needs and even higher support expectations. Members of the firm—our customers—and its clients expect the Help Desk to deliver the highest quality services and to provide lasting value. To achieve this, every member of the IT team must be a leader who generates enthusiasm and responds with extra effort to meet the firm's needs and the needs of its clients. We have come a long way in a short period of time, but we're not resting on our laurels. We will continuously reevaluate our support efforts and seek out best practices so that we can continuously improve and contribute to the firm's business goals.

INDIVIDUAL PERFORMANCE MEASURES

Team performance is only as good as the performance of the analysts on the team. Every analyst influences the team's ability to achieve its goals and expected service levels. If every analyst in the help desk achieves his or her individual performance goals, then the team will achieve its goals. Like team performance measures, individual performance measures gauge and try to balance characteristics such as efficiency, effectiveness, and quality. The goals of measuring individual performance are to:

- Set performance expectations.

- Reward positive performance.

- Set up a plan to improve weak performance.

- Measure changes in performance throughout the year.

- Document when an improvement plan is successful and when it is unsuccessful.

Figure 6-8 lists the most common ways that help desks measure individual performance.

- Individual performance goals

- Employee Service Level Agreements

- Monitoring

- Skills inventory matrix

Figure 6-8   Common individual performance measures

These techniques provide help desk management and staff with a framework for setting performance expectations and identifying the data they will use to measure and manage individual performance. Help desk analysts often create the data that will measure their performance. Some analysts dislike performance measures and mistakenly believe that management cannot measure their performance if the data are not available. The flaw in this line of thinking is that management still measures performance, they simply do it without facts. In other words, management measures performance based on what they *perceive* an analyst has accomplished. By capturing data, and learning to use data to create information, analysts can maximize their contribution to help desk goals and communicate that contribution to management.

Individual Performance Goals

Individual performance goals are measurable objectives for analysts that support the help desk mission. These goals are communicated to analysts at the time they are hired and during performance reviews. How and when performance reviews are conducted varies from one company to the next. Some companies informally review metrics with analysts on a weekly basis and conduct more formal reviews quarterly, semi-annually, or annually. Other companies conduct, for example, a semi-annual review to discuss performance. Most companies then conduct an annual review that determines any changes to the employee's compensation package (that is, salary, benefits, training or certification allotment, and so forth). Frequent performance reviews are best because they enable analysts to know how they are doing and they provide a forum for discussing ways that analysts can improve.

As with team performance goals, a number of different help desk tools are used to create individual performance metrics, such as an automatic call distributor (ACD) and the incident tracking and problem management systems. Sample individual performance metrics captured with an ACD include:

- **Availability**—The length of time an analyst was signed on to the ACD compared to the length of time the analyst was scheduled to be signed on.

- **Average call duration**—The average length of time required to handle a call.

- **Time idle**—The average length of time an analyst was idle during a given period of time. Recall that an idle state means an analyst does not answer a call routed to his or her phone within the specified number of rings and the ACD transfers the call to the next available analyst.

- **Wrap-up time**—The average length of time an analyst was in wrap-up mode during a given period of time. Recall that wrap-up mode is a feature of an ACD that prevents the ACD from routing a new inbound call to an analyst's extension.

An excessive amount of idle time or wrap-up time is undesirable because it delays service to the customer. However, most help desk managers take into consideration the fact that some idle or wrap-up may not mean that an analyst is being unproductive. For example, an analyst may be in the middle of providing critical information to a coworker or a supervisor who is at his or her desk when a call arrives. On the other hand, some analysts forget to log off the ACD when they step away from their desk or to make themselves unavailable when extra time is needed to escalate a call. In such cases, the help desk manager or supervisor will counsel the analyst on the importance of avoiding unnecessary or excessive idle or wrap-up time.

Some companies avoid excessive amounts of idle or wrap-up time by dedicating senior level one analysts or specialists to the resource desk. Recall that a resource desk is a reference desk where level one analysts can get help with difficult incidents and training to handle similar incidents in the future. Resource desk specialists do not log on to the ACD when they are working on the resource desk and are thus are not eligible to receive calls.

These metrics are combined with metrics produced using the help desk's incident tracking and problem management system. Sample individual performance metrics captured with incident tracking and problem management systems include:

- **Reopen percent**—The percentage of incidents an analyst opens back up compared to the total number of incidents that analyst closed during a given period of time.

- **Resolution percent**—The percentage of incidents an analyst resolves compared to the total number of incidents that analyst handled during a given period of time.

- **Application of training investments**—A comparison of an analyst's resolution percent before and after attending training.

6

Customer satisfaction is a common individual performance metric. It is captured through the results of event-driven customer satisfaction surveys, which capture information about an analyst's performance as opposed to the overall team performance. Help desk management in conjunction with customer management establish these individual goals, such as maintaining an average customer satisfaction rating of four out of five. Conducting customer satisfaction surveys and monitoring calls are excellent ways to measure the quality of an individual's performance and determine whether an analyst is meeting his or her individual goals.

Certification also can be used to measure individual performance. **Certification** is a document awarded to a person who has demonstrated that he or she has certain skills and knowledge about a particular topic or area. Often, the person must pass a test after receiving instruction or doing self-study. Because certification requires analysts to demonstrate their mastery of a subject by taking a test, companies consider it an excellent way to measure an analyst's knowledge.

 Certification is discussed in detail in Chapter 8.

As with team performance measures, no single metric can measure individual performance accurately. They work together and can influence each other. By monitoring all of these metrics, individuals can identify areas where they can improve. Help desks often incorporate individual performance goals into employee Service Level Agreements. Help desks that do not use employee Service Level Agreements or provide job descriptions with measurable objectives also set individual performance goals.

Employee Service Level Agreements

An **employee Service Level Agreement (employee SLA)** is a document that clearly describes an analyst's performance requirements and individual improvement objectives. Unlike job descriptions, which can be generic and static, employee SLAs change as the employee's performance improves or deteriorates. Figure 6-9 shows a sample employee SLA.

Employee SLAs are most effective when analysts are given the tools—in this case, reports—they need to monitor their daily performance. Analysts then can meet weekly or monthly with their supervisor or team leader to review and discuss the results. At that time, they can refine the employee SLA as needed.

Monitoring

Monitoring occurs when a supervisor or team leader listens to a live or recorded call or watches an analyst take a call in order to measure the quality of an analyst's performance during the call. Used properly, monitoring is an excellent quality metric. In addition, it promotes the consistent handling of telephone calls and provides employees and supervisors with information on which they can base performance improvement plans.

Monitoring is also an excellent training technique because supervisors and team leaders can give analysts specific feedback on how they could have handled a call better and how they can handle similar calls in the future. Some supervisors and team leaders occasionally watch analysts take calls so they can also provide guidance in areas such as the ergonomics of the analyst's workspace, the analyst's use of tools, and the analyst's ability to stay organized and calm while working.

Chapter 7 explores in detail how to set up an ergonomic workspace.

Used properly, monitoring encourages analysts to put themselves in the customer's shoes and objectively assess the quality of their service from the customer's perspective. Some companies use monitoring only for training purposes rather than as a way of measuring performance. Others use monitoring both as a training tool and as a way of measuring performance.

A monitoring program must be implemented carefully in order to be effective, rather than demoralizing and invasive. Most companies involve the help desk staff when designing their monitoring programs. Management and staff jointly define guidelines for how and when employees will be monitored. For example, they may agree to monitor recorded calls or to silently monitor live calls five times each month. Other guidelines include agreeing not to monitor partial calls or personal calls.

6

EMPLOYEE SERVICE LEVEL AGREEMENT

My personal mission is to provide the highest-quality technical support in a courteous and professional manner. I also am committed to communicating customer needs to the appropriate teams within the IT organization. In order for the help desk to be successful, I will strive to meet the following goals:

Technical Knowledge

- Maintain a high level of knowledge in the products, tools, and systems for which I am recognized as an expert.
- Increase my level of knowledge in the following products, tools, and systems over the next three months:
  - ➤ Microsoft Windows XP
  - ➤ Microsoft Excel
- Continuously seek out ways to improve my technical support skills.

Customer Service Quality

- Provide courteous, quality, responsive, and responsible telephone support.
- Show genuine interest in every customer concern.
- Maintain a high level of support policy knowledge.
- Utilize all available tools and procedures to resolve customer issues.
- Continuously seek out ways to improve my customer service skills.

Call Resolution and Work Quality

- Log all calls received.
- Reduce the number of calls I escalate by $x\%$ within the next three months.
- Improve my Average Call Duration from _____ to _____ minutes per call within the next three months.

Teamwork

- Work well with others, participate constructively in team meetings, and assist other team members when needed.
- Adhere to assigned shift schedules.

Figure 6-9 Sample employee Service Level Agreement

One of the keys to a successful monitoring program is a checklist given to analysts that describes the specific criteria supervisors or team leaders are using to measure the quality of a call. Figure 6-10 shows a sample monitoring checklist.

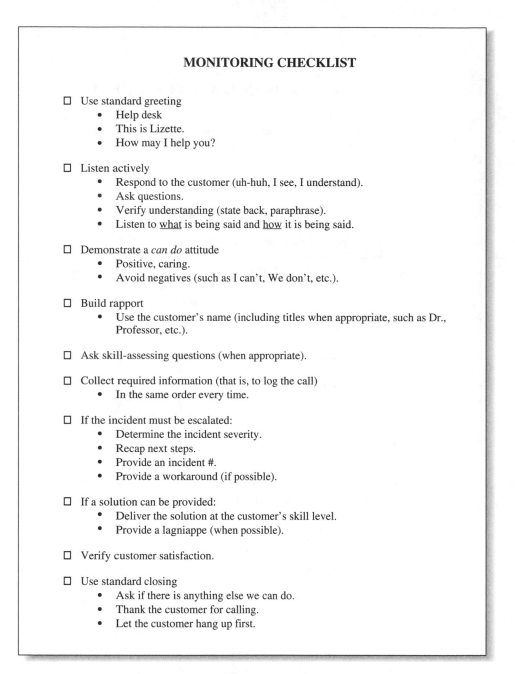

MONITORING CHECKLIST

☐ Use standard greeting
  - Help desk
  - This is Lizette.
  - How may I help you?

☐ Listen actively
  - Respond to the customer (uh-huh, I see, I understand).
  - Ask questions.
  - Verify understanding (state back, paraphrase).
  - Listen to <u>what</u> is being said and <u>how</u> it is being said.

☐ Demonstrate a *can do* attitude
  - Positive, caring.
  - Avoid negatives (such as I can't, We don't, etc.).

☐ Build rapport
  - Use the customer's name (including titles when appropriate, such as Dr., Professor, etc.).

☐ Ask skill-assessing questions (when appropriate).

☐ Collect required information (that is, to log the call)
  - In the same order every time.

☐ If the incident must be escalated:
  - Determine the incident severity.
  - Recap next steps.
  - Provide an incident #.
  - Provide a workaround (if possible).

☐ If a solution can be provided:
  - Deliver the solution at the customer's skill level.
  - Provide a lagniappe (when possible).

☐ Verify customer satisfaction.

☐ Use standard closing
  - Ask if there is anything else we can do.
  - Thank the customer for calling.
  - Let the customer hang up first.

Figure 6-10   Sample monitoring checklist

Without this checklist, analysts are unsure what supervisors and team leaders are looking for when they monitor the calls, and, therefore, may perceive the results as subjective.

Skills Inventory Matrix

A **skills inventory matrix** is a grid that rates each analyst's level of skill on every product, system, and service supported by the help desk. A skills inventory matrix is an excellent tool that management can use to determine hiring needs, develop training and cross-training plans for both individual analysts and the help desk team, and establish and measure how well analysts are attaining their improvement goals. Also, recall that companies that use skills-based routing typically require analysts to create and maintain a skills inventory. Some companies have analysts complete the skills inventory matrix during their job interview in an effort to compare the knowledge and expertise of job candidates. Analysts can also use the skills inventory matrix to assess and document their skill levels and identify required improvement areas. Furthermore, analysts can use the skills inventory matrix to determine the best person to consult when they need assistance in a particular area. Figure 6-11 shows a sample skills inventory matrix. Note that a skills inventory matrix reflects soft skills as well as technical skills and may also reflect business and self-management skills.

Team Members	Customer Service	Windows XP	Microsoft Word	Add new required skills as they are identified
Jane	3	1	Jane	4
John	1	3	John	2
Bill	1	3	Bill	1

Sample Rating Scale:
1   Expert; Certified expert
2   Expert; Able to train; write documentation; install
3   Confident; Able to assist; Not able to train
4   Somewhat able to assist; Not totally confident
NA   Not Applicable; No skill required

Figure 6-11   Sample skills inventory matrix

Employee SLAs, individual performance goals, monitoring, and the skills inventory matrix are all ways help desk management can measure the performance of individual analysts. Organizations can use one, all, a combination, or none of these techniques. Although these techniques are interrelated, they are independent. All of these tools require and use information and, when rigorously supervised, will result in customer and employee satisfaction.

INDIVIDUAL CONTRIBUTIONS TO TEAM GOALS

Although management directs most of the performance metrics analysts must meet, energetic analysts can suggest additional metrics and supply other information that further demonstrates their contribution to the team's goals. Many managers in a team setting try to involve their staffs when establishing performance measures and encourage their staff to suggest how team and individual performance can be measured and improved. Even simple things such as suggesting possible solutions to a problem rather than finding fault or complaining will raise an analyst's standing in management's eyes.

 By embracing performance metrics and, when appropriate, suggesting additional performance metrics, you can show management that you are a team player. For example, if the company you work for seems very focused on efficiency, you may want to propose an effectiveness metric or a quality metric that can balance the help desk's services. If you make a suggestion that you believe will make the help desk operate more efficiently or effectively, make sure to capture a baseline metric to use for comparison purposes once your proposed change is implemented. This way, you can illustrate the fact that your suggestion was a success.

Management appreciates summarized information and can make decisions more quickly and in a less arbitrary manner when they have facts. A powerful technique is to statistically communicate information about a cause and effect to management. This information can indicate both positive and negative trends. For example, help desk management might report to senior management that "we've taken on support for a new product without increasing our staffing levels and as a result we're experiencing a longer Average Speed of Answer (ASA)." Or, help desk management might report "we implemented a new knowledge management system and can now resolve 15 percent more incidents than before." Capturing data and using information also moves the help desk from a reactive state to a proactive state—which is a much less stressful state for help desk analysts.

In business, everyone's performance is measured, from the most junior associate to the most senior executive. Employees cannot just work hard and *hope* that management recognizes their efforts. To be successful, you must *show* management your commitment and competency. The best way to do that is to ensure that you understand the goals of your department and become skilled at using information to demonstrate how you personally are contributing to those goals.

CHAPTER SUMMARY

- ❏ Today's savvy customers have high expectations for the help desk, and business managers have high expectations for their employees. Every department, including the help desk, is expected to contribute to the goals of the business, and every employee is expected to contribute to the goals of his or her department. The most important goal for the entire company is customer satisfaction. Companies focus on customer satisfaction by understanding their customers' needs and expectations in all areas of the business. They do this by analyzing data and creating information.

❐ Data and information are resources in the same way that well-trained employees, well-defined processes, and well-implemented technology are resources. Help desks that recognize information as a resource are more proactive than reactive. A reactive help desk simply reacts to events that occur each day, whereas a proactive help desk uses information to anticipate and prevent problems and prepare for the future.

❐ Help desks that capture information divide that information into various data categories such as customer, incident, status, and resolution data. Help desk analysts and managers use these data categories, typically captured through fields in the help desk's incident tracking or problem management system, to create detailed tracking and summary reports and to perform trend analysis. In addition, managers use these data fields to calculate many team and individual performance measures.

❐ Help desk performance measures typically reflect the efficiency, effectiveness, and quality of the services being delivered by the help desk team and by individuals within the team. Common team performance measures include help desk goals, Service Level Agreements (SLAs), customer satisfaction surveys, and benchmarking. Common individual performance measures include individual performance goals, employee SLAs, monitoring, and a skills inventory matrix.

❐ In business, everyone's performance is measured, from the most junior associate to the most senior executive. Employees cannot just work hard and *hope* that management recognizes their efforts. To be successful, you must understand the goals of your department and become skilled at using data and information to demonstrate how you are personally contributing to those goals.

KEY TERMS

abandon rate percent — The percentage of abandoned calls compared to the total number of calls received.

abandoned call — A call where the caller hangs up before an analyst answers.

application of training investments — A comparison of an analyst's resolution percent before and after attending training.

availability — The length of time an analyst was signed on to the ACD compared to the length of time the analyst was scheduled to be signed on.

average call duration — The average length of time required to handle a call.

Average Speed of Answer (ASA) — The average time it takes an analyst to pick up an incoming call.

average wait time — The average number of minutes a caller waits for an analyst after being placed in the queue by an ACD; also known as average queue time.

baseline — A metric used to show a starting point.

benchmarking — The process of comparing the help desk's performance metrics and practices to those of another help desk in an effort to identify improvement opportunities.

certification — A document awarded to a person who has demonstrated that he or she has certain skills and knowledge about a particular topic or area.

cost per contact — Historically called cost per call; the total cost of operating a help desk for a given period (including salaries, benefits, facilities, equipment, and so on) divided by the total number of contacts (calls, e-mails, faxes, Web requests, and so on) received during that period.

cost per unit — The total cost of operating a help desk for a given period (including salaries, benefits, facilities, equipment, and so on) divided by the total number of units (such as devices, systems, and so on) supported during that period.

customer data — Identifying details about a customer, including the customer's name, telephone number, department or company name, address or location, customer number, and employee number or user ID.

customer record — All of the fields that describe a single customer.

customer satisfaction surveys — A series of questions that ask customers to provide their perception of the support services being offered.

data — Raw facts that are not organized in a meaningful way.

effectiveness — How completely and accurately services are delivered.

efficiency — How quickly services are delivered.

employee Service Level Agreement — A document that clearly describes an analyst's performance requirements and individual improvement objectives.

event-driven surveys — Customer satisfaction surveys that ask customers for feedback on a single, recent service event.

exit poll — A measurement technique that, on the Internet, combines questions such as "Was this information helpful to you?" with Yes and No buttons that customers can use to provide feedback.

field — A location in a database that stores a particular piece of data.

first call resolution rate percent — The percentage of calls resolved during a customer's initial telephone call compared to the total number of calls received at the help desk for a given period of time.

help desk goals — Measurable objectives that support the help desk's mission.

incident data — The details of a problem or request, including incident type (such as a problem or request), channel used to submit (such as telephone or e-mail), category (such as hardware or software), affected component or system (such as a printer or monitor), symptom, date and time incident occurred, date and time incident was logged, analyst who logged incident, incident owner, description, and severity.

incident record — All of the fields that describe a single incident.

incidents resolved within target time percent — The percentage of incidents resolved within a target resolution time.

individual performance goals — Measurable objectives for analysts that support the help desk mission.

information — Data organized in a meaningful way.

level one resolution rate percent — The percentage of incidents resolved at level one, but not necessarily during the customer's initial telephone call.

metrics — Performance measures.

monitoring — When a supervisor or team leader listens to a live or recorded call or watches an analyst take a call in order to measure the quality of an analyst's performance during the call.

overall satisfaction surveys — Customer satisfaction surveys that ask customers for feedback about all calls they made to the help desk during a certain time period.

page hit — a Web page visit.

proactive help desk — A help desk that uses information to anticipate and prevent problems and prepare for the future.

quality — How well services meet customer expectations.

reactive help desk — A help desk that simply reacts to events that occur each day.

record — A collection of related fields.

reopen percent — The percentage of incidents an analyst opens back up compared to the total number of incidents that analyst closed during a given period of time.

reopened percent — The percentage of closed incidents that had to be opened back up within a given period of time.

resolution percent — The percentage of incidents an analyst resolves compared to the total number of incidents that analyst handled during a given period of time.

resolution data — Details that describe how an incident was resolved, including all fields required to track service level compliance and perform root cause analysis, such as the person or group who resolved the incident, resolution description, date and time resolved, customer satisfaction indicator, date and time closed, and root cause.

response time — The length of time a customer waits for a reply to a fax, e-mail, or Web-based request.

skills inventory matrix — A grid that rates each analyst's level of skill on every product, system, and service supported by the help desk.

status data — Details about an incident that are used to track incidents not resolved at level one, including incident status (such as assigned, awaiting parts, resolved, closed), the person or group assigned, date and time assigned, and priority.

time idle — The average length of time an analyst was idle during a given period of time.

wrap-up time — The average length of time an analyst was in wrap-up mode during a given period of time.

6

REVIEW QUESTIONS

1. What are metrics and how are they created?
2. What is the difference between data and information?
3. What causes an organization to stay in a reactive state?
4. List at least three ways that proactive help desks use information.
5. How can a help desk move to a proactive state?
6. What factors influence the amount of data captured by a help desk?
7. List the four main data categories captured by most help desks.
8. How is resolving an incident different from closing an incident?
9. List and describe the three characteristics assessed by help desk team and individual performance measures.
10. List the four most common ways that help desks use to measure team performance.
11. How is cost per contact calculated?
12. What is the distinction between help desk goals and operational performance measures?
13. Why is the use of SLAs on the rise in internal support organizations?
14. List three service level metrics that measure the efficiency of the help desk team.
15. List three service level metrics that measure the effectiveness of the help desk team.
16. What is the difference between first call resolution rate and level one resolution rate?
17. What is target resolution time based on?
18. What performance characteristic does a customer satisfaction survey measure?
19. How are event driven surveys used differently than overall satisfaction surveys?
20. What is the benefit of benchmarking?
21. Why is it important that companies thoroughly analyze benchmarking results?
22. What are the goals of individual performance management?
23. What are the four most common ways that help desks measure individual performance?
24. List two ways to measure an individual's efficiency.
25. List two ways to measure an individual's effectiveness.
26. List two ways to measure the quality of an individual's performance.
27. Used properly, how does monitoring encourage analysts to view the services they are delivering?
28. List two ways that managers use a skills inventory matrix.
29. List two ways that analysts use a skills inventory matrix.

30. How do help desk analysts benefit when help desks use information to move from a reactive state to a proactive state?

31. How can you ensure that management recognizes your efforts?

HANDS-ON PROJECTS

Project 6-1

Learn how data is captured and used. Use one of the demonstration or trial versions of an incident tracking and problem management system that you downloaded in Chapter 5 to learn more about data fields captured by help desks. Explore the Web site and demonstration version of the system you select and prepare a table or spreadsheet that shows what data fields the system collects for each of the data categories: customer, incident, status, and resolution. Also, provide a paragraph or two describing how the data is used—for example, the types of reports that can be created, the types of metrics that can be produced, the types of knowledge base searches that can be performed, and so forth.

Project 6-2

Learn how a help desk measures performance. Select a class representative who can arrange to have a manager or analyst from a local help desk come and speak to your class. Prior to the presentation, prepare a list of the team and individual performance measurements discussed in this chapter. As a courtesy, have the representative send this list to your speaker ahead of time so that he or she knows the goal of your class is to learn how these techniques are used. Prepare a report that answers the following questions:

❑ What metrics do they use to measure team performance?

❑ What metrics do they use to measure individual performance?

❑ What tools do they use to capture their metrics?

❑ What is their philosophy with regard to capturing data and creating information?

❑ What is their philosophy with regard to performance measurements?

Project 6-3

Evaluate performance measurements. Assemble a team of at least three of your classmates. Discuss the metrics being captured by the company you interviewed in Project 6-2 and its philosophy toward performance measurements. Discuss the following questions and then document your team's conclusions:

❑ Is this company collecting a balanced set of metrics? In other words, is it measuring efficiency, effectiveness, and quality?

❑ If not, what metrics does your team recommend the company begin capturing in an effort to be more balanced? Explain.

❑ What, if any, observations can you make concerning the company's philosophy with regard to performance measurements?

Present and compare your conclusions with the rest of the class.

Project 6-4

Learn about collecting data for help desk metrics. Visit the Web sites of Metricnet (**www.metricnet.com**) and supportindustry.com (**www.supportindustry.com**). Explore both sites and determine the following:

❑ How do these sites collect the data needed to create help desk metrics?

❑ What help desk metrics do these sites publish? To learn this at metricnet.com, you can view its Help Desk Metrics report. To learn this at supportindustry.com, you can click the research icon and view its Service and Support Metrics report.

❑ How are the help desk metrics published by these sites similar? How are they different?

Prepare a brief report that describes what you learned by visiting these sites and any conclusions you can draw about help desk metrics from reading this chapter and visiting these sites.

You will have to register free-of-charge at each site. When you register at Metricnet you will earn 40 data credits, which is enough to view its Help Desk Metrics report. Print the report or save it to a disk so that you will have it for future reference.

Project 6-5

Learn how companies measure customer satisfaction. Visit the Web site of an organization you do business with (such as the company that manufactured your computer or published a software package you use).

❑ Does the site contain a customer satisfaction survey? If not, does it provide some other way for customers to provide feedback?

❑ What kind of feedback does it request (for example, feedback on its efficiency, effectiveness, or quality)?

❑ Does the organization give any indication of how it will use customer feedback?

❑ Did you feel compelled to give feedback? In other words, did the company make you feel that your feedback was important, and did the site make it easy for you to provide it?

Project 6-6

Identify ways to reduce abandoned calls. Recall that an abandoned call means the caller hangs up before an analyst answers the call. Prepare a list of reasons that customers may abandon calls. Then, using everything you have learned, prepare a second list that proposes ways to reduce the number of abandoned calls. Assemble a team of at least three of your classmates. Compare and discuss your lists. Can you, as a team, add any additional items to your lists?

Project 6-7

6

Learn how team and individual performance is measured. Interview a friend, family member, or classmate who works in a team setting. (It does not have to be a help desk.) Ask this person the following questions:

❑ How is the team's performance measured?

❑ How is the person's individual performance measured?

❑ Does this person feel that his or her manager has communicated clearly what he or she must do to receive a positive performance evaluation?

❑ What techniques does this person use to communicate his or her achievements to management?

❑ How does this person feel about the amount of information management requires about his or her personal performance? If the person feels it is a burden, ask why.

Prepare a brief report that presents any conclusions you can draw from this discussion.

Project 6-8

Evaluate a single performance characteristic. Choose between the characteristics of efficiency, effectiveness, and quality. List the pros and cons of focusing on this single performance characteristic. For example, list the pros and cons of focusing only on how efficiently the help desk is performing while ignoring its effectiveness or the quality of its services.

You may want to work with two of your classmates to complete this project by holding a debate. Each classmate could present the merits of a single performance characteristic and state why he or she believes that characteristic is more important than the others. You could then end the debate by summarizing the pros and cons of focusing on a single performance characteristic.

Project 6-9

Learn how help desk outsourcing services measure performance. Search the Web to locate two companies that provide help desk outsourcing services. For each company, summarize in a few paragraphs what you were able to learn about its performance management program from the Web site. In your summary, include the answers to such questions as:

❑ Does the company appear to use any of the techniques discussed in this chapter to measure overall team performance?

❑ Does it give any indication of how it measures the performance of individual staff members?

❑ How does it measure customer satisfaction?

❑ Can you determine from the company's Web site if the company addresses all of the performance characteristics (efficiency, effectiveness, and quality)?

Project 6-10

Interview a manager. Talk to someone you know who is in a management position. (The person doesn't have to be the manager of a help desk.) Document his or her answers to the following questions:

❑ How does this person measure the performance of his or her team?
  - Overall?
  - Individually?

❑ Does this person feel he or she has all the information needed to, for example, justify resources, enhance productivity, and evaluate performance? If not, why?

❑ How does this person communicate to upper management the contribution of his or her team to the organization's goals?

❑ How does this person communicate to upper management his or her individual contribution to the organization's goals?

Summarize any conclusions you can draw from this discussion about the importance of using information as a resource.

CASE PROJECTS

1. ABC Electronics

You've recently been promoted to help desk supervisor at ABC Electronics. The help desk does not currently capture any team or individual performance measures. Everyone is extremely busy, but you're not having any luck convincing management that additional resources are needed. Your help desk does not have a sophisticated telephone system such as an ACD, but you do have a simple incident tracking system. Currently, only high-severity problems that must be assigned to other groups are logged and very little information is captured.

The help desk manager asks you to recommend ways the help desk can justify additional resources and communicate its value to management. Prepare a brief report outlining your recommendations.

2. Technology Support Unlimited

You have been hired as a consultant to help Technology Support Unlimited (TSU) measure customer satisfaction with its support services. TSU provides help desk outsourcing services. It has SLAs with all of its customers that describe measurable performance goals regarding the efficiency and effectiveness of its services. It wants to use customer satisfaction surveys to measure the quality of its services and identify opportunities to offer additional services. It has asked you to develop a survey.

Begin by interviewing several of TSU's customers. (You can use classmates, friends, family members, or coworkers who have contacted a help desk in the past.) Determine what they feel are the characteristics of quality help desk service. Narrow their suggested list of characteristics down to no more than five key characteristics. Create a one-page survey that asks customers to rate TSU's performance in those areas. Remember also to ask customers if they have any suggestions about how TSU can improve its services. You may want to look on the Web or collect sample surveys from restaurants and so forth to get ideas for the format of your survey.

3. Communicate Your Value

You work for a small company that does not have a formal performance management program. Your manager is extremely busy and often is not aware of everything you are doing. You want to keep your manager informed, and you also would like to be considered for a promotion to supervisor. You've tried preparing lengthy status reports, but your manager doesn't seem to have the time to read them.

Develop the format for a one-page status report that you can use to demonstrate your accomplishments. In addition to your accomplishments for the current month, you may want to include comparisons to previous period(s) as well as to your stated goals. Make sure your status report is balanced and stated in the form of measurements (as opposed to a narrative form). Include in your status report all of the qualities you feel demonstrate your commitment to delivering excellent customer support.

7

THE HELP DESK SETTING

In this chapter you will learn:

♦ Factors that influence the location and layout of a help desk

♦ How analysts can improve the ergonomics of their personal workspace

♦ Work habits to keep you organized and help you achieve personal success

Having the right processes, tools, and technologies—and knowing how to use them properly—is only part of supporting customers effectively. In order to provide top-quality customer service and support, an analyst needs a good work environment, good work habits, and a great attitude. Some days, walking into a help desk is like walking into an amusement arcade. Lights are flashing, alarms are ringing, and everyone is talking at once. The larger the help desk, the more active and intimidating it can be. Focused, organized people who thrive on challenge will find this dynamic environment invigorating.

Help desks—whether large or small—are high-energy and high-activity places to work. The constant stream of contacts from customers in need requires friendly and patient analysts. Companies that create a pleasant, comfortable working environment make it easier for their analysts to be understanding and effective. But whether or not a company provides the optimal working environment, analysts can take care to set up their personal workspace for optimum comfort and functionality. They can also establish routines to organize their days.

To be a successful help desk analyst, you need to understand how the physical layout of your workspace can benefit, and sometimes detract from, your performance. Also, it is important to understand that you can adopt behaviors and arrange your physical workspace to increase your comfort and productivity.

HELP DESK SETUP

Help desks come in all shapes and sizes, and the setup of help desks varies from one company to the next. The setup of the help desk includes both its location and physical layout. Factors such as accessibility, the need for security, and the company's commitment to the well-being of its staff influence the help desk's location. Factors such as size, technical sophistication, and the nature of problem solving done by analysts influence the help desk's physical layout. All of these factors together affect analysts' comfort in the workplace and how efficiently they work.

Location of the Help Desk

Location refers to the physical site of the help desk in the building. When choosing a location, companies may place the help desk near other groups in the department that the help desk reports. Because those other groups are very often level two support groups, this physical proximity allows the help desk to interact more easily with those groups and vice versa. The help desk may be placed near groups that report to a different department but that interact regularly with the help desk. For example, an external help desk may be located near the sales group. Companies may also place the help desk near their customers. This allows the help desk to build rapport with its customers and develop an understanding of the environment in which its customers work. Location may also be influenced by the need to provide for continuous operations in the event of an emergency. For example, some companies have multiple help desks that are linked by technology. This enables the company to transfer help desk operations to an alternate site in the event that one site is affected by a natural disaster, such as a hurricane or tornado, or other extreme conditions. Figure 7-1 lists other factors that influence the location of the help desk.

- Accessibility
- Security
- Wellness

Figure 7-1   Factors that influence help desk location

A company's commitment to creating a safe and attractive workplace for its employees and its willingness to make the financial investment required to do so also have considerable bearing on the help desk location.

Accessibility

Accessibility determines how easily the help desk can be reached by help desk staff, other employees of the company, and customers. Historically, many help desks were located behind closed doors in the confines of the computer room. Today, help desks are situated in a more centralized location. Accessible help desks enable analysts to interact more freely with level two and level three support groups and, when appropriate, with internal or external customers. For example, some help desks offer walk-in service. This can be distracting if customers begin speaking to an analyst who is on the phone—it's sometimes hard to tell with headsets. As a result, many help desks set up a desk or counter that customers report to when they arrive at the help desk for walk-in service. They then receive service on a first-come, first-served basis.

Some help desks offer tours of their facilities to customers, visitors from other companies, remote employees who have come to corporate headquarters for a meeting or training, and so forth. When efforts are made to ensure that visitors do not disrupt analysts who are on the telephone, having customers and other support groups visit the help desk is an excellent way to let them see the help desk in action and help them understand the help desk's role.

Security

Data and equipment protection along with the personal safety of employees affect where a help desk is located and the measures taken to secure the area. Some help desks are in remote parts of the building or can be accessed only by using a key or a card key or by signing in with a guard. The permissions or authority the help desk has to make system changes also influence the need for security. For example, help desks with access to master computer consoles need greater security to prevent unauthorized changes to the system that could result in serious damage. The safety of the help desk staff is also a consideration. Help desks that operate 24 hours per day, 7 days per week need more security than those that function only during regular business hours. Help desks that are open around the clock often secure the help desk area by, for example, locking the doors and requiring the use of a key or a card key to enter the help desk after business hours so their after-hours workers feel safe.

Wellness

Wellness is the condition of good physical and mental health, especially when maintained by proper diet, exercise, and habits. Light, clean air, and the ability to exercise are just a few things that influence workers' physical and emotional well-being both at and away from the workplace. A well-lit environment encourages the positive attitude help desk analysts need. Many people prefer to work in an area that has good ventilation or windows they can open for fresh air and that is located far from a designated smoking area. People are also more comfortable when they work in an open workspace that allows them to move about or in a building that has an indoor gym or other room where they can exercise when it is too hot or cold outside. Companies that promote wellness design their workplaces to provide these types of positive influences. A well-designed workspace that takes into consideration the comfort and safety of employees prevents workplace injuries, reduces fatigue and stress, and increases productivity.

WALTER HUNDLEY
IT SERVICE DESK MANAGER
ENTERGY CORPORATION (UTILITY)
SCIENCE APPLICATIONS INTERNATIONAL
CORPORATION (SERVICE AGENCY)
LITTLE ROCK, ARKANSAS
WWW.ENTERGY.COM
WWW.SAIC.COM

Entergy Corporation is a major integrated energy company engaged in power production, distribution operations, and related diversified services, with over 2.6 million customers and 15,000 employees. In 1999, Entergy outsourced all of its IT services, including the IT Service Desk, to Science Applications International Corporation (SAIC). SAIC is the largest employee-owned research and engineering company in the United States. As the Entergy-SAIC agreement allowed Entergy IT employees to remain Entergy employees or to join SAIC, many of the SAIC employees who now support the energy company are former Entergy employees. Entergy's IT Service Desk is part of SAIC's Integrated Services Management Center (ISMC).

Tasks. The IT Service Desk (service desk) provides technical support to over 17,000 Entergy employees and contractors. The service desk provides support 14 hours per day, 5 days a week, plus 4 hours a day on weekends. Entergy's Network Operations Center (NOC), which is also run by SAIC, handles calls outside of the help desk's normal business hours. Thus customers have access to 24 X 7 support. As part of the outsourcing agreement with Entergy, SAIC is required to meet two primary performance goals: (1) answer all calls in less than 45 seconds, and (2) resolve at level one 80 percent of the problems that are within the scope of the service desk's responsibility.

Entergy's service desk is "virtual" with SAIC agents housed at two Entergy locations: Little Rock, Arkansas, and New Orleans, Louisiana. Entergy uses a sophisticated voice response unit (VRU) to route calls to available agents at either of these locations. Having two locations enables the service desk to provide continuous operations in the event of a disaster, such as a hurricane in New Orleans or an ice storm in Little Rock.

7

Because Entergy employees use more than 200 applications to do their work, each location also has access to application experts who provide support for internal applications such as Entergy's fossil, nuclear, transmission, distribution, retail, and corporate software. Some of these applications are still supported by Entergy, some are supported by SAIC, and some are supported by other contractors. Regardless of who supports an application, all calls are logged by the service desk, and calls that cannot be resolved during the first call are either escalated to the appropriate support group, or they are saved to the help desk Inbox and later retrieved by agents with the needed expertise. Well-defined business processes ensure that each group assumes responsibilities for problems it is assigned.

Organization. The number of staff working within the service desk varies depending on call volume predictions for the time of day, day of week, and so forth. There is one manager at each site in addition to the 19 agents who are split between the two locations. Due to the variety of systems the service desk supports, it takes from 3 to 6 months for agents to become fully versed in the company's desktop applications (Microsoft is its standard), internally developed applications such as Entergy's Customer Information System (CIS), and its extensive LAN/WAN infrastructure. Agents have the opportunity to take classes once a quarter, and choose the class they take from the course catalog offered by New Horizons. The job is considered a professional position, not an hourly position.

In addition to their normal service desk duties, staff members may be given other responsibilities. For example, staff members may develop procedures, participate on rollout teams, serve as Webmaster, or prepare self-help information. Team and individual goals are well defined, and performance reviews are based on those goals and the ultimate goal—customer satisfaction. The help desk's problem management system automatically sends an electronic customer satisfaction survey to the user on 20 percent of cases when they are closed. Survey responses are monitored closely, and the case is reopened if a customer is not satisfied.

The service desk works closely with Entergy's Network Operations Center (NOC), which handles tasks such as monitoring the company's extensive LAN/WAN and voice networks. The NOC, like the service desk, is located in both New Orleans and Little Rock for redundancy. In New Orleans, service desk and NOC staff reside in Entergy's Data Center. The Data Center is home to the Entergy Command Theater, a state-of-the-art facility with large screen display monitors that provide real-time information about everything from the status of the network and mainframe production jobs to the weather conditions that may be affecting Entergy's external customers. The service desk and NOC mirror this information electronically on each desktop, so that all sites have the latest status on known issues, applications, and network outages. In addition to service desk and NOC staff, Tier II and Tier III technical support staff work together in the Command Theater or remotely at other corporate sites with one common purpose: To solve the customer's problem, no matter what it takes.

Final responsibility for problem management resides with Entergy's Service Management Coordinators (SMCs). The SMCs, located in New Orleans and Little Rock, coordinate resolution and communication on high and critical priority problems that may require multiple departments, and even multiple companies, working together to determine the root cause. This one point of coordination transcends departmental and company boundaries and promotes teamwork that enables the different departments and companies to communicate openly.

Philosophy. Both Entergy and SAIC are deeply committed to delivering quality products and services to their respective customers. In Entergy's case, the agreement with SAIC allows Entergy to focus on its core business, increase its flexibility to respond to changing business needs, leverage technology to improve service to its customers, and improve unit cost for information technology. In SAIC's case, the agreement with Entergy allows SAIC employees to do what they do best: deliver best-value services and solutions based on innovative applications of science and technology. Proof that both companies are benefiting from this agreement came from an independent source when, in 2000, Entergy benchmarked its help desk services and was rated best-in-class by Gartner, Inc.

Physical Layout of the Help Desk

Physical layout refers to how the help desk is arranged into workspaces. A **workspace** is an area outfitted with equipment and furnishings for one worker. Figure 7-2 shows a sample help desk workspace.

Figure 7-2   Sample help desk workspace

The physical layout might be a result of how the help desk was formed. Recall that some large help desks grew from small help desks, whereas others have evolved from the consolidation of several smaller help desks or from a corporate merger or acquisition. A company's desire to create an attractive workplace also has considerable bearing on its physical layout. Figure 7-3 lists other factors that influence the physical layout of the help desk.

- Size
- Tools and technology
- Interaction

Figure 7-3   Factors that influence the help desk's physical layout

Size

The number of analysts who work at a help desk greatly influences its physical layout or how the workspace is arranged. For example, smaller help desks place analysts close together to enhance their ability to work together as a team. Larger help desks want analysts to be able to work together as a team but must also accommodate the needs of help desk management and other supporting groups such as knowledge base administration, a resource desk, and perhaps a training group.

In a very small help desk—consisting of one or two people—the analysts typically sit in cubicles. The analysts in a small help desk with more than two people may sit side-by-side in large cubicles that face each other across an aisle so they can communicate easily. These help desks also may devote some space to a white board and extra equipment such as a fax machine and network monitors. Figure 7-4 illustrates a small help desk setting.

Courtesy of Utility Partners, Inc.

Figure 7-4   Small help desk setting

In very small help desks, the help desk supervisor or manager (if there is one) may reside in the help desk and take customer calls. As the help desk grows, the help desk supervisor or manager often moves to a cubicle or office near the help desk.

Medium help desks use a different layout than small help desks do. Recall that medium help desks have between 10 and 25 people on staff and can take on the characteristics of both small and large help desks. As the help desk grows to 25 people or so, some companies arrange cubicles around an enclosed common area—sometimes called a "bullpen"—to minimize the noise entering and leaving the help desk as well as to enable analysts to share resources such as equipment, books, and training manuals. Communication tools such as a white board, an electronic reader board, or network monitors are positioned so they can be viewed easily by all analysts. Figure 7-5 shows a medium help desk setting.

Courtesy of National Association of Securities Dealer's, Inc.

Figure 7-5   Medium help desk setting

 Medium and large help desk settings sometimes set aside an extra cubicle or two, which may be used by level two staff who periodically visit the help desk for informal training or are on-site when a new system is launched. These cubicles may also be used for testing, such as certification testing or testing of job applicants.

Large help desks that grew from small or medium help desks sometimes did so without the benefit of a plan. In those instances, team members may reside in long rows of standard cubicles and must leave their cubicles to communicate with coworkers and help desk management. Worse yet, they may shout through cubicle walls or stand on their chairs in an effort to communicate. Although such help desks might contain common areas such as a lab or meeting area, they may not be easily accessible and, as a result, may be underutilized.

In contrast to these unplanned settings, some large help desks are created with employee comfort, safety, and productivity in mind. These help desk settings consider factors such as noise, lighting, and the analyst's personal workspace in their layout. Workspaces are often arranged in clusters or "pods" designed to reduce noise, facilitate communication, and increase teamwork. These clusters may represent teams of analysts within the help desk who have similar skills such as hardware skills or PC software skills. In an external help desk or service agency, these teams may consist of analysts who support a single large external customer, or they may consist of analysts who support several customers, such as several small companies that require a limited amount of support.

In a well-designed setting, the cubicle walls between the workspaces typically are low—three to four feet—enabling analysts to interact easily and view electronic reader boards, network monitors, and even pictures mounted around the perimeter of the help desk. Figure 7-6 illustrates a large help desk setting.

 Regardless of a help desk's size, the physical layout of the help desk must facilitate efficient communication between analysts in an effort to avoid situations such as having more than one analyst working on the same problem. It is also important to have a mechanism such as a white board or a reader board that can be used to quickly notify all analysts when there is a major problem.

Courtsey of CompuCom Systems, Inc.

Figure 7-6   Large help desk setting

The size of the help desk often reflects its use of tools and technology.

Tools and Technology

The tools and technology the help desk uses influence its physical layout. Furthermore, the size of the help desk and its technical sophistication often go hand in hand. For example, smaller help desks may simply need a fax machine and a white board, whereas larger help desks may use electronic reader boards and network monitors. Some help desks—regardless of size—have lab areas with the same hardware and software configurations as its customers. Analysts can use these lab areas to obtain hands-on training, simulate customers' problems, and develop and test potential solutions. All help desks can benefit from technology, and the help desk's physical layout must accommodate whatever tools and technology the help desk uses or plans to use in the future.

Interaction

The level of interaction and the nature of problem solving that analysts perform influence the design of the help desk. For example, help desks in which analysts interact constantly and work together to solve problems use low-walled, open cubicles arranged to face a common area. Help desks where analysts work independently researching problems or debugging programs use higher cubicle walls and, perhaps, even private offices.

Growing help desks often add on to their existing location without considering or being able to consider these factors—size, tools and technology, and interaction. This ad hoc design hinders productivity. Companies that are designing new help desks, or redesigning existing ones, are in the best position to consider all of these factors in their physical layout plans. More and more, companies are recognizing that a well-designed work environment enhances the help desk's productivity and improves analysts' ability to communicate and share information. In fact, many organizations conduct research on work environments and recommend ways to prevent work-related injuries and illnesses. For example, the **National Institute for Occupational Safety and Health** (**NIOSH**) is a part of the Centers for Disease Control and Prevention (CDC) that is responsible for conducting research and making recommendations for the prevention of work-related illnesses and injuries (**www.cdc.gov/niosh/homepage.html**). The **Occupational Safety and Health Administration** (**OSHA**) is an agency of the U.S. Department of Labor that is dedicated to reducing hazards in the workplace and enforcing mandatory job-safety standards (**www.osha.gov**). OSHA also implements and improves health programs for workers. These organizations provide companies with the information needed to create safe and comfortable workspaces.

ANALYSTS' PERSONAL WORKSPACE

Analysts often have no control over the location and the physical layout of the help desk, but they can improve the ergonomics of their personal workspace. **Ergonomics** is the science of people-machine relationships and is intended to maximize productivity by reducing operator fatigue and discomfort. Some symptoms of a poorly designed workplace include headaches, wrist and shoulder pain, backaches, and swollen ankles. Ergonomics helps reduce these symptoms and prevent repetitive stress injuries. **Repetitive stress injuries** (**RSIs**) are physical symptoms caused by excessive and repeated use of the hands, wrists, and arms; they occur when people perform tasks using force, repeated strenuous actions, awkward postures, and poorly designed equipment. RSIs include carpal tunnel syndrome, tendonitis, bursitis, and rotator-cuff injuries. **Carpal tunnel syndrome** (**CTS**) is a common repetitive stress injury that affects the hands and wrists and is linked to repetitious hand movements, such as typing on a computer keyboard, pinching a mouse, or repeatedly clicking a mouse. CTS is caused by constant compression of the main nerve to the hand as it passes through the carpal tunnel of the wrist. The help desk team is susceptible to RSIs such as CTS because analysts do a considerable amount of keyboarding and mousing. Analysts will become more susceptible as e-mail and chat become more common methods of communicating with customers.

 To learn more about ergonomics and how to prevent and treat conditions such as carpal tunnel syndrome and computer vision syndrome, go to **www.healthycomputing.com**. **Computer vision syndrome** encompasses a variety of ailments such as headaches and eyestrain that occur as a result of staring at a computer monitor.

A majority of ergonomic problems can be eliminated by making simple, no-cost adjustments to the analyst's personal workspace. Analysts can easily adjust the chair, monitor, keyboard and mouse, telephone and headset, and lighting to create a workspace that fits their needs. Making these adjustments goes a long way to helping analysts stay healthy on the job.

Chair

In each workspace, the placement and use of the chair, monitor, keyboard, and mouse are related, and all must be aligned properly with each other and with the analyst. How analysts adjust and sit in their chairs are equally important. Analysts should adjust the chair until the back is erect, slightly back, and firm against the backrest. Figure 7-7 illustrates a typical office chair that can be adjusted to promote good posture and back support. Adjustment features may include the ability to adjust arm height, arm width, seat height, seat tilt, and support for the lumbar region, also known as the small of the back.

Figure 7-7   Typical office chair

If necessary, analysts can further support their backs with a lumbar pillow or a rolled-up towel. Legs should be relaxed and feet should be flat on the floor. Analysts can also place a footrest or a box under the desk to keep their feet from dangling.

 To learn more about how to adjust your chair, go to **www.osha.gov/SLTC/ computerworkstations_ecat/chair.html**. This site also offers information about how to adjust your keyboard and mouse and how to improve the lighting in your workspace.

Monitor

The chair height can both affect and be affected by the monitor placement. The best position for a monitor is directly in front of the analyst at or just below eye level. When analysts are sitting straight with their heads erect, the monitor should be no more than 24 inches away from their eyes. If necessary, analysts can place a book under the monitor to raise it up to the right level. If the monitor is too high, they can remove anything under it to lower it, adjust their chair, or replace the desk or table with a lower one as a last resort.

 Don't forget to treat the glass surface with an anti-glare coating or install a filter if you're encountering monitor glare.

Liquid crystal display (LCD) monitors, also known as LCD flat screen monitors, are becoming increasingly popular and are expected in time to replace cathode ray tube (CRT) monitors. LCD monitors typically offer a large viewing screen and high-resolution graphics, and are resistant to glare. These monitors also have a smaller footprint, which means they take up less space on a desk. Figure 7-8 shows a sample LCD monitor.

Figure 7-8   Sample LCD monitor

Keyboard and Mouse

Correct placement and use of the keyboard and mouse combined with good work habits can help analysts avoid repetitive stress injuries. The proper form for keyboarding and using the mouse is to keep wrists straight and avoid resting them on hard surfaces. Keys should be pressed gently rather than pounded to prevent injury to both the hands and the keyboard. Also, the mouse should be gripped loosely. Analysts can also consider using ergonomic keyboards and sloping keyboard trays to reduce the symptoms of carpal tunnel syndrome. A wrist rest—a firm cushion that lays parallel to the keyboard—can also help. Too-soft wrist wrests that wrists sink into put unnecessary pressure on the wrists. Figure 7-9 illustrates how a wrist rest can be used in front of a keyboard as well as in front of a mouse.

Figure 7-9   Sample keyboard and mouse wrist rest

7

 Periodically shake out your hands and perform shrugging exercises to relax your shoulders. Keep it loose!

All these components—chair, monitor, keyboard, and mouse—work together. The chair should be aligned with the monitor and keyboard so that when analysts sit up straight in the chair the monitor is at or below eye level and their wrists are straight on the keyboard. Whenever analysts adjust their chair, they will most likely need to readjust their monitor and their keyboard and mouse as well. Figure 7-10 illustrates the relationship between the chair, monitor, and keyboard.

Notice that the person in this figure is sitting up straight with her feet resting comfortably on the floor and with the chair supporting her lower back. Notice also that the monitor is at eye level, the person's wrists are straight, and her fingers are resting lightly on the keyboard.

Figure 7-10   Ergonomically aligned chair, monitor, and keyboard

 To view a diagram that shows a person in relation to correctly placed office components, go to **www.techweb.com/encyclopedia/defineterm?term=ergonomics**.

Telephone and Headset

A telephone is one of the most basic pieces of equipment at help desks. The type or style of telephone is less important than the correct position in relation to the computer. Analysts who have to stretch or turn around to answer the telephone are at risk for a repetitive stress injury. A good rule of thumb for analysts is to place the telephone either directly in front of them or at less than a 25° angle and no more than 10 inches away.

Telephone headsets rid analysts of the traditional handheld receiver. Headsets relieve stress and tension by freeing analysts' hands for typing and prevent neck pain by eliminating the need for analysts to balance a receiver between their tilted head and shoulder. In fact, a study conducted at Santa Clara Valley Medical Center in San Jose, California, found that headset users reduce neck, shoulder, and upper back tension by as much as 41 percent. Wireless headsets are also available that provide the added ability to stand up and move about the help desk. As shown in Figure 7-11, there are numerous styles of headsets, including over-the-ear models and headbands that fit over one ear or both ears.

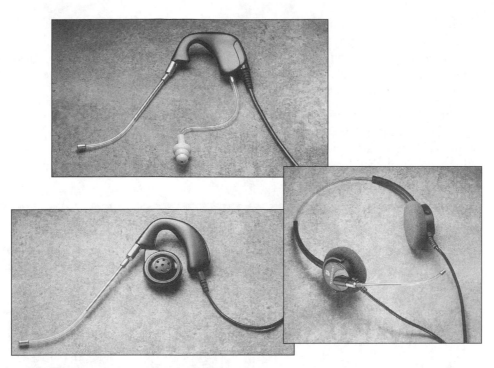

Figure 7-11   Sample headset styles

If possible, analysts should try on several models before making a final selection. Although the style of headset a person selects is a matter of personal choice, each style changes how much the wearer can hear. For example:

- Some headsets cover only one ear so people can remain aware of what is going on around them.

- Some headsets cover both ears so people can block out noise.

- Some headsets offer a noise-canceling microphone to help filter out noise from the help desk that the customer may hear.

Regardless of the style, a headset should keep the user's head and neck in a neutral position and free the hands for activities such as keyboarding.

 Your head is the heaviest part of your body. Although headsets are fairly light, do not use a headset that encourages you to tilt or hang your head. Leaving your head tilted for even a short period of time causes tension in your neck, shoulders, and back.

Lighting

The brightness of a workspace can greatly affect an analyst's well-being. Too much overhead lighting or ambient light from a window can produce a glare on the monitor, which can cause eyestrain, headaches, and fatigue. Glare can also prompt analysts to shift their posture to a more awkward position, increasing the chance of neck or back strain. Analysts can reduce this glare by spraying an anti-glare coating on the glass surface or by installing an anti-glare filter. Too little lighting can cause analysts to squint and strain in order to see paperwork or the monitor.

Adjustable task lighting on the desk provides directed lighting to supplement the overhead lighting and can be shifted to prevent glare. Task lighting can be used to spotlight desk tasks such as writing and reading and can also be used to reduce the high contrast of light and dark areas that occur in a workspace. Figure 7-12 shows the use of task lighting.

Figure 7-12   Sample task lighting

When using a task light:

- Position the light away from your computer screen to prevent glare.

- If you are working with a document holder next to the computer screen, make sure that the light shines directly down on the document holder and not on your computer screen.

- Position the light 15 to 20 inches (depending on your height) directly over paper documents that are placed on your desk.

- Position the light slightly below eye level.

- Always keep the light head facing down so that it does not shine in your eyes.

- Place the task light where it can be easily adjusted by hand or moved to the area of the desk where you are working.

In addition to overhead and task lighting, analysts need regular or periodic exposure to natural light. This is because natural light, or the lack of it, can influence analysts' moods. A study conducted by the National Institute of Mental Health found that the shorter days and fewer sunlight hours during winter triggers a change in many people's brain chemistry. The change may set off a cycle of depression, which is now recognized in medical literature as Seasonal Affective Disorder (SAD). Also, lightbulbs emit light in only a narrow scope of the visual spectrum whereas natural light has a balanced spectrum that renders colors perfectly. Because of this, natural light is much more pleasing than artificial light. Analysts can experience a positive psychological lift by making a conscious effort to look out a window periodically throughout the day or by going outside, even if only for a brief period of time.

 Remember that your work habits contribute to the amount of stress and tension you experience on the job. Take regular breaks, periodically look out a window, stretch, and be aware of your posture and wrist positions.

At any new office or workstation, analysts should take the time to arrange the equipment to meet their requirements. If they need additional equipment, such as a task light or footrest, they should request it from their managers. In addition to these physical equipment adjustments, analysts can adapt their work habits as well.

GOOD WORK HABITS FOR ANALYSTS

Customer support is a tough job. In fact, it's one of the most stressful professions you can have. This is because analysts cannot predict what crisis will occur on any given day. Difficult customer situations and a lack of time to update one's skills or insufficient resources such as tools, procedures, and knowledge sources also contribute to the stress that can occur in a help desk setting. To reduce stress and the possibility of getting injured on the job, analysts can ensure that they are ready to *respond*, not react, to whatever comes their way. Figure 7-13 lists good work habits analysts can use to get and stay organized and to achieve personal success.

> Create a beginning of day (BOD) procedure.
>
> Manage priorities.
>
> Create a "What I Need to Know" list.
>
> Create a "What Coworkers Need to Know" list.
>
> Utilize peak productivity times.
>
> Eliminate or minimize time robbers.
>
> Place a mirror on your desk.
>
> Take breaks.
>
> Recognize learning as the labor of the information age.

Figure 7-13   Good work habits for help desk analysts

Each of these items helps reduce the stress that can occur in a help desk setting and contributes to the personal success of help desk analysts and, ultimately, to the success of the help desk and the company.

Create a Beginning of Day (BOD) Procedure

Successful analysts develop routines that enable them to stay organized and remember things. A **beginning of day** (**BOD**) procedure is a list of tasks an analyst performs at the start of each workday. For example, an effective BOD includes:

- Greet coworkers.

- Check and respond to your voice mail and e-mail messages.

- Check the status of problems you own through the problem management system.

- Follow-up on any critical issues from the previous day.

- Create or update a "To Do" list for the day.

- Straighten desk.

- Note any current "hot" (or system-wide) problems.

- Take a deep breath and get ready for anything!

Try to arrive at your help desk a few minutes early so that you can complete your BOD before signing on to take calls. A BOD is a habit that sets the tone for the rest of the day. Start the day off right.

In addition to a BOD procedure for each analyst, some help desks create a BOD for the entire help desk. An EOD (end of day) procedure is also a good idea. Help desks that work in shifts also may have a beginning and end of shift procedure, also known as a shift turnover procedure. The policies of the help desk determine what tasks are included in these procedures.

Manage Priorities

Once analysts are organized for the day, they need to determine in what order they will complete the tasks on their "To Do" list. A "To Do" list must be prioritized daily. Analysts assign a priority to each task on their "To Do" list to indicate the order they will work on tasks that day. A simple priority scale rates each task on a scale from A to D, as shown in Table 7-1.

Table 7-1 Simple priority scale

Rating	Priority
A	Urgent, must do today
B	Important, should do this week
C	Do when time permits
D	Delegate

After each task has a priority rating, the analysts should check for a balance of priorities. When faced with more "A" priority tasks than can be completed in one day, analysts can consider the following questions about each task:

1. **Who asked me to complete this task?**
   A task assigned by a customer or a manager may have a higher priority than a task assigned by a coworker.

2. **Am I the proper person to complete this task?**
   You don't have to accept a task just because someone asks. The person asking you to complete a task may not know that another person on the team is responsible for the work being requested. If your manager is asking you to complete a task that you do not feel qualified to complete, discuss the matter with your manager and ask him or her for any help you need prior to proceeding.

3. **What is the risk if I don't complete this task? What is the value if I do complete this task?**
   Failing to complete a task may cause the analyst (or someone waiting on the analyst's input) to miss a critical deadline. Consistently completing tasks on time helps make an analyst eligible for a raise or a promotion.

4. **When am I expected to have this task done? That is, what is my deadline for this task?**
   If the task is due that day, it is a high priority for the day. If it is not due for several weeks, the analyst can assign a lower priority and strive to simply start the task even though it may not get completed that day.

 When accepting a task, avoid putting pressure on yourself—ask the person assigning the task when he or she needs it, rather than offering to complete it immediately. The person may not need the task completed immediately, so you can assign it an appropriate priority and incorporate it into your workload. If your manager is asking you to complete a new task and you are unsure about its priority, ask him or her how important this task is relative to other work you've already been assigned.

Based on their answers to these questions, analysts can refine the priorities of the tasks on their "To Do" list.

Create a "What I Need to Know" List

Lists of commonly used information are a great way for analysts to get and stay organized. Analysts should create a list of important telephone numbers, filenames, dates, and so on that they need on a fairly regular basis and place it in clear view. These items are not necessarily ones they use on a daily basis, which analysts tend to memorize, but are pieces of information they may use often during a short period of time, such as the roll-out date of a new system.

Create a "What Coworkers Need to Know" List

Similar to the "What I Need to Know" list, the "What Coworkers Need to Know" list contains important information coworkers may need to know if an analyst is out of the office for a few days or weeks. For example, the analyst could be at a training class, on vacation, and so forth. This list should include the status of any current and ongoing projects, the names of folders, or the location of documents the analyst is responsible for maintaining, the dates during which the analyst will be gone, and the names of people who provide backup in their absence. During work-related travel, such as attending a training class or offsite meeting, analysts may include a way for coworkers to reach them in the event of an emergency.

Utilize Peak Productivity Times

Are you an early bird or a night owl? Most people have about four hours each day during which they are most productive and alert. Because this time varies from person to person, each analyst should determine his or her personal peak productivity time. If possible, they should schedule their work to take advantage of the time during which they function best.

Eliminate or Minimize Time Robbers

Time robbers are activities that take up time and do not add value to the work that analysts perform. In fact, time robbers usually decrease productivity and increase stress levels. Analysts can use the following techniques to avoid time robbers:

- **Log calls as they come in.** This avoids the need to handle the call twice, eliminates the possibility that analysts forget critical information, and ensures that the time stamps that indicate when the incident record was entered correspond to when the incident was actually reported by the customer. Logging calls real-time also ensures that other analysts and customers who may be checking the status of tickets online can get the information they need, when they need it, thus preventing a waste of their time.

- **Avoid distractions.** Overall, analysts should stay focused on their work and resist the temptation to get involved in every conversation going on around them. It is, however, appropriate for analysts to get involved when it appears there is a system-wide problem and they need a status update, or to participate in joint problem solving with a coworker.

- **Avoid procrastination.** Putting off a task until the last minute can cause analysts to miss a critical deadline or produce a low-quality product. The best way for analysts to avoid this is to break large tasks into smaller ones and try to complete the task a little bit at a time. Also, they can set a time limit and work on a task for at least that period of time. Even if it's only 10 minutes, at least they will have started. Who knows—they may find that the project captures their interest and they will want to keep going.

- **Ask for help when you need it.** It's human nature to want to figure things out on our own, but sometimes we all need help. Analysts need to try to distinguish between just "taking a little more time to figure things out" and needing help and guidance to avoid aggravation and wasted time.

- **Keep desk and files organized.** Organization is a key to success. Analysts should devise a system that they can use to get and stay organized. Then they should get in the habit of always putting away files after they use them and handling papers and folders only one time. A good rule of thumb is: Do it, file it, or dump it (that is, throw away junk mail or other unneeded paperwork).

- **Suggest constructive ways to make improvements.** Complaining wastes time, is typically perceived as whining, and can give an analyst a bad reputation. The analyst may be viewed as negative and uncooperative, or unwilling to be a team player. If analysts see opportunities to make improvements, they should—in a constructive manner—tell their team leader or send an e-mail or memo that outlines the steps they think could help eliminate or minimize a problem.

- **Automate recurring tasks.** Every job contains tasks that must be done repeatedly. Analysts should identify these tasks and then set up shortcuts and function keys that they can use, for example, to access frequently used Web sites or perform routine lookups in the incident tracking system. Analysts can also create and use macros for Windows-based applications such as Microsoft Word, Excel, and Access. A **macro** is series of menu selections, keystrokes, and/or commands that have been recorded and assigned a name or key combination.

Developing excellent time management skills will serve you well throughout your life.

Your local library has numerous books on time and stress management. These sources contain many excellent tips about how to manage your time wisely and how to avoid and alleviate stress.

To learn more about time management on the Web, go to **www.time-management-guide.com**. For time management tips for students, go to **www.d.umn.edu/student/loon/acad/strat/time_man_princ.html**. To learn more about stress management, go to **stress.about.com** or **my.webmd.com/encyclopedia/article/1674.52486**.

Place a Mirror on Your Desk

Facial expression mirrors mood, and mood mirrors facial expression. Also, good posture improves the quality of the voice and makes it easier for customers to understand what analysts are saying. To monitor their facial expressions and posture, analysts can place a mirror at eye level when they are sitting straight. By taking a quick look in the mirror before they answer the phone, analysts can ensure that they have a relaxed and pleasant facial expression. They can put a smile on their face, give the customer (whom they pretend to see in the mirror) their full attention, take a deep breath, if needed, to get focused, and then answer the telephone. This mirror technique also helps analysts ensure that they demonstrate concern when a customer is dissatisfied and when they sense anger building (their own or the customer's). Again, they should relax their faces and assume a caring expression, give their full attention to the customer (whom they pretend to see in the mirror), take a deep breath, if necessary, to get focused and to stay calm, and make sure they are listening actively to the customer. A mirror also enables you to see a person who walks up behind you, thus preventing you from being startled when you are on the telephone or focused on a task.

Take Breaks

Working nonstop often leads to fatigue and burnout. Analysts should take time throughout the day to rejuvenate themselves: Stretch, spend a moment looking out the window, or simply close their eyes and take a few deep breaths to regain a sense of calm. They can take a short walk, even if it's only to the restroom or to get a drink of water. Fatigue is one of the first signs of dehydration, so analysts should make sure they are drinking plenty of water. Drinking plenty of water increases your energy level and mental capacities. A side benefit is that when you drink plenty of water, your body lets you know when it's time to take a break.

Taking a break can also involve performing a low-stress task such as opening mail, filling out your time sheet, putting away reference books or magazines, or tidying up your desk. Completing such small, seemingly trivial tasks provides a rejuvenating sense of accomplishment; eliminating clutter from your workspace will enable you to refocus your energies.

Recognize Learning as the Labor of the Information Age

Friends, family, and coworkers often refer to analysts as "computer experts," and at any given point they *are* experts. However, technology changes quickly. The skills and experience that served an analyst well in the past may, at any time, outlive their usefulness or relevance. Then it is time to replace them with new skills. True experts take the time and energy to continually update and improve their knowledge and skills. Working at a help desk provides constant opportunity for change, which an analyst can resist or embrace. Choose to embrace it!

Good work habits represent the discipline analysts need to feel in control during exceptionally busy times at the help desk and to stay motivated during slow times. Getting and staying organized and knowing how to manage stress and continuously rejuvenate oneself are habits that enable people to view work as a challenge to be enjoyed. These habits, combined with a properly set up workspace, enable analysts to maintain physical and mental fitness on the job and to achieve personal success.

CHAPTER SUMMARY

❑ In order to provide top-quality customer service and support, an analyst needs a good working environment, good work habits, and a great attitude. Companies that create a pleasant, comfortable working environment make it easier for their analysts to be friendly and patient when interacting with customers. Whether or not a company provides the optimum working environment, analysts can take care to set up their personal workspace for optimum comfort and functionality. They can also establish routines to organize their days.

❑ Factors such as accessibility, the need for security, and the company's commitment to the wellness of its staff influence the help desk's location. Factors such as size, the tools and technology the help desk uses, and the level of interaction and the nature of problem solving that analysts perform influence the help desk's physical layout. All of these factors affect how safe and comfortable analysts are in the workplace.

❑ Analysts often have no control over the location and the physical layout of the help desk, but they can improve the ergonomics of their personal workspace. A well-arranged workspace can reduce the chances that analysts will suffer repetitive stress injuries such as carpal tunnel syndrome. Analysts can easily adjust their chair, monitor, keyboard and mouse, telephone and headset, and lighting to create a workstation that fits their personal needs.

❐ Customer support is a tough job. In fact, it's one of the most stressful professions you can have. Good work habits help to reduce stress and the possibility of getting injured on the job. They also enable analysts to get and stay organized and to achieve personal success. Analysts working in a help desk setting must strive to *respond*, not react, to daily events. Good work habits can help.

KEY TERMS

accessibility — How easily the help desk can be reached by help desk staff, other employees of the company, and customers.

beginning of day (BOD) — A list of tasks an analyst performs at the start of each workday.

carpal tunnel syndrome (CTS) — A common repetitive stress injury that affects the hands and wrists and is linked to repetitious hand movements, such as typing on a computer keyboard, pinching a mouse, or repeatedly clicking a mouse.

computer vision syndrome — A variety of ailments such as headaches and eyestrain that occur as a result of staring at a computer monitor.

ergonomics — The science of people-machine relationships, intended to maximize productivity by reducing operator fatigue and discomfort.

location — The physical site of the help desk in the building.

macro — A series of menu selections, keystrokes, and/or commands that have been recorded and assigned a name or key combination.

National Institute for Occupational Safety and Health (NIOSH) — A part of the Centers for Disease Control and Prevention (CDC) responsible for conducting research and making recommendations for the prevention of work-related illnesses and injuries; located on the Web at **www.cdc.gov/niash/homepage.html**.

Occupational Safety and Health Administration (OSHA) — An agency of the U.S. Department of Labor that is dedicated to reducing hazards in the workplace and enforcing mandatory job-safety standards. OSHA also implements and improves health programs for workers; located on the Web at **www.osha.gov**.

physical layout — How the help desk is arranged into workspaces.

repetitive stress injuries (RSIs) — Physical symptoms caused by excessive and repeated use of the hands, wrist, and arms; these symptoms occur when people perform tasks using force, repeated strenuous actions, awkward postures, and poorly designed equipment.

time robbers — Activities that take up time and do not add value to the work that analysts perform. In fact, time robbers usually decrease productivity and increase stress levels.

wellness — The condition of good physical and mental health, especially when maintained by proper diet, exercise, and habits.

workspace — An area outfitted with equipment and furnishings for one worker.

REVIEW QUESTIONS

1. Briefly describe the three factors that influence where a help desk is located.

2. Why is the help desk often situated in a centralized location?

3. Describe three ways that companies promote wellness when designing a workplace.

4. What is a workspace?

5. What are the benefits of a well-designed workspace?

6. Briefly describe the three factors that influence a help desk's physical layout.

7. Describe a typical layout for a small help desk.

8. What are the benefits of arranging workstations in clusters, or "pods?"

9. Why do companies install lower cubicle walls in a help desk setting?

10. Define the term *ergonomics*.

11. List four symptoms analysts may experience if their workspace is not arranged ergonomically.

12. What help desk activities put analysts at risk for carpal tunnel syndrome?

13. How should analysts adjust and sit in their chair?

14. How should a monitor be situated on the analyst's desk?

15. When typing and using the mouse, what four work habits can analysts adopt to avoid carpal tunnel syndrome?

16. Describe two benefits of using a headset.

17. What are two factors you might consider when selecting a headset?

18. Briefly explain the impact of having too much light in a workspace, and suggest two ways to alleviate that problem.

19. Briefly explain the impact of having too little light in a workspace, and suggest a way to alleviate that problem.

20. Why is natural light important, and what are two ways that analysts can reap its benefits?

21. What should you do anytime you move into a new office or workspace?

22. What is a BOD, and why is it an important habit?

23. Briefly explain what you should do if faced with more "A" priority tasks than you can complete in one day.

24. What are time robbers, and why should they be eliminated?

25. What can happen if you procrastinate the completion of a task?

26. Why is it important to take breaks?

27. What are the benefits of drinking plenty of water?

28. Why must analysts recognize learning as the labor of the information age?

29. Describe two work habits that enable people to view work as a challenge to be enjoyed.

HANDS-ON PROJECTS

Project 7-1

Learn about ensuring employee comfort and safety. Interview a manager in any business setting (it doesn't have to be a help desk manager) and determine what that person has done to ensure the comfort and safety of his or her employees. Document his or her answers to the following questions:

❑ What have they (or their company) done to:

- Provide for the comfort and safety of their employees?

- Facilitate communication and the sharing of resources?

❑ Do they teach their employees about ergonomics? If so, what components of their work environment can employees adjust?

- If they do teach their employees about ergonomics, do they feel these efforts are beneficial? If so, in what ways?

- If they do not teach their employees about ergonomics, do they feel it would be beneficial to do so? If so, in what ways?

Project 7-2

Learn about carpal tunnel syndrome. Research the following about carpal tunnel syndrome: what causes it, how it is treated, and how it can be prevented. Web sites you may want to visit include **www.ctsplace.com** and **www.webmd.com** (search for "carpal tunnel syndrome"). Prepare a paper that answers the following questions:

❑ What are the symptoms of carpal tunnel syndrome?

❑ How is it caused?

❑ How is it treated, or how can its symptoms be controlled?

❑ How long does it take to relieve the symptoms?

❑ How can it be prevented?

Project 7-3

Evaluate your workspace. A properly arranged workspace increases productivity and reduces stress and fatigue. Look closely at the workspace where you complete most of your writing, computer work, and reading or studying. This workspace could be at home, work, or school. Then, briefly outline your answers to the following questions:

❏ Have you ever experienced any of the negative symptoms of a poorly designed workspace, such as headaches, wrist and shoulder pain, back pain, or swollen ankles?

- If so, given what you have learned in this chapter, were your symptoms the result of poor workspace design or poor work habits?

❏ In what ways can you improve the ergonomics of your workspace?

❏ In what ways can you improve your work habits?

Unless you share your workspace, arrange your workspace so that it meets your ergonomic requirements.

7

Project 7-4

Correct your workspace lighting. Assess the lighting in the area where you do most of your reading, writing, and computer work. Do you have adequate lighting to read, write, use your computer (if you have one), and so on without experiencing negative side effects. If not, use the information presented in this chapter to determine what you can do to correct the lighting in this space. Prepare a paper that describes the steps you can take to improve the lighting situation and the negative side effects the steps will alleviate. If the lighting situation is acceptable, explain why.

Project 7-5

Reduce noise in the help desk. Assemble a team of at least three of your classmates. Brainstorm and prepare a list of ways that help desk staff can work as a team and as individuals to reduce the noise that can occur in a help desk setting. For example, the help desk might avoid the use of speakerphones.

Project 7-6

Create a BOD for a typical day. For example, if your day usually involves going to school and going to work, prepare a list of tasks you must complete before leaving the house to ensure that you are ready for both. While creating your BOD, consider the last couple of weeks. Were there days when you felt disorganized or when you forgot items you needed? Include tasks on your BOD that can prevent the frustration of this type of situation. Were there days when you felt you had your act together? Include tasks on your BOD that enable you to regularly feel confident and organized. Post your BOD somewhere you can view it each day in an effort to make these tasks a habit.

Project 7-7

Practice using a mirror. Place a mirror near the telephone you usually use, and then look in it before you answer the phone and while you are talking on the phone to a friend or family member. Regardless of how you feel, practice putting a smile on your face and using a pleasant upbeat tone every time you answer the telephone. Experiment with different facial expressions while you are on the telephone. For example, if you are laughing, try to look sad. Or if you are frustrated, try smiling. Notice how these different facial expressions affect the tone of your voice and your interactions with the person on the other end of the telephone. Pretend that what you are seeing in the mirror is what the person on the telephone would see if you were speaking with them in person, and make sure you are using appropriate expressions. Write down how the mirror has affected your conversations.

Project 7-8

Identify time robbers. Review the list of time robbers discussed in this chapter. Make a list of any time-robbing activities that regularly cause you to waste time. For example, you may regularly procrastinate tasks or allow your desk and files to become unorganized. Go to the library or search the Web for information about time management. Identify three specific things you can do to eliminate or minimize the source of your time robbers. Prepare a brief paper describing (1) your time robbers, (2) your course of action, and (3) any goals you may choose to set. For example, you may set a goal to clean off your desk within three days.

Project 7-9

Learn about the benefits of water. This chapter briefly discussed the benefits of drinking plenty of water. Visit a Web site such as **www.avsands.com/Health/Advice/benefitsdrink_ayj_av.htm** or enter "health benefits of drinking water" into your Web browser. Prepare a report that provides additional detail about the benefits of water. Include the following:

❏ The amount of water you should drink each day.

❏ The symptoms of not drinking enough water.

❏ The symptoms of drinking a sufficient amount of water.

❏ Tips for consuming an adequate amount of water each day.

CASE PROJECTS

1. Design New Help Desk Facilities

You are the supervisor of a small help desk (seven analysts) and your manager has just informed you that you will be moving to a new building at the end of the year. Your manager asks you to suggest the best way to design the new facilities. She would also like you to recommend ways to make your new facilities "analyst-friendly." Prepare a sketch of your suggested layout, and provide notes that outline the rationale for your design. You may want to look on the Web or do research at the library to get ideas for the layout.

2. Report on the Benefits of Headsets

The company where you work has decided to acquire headsets. Your manager asks you to do some research and present a brief report to the help desk team about the different styles of headsets that are available. Prepare a report that includes a table listing at least five headset styles and the benefits of each.

3. Ergonomics 101

You've been hired as a consultant to help a large help desk implement an ergonomics program. Do research to determine the steps involved in setting up an ergonomics program. Prepare a brief report for management outlining the steps to be taken and the benefits to be derived. Include in your report steps management should take to ensure the ongoing success of this program.

7

8

CUSTOMER SUPPORT AS A PROFESSION

> **In this chapter you will learn:**
> - Help desk industry trends and directions
> - The role of certification in the help desk
> - How to maintain your technical skills while learning help desk management skills
> - How to prepare for a future as a help desk professional

Tremendous opportunities exist for people interested in pursuing a help desk career. There are an increasing number of opportunities in the help desk industry because companies worldwide realize that they must provide high-quality customer service and support or lose their customers to a company that does. Departments that deliver internal customer support realize that they too must provide high-quality service and support and that they must understand and align their services with their company's business goals. The most successful companies in the future will be those that keep a close eye on business and help desk industry trends and embrace the ones that enable them to achieve their goals. These companies need and reward people who are innovative, flexible, and professional, and who thrive on satisfying customers.

Companies and departments worldwide are working hard to attract and keep people who have the energy, enthusiasm, and skills needed to deliver the quality support services their customers demand. These organizations are seeking people who have the desire and ability not only to support the increasingly complex technologies being used by customers, but also to utilize and promote the equally complex technologies that help desks use to deliver support. These companies also need people who can assume the increasingly important supporting roles in a help desk such as knowledge base administration, service management and improvement, and technical support for the help desk's tools and technologies.

The support industry is growing and changing at the speed of light. To seize the opportunities offered by this dynamic industry you must be aware of help desk industry trends and objectively evaluate how those trends affect your skills. You must determine your strengths and interests and seek out jobs and experiences in which you can excel. A successful help desk career occurs when you continuously leverage your experiences, refine your skills, and keep an eye on the future.

HELP DESK INDUSTRY TRENDS AND DIRECTIONS

An irreversible dependence on technology has prompted customers to demand ever-cheaper, faster, and better support services. This demand has prompted companies to considerably expand the role of the help desk. Although in the past companies considered help desk jobs to be entry-level positions, today they elevate the help desk to a more strategic position in recognition that the help desk can and does contribute to the company's bottom line.

The help desk offers—and will for the foreseeable future continue to offer—considerable opportunities to people who want to be a part of this dynamic and growing industry. For example, pursuing a career in the help desk provides the opportunity to:

- Use and support state-of-the-art technology.

- Work with people and with technology.

- Use previously acquired skills, such as customer service skills, to gain entry into the computer industry.

- Gain entry into a company at which you want to work.

- Learn about all the different departments within a company and gain a full appreciation of the opportunities available within that company.

- Advance your career either along a technical career path or a managerial career path.

As help desks continue to evolve, they face many challenging business trends. These trends influence the direction in which the help desk industry is heading and the opportunities available to people pursuing a help desk career. These trends, many of which were touched on in previous chapters, include those listed in Figure 8-1.

- 24 × 7 support
- Fee-based support
- Global support
- Help desk as a profession
- Increased dependence on technology
- Increased workload
- Mobile workforce support
- Multi-channel support
- Outsourcing
- Web-based support

8

Figure 8-1   Help desk industry trends

Each of these trends affects how help desks are run and the opportunities they present to help desk analysts.

24 × 7 Support

Customers are challenging companies to provide **24 × 7 support**, which means that help desk services are provided 24 hours a day, 7 days a week. According to the Help Desk Institute, 31 percent of its members have at least one employee on-site 24 hours a day, up from 21 percent in 2001 ("Help Desk Institute Practices Survey," Help Desk Institute, 2002). The need to support an increasingly self-sufficient customer base, a global customer community, a mobile workforce, or a part of the business that operates around the clock, such as a manufacturing facility, leads to this demand for continual support.

24 × 7 support does not, however, mean that help desk analysts must be on-site at all times. Many help desks use their phone system to direct customers to their Web site after hours where they can help themselves, submit a problem or request, or obtain the status of an outstanding problem or request. Some help desks use their phone system to transfer callers to analysts who are working at home or instruct callers about how to obtain emergency support if needed—typically by using a pager to contact an on call analyst.

Emergency support is often provided by on call analysts who carry pagers. The compensation that on call analysts receive varies by company. For example, some companies pay an hourly overtime rate, which is typically 1.5 times the analyst's base rate. Some companies offer analysts compensatory time (comp time), which means they give employees time off when they work extra-long hours. Some companies convert pager availability time to comp time. For example, two to four hours of pager time equals one hour of comp time. Other companies are more generous. A night of pager time equals a day off. Conversely, some companies simply expect analysts to carry a pager as a regular part of their job. They may, however, pay a flat rate per incident, which means analysts are compensated only when they actually handle customer contacts, or they may pay a bonus when an analyst spends a lot of time working on a particularly severe or complex problem.

This 24 × 7 support trend creates many opportunities for help desk professionals. It creates positions for help desk analysts as well as positions for team leaders and supervisors. Companies that provide 24 × 7 support often employ three work shifts: a day shift, a midday (or mid) shift, and a night shift. The hours that these shifts work vary from company to company.

 Companies often pay a shift premium, or shift differential, to employees who work an undesirable shift such as the night shift. The shift periods that qualify for a premium and the amount paid varies from one company to the next. Most shift premiums range from 5 percent to 8 percent of an employee's salary.

Companies that provide 24 × 7 support may also offer very flexible schedules for their employees. For example, people may work 10 hours per day for 4 days and then have 3 days off. Or they may work part-time, such as 20 hours per week. These scheduling alternatives help accommodate the needs of people who want to continue their education, have family demands, and so forth.

This trend also creates opportunities for people who assume supporting roles in the help desk. For example, the help desk's technical support staff maintains the help desk's Web site and makes it possible for customers to gain access to Web-based self-services after hours. Knowledge engineers also make it possible for customers to get answers to FAQs and search knowledge bases for solutions after hours.

For most companies, demand for support is typically light after hours. As a result, support may be provided by a service agency (discussed below), by an on-call employee, or via the Web. Customers may not receive the same depth of service after hours that they receive during normal business hours. Most customers are satisfied, however, if they are at least able to find answers on their own, submit a request to obtain service during normal help desk business hours, or obtain support in the event of an emergency.

Fee-Based Support

With **fee-based support**, customers pay for support services on a per-use basis. In other words, each time a customer calls the help desk or each time a customer accesses the company's Web site for support, a fee is charged. Help desks that charge for support then have funds available to acquire resources and continuously improve their services. This creates job opportunities. Also, charging for support is an effective way to manage customer expectations. For example, the help desk can charge a higher rate for premium or value-added services. As a result, higher-level, more challenging, and higher-paying job positions are created.

Chapter 2 discussed some of the advantages and disadvantages of this practice in the "Help Desks as Cost Centers or Profit Centers" section.

The trend is that some Web-based support services will most likely continue to be free, such as FAQs, online knowledge bases, downloadable software fixes, and so forth. However, more help desks will likely charge for at least some of their services; for example, their premium services.

People entering the help desk industry need to be aware of this trend and determine whether and how their employer, or prospective employer, charges for support. A company's policy on this practice greatly influences how analysts account for their time and effort as well as how they interact with customers. For example, analysts who work at help desks that charge for their services are typically required to verify that a customer is entitled to support before they begin working on a problem. Help desk managers value people who understand that the help desk is a "business within a business" that must justify its existence and that can be run profitably.

Global Support

Some companies are being challenged to support customers anywhere in the world. This demand for **global support** may be caused by the need to support a large company that has foreign divisions and subsidiaries or by the need to support customers who are doing business with the company through the Web. Companies providing global support must address the culture, language, and legal issues that come with working in an international market. There are several ways they can do that, including:

- **Regional, in country help desks**—Traditionally, large companies establish multiple, in country help desks that each provide localized support. These in country help desks are able to provide highly personalized service because they understand issues such as language, culture, and local expectations. Some companies prefer this highly personalized form of support even though it can be expensive. To mitigate their costs, these companies may require that all help desks use the same processes and technologies. Each help desk may also produce a standard set of metrics that are forwarded to the corporate headquarters for review. Conversely, some companies allow each help desk to establish its own processes and technologies and focus only on its own needs and the needs of its customers.

■ **Follow the sun support**—Follow the sun support means that companies establish several help desks (typically three); each on a different continent, and as one help desk closes, another automatically opens and begins supporting customers. For example, if a company has help desks in the United States, the United Kingdom, and Australia, when the United States completes its normal business day it transfers support to the help desk in the United Kingdom. When its business day is complete, the United Kingdom help desk transfers support to the Australian help desk, which transfers support back to the United States when its day is done. These help desks use common tools and common processes and are able to share common data sources such as knowledge bases and asset and configuration management databases. The advantage of this approach is that the company is able to leverage technology and maximize its ROI, while analysts within each help desk are able to deliver personalized service to their customers—that is, service that addresses issues such as language and culture. Large, multinational companies often take a follow the sun approach.

■ **One global support desk**—One global support desk means that one physical help desk provides 24 × 7 support. This approach tends to be less costly than follow the sun support because companies are not required to set up and staff multiple facilities, nor are they required to replicate their processes and technologies across multiple sites. These companies must, however, address issues such as language and culture, and they must also determine how to deliver localized support when necessary. For example, a help desk may need to determine how to ship a replacement laptop to a mobile worker in another country. Companies that need to provide global support but lack a large support staff, such as a small Web-based company, often opt to have a single global support desk.

Regardless of how companies provide global support, this trend presents a number of opportunities for people pursuing a help desk career. First, companies that provide global support often operate 24 hours a day, 7 days a week, which means more job opportunities. Second, people with the right skills may be given the opportunity to travel and gain experience working abroad. Third, global support often requires people who speak multiple languages and understand the cultural issues that are unique to a particular part of the world. For example, in Germany people consider it rude to address someone by their first name prior to being given permission. In the United States, however, people rarely use last names anymore. Also, while some companies provide information and deliver support through the Web in English only, others offer a choice of languages. These companies depend on their analysts to translate solutions and publish them in a variety of languages. Companies that provide global support value and are willing to reward people who understand cultural differences and can read and write multiple languages as well as speak them. Rewards may include higher salaries and perks such as the opportunity to telecommute or travel abroad.

Help Desk as a Profession

Historically, the help desk was considered a stepping stone to other professions. Today, a number of trends indicate that the help desk has been elevated to a profession in and of itself. For example:

- According to the Help Desk Institute, more than 69 percent of help desks report to a Chief Information Officer (CIO) or senior executive. This shows the growing importance of help desks within companies.

- Many companies have rewritten their help desk job descriptions to create higher-level job positions, which reflects the expanded responsibility of the help desk. Because the expanded responsibility includes the help desk being asked to solve more problems at level one, many companies are increasing the amount of training and authority given to analysts. In addition, some companies have been raising the starting salaries for help desk positions.

- An increasing number of organizations offer bonuses based on a person's performance and ability to satisfy customers.

- Some companies are creating new team leader and supervisor positions within the help desk in recognition of the need to provide feedback, coaching, and counseling to front-line staff. As a result, more management positions are available.

- Some companies rotate personnel through different positions in the department or company in an effort to reduce burnout and increase the experience and skill of help desk analysts. This practice enables front-line staff to acquire a broad base of experience and to better understand the needs of the business. This practice also enables help desks to reduce turnover and retain the knowledge and experience of seasoned analysts.

- Individual and site certification programs (discussed below) are increasingly being used by help desk managers and help desk analysts to demonstrate their business, technical, soft, and self-management skills.

The help desk is no longer an entry-level position that people enter and leave as if through a revolving door. The number of opportunities the help desk offers continues to expand, as shown in Figure 8-2.

8

Figure 8-2   Career path opportunity within and beyond the help desk

This figure illustrates the numerous career path opportunities that exist within and beyond the help desk.

Increased Dependence on Technology

Our dependence on computing technology and on technology in general is becoming increasingly prevalent. Even the smallest businesses tend to use computers to manage some aspect of their operations. Children regularly use computers in class and often need one to do their homework. At home, many people use computers to manage their personal finances, research vacation destinations and make travel arrangements, or run a home-based business. Many people would not think of leaving home without a cell phone, laptop, or a handheld computing device such as a PDA. This dependence on technology has caused a huge technology support demand, which will continue to grow.

The fact that computing technology is beginning to converge with communications technology is further increasing our dependence on technology. Soon, many living rooms will house a device that looks like a TV and functions like a computer. These WebTV devices are already in the marketplace and, in the coming years, this technology will inevitably become cheaper, more readily available, and eventually the norm.

Also, the ubiquitous computing wave is beginning to arrive. **Ubiquitous computing** is an environment where people have access to their information and computing systems from public shared access points, such as airports automated teller machines

(ATMs), hotel rooms and lobbies, libraries, retail stores, and supermarkets. As illustrated in Figure 8-3, access to these computing devices will be much like today's access to public telephones or ATMs.

Figure 8-3   Ubiquitous computing devices

We can only guess how this need to ensure access whenever and wherever customers want it will impact the support industry. You can be sure, however, that the demand for support will be great while this technology is maturing.

Increased Workload

The help desk is experiencing an increased workload due to several trends, including the expanded role of the help desk evidenced by the shift toward the support center. This convergence of the help desk with other support functions, such as network support, field support, and systems administration, has broadened the help desk's scope of responsibility and created jobs that require more advanced skills, pay better, and offer a greater diversity of advancement opportunities for help desk analysts

The increasing complexity of technology and the speed with which companies introduce new technologies also lead to a great demand for support. META Group estimates that the adoption of handheld personal computing devices and wireless devices alone will cause IT service and support demands to double through 2004 ("New-Age Support Requirements," META Group, Inc., October 2002).

This constant barrage of new technologies not only creates job opportunities, it also requires people in support positions to continuously update their skills. Many companies offer a considerable amount of training in an effort to attract and retain analysts who have, and want to maintain, state-of-the-art skills.

A third trend that is causing increased workload is the growing number of multivendor incidents that help desks must handle. **Multivendor support** is support for customers who use products developed by a number of different vendors. Multivendor support can be difficult and time-consuming to provide because it may not be clear if the problem lies in the product the customer is using, in a related or dependent product developed and supported by another vendor, or somewhere in between. For example, when a printer doesn't work, the problem may be with the printer, the printer drivers, the software application being used to print, a network device, or the network connection, all of which may be manufactured by different vendors. Multivendor support incidents can cost many times more than those that involve a single vendor. Some companies strive to minimize this cost by hiring people who have strong problem-solving skills and a broad base of product knowledge and experience, as opposed to extensive knowledge of a single product. Because customers quickly become dissatisfied when they are repeatedly told, "it's someone else's problem," companies are also seeking people who take ownership of incidents and follow through to ensure that problems are resolved.

Mobile Workforce Support

A growing mobile workforce is another of the reasons that many help desks are experiencing an increased demand for support. According to International Data Corporation (IDC), the number of mobile workers in the United States will increase from 92 million in 2001 to 105 million by 2006. This means that roughly 66 percent of the U.S. workforce will be working in a mobile capacity ("U.S. Mobile Workforce to Grow," International Data Corporation, July 2002). IDC estimates there will be over 20.1 million mobile workers in Europe by 2005, up from 6.2 million in 2000 ("Western European Teleworking: Mobile Workers and Telecommuters, 2000-2005," International Data Corporation, October 2001).

The variety of mobile and wireless devices and applications and the speed at which individuals are adopting these devices make supporting mobile workers particularly challenging for help desks. Gartner, Inc. estimates that by 2004, 60 percent of office workers will carry or own at least three mobile devices. This constant barrage of new technologies and a lack of standards in this area are causing help desks to realize that they must assess the skills of their staff, redesign their business processes, evaluate their tools, and rethink their data and information needs in order to address mobile computing requirements.

Increasingly, help desks are helping to define standards in terms of what mobile devices and applications best serve the needs of users and ensure the security of corporate data assets. Help desks are also modifying SLAs to include mobile computing policies and procedures, and address asset management and configuration issues such as when and how to swap out failing devices with usable devices.

Multi-Channel Support

For years most help desks have offered customers alternatives to the telephone such as voice mail, e-mail, and some Web-based support. Help desks have historically, however, viewed the telephone as the "official" support channel. Accordingly, help desks require analysts to log all or most telephone calls, and telephony-centric metrics such as average speed of answer and abandon rate are the primary measures used to gauge help desk performance. Alternative support channels are often handled informally—for example, they may not be logged—and few, if any, metrics are captured.

Several factors are causing help desks to look at multi-channel support differently now.

1. Customers are increasingly using alternative channels, prompting help desks to realize that they must handle these support channels in a more formal manner. All contacts must be logged, and metrics such as response time must be used to ensure that all contacts are handled in a timely manner.

2. Customers' expectations relative to alternative channels are changing, particularly relative to response time. Customers increasingly expect help desks to respond to e-mail messages and Web submissions in a more real-time manner.

3. Customers are increasingly willing to use the help desk's Web site first, and use e-mail or the telephone only when additional help is needed.

And herein lies the trend. Web technology is becoming more and more ubiquitous. Help desk Web sites are becoming more robust and real-time. Smart help desks know that customers will embrace their Web site only if its content is current, well organized, and easy to use. These same help desks also know that, as discussed previously, some customers are still going to use channels such as the telephone and e-mail to obtain support.

As a result, help desks face the challenge of ensuring that they are capturing the data needed to efficiently and effectively manage the various support channels they offer to customers. This means they must determine how best to integrate the various tools needed to capture this data, such as ACDs, e-mail response management systems, incident tracking systems, and Web-based systems, to name just a few. Help desks must also begin to produce meaningful metrics such as response time and cost per contact relative to each channel they offer. They must understand that when sites are well designed, Web-based contacts cost *less* than contacts that involve analysts, but they are not free. Companies must bear the cost of maintaining their Web sites and they must work hard to keep them useful and up-to-date, or customers will return to the telephone. Companies must also understand that telephone contacts will increase in cost more, because they represent complex and unique problems that typically cannot be resolved using self-services.

Multi-channel support requires help desks to determine how best to utilize each of the components discussed throughout this book: people, processes, technology, and information. Many companies are taking the first step toward meeting this challenge by redesigning their business processes. By redesigning

8

their business processes, help desks are able to determine how best to utilize their existing people and technology, before hiring new people or acquiring new technology. Help desks can use information to determine which processes need to be redesigned, or designed, and they can also use information to measure the efficiency and effectiveness of their new processes.

Outsourcing

Many of the trends discussed above such as 24×7 support, global support, increased dependence on technology, increased workload, and mobile workforce support are prompting an increase in help desk outsourcing. Recall that outsourcing is when companies have help desk services provided by an outside supplier (service agency or outsourcer), instead of providing them in-house. Factors that prompt companies to consider outsourcing include outsourcer experience, flexibility such as an outsourcer's ability to accommodate peak periods, seasonal call volumes, or after-hours call volumes, and the opportunity to leverage an outsourcer's investment and use of new technologies. Frequently, companies are partnering with these external service agencies to deliver high-quality support services at a reduced cost. Some companies outsource all of their support services. Others outsource a portion of their services, such as after-hours support, hardware support and repair, or off-the-shelf PC software support. Some companies outsource support for these industry standard hardware and software products so they can dedicate their resources to supporting systems developed in-house. This desire to outsource all or some support services has spawned a tremendous increase in the number of companies that offer help desk outsourcing services and, consequently, the number of job opportunities.

 Outsourcing requires that the two companies involved—the service agency and the company that hires them—work closely together to define the services to be delivered and the expected level of performance.

This outsourcing trend represents a great opportunity for people who want to pursue a help desk career because it has created many jobs that offer a lot of flexibility. Each outsourcer needs the right number of people with the right skills to support its clients. Outsourcers are constantly looking for people who have great customer service skills along with the necessary mix of business and technical skills to satisfy their customers' needs, which naturally vary considerably from one customer to the next. As a result, people have the opportunity to work with a diversity of customers while being employed by one company. Outsourcers often base raises and bonuses on people's performance and ability to satisfy customers. The best and the brightest people are regularly rewarded and promoted. Service agencies also tend to offer flexible work hours and even the opportunity to work on a contract basis. This means that people who want to work for a time and then take time off (for example, to go to school or to care for a child or family member) have the opportunity to do so as long as they give the service agency adequate notice.

People working in help desks tend to be frightened by the prospect of outsourcing because it can result in the loss of jobs. However, successful outsourcing *creates* job opportunities for the external service agency, which they may then offer to help desk employees. It is not uncommon for companies to allow a service agency to hire qualified members of their help desk staff when it takes over support because knowledge about the customer community is very important. This is particularly true when a company decides to **insource** its support services, which means the service agency employees who deliver support services are physically located at the company's facilities. Companies may insource for security reasons, or because they want to leverage an existing investment in technology. Whether a company outsources or insources its support services, people with the right skills are valued.

Web-Based Support

Customers have come to expect support organizations to offer Web-based services such as knowledge bases, FAQs, Web forms that can be used to submit problems and requests, and so forth. This trend has and will continue to have a considerable impact on the support industry because the Web is changing the way support is delivered and the skills required to deliver it.

A common misconception is that Web-based services eliminate the need for help desk analysts. For example, some companies believe that if they provide self-services such as FAQs and solutions to known problems on the Web, customers will find the answers on their own and the company can downsize its help desk. Although it is true that some companies may be able to downsize their help desks, there will always be a need for qualified analysts. Some customers simply prefer to speak with a human being, whereas others want to interact real-time with analysts online. Also, new technologies are being introduced regularly that arrive with a whole new set of questions and problems. Finally, complex problems require the attention of people with strong problem-solving skills or perhaps even a team of resources working together to identify a resolution. Help desk analysts—not technology—accommodate these varying customer requirements.

Although Web-based support does not eliminate the need for qualified help desk analysts, it does change the skills they must have and the types of problems and requests they resolve. Because customers can handle their simpler problems through the Web, they contact the help desk with their more complex problems. As a result, good problem-solving skills are increasingly important for analysts. Writing skills have greater importance because analysts: (1) use these skills to interact with customers through e-mail and Web-based systems, and (2) contribute to the written information that customers access on the Web. Internet skills such as the ability to use browsers, find content online, and use Internet-based diagnostic tools (for example remote control systems) also are increasingly imperative.

Web-based support also creates a need for people to develop, maintain, and support the help desk's systems. Roles such as technical support and knowledge base administration have greater importance as help desks rely more heavily on their support systems, and use these systems to collect and maintain content for their Web sites. Help desks also need

8

people to embrace trends such as self-healing, mass-healing, and assisted service, and to evaluate and deploy the technologies that enable these services. Recall that self-healing systems are hardware devices and software applications that have the ability to detect and correct problems on their own. **Mass-healing** systems enable help desks to detect and repair problems across the entire enterprise. For example, mass-healing systems provide help desks with the ability to detect and eliminate viruses that may be infecting the company's networked PCs. Help desks also need people to evaluate and deploy assisted services such as remote control systems that enable analysts to diagnose and correct problems, provide training, and distribute software to customers via the Web.

Web-based support does not reduce the need for a well-trained, professional help desk staff. It does, however, free analysts to handle more challenging problems and work on projects aimed at increasing help desk efficiency and enhancing customer self-sufficiency.

DAVID LISS
USER SUPPORT COORDINATOR
SOUTHWEST MISSOURI STATE UNIVERSITY
SPRINGFIELD, MISSOURI
HELPDESK.SMSU.EDU

Southwest Missouri State University (SMSU) is a major university with more than 18,000 students from the United States and 85 other countries. The Computer Services Help Desk at SMSU is a division of the User Support department within Computer Services. It is part of a decentralized network of support organizations that deliver campus user support.

Tasks. User Support is the point of first contact for information and problems regarding University computing resources. The User Support Group maintains three open-access computer labs—one of which is open 24 hours a day—that provide students availability on more than 250 computers. Students obtain support through the computer labs by calling, visiting, or accessing the Open-Access Labs Web site. Students who are staying in the residence halls and connecting their computers to the campus network obtain support from a help desk that reports to the Department of Residence Life and Services—as opposed to Computer Services.

User Support also runs the Computer Services Help Desk, which answers questions, provides technical support, and delivers self-services via the Help Desk's Web site to faculty and staff on campus. Additionally, we assist faculty and staff with the installation of new computers, software, hardware, and peripherals as well as provide training and documentation on topics such as Web development, off-campus dial-up, and various application programs.

The Help Desk's Web site provides a one-stop resource for people to learn about the services offered by User Support and to get answers to their technology-related questions. The Web site serves as a portal where faculty and staff can learn how to contact the Help Desk and view important Help Desk news. The site also provides a series of links designed to direct users to categories of information such as Need Help?, Accounts & E-Mail, IT Training, Supported Software, Lab & Classroom support, Anti-Virus, Internet Access, and IT Resources.

University faculty and staff with computer-related problems can visit the Help Desk's Web site 24 hours a day and access the IT Knowledge Base, obtain answers to frequently asked questions (FAQs), change or reset their password, obtain information about the latest virus threat, or use an online form to enter a service request. They can also call, visit, or e-mail the Help Desk during its normal business hours to request service. Priority is given to answering the telephone, followed by walk-ins, self-service requests, and then e-mail.

Per their Service Level Agreement (SLA) with SMSU faculty and staff, the Help Desk aims for an 80 percent first-call resolution of all problems reported to the Help Desk. To ensure it has the knowledge and resources needed to achieve this objective, the Help Desk regularly evaluates software and maintains a list of software

8

for which it provides Full or Limited support. The products that fall into the Full and Limited support categories are determined by factors such as campus standardization on the software application, support availability from the manufacturer, and compatibility considerations. The supported software list also contains products that are unsupported, which means that User Support will not load the software on University computers nor will it provide support in the event of a problem.

Organization. We have a number of different job positions within User Support including Lab Support Specialists and a Lab Support Administrator who oversee the open-access computer labs, a Technical Trainer, an Assistive Technology Support Specialist who provides assessment and support services to individuals with disabilities, and Microcomputer Support Specialists and a Microcomputer Support Administrator who run the Help Desk.

Monday through Friday from 8 a.m. to 5 p.m. the Help Desk is staffed with Microcomputer Support Specialists who serve as Level 1 and Level 2 analysts. Level 1 analysts attempt to answer technical support calls over the phone. If the support call is not resolved within roughly 5 minutes, the call may be transferred to a Level 2 analyst. If a Level 1 analyst determines that the support call will require an on-site visit, an "active" service ticket is entered and the customer is sent an e-mail containing his or her ticket number and an estimated turnaround time that is determined by the priority of the problem. A Microcomputer Support Specialist is then assigned to the ticket and becomes responsible for its resolution.

Four full-time Microcomputer Support Specialists and 10 student workers rotate daily between taking calls and handling on-site visits. During a typical shift, one full-time analyst and one student worker take calls on Level 1 support, while two full-time analysts and the student workers, who work varying shifts, make site visits. The four full-time Microcomputer Support Specialists also rotate through the Level 2 analyst role. The Level 2 analyst handles complex problems along with e-mail and self-service requests. The Level 2 analyst also serves as supervisor for the day, which involves handling critical problems, assigning tickets to analysts handling site visits, and so forth.

The supervisor also forwards tickets, based on the area of responsibility, to any of the 15 Distributed User Support Specialists who work directly for one of the seven colleges that make up the University—as opposed to working for Computer Services—and who specialize in the needs of that college.

Besides managing all aspects of the Help Desk, the Microcomputer Support Administrator handles a variety of tasks such as administering the User Support and Lab Support servers, assisting VIP customers, and maintaining the Help Desk's

Web site. He also administers the IT Knowledge Base by reviewing submitted articles, putting them into a standard format, and adding them to the knowledge base.

Philosophy. A central goal of the Computer Services department is customer satisfaction and so when hiring, we look for individuals with excellent communication skills and experience dealing with people. Without discounting technical skills and abilities, we look for people who possess exceptional interpersonal skills and will take care of our customers before, during, and after their technical situation. We meet regularly as a group as well as with the other 15 Distributed User Support Specialists to ensure that everyone involved in supporting the University's technology users has the information and resources they need to achieve our goals.

Our job is to ensure that the University's faculty, staff, and students have the technology they need and to make that technology easy for people to use. It is bothersome to see people struggling with technology and, because our focus is on people first and technology second, we look for individuals who have the attitude, experience, and desire to help people and make their computer-related problems go away. If we can make technology an "invisible" tool that our customers use to do their jobs more effectively and efficiently, then we have accomplished a goal that many IT departments seldom achieve.

8

ROLE OF CERTIFICATION IN THE HELP DESK

The idea of certifying professionals has existed for years. Examples include certified public accountants (CPAs), certified electricians, and certified mechanics. Recall that certification is the act of awarding someone a document after that person demonstrates that he or she has certain skills and knowledge about a particular topic or area. Often, the person must pass a test after receiving instruction or doing self-study. Some certification programs require people to pass an oral exam or complete a project. As a result, companies find that certification is an excellent indicator of a person's knowledge about a given subject. Many certification programs require people to periodically renew their certificates. Companies view a person who maintains his or her certification as willing to learn new skills and stay current, which are desirable characteristics in today's ever-changing workplace.

Only since the late 1980s have managers recognized the importance of certifying IT professionals. This recognition was prompted by the growing complexity of technology coupled with the shortage of people with IT skills. Early IT certification programs focused primarily on analysts' technical skills. In the early 1990s, the support industry, in an effort to elevate the role of the help desk, began to offer certification programs geared specifically to help desk professionals. These certification programs consider the soft and self-management skills needed by help desk professionals. Now that certification is available, companies more and more often use it to distinguish between job candidates. Some companies even require certification as a condition of employment. Although these companies might hire people who are not certified, uncertified employees may receive a lower salary and be required to obtain their certification within a predefined time.

There are two types of certification programs available to help desk professionals: *technical certifications* that are vendor specific and *help desk certifications* that are vendor neutral. Help desk certifications enable companies to certify the individual managers and analysts within their help desk or their entire help desk. Figure 8-4 lists the leading help desk certification programs:

- Help Desk Institute certification
- Service & Support Professionals Association (SSPA) certification
- STI Knowledge certification

Figure 8-4   Help desk certification programs

These certification programs enable individuals to focus on and demonstrate that they possess the industry knowledge and soft skills needed to deliver excellent customer support, and enable help desks to benchmark their practices against industry best practices.

Help Desk Institute Certification

Help Desk Institute certification is an open, standards-based, internationally recognized certification program for help desk professionals (**www.thinkhdi.com/cert/ certoverview.asp**). Certification levels include Customer Support Specialist (CSS), Help Desk Analyst (HDA), Help Desk Senior Analyst (HDSA), and Help Desk Manager (HDM).

Service & Support Professionals Association (SSPA) Certification

The SSPA individual certification training program is designed to prepare support professionals at all levels to perform within industry standards and to earn international certification (**www.thesspa.com/programs/certifications/indiv.asp**). The five levels of SSPA individual certification available include: Customer Service Qualified, Certified Support Professional, Certified Support Specialist, Certified Support Manager, and Certified Support Executive. The SSPA also offers the Support Center Practices (SCP) site certification program that evaluates help desk performance relative to 11 major criteria such as people programs, total quality management, productivity tools, and performance metrics (**www.thesspa.com/programs/certifications/site.asp**). SSPA's programs are geared to companies that provide external customer support.

STI Knowledge Certification

STI Knowledge offers Help Desk 2000 certification (**www.stiknowledge.com/ certification_advisory/courses.asp#hd2k**) for help desk analysts, managers, and directors. Help Desk 2000 programs involve a stringent testing process that includes a three-hour written exam along with an oral exam or a specific help desk project. Certification levels include: Certified Help Desk Professional, Certified Help Desk Manager, and Certified Help Desk Director. STI Knowledge also offers the Core 2000 certification program, which enables companies to certify their entire help desk (**www.stiknowledge.com/ certification_advisory/comp_certification.asp**).

Certification programs can be costly and time-consuming to complete successfully, and so individuals and sites that become certified truly exemplify world-class service providers. Certification represents industry recognition and the ability to demonstrate a level of competency based on industry best practices. Help desk certification also offers individuals and sites education about the support industry—how it works, and how help desks and individuals within help desks contribute to their company's strategic business goals. As a result, individuals and sites that complete help desk certification programs gain a bigger picture perspective than technical certification programs tend to offer.

That does not mean that technical certification programs aren't important and valuable. Many individuals are opting to obtain technical certification from third-party vendors. Figure 8-5 shows the top ten technical certification programs viewed as most important by participants in a 2001 study conducted by the Association of Support Professionals:

● Microsoft	● Sun
● Cisco	● Hewlett-Packard
● Oracle	● Compaq
● CompTIA	● IBM
● Novell	● Citrix

Figure 8-5   Important technical certification programs

Although becoming certified does not automatically guarantee an individual will be hired or promoted, being certified does enable individuals to distinguish themselves from other job candidates and may make them eligible for raises or bonuses. For example, some companies have a formal policy about raises for certification, whereas others leave it to the discretion of the employee's manager. Some companies pay a one-time bonus— typically between $250 and $1,000—to employees who become certified.

One of the most common incentives is for companies to pay for the training and for the cost of the exam that leads to certification. Many companies pay for certification to

8

reward their employees, and they view it as a way to retain people who have the skills needed to support today's sophisticated technology environments. As this cost can be substantial, some companies require individuals to sign a contract that requires them to stay at the company for a specified period of time once they become certified. Employees who choose to leave the company before the specified time may be required to reimburse the company all or a portion of the cost of certification.

Some companies also reward individuals who demonstrate that they are applying the lessons learned through certification and sharing those lessons with others. For example, some companies compare metrics before certification—such as first contact resolution and customer satisfaction—to metrics after certification, in an effort to validate, quantify, and ultimately reward an increase in a person's level of competence.

Certifications are becoming a necessary credential for help desk professionals. Managers value people who dedicate the time and effort necessary to get certified. As a result, certified individuals often get better jobs, receive higher salaries, and advance more quickly.

BILL ROSE
FOUNDER AND CEO
SERVICE & SUPPORT PROFESSIONALS ASSOCIATION
SAN DIEGO, CALIFORNIA
WWW.THESSPA.COM

The fact that help desk certification programs exist serves as true validation that customer support is now a recognized profession. These programs emphasize the importance of interpersonal skills as well as technical skills, and ultimately will ensure that people who choose customer support as a career are rewarded for those skills. To have a successful customer support career: **(1) Decide to make it your career.** In other words, rather than viewing technical support as just a job, or as a stepping stone to some other profession, decide you're going to pursue technical support as a career. Paramount to this decision is understanding that to be successful you must thrive on dealing with customers, not just technology. Furthermore, you've got to love complaining and demanding customers. You've got to be confident that in difficult situations, you can really shine. **(2) Become a specialist.** Customer support is a very broad term that spans many opportunities. To make the most of your opportunities, become a specialist in *something*—a product, a platform, help desk tools, you decide. Becoming a specialist will not only give you intrinsic confidence, it will enable you to know when you need to consult another specialist, and it will give you the confidence you need to interact with other specialists. Technical specialists can be like deer or moose meeting in the wild; they occasionally lock antlers. Being a specialist will let you grow really big antlers. **(3) Become an expert generalist.** Once you've become a specialist, determine all of the areas where you lack experience, and begin to fill in the blanks. Learn more about business, learn more about your company's business, attend sales meetings and learn how you can help your company sell new products and attract new customers. The more you know, the easier it is to do new things, and in this day and age, the only thing constant in any career is change. **(4) Market your skills and gain exposure outside of your department and company.** While we all hope that our boss or a perspective employer will just know what a great person we are and what a great job we do, the reality is you've got to market yourself. In other words, you've got to create your own opportunities. One way to do this is to hone your writing skills and get published. There are literally thousands of Web sites, magazines, and ezines to which you can submit articles, or white papers, or solutions to technical problems. If you need to, take a technical writing class or use books about writing to improve your skills. You can also hone your presentation skills and speak at conferences, user group meetings, and within your company. If you don't feel comfortable speaking or want to improve your interpersonal skills, use training programs such as Toastmasters, Dale Carnegie, or speech classes to gain the confidence you need. Publishing articles and speaking will not only cause more people to recognize your name and abilities, it will also enable you to build a portfolio over time that you can share with prospective employers or clients. You can also work at building relationships with employees in other parts of your company. For example, get to know the folks in your company's training department or quality department. Let them know what's happening in the support department, and learn about what they do and how they can help you and your team.

Once perceived as a profession that simply required people to be nice, customer support is increasingly complex and challenging. The technologies we support are complex, the tools we use to deliver support are complex, our customers are demanding, and our employers are demanding. That represents a lot of opportunity for people who want to use the best of all their skills—interpersonal, technical, and analytical—to have a rewarding career. Do you want to make customer support your career?

8

PREPARING FOR A CAREER IN THE HELP DESK

Every day, the world changes dramatically. People and businesses are being called upon to continuously reinvent themselves in order to compete. Unlike in days past when people worked for the same company most of their lives, today's college graduates will have 10 to 12 jobs during three to five careers. If you choose to pursue a help desk career as one of those, the skills you develop will serve you well throughout your life because they are very transferable and relevant to any number of endeavors.

A successful help desk career begins with the decision that you want a help desk career. This is easily determined by asking yourself a few simple questions: Do you have a positive attitude? Do you enjoy helping others? Do you enjoy solving problems? Do you like change? Do you enjoy learning new skills and acquiring new knowledge? Do you have the ability see the good in people and be objective in difficult situations? If you answer yes to these questions, you possess the fundamental characteristics needed to be successful.

A second set of questions deals with your ascent through the help desk. Are you interested in pursuing a technical career? Are you interested in pursuing a management career? Are you interested in pursuing a customer service career? Your answers to these questions will determine the work experience you seek, the focus of your education and training, and the nature of your self-study.

Work Experience

Although prior help desk experience is optimal when looking for a job in the help desk industry, companies that are hiring people for help desk positions will also consider relevant work experience that represents some form of customer service. For example, working at a store in the mall or at a restaurant is valuable experience because these jobs require a lot of customer interaction. Other relevant fields include teaching and social work because they require someone who enjoys working with people and who can communicate effectively. Having relevant work experience can help in that search for your first help desk job.

Education and Training

Not all companies require candidates to have an MIS or Computer Science degree when applying for help desk positions. Because communication skills are so important, companies also consider candidates with English or Communications degrees. Increasingly, companies are hiring degreed Technical Writers. In addition, certifications are valuable and differentiate one candidate from another. Good computer literacy and software skills also are important. Regardless of the type of technology they support, most companies require that their employees *use* technology to do their jobs. A high level of comfort using technology will give you a competitive edge over other candidates.

Self-Study

No one can predict what the future holds. Today's trends, however, provide some insight. Take it upon yourself to do reading and studying over and above that which is required at work or at school. To be successful in the help desk, continuously follow help desk and general business trends, gain an understanding of their impact on your skills and on the support industry, and determine how you can seize the opportunities they present. Ongoing study will keep you competitive and prepared for changes.

 Appendix B lists books, magazines, and organizations you can use to obtain additional information about the support industry and stay informed.

TRANSITIONING TO A MANAGEMENT POSITION

Whether you plan to pursue a career in management or at some point are promoted into a management position as a reward for excellent technical performance, the transition to a management position can be trying. This is especially true for people who pride themselves on their technical abilities. Technicians often have a hard time "giving up" the technical skills they have worked so hard to develop in order to acquire the business skills they need to be a manager. Also, technicians often believe the amount of respect they receive from other technicians is based solely upon their technical ability. The tips listed in Figure 8-6 are designed to ease this transition.

8

- Focus on the big picture.
- Serve as a consultant to your staff.
- Learn to delegate.
- Lead and coach your staff.
- Learn to use information.
- Broaden your skills base.

Figure 8-6   Tips for transitioning to management

Following these tips will give people with strong technical skills who choose to pursue a management career the confidence to focus on management issues.

Focus on the Big Picture

Successful managers strive continuously to understand how their group or department fits into the company as a whole and how it contributes to the company's goals. This perspective enables them to understand how the actions of their team impact the company's performance. Understanding the big picture also enables managers to continuously identify ways their team can improve and more fully contribute to the company's bottom line. The best managers can communicate this bigger-picture perspective to their staff.

Serve as a Consultant to Your Staff

A consultant is a professional who analyzes clients' needs and helps them develop systems to improve employee performance, company productivity, customer satisfaction, and so on. Good consultants do not always have all the answers between their ears. They do, however, know where to get information when they need it. Also, consultants typically have a broad base of experience and can offer alternative ways of getting things done.

Serving as a consultant to their staff allows managers to stay focused on the bigger picture, while providing their staff with what they need to focus on the details.

Learn to Delegate

Delegating is a tough lesson for every new manager to learn, but it is particularly difficult for people with strong technical skills. This is because technicians often fear that if they do not use their technical skills they will lose them. Also, many technicians learn new skills by doing a task. They roll up their sleeves and figure out how to do what they need to do by trial and error. Although delegating tasks may make new managers feel like they are depriving themselves of the opportunity to practice and learn new technical skills, it will free up the time they need to acquire management skills.

Lead and Coach Your Staff

A good manager understands that he or she can't motivate other people. Motivation comes from within. What managers can do, however, is to provide leadership and a motivating, well-managed environment. A leader guides people by communicating a vision and inspiring people to achieve that vision. A leader also coaches people and teaches them how to be self-motivated and empowered.

Successful help desk managers lead their staff by helping them to understand the role of the help desk in its company or its department, the help desk's importance to the company or the department, and the scope of the help desk's responsibilities. Managers must also create a clear vision of where the help desk is heading in the future, and passionately move the help desk toward that future state by setting clear, attainable goals. Furthermore, managers must help people understand the bigger issues that are involved in their management decisions and activities. In other words, *why* the help desk is doing things the way it is doing them and *why* the help desk is heading in the direction it is heading. Educating their staff about these higher-level activities enables managers to engage their staff in the decision-making process when appropriate, thus instilling a sense of responsibility and a feeling of ownership relative to the results.

Responsibility is one of the factors that leads to job satisfaction according to Frederick Herzberg, a behavioral scientist who developed a theory about motivation that continues to be relevant today ("The Motivation to Work," Wiley & Sons, New York, 1959). Herzberg studied motivational influences and concluded that the things that satisfy workers, such as responsibility, are entirely different than the things that dissatisfy workers. Furthermore, Herzberg concluded that the things that dissatisfy workers are not just the opposites of things that satisfy workers. Figure 8-7 lists some of the work dissatisfiers that Herzberg found in his studies.

- Company policy administration

- Lack of job security

- Poor working conditions

- Insufficient or unfair salary and compensation

- Too much or too little supervision

Figure 8-7   Herzberg's work dissatisfiers

Table 8-1 lists some of the work satisfiers that Herzberg found in his studies, along with examples of these work satisfiers in a help desk setting.

8

Table 8-1   Herzberg's work satisfiers and examples in a help desk setting

Herzberg's Work Satisfiers	Examples of Satisfiers in a Help Desk Setting
Achievement	■ Clearly defined goals ■ Special projects ■ Team-building activities
Interesting work	■ Job shadowing ■ Complex problem solving ■ Using a variety of skills
Opportunity	■ Technical and managerial career paths ■ Project management ■ Training and certification
Recognition	■ Incentive programs ■ Peer recognition programs ■ Thanks, praise, and feedback
Responsibility	■ Flexible work hours ■ Mentoring ■ Representing the team at meetings and on projects

Herzberg theorized that managers should not assume that by eliminating dissatisfiers, they have created satisfaction. Herzberg also concluded that job satisfiers are the source of motivation, as they have a positive, intrinsic impact on workers.

Herzberg's theory makes perfect sense when you assume the perspective of a worker. For example, have you ever had a bad boss or have you ever felt you weren't being paid fairly? Such scenarios cause dissatisfaction. Eliminating these dissatisfiers may not, however, cause job satisfaction. If you are doing a job that is boring and, from your perspective, meaningless, you will be dissatisfied, regardless of a great boss or a good salary. In other words, it is possible to love your boss or to be making a lot of money, and hate your job.

Remember, motivation comes within. As a manager, all you can do is create a motivating environment. You can do that through:

- **Teamwork**—Creating a shared vision and positive relationships.

- **Education**—Continuously promoting the benefits of your vision and providing people with the training and education they need to be successful.

- **Setting goals**—Breaking the vision into smaller attainable goals, thus enabling a sense of achievement.

- **Empowerment**—Communicating values (that is, right and wrong ways of doing things) and requiring each and every person on your team to take responsibility for their actions and for their role in attaining the desired future state.

Remember, too, that not all workers are highly motivated. Managers must sometimes deal with poor performers or risk damaging the morale of the whole team. Successful managers continuously coach their employees by providing constructive feedback and guidance. The best managers regularly tell people what they are *specifically* doing right and, when necessary, what they are *specifically* doing wrong and how they can improve.

 Your local library has numerous books on leadership, motivation, and coaching. Some excellent examples include *Coaching for Improved Work Performance* by Ferdinand Fournies; an "oldie but goodie" *The One Minute Manager* by Kenneth Blanchard and Spencer Johnson; and *Zapp! The Lightning of Empowerment: How to Improve Productivity, Quality, and Employee Satisfaction* by Jeff Cox.

Successful managers also regularly recognize the efforts of their workers in meaningful ways. One of the best ways to do this is by learning about employees as individuals: What is important to them? What are their personal goals? How do they take in information?

People take in information differently. Some people are auditory, which means they take in information by listening. Auditory workers like to be told they are doing a good job. Saying "thank you" or "great job" to an auditory worker, in person when possible, is an excellent way to acknowledge his or her efforts. Some people are visual, which means they take in information by seeing. You can usually tell visual people as they have "stuff" all over their desks. Visual people really appreciate being given something they can look at such as a thank you note, a letter of recognition, or a certificate. Some people are kinesthetic, which means they take in information by touching; they like a "hands on" approach. You can acknowledge a kinesthetic person's efforts by shaking her hand or by giving him a pat on the back.

 Learning about people as individuals is a life skill that will serve you well, whether or not you are a manager and regardless of your chosen profession.

Learn to Use Information

It is imperative that help desk managers understand that information is a resource, just as people, processes, and technology are resources. It is not enough for managers to ensure that their staff is collecting information; they must add value to that information and share it with others throughout the company. Managers who request resources without being able to justify the cost versus the benefit of those resources rarely receive what they need. Similarly, managers who cannot give other managers in their department or company the information they need to improve the quality of products and services rarely earn the respect and cooperation they want.

Broaden Your Skills Base

Managers need to add to the business, technical, soft, and self-management skills that they depended upon as analysts. They must quickly acquire or fine-tune skills such as team building, project management, presentation, and meeting skills. These skills involve building relationships and working with others to obtain their confidence and commitment. Classes are available, and libraries and bookstores are filled with books and tapes that can help managers expand their knowledge in these areas.

It is important to understand that promotion to a management position means that you will be expected to acquire and demonstrate management skills. Analysts don't always realize the impact this will have on their ability to maintain their technical skills. Furthermore, not all technicians enjoy doing the work that managers are required to do. Because not everyone on the help desk team is interested in pursuing a management career, many companies are developing technical and managerial career paths that enable people to focus on their personal strengths and interests. Continuous self-assessment and the exploration of available opportunities will help you to determine and choose what path to take on your way to a long and rewarding career.

The future is bright for people who can find and fill the gaps that may exist in their company's help desk organization or in the help desk of a prospective employer. To locate and fill these gaps, you need to be aware of help desk industry trends and be able to objectively evaluate how those trends affect your skills. You must develop a balanced set of business, technical, soft, and self-management skills and be able to communicate the value of those skills. What is most important, you must learn to employ help desk people, processes, technology, and information and use them as stepping-stones to the future.

CHAPTER SUMMARY

❑ Tremendous opportunities exist for people interested in pursuing a help desk career. This is because companies and departments worldwide are working hard to attract and keep people who have the energy, enthusiasm, and skills needed to deliver the high-quality services their customers demand. These companies also need people who can assume the increasingly important supporting roles in a help desk such as knowledge base administration, service management and improvement, and technical support for the help desk's tools and technologies. To seize the opportunities offered by this dynamic industry, you must be aware of help desk industry trends and objectively evaluate how those trends affect your skills. You must determine your strengths and interests and seek out jobs and experiences in which you can excel.

❑ An irreversible dependence on technology has prompted customers to demand ever-cheaper, faster, and better support services. This demand has prompted companies to considerably expand the role of the help desk. Trends such as the need to provide 24 × 7 support, fee-based support, global support, mobile worker support, multi-channel support, and Web-based support are further influencing the direction in which the help desk industry is heading. Each of these trends affects how help desks are run and the opportunities they present to help desk analysts.

❑ The idea of certifying professionals, such as accountants and electricians, has existed for years. Since the late 1980s, managers have recognized the importance of certifying IT professionals. There are two types of certification programs available to help desk professionals: *technical certifications* that are vendor specific, and *help desk certifications* that are vendor neutral. Help desk certification programs enable individual managers and analysts to focus on and demonstrate that they possess the industry knowledge and soft skills needed to deliver excellent customer support, and also enable entire help desks to benchmark their practices against industry best practices. Certification programs can be costly and time-consuming to complete successfully, so individuals and sites that become certified truly exemplify world-class service providers.

❑ A successful help desk career begins with the decision that you want to have a help desk career and the type of career you want to pursue. Are you interested in pursuing a technical career? Are you interested in pursuing a management career? Many companies are developing both technical and managerial career paths that enable people to focus on their personal strengths and interests. Continuous self-assessment and the exploration of available opportunities will enable you to determine and choose what path to take on your way to a long and rewarding career.

❑ Technicians who choose or are promoted into a management position must work hard to acquire the business skills needed to be a manager. Tips for making this transition include focusing on the big picture and serving as a consultant to your staff. Managers must also learn to delegate, provide leadership, and create a motivating environment.

They must understand that information is a resource, just as people processes, and technology are resources, and they must add to the business, technical, soft, and self-management skills that they depended upon as analysts. Not everyone is interested in pursuing a management career and so many companies are developing technical and managerial career paths that enable people to focus on their personal strengths and interests. Continuous self-assessment and the exploration of available opportunities will help you to determine and choose what path to take on your way to a long and rewarding career.

KEY TERMS

24 × 7 support — Help desk services that are provided 24 hours a day, 7 days a week.

fee-based support — Support services that charge the customer on a per-use basis.

global support — Support for customers anywhere in the world; may be caused by the need to support a large company that has foreign divisions and subsidiaries or by the need to support customers who are doing business with the company through the World Wide Web.

insourcing — When service agency employees are physically located at the facilities of the company that has hired them to provide support services.

mass-healing systems — Systems that enable help desks to detect and repair problems across the enterprise.

multivendor support — Support for customers who use products developed by a number of different vendors.

ubiquitous computing — An environment where people have access to their information and computing systems from public shared access points, such as aiports automated teller machines (ATMs), hotel rooms and lobbies, libraries, retail stores, and supermarkets.

REVIEW QUESTIONS

1. Why is there an increasing number of opportunities (a) in companies that deliver external customer support, and (b) in departments that deliver internal customer support?

2. Why have companies elevated the help desk to a more strategic position?

3. What are four ways that companies provide 24 × 7 support?

4. Why do people need to determine whether or how their employer, or prospective employer, charges a fee for support?

5. What three issues must companies providing global support address?

6. What trend shows the growing importance of help desks within companies?

7. What impact will ubiquitous computing have on the support industry?

8. Describe three trends that are causing the help desk to have increased workload.

9. How can help desks ensure that mobile devices and applications best serve the needs of users and ensure the security of corporate data assets?

10. List three factors that are causing help desks to look at multi-channel support differently.

11. What are four factors that prompt companies to consider outsourcing?

12. Why do some companies outsource support for industry standard hardware and software products?

13. List three skills that are increasingly important for people in a help desk to have in order to provide Web-based support.

14. Why are roles such as technical support and knowledge base administration important to help desks that provide Web-based support?

15. What two trends initially prompted corporate managers to recognize the importance of certifying IT professionals?

16. How do help desk certification programs enable individuals to gain a bigger picture perspective than technical certification programs tend to offer?

17. What are three ways that managers show they value the time and effort that individuals put into becoming certified?

18. List at least three of the fundamental characteristics you must posses to have a successful help desk career.

19. What type of work experience will companies consider when hiring people for help desk positions?

20. Why is it important to continuously follow help desk and general business trends?

21. Describe three ways that people with strong technical skills can ease the transition to a management position.

22. Describe two traits of a leader.

23. When requesting resources, help desk managers must use information to _____.

24. What skills must you develop to have a balanced set of skills?

25. What components of a help desk must you learn to leverage and use as a stepping-stone to the future?

HANDS-ON PROJECTS

Project 8-1

Evaluate a local help desk. Visit the help desk where you work or at your school or at a company in your community. Determine the following:

❑ What services does the help desk provide?

❑ What skills does it require of its employees?

❑ Does it encourage or require its employees to become certified? If so, how? Technical? Help desk?

❑ How does it interview job candidates? What qualities does it look for in job candidates?

❑ How does it measure the performance of its analysts?

❑ What processes does it have in place?

❑ What technologies does it use?

❑ What data does it capture? How does it use that data to crete information?

❑ Does it provide 24 × 7 support? If so, how? If not, does it provide after–hours support? If so, how?

❑ How does the manager envision meeting his or her customers' needs in the next five years?

Given everything you have learned in this book, what conclusions can you draw from visiting this help desk? Write a report that summarizes your findings and conclusions.

8

Project 8-2

Interview a help desk employee. Arrange to interview a manager or analyst who works in a help desk either at your school or in the community. Before the interview, prepare a list of questions you would like answered and send it to the person so that he or she can prepare. For example, you may ask the person to describe:

❑ How is the help desk organized? (If possible, obtain a copy of the company's organization chart.)

❑ What job categories are included in the organization chart?

❑ What skills are required for each job category?

❑ What, if any, certifications are encouraged or required?

❑ What career path opportunities exist within the help desk?

❑ What career path opportunities exist beyond the help desk?

❑ What processes determine the work that person performs on a daily basis?

❑ What technologies are used by the help desk?

❑ What data is that person required to collect? How is this data used?

❑ What terminology is used? Obtain an understanding of any new terms that person introduces or terms that are used differently than those described in this book.

Write a report that summarizes what you learned from this person.

Project 8-3

Learn about help desk certification. Visit the Web site of one of the companies or organizations discussed in this chapter that certifies help desk professionals. Determine the following:

❏ What levels of certification are available?

❏ What skills are certified?

❏ What must you do to get certified?

❏ What are the benefits of being certified?

Write a report that summarizes what you have learned about certification from visiting this Web site.

Project 8-4

Learn about cultural differences. Select a region of the world other than the United States such as Africa, Asia, Europe, and so forth. (See how many different regions of the world your class can learn about.) Research and prepare a brief report that describes the cultural differences the help desk should be aware of when supporting this region of the world. Include information about the steps the help desk can take to acknowledge and facilitate these differences. Present your report to the class.

Project 8-5

Discuss the impact of ubiquitous computing. In the foreseeable future, people will have access to computing devices in much the same way they have access to public telephones today. Assemble a team of at least three classmates and briefly discuss the concept of ubiquitous computing as it is presented in this chapter. Each person should share his or her knowledge and thoughts about ubiquitous computing. As a team, predict the impact that ubiquitous computing will have on the support industry. How can the support industry facilitate ubiquitous computing? How can companies, libraries, and so forth prepare for ubiquitous computing? Present your predictions to the class.

Project 8-6

Reduce the cost of multivendor support. Assemble a team of at least three classmates. Discuss the challenges that multivendor support presents to companies. Brainstorm ways that the help desk can reduce the cost associated with this kind of support. Prepare a list of suggested techniques for reducing these costs. Compare your team's ideas with those developed by other groups in your class.

Project 8-7

Learn about managerial skills. Interview a friend or family member who is in a management position. Ask this manager how he or she developed skills such as team-building skills, project management skills, presentation skills, and meeting skills. How important does this person feel it is for a manager to have these skills? What other skills does this person feel are needed to be a manager? Summarize what you learned from this interview.

Project 8-8

Learn what motivates workers. Assemble a team of three to five classmates, optimally classmates of varying ages. Discuss what motivates workers who are part of the baby-boom generation, generation X, and generation Y. How are these workers different? How are these workers the same? For each generation, prepare a list of the following:

- Three work dissatisfiers
- Three work satisfiers
- Three specific examples of each work satisfier

Present and discuss your conclusions with the class.

Project 8-9

State your career goals. The section "Preparing for a Career in the Help Desk" presented a series of questions that describe the fundamental characteristics needed to have a successful help desk career. Ask yourself these questions, and assess your desire to pursue a help desk career. The section also presented a second set of questions that relate to your ascent through the help desk. Ask yourself these questions and again assess your desire to pursue a help desk career. Write down a description of your help desk career goals based on your answers to these questions. Explain why you want to pursue this direction.

CASE PROJECTS

1. Bayside Legal Services, Inc.

You are the supervisor for a help desk that supports the internal customers of Bayside Legal Services, Inc., a small law firm that has recently outfitted all of its lawyers with laptop computers. As a result, you are expanding your help desk. You are very committed to satisfying customers and resolving a high percentage of incidents, and you know that many of the traditional techniques used to support workers such as going to the worker's office to diagnose a problem or upgrade a system aren't going to be possible or practical now that lawyers have the ability to work remotely. Search the Web for articles about topics such as "supporting remote workers" and "supporting telecommuters." Use the articles to prepare a brief presentation outlining the people, process, technology, and information issues you must address at the help desk in preparation for this change. Outline how the responsibilities of your customers must change as well.

2. Support Services, Inc.

Support Services, Inc., a company that provides help desk outsourcing services, has built a new local support center and has a number of openings for entry-level support analysts. The company's motto is "Customer Satisfaction Is Our Number 1 Priority." The job ad states that "relevant experience will be considered." Review your education, training, and work experience and prepare for your interview. Present to your class a three- to five-minute description of the skills you have that you believe qualify you for consideration for this position.

3. Marconi Company

You work as a help desk analyst for Marconi Company, which manufactures television sets. For many years, customers have reached the company's help desk using a 1–800 number. You have just found out that your company will soon begin distributing a line of WebTV systems. You're not really sure what this means to your help desk so you decide to do a little research on the Web. After you finish your research, prepare a brief report of your findings for management. The report could outline, for example, what the introduction of WebTV will mean to your customers. Provide any information you can about how other companies that offer WebTV systems are supporting their customers. Finally, prepare a list of changes you recommend making to your help desk so that your team will be prepared to support this new product line.

A

JOB DESCRIPTIONS FOR THE HELP DESK

This appendix provides sample help desk job descriptions. These job descriptions provide you with a basic overview of the job responsibilities and activities as well as the professional experience and education required for each position. Be aware that these job titles and descriptions will vary from company to company. Sample job descriptions provided include:

- Level One Analyst
- Level One Specialist
- Help Desk Team Leader
- Help Desk Manager
- Knowledge Engineer

LEVEL ONE ANALYST

REPORTS TO

Help Desk Team Leader

POSITION CONCEPT

As directed by the Help Desk Team Leader, delivers quality customer service to help desk customers by providing them with a single point of contact to report problems or to make inquiries. Handles day-to-day service delivery problems and works on special projects as assigned.

DUTIES AND RESPONSIBILITIES

1. Ensures customer satisfaction by responding to calls to the help desk. Logs all customer questions and problems and tracks the same through to resolution.

2. Ensures customer problems are handled in a timely manner by documenting the impact to the customer and by assigning an appropriate severity and target resolution time.

3. Conducts level one problem determination using documented procedures and available tools. Records problem symptoms and status information in a timely fashion in an effort to communicate with and properly use senior IT staff.

4. Ensures problem resolution by maintaining an action plan for problem resolution, by initiating and tracking problem assignments to technical resources, vendors, and so forth, and by keeping the customer updated on the status of problem resolution.

5. Ensures management awareness of problems that are severe in nature or that are exceeding documented targets.

6. Builds team spirit by assisting and coaching other staff members.

REQUIRED SKILLS AND ABILITIES

1. Strong dedication to quality customer service and a working knowledge of enterprise-wide service delivery procedures.

2. Strong verbal and written interpersonal and communication skills. Superior telephone and e-mail etiquette and an ability to interact effectively with customers, vendors, peers, and management.

3. Strong problem-solving skills and inherent decision-making ability.

4. Good initiative and assertiveness. Good project management skills and the ability to organize work efficiently, in addition to the capacity to work well under stress and time pressures.

5. Good working knowledge of the day-to-day operating environment, available tools, operating techniques, and customer applications.

Education: Associate's degree or equivalent technical training.

Experience: One to three years of computer-related support experience.

LEVEL ONE SPECIALIST

REPORTS TO

Help Desk Team Leader

POSITION CONCEPT

Acts in a liaison role for IT with all internal technology users throughout the company. Demonstrates a broad understanding of the company's information technology along with a depth of expertise in a specific subject area. Resides in the customer support center for his or her assigned shift and is also responsible for developing, coordinating, and managing the relationship between the customer and IT to ensure that desired levels of service are maintained.

DUTIES AND RESPONSIBILITIES

1. Resides in the customer support center for assigned shift.

2. Services and resolves customer problems referred by Level One Analysts.

3. Researches complex incidents and develops solutions.

4. Participates on project teams related to his or her area of expertise and determines the help desk's needs with regard to new products and systems.

5. Demonstrates excellent oral and written communication skills.

6. Demonstrates commitment in areas of strategic importance to the organization.

REQUIRED SKILLS AND ABILITIES

Level One Specialists are fully qualified to answer customer support questions and to resolve the majority of customer problems. Additional or more specific educational or professional background may be required for a candidate to be selected for a support position associated with a particular client organization. The following criteria are considered minimal for the position:

Education: Bachelor's degree or equivalent technical training.

Experience: Three to five years of computer-related support experience; considerable work experience in area of specialty.

HELP DESK TEAM LEADER

REPORTS TO

Help Desk Manager

POSITION CONCEPT

Oversees the day-to-day operation of the help desk. Works closely with front-line service providers to ensure that they have the resources needed to perform their duties efficiently. Ensures that all problems and requests reported by both IT customers and staff are recorded and monitored. Ensures that the help desk is meeting its Service Level Agreement (SLA) commitments.

DUTIES AND RESPONSIBILITIES

1. Ensures that all problems are logged.

2. Ensures prompt, accurate status and feedback of all problems to customers and management.

3. Monitors SLA compliance.

4. Performs trend analysis to alleviate recurring problems experienced by customers.

5. Ensures that front-line service providers have the resources needed to resolve as many problems as possible.

6. Develops and maintains help desk procedures and ensures that procedures are followed.

7. Works with the Help Desk Manager to monitor and evaluate the performance of help desk staff.

8. Develops training plans and ensures that help desk staff are properly trained.

9. Performs other duties when required.

REQUIRED SKILLS AND ABILITIES

Strong supervisory, communication, and teamwork skills are essential, as well as a demonstrated ability to provide excellent customer service.

Education: Bachelor's degree or equivalent work experience.

Experience: Five years of customer service and support experience.

HELP DESK MANAGER

REPORTS TO

Senior Help Desk Manager

POSITION CONCEPT

Provides the primary interface between IT management and customer management. Engages management in activities such as reviewing reports and analyzing statistics, establishing SLAs, and ensuring that the help desk's processes and technologies are meeting the needs of the company. Works closely with the Senior Help Desk Manager to prepare the help desk's budget and plan its activities for the coming year.

DUTIES AND RESPONSIBILITIES

1. Plans and directs training activities for the development of personnel.

2. Supervises all help desk personnel and maintains proper staffing to ensure that objectives are met.

3. Coordinates the implementation of system changes that impact help desk customers.

4. Analyzes and reports on the performance and availability of the supported products and services.

5. Interfaces with multiple vendors regarding service, maintenance, and performance.

6. Makes recommendations to management for the purchase of help desk tools and technologies.

7. Performs other duties as assigned.

REQUIRED SKILLS AND ABILITIES

Extensive management experience is required. Necessary skills include the ability to prepare budgets and reports along with the ability to analyze statistics. Must demonstrate the ability to establish goals and plan improvement initiatives.

Education: Bachelor's degree or equivalent business training.

Experience: Five to 10 years of customer service and support experience.

KNOWLEDGE ENGINEER

REPORTS TO

Help Desk Manager

POSITION CONCEPT

Responsible for the content, maintenance, and administration of knowledge resources such as the problem management system resolution database, the help desk Web site's FAQ list and solution database, and commercially available knowledge bases that are applicable to the technology environment supported by the help desk. Identifies and promotes Web-based knowledge resources that are applicable to the technology environment supported by the help desk.

DUTIES AND RESPONSIBILITIES

1. Promotes and facilitates knowledge sharing throughout the organization.

2. Maintains the problem management system resolution database.

   a. Develops and distributes resolution documentation standards such as the format and writing style to be used when preparing resolutions.

   b. Reviews resolutions submitted by help desk analysts, technical resources, subject matter experts, vendors, and so forth.

   c. Ensures that resolutions (1) are technically valid, (2) are reusable, (3) are presented in a clear, consistent, logical manner, (4) conform to knowledge management standards, and (5) do not duplicate an existing resolution.

   d. When necessary, confers with technical staff to clarify resolution procedures, verbiage, or placement within the resolution database.

   e. Approves or rejects resolutions as appropriate.

   f. Ensures that analysts can quickly and easily retrieve resolutions added to the resolution database.

   g. Provides education and counseling as needed to improve the quality of submitted resolutions.

3. Reviews problem management system trend data, technical bulletins, and vendor forums and proactively includes resolution information relative to the technology environment in the problem management system resolution database.

4. Identifies and recommends improvements to the design and functionality of the company's technical resolution resources.

5. Leads or participates on project teams dedicated to improving the efficiency, effectiveness, and quality of technical resolution resources.

6. Acts as a consultant to the help desk manager with regard to how technical resolution resources are being used.

REQUIRED SKILLS AND ABILITIES

1. Excellent problem-solving and problem analysis skills.

2. Strong oral and technical writing skills.

3. Extensive experience with the company's technical environment (including operating systems, local and wide area networks, telecommunications, hardware, and system and application software).

4. The ability to identify and verify valid resolutions to technical problems.

5. The ability to provide technical resolution data in a form that analysts can easily retrieve and apply to reported problems and requests.

6. An in-depth understanding of help desk operations.

7. An interest in keeping abreast of the most recent technical bulletins and vendor forums related to relevant product defects, resolutions, and available workarounds.

Education: Bachelor's degree or equivalent work experience.

Experience: Three to five years experience providing technical customer support.

B

HELP DESK RESOURCES

This appendix lists resources for additional information about the help desk industry that you can use to learn more about this dynamic industry and advance your career. Many of these resources can be obtained through your local library or via the Web. Many of the magazines can be obtained free of charge by subscribing through the magazine's Web site. The magazines and the membership organizations are excellent sources of the most up-to-date information about the industry. Resources include:

- Books
- Certification programs
- Self-study programs
- Magazines
- Membership organizations

BOOKS

Building and Managing a World Class IT Help Desk. B. Wooten. McGraw-Hill Osborne Media, 2001.

The Complete Idiot's Guide to MBA Basics. T. Gorman, E. Paulson. Alpha Books, 1998.

The Complete Idiot's Guide to Technical Writing. K. Van Laan. Alpha Books, 2001.

Dictionary of Business Terms, Third Edition. J. Friedman. Barron's Educational Series, 2000.

The Elements of Technical Writing. G. Blake. Macmillan General Reference, 1993.

The Essential Drucker. P. Drucker. HarperBusiness, 2001.

A Guide to Computer User Support for Help Desk & Support Specialists, Second Edition. F. Beisse. Course Technology, 2001.

A Guide to Customer Service Skills for Help Desk Professionals. D. Knapp. Course Technology, 1999.

A Guide to Help Desk Technology, Tools, & Techniques. D. McBride. Course Technology, 2000.

The Handbook of Technical Writing. G. Alred. St. Martin's Press, 2003.

IT Help Desk Survival Guide (CD-ROM). TechRepublic, 2002.

IT Problem Management. G. Walker. Prentice Hall PTR, 2001.

PC Help Desk in a Book: The Do-it-Yourself Guide to PC Troubleshooting and Repair. M. Soper. Que, 2002.

The Portable MBA, Third Edition. R. Bruner (Contributor), M. Eaker, R. Freeman (Contributor), R. Spekman. John Wiley & Sons, 1997.

Root Cause Analysis: Simplified Tools and Techniques. B. Anderson. American Society for Quality, 1999.

Running an Effective Help Desk, Second Edition. B. Czegel. John Wiley & Sons, 1998.

Service Delivery (IT Infrastructure Library Series). The Stationary Office, 2001.

Service Support (IT Infrastructure Library Series). The Stationary Office, 2000.

Technical Support on the Web: Designing and Managing an Effective E-Support Site. B. Czegel. John Wiley & Sons, 2000.

CERTIFICATION PROGRAMS

Help Desk Institute
(719) 268-0174
(800) 248-5667, Toll-Free
www.helpdeskinst.com

Help Desk Institute certification is an open, standards-based, internationally recognized certification program for help desk professionals (**www.thinkhdi.com/cert/certoverview.asp**).

Service & Support Professionals Association (SSPA)
(858) 674-5491
www.thesspa.com

The SSPA offers an individual certification training program that is designed to prepare support professionals at all levels to perform within industry standards and to earn international certification (**www.thesspa.com/programs/certifications/indiv.asp**). The SSPA also offers the Support Center Practices (SCP) site certification program that evaluates help desk performance relative to 11 major criteria such as people programs, total quality management, productivity tools, and performance metrics (**www.thesspa.com/programs/certifications/site.asp**). SSPA's programs are geared to companies that provide external customer support.

STI Knowledge
(770) 280-2630
(800) 350-5781, Toll-Free
www.stiknowledge.com

STI Knowledge offers Help Desk 2000 certification for help desk analysts, managers, and directors (**www.stiknowledge.com/certification_advisory/courses.asp#hd2k**). STI Knowledge also offers the Core 2000 certification program, which enables companies to certify their entire help desk (**www.stiknowledge.com/certification_advisory/ comp_certification.asp**).

SELF-STUDY PROGRAMS (AUDIO TAPES, VIDEO TAPES, ETC.)

American Management Association
(800) 262-9699, Toll-Free
www.amanet.org

Titles include *Delivering Knock Your Socks Off Service*; *Finance and Accounting for Nonfinancial Managers; How to Build High-Performance Teams; Taking Control with Time Management; Motivating Others*; and *How to Manage Conflict in the Organization.*

CareerTrack, Inc.
(800) 488-0928, Toll-Free
www.careertrack.com

Titles include *How to Give Exceptional Customer Service*; *Professional Telephone Skills*; and *Pleasing Your Hard-to-Please Customers.*

Crisp Publications, Inc.
(650) 323-6100
(800) 442-7477, Toll-Free
www.crisplearning.com

Titles include *Calming Upset Customers*; *Measuring Customer Satisfaction*; *Technical Writing in the Corporate World*; and *Telephone Courtesy and Customer Service.*

Help Desk Institute
(719) 268-0174
(800) 248-5667, Toll-Free
www.helpdeskinst.com

Titles include *Call Escalation and Management*; *Customer Care!*; *Every Call Comes with an Attitude*; *Help Desk Professionals Make a Difference*; *Managing Customer Attitudes*; and *Self-Motivation for Help Desk Professionals.*

JWA Video
(800) 327-5110, Toll-Free
www.jwavideo.com

Titles include *50 Ways to Keep Your Customer*; *How to Develop Effective Communication Skills*; and *Listen and Win*.

The Telephone Doctor
(800) 882-9911, Toll-Free
www.telephoneskills.com

Titles include *Do's & Don'ts of Customer Service*; *How to Handle the Irate Caller*; and *Telephone Skills from A–Z*.

MAGAZINES

Call Center Magazine
(888) 824-9793, Toll-Free
www.callcentermagazine.com

Contact Professional
(800) 899-2676, Toll-Free
www.contactprofessional.com

Field Force Automation
(323) 964-4800
www.destinationffa.com

SupportWorld
(800) 248-5667, Toll-Free
www.thinkhdi.com/publications/supportmag.asp

MEMBERSHIP ORGANIZATIONS

Association of Support Professionals
(617) 924-3944
www.asponline.com

The Association of Support Professionals is a membership organization that represents support managers and other professionals in hundreds of PC software companies, large and small.

Help Desk Institute
(800) 248-5667, Toll-Free
www.helpdeskinst.com

Help Desk Institute (HDI) provides targeted information about the technologies, tools, and trends of the help desk and customer support industry. HDI offers a variety of services to meet the evolving needs of the customer support professional.

Service & Support Professionals Association
(858) 674-5491
www.thesspa.com

The Service & Support Professionals Association (SSPA) provides a value-added forum in which service and support professionals in the software industry can share ideas, discuss developing trends, and network with their peers, who are skilled professionals working with every conceivable platform, application, and operating system in the industry.

Glossary

24 × 7 support — Help desk services that are provided 24 hours a day, 7 days a week.

abandon rate percent — The percentage of abandoned calls compared to the total number of calls received.

abandoned call — A call where the caller hangs up before an analyst answers.

accessibility — How easily the help desk can be reached by help desk staff, other employees of the company, and customers.

account management — A process that dedicates an account manager to each business unit within a company or to large or important clients who receive external support.

account manager — An employee who has in-depth knowledge of a specific customer community and serves as the primary contact for the customer and the help desk staff supporting the customer.

ACD supervisor console — A system that works with ACD systems and enables supervisors to monitor call volumes and the performance of individual help desk analysts or groups of analysts.

active listening — When the listener participates in a conversation and gives the speaker a sense of confidence that he or she is being heard.

announcement system — A technology that greets callers when all help desk analysts are busy and can provide answers to routine questions or promotional information.

application of training investments — A comparison of an analyst's resolution percent before and after attending training.

asset and configuration management — The process of collecting and maintaining information about IT assets (such as hardware, software, network, and communication components) and showing the relationships that exist among those assets; it also captures financial information, such as license and warranty information.

asset and configuration management systems — Technology that allows an analyst to "see" what hardware and software is installed on a computer or network along with financial information such as license and warranty information.

automated attendant — An ACD feature that routes calls based on input provided by the caller through a touch-tone telephone.

automatic call distributor (ACD) — A technology that answers a call and routes, or distributes, it to the next available analyst. If all analysts are busy, the ACD places the call in a queue and plays a recorded message, such as "We're sorry, all of our service representatives are currently assisting other customers; your call will be answered in the order it has been received."

automatic number identification (ANI) — A service provided by a *long distance* service provider that delivers the telephone number of the person calling.

availability — The length of time an analyst was signed on to the ACD compared to the length of time the analyst was scheduled to be signed on.

available state — An ACD state that occurs when an analyst is ready to take calls.

average call duration — The average length of time required to handle a call.

Average Speed of Answer (ASA) — The average time it takes an analyst to pick up an incoming call.

average wait time — The average number of minutes a caller waits for an analyst after being placed in the queue by an ACD; also known as average queue time.

baseline — A metric used to show a starting point.

beginning of day (BOD) — A list of tasks an analyst performs at the start of each workday.

benchmarking — The process of comparing the help desk's services, standardized metrics, and practices to those of a rival or world class company in an effort to identify ways it can improve.

best practice — An innovative process or concept that moves a company or department to a position of improved performance.

best-in-class — A company that is the finest in its relative industry peer group. For example, a best-in-class manufacturing company is considered excellent by its customers when compared only to other manufacturing companies.

blended call centers — Call centers that receive incoming calls *and* make outgoing calls.

business skills — The skills people need to work successfully in the business world, such as the ability to understand and speak the language of business (business knowledge); the skills that are unique to the industry or profession the help desk supports, such as accounting skills or banking skills (industry knowledge); and also the skills that are specific to the customer service and support industry, such as understanding the importance of meeting customers' needs and knowing how to manage their expectations (service industry knowledge).

call center — A place where telephone calls are made, or received, in high volume.

caller identification (caller ID) — A service provided by a *local* telephone company that delivers the telephone number of the person calling.

Capability Maturity Models (CMMs) — A set of quality-oriented management practices that assist organizations in maturing their people, processes, and technology assets to improve long-term business performance.

carpal tunnel syndrome (CTS) — A common repetitive stress injury that affects the hands and wrists and is linked to repetitious hand movements, such as typing on a computer keyboard, pinching a mouse, or repeatedly clicking a mouse.

case — A unit of information, such as an online document, a database record, or the solution to a common problem, which is indexed so an analyst can easily locate it when needed.

case-based reasoning (CBR) — A searching technique that uses everyday language to ask users questions and interpret their answers.

case-based system — A system made up of (1) cases and (2) a set of question and answer pairs that can be used to confirm the solution to the problem.

centralized help desk — A single help desk that supports all of the technologies used by its customers.

certification — A document awarded to a person who has demonstrated that he or she has certain skills and knowledge about a particular topic or area.

change categories — A consistent way to communicate the potential risk and impact of a change.

change management — The process of controlling changes to the production environment while minimizing service disruptions.

channels — Routes of communication to and from the help desk, such as the telephone, voice mail, e-mail, and the Web.

collaboration products — Products that enable multiple users to work together on related tasks.

computer-based training (CBT) — Computer software packages used to train and test people on a wide range of subjects.

computer telephony integration (CTI) — The linking of computing technology with telephone technology to exchange information and increase productivity.

computer virus — A software program that can "infect" a computer by storing itself in the computer's memory or attaching itself to program or data files. Some viruses won't harm an infected system, whereas others are destructive and can damage or destroy data.

computer vision syndrome — A variety of ailments such as headaches and eyestrain that occur as a result of staring at a computer monitor.

configuration items (CIs) — The individual records that are stored in an organization's configuration management database, such as IT assets, Service Level Agreements (SLAs), and knowledge assets.

configuration management database (CMDB) — A central database for IT asset information.

contact center — A call center that uses technologies such as e-mail and the Web in addition to the telephone.

cost benefit analysis — A business calculation that compares the costs and benefits of two or more potential solutions in order to determine an optimum solution.

cost centers — A help desk in which the budget items required to run the help desk are considered a cost (expense) to the company.

cost per contact — Historically called cost per call; the total cost of operating a help desk for a given period (including salaries, benefits, facilities, equipment, and so on) divided by the total number of contacts (calls, e-mails, faxes, Web requests, and so on) received during that period.

cost per unit — The total cost of operating a help desk for a given period (including salaries, benefits, facilities, equipment, and so on) divided by the total number of units (such as devices, systems, and so on) supported during that period.

costs — The amounts paid to produce a product, such as workers' wages, salaries, and benefits; the facilities and equipment workers use; any materials and supplies they consume; and so on.

customer — A person who buys products or services.

customer data — Identifying details about a customer, including the customer's name, telephone number, department or company name, address or location, customer number, and employee number or user ID.

customer entitlement — The determination of whether the customer is authorized to receive support and, if so, the level of support the customer should receive.

customer memory — A record that includes all the information and transactions relevant to a given customer.

customer record — All of the fields that describe a single customer.

customer relationship management (CRM) — A program that involves using customer contact and relationship information to generate additional sales and increase levels of customer service and retention.

customer satisfaction — The difference between how a customer perceives he or she was treated and how the customer expects to be treated.

customer satisfaction surveys — A series of questions that ask customers to provide their perception of the support services being offered.

customer service — Services that ensure customers receive maximum value for the products or services they purchase.

customer support — Services that help a customer understand and benefit from a product's capabilities by answering questions, solving problems, and providing training.

customer surveying systems — Systems that are used to create and distribute questionnaires to customers and to collect and tabulate the results of their feedback.

data — Raw facts that are not organized in a meaningful way.

decentralized help desks — Multiple help desks, each of which supports specific products or customer communities.

decision tree — A branching structure of questions and possible answers designed to lead an analyst to a solution.

development — The construction of new systems.

dialed number identification service (DNIS) — A service that provides the number the person called when they call using a toll-free number or a 1-900 service.

dispatch — To send or route.

dispatcher — The person who initially handles customer problems, requests, or inquiries; also called a help desk agent, customer care agent, customer service representative, or call screener.

effectiveness — How completely and accurately services are delivered.

efficiency — How quickly services are delivered.

electronic reader boards — Bright displays that send out visual and, in some cases, audible messages to help desk staff and to customer sites that have reader boards installed.

e-mail response management systems — Systems that enable help desks to manage high volume chat, e-mail, and Web form messages.

employee Service Level Agreement — A document that clearly describes an analyst's performance requirements and individual improvement objectives.

enterprise solutions — A suite of systems that companies use to manage their problem, request, knowledge management, change, and asset and configuration management processes; also called integrated enterprise solutions.

ergonomics — The science of people-machine relationships, intended to maximize productivity by reducing operator fatigue and discomfort.

escalation (or escalate) — To raise a problem from one level to another, such as from level one to level two, in order to dedicate new or additional resources to the problem.

ethics — The rules and standards that govern the conduct of a person or group of people.

event-driven surveys — Customer satisfaction surveys that ask customers for feedback on a single, recent service event.

exit poll — A measurement technique that, on the Internet, combines questions such as "Was this information helpful to you?" with Yes and No buttons that customers can use to provide feedback.

expert system — A computer program that stores human knowledge in a knowledge base and has the ability to reason about that knowledge.

external customer — A person or company that buys another company's products and services.

external help desks — Help desks that support customers who buy their company's products and services (external customers).

fax — An electronic device that sends or receives printed matter or computer images.

fax-on-demand — Technology that enables customers to use their touch-tone telephone to request that answers to FAQs, procedures, forms, or sales literature be delivered to the fax machine at the number they provide.

feature and functionality requirements — The specifics of how the selected tool must perform in order to support its associated business processes.

fee-based support — An approach wherein customers pay for support services on a per-use basis.

field — A location in a database that stores a particular piece of data.

first call resolution rate percent — The percentage of calls resolved during a customer's initial telephone call compared to the total number of calls received at the help desk for a given period of time.

flow chart — A diagram that shows the sequence of tasks that occur in a process.

form — A predefined document that contains text or graphics users cannot change and areas in which users enter information.

front-line service providers — Help desk staff who interact directly with customers.

fuzzy logic — A searching technique that presents all possible solutions that are similar to the search criteria, even when conflicting information exists or no exact match is present.

global support — Support for customers anywhere in the world; may be caused by the need to support a large company that has foreign divisions and subsidiaries or by the need to support customers who are doing business with the company through the World Wide Web.

groupware software — Software that enables multiple users to coordinate and keep track of ongoing projects.

help desk — A single point of contact within a company for managing customer problems and requests and for providing solution-oriented support services.

help desk goals — Measurable objectives that support the help desk's mission.

help desk manager — A person who works closely with the senior help desk manager to prepare the help desk's budget and plan its activities for the coming year.

help desk supervisor — A person who oversees the day-to-day operation of the help desk, which includes making sure the help desk is meeting its SLA commitments, monitoring and evaluating the performance of help desk staff, and ensuring that the staff is properly trained; also called team leader.

high-level requirements — The broad needs for a system.

hyperlinks — Colored and underlined text or graphics in a hypertext or hypermedia document that allow readers to "jump" to a related idea, regardless of where that idea occurs in the document.

hypermedia — A storage method that stores information in a graphical form so users can access the information in a nonlinear fashion using hyperlinks.

hypertext — A storage method that stores information in a nongraphical form so users can access the information in a nonlinear fashion using hyperlinks.

idle state — An ACD state that occurs when an analyst did not answer a call routed to his or her telephone within the specified number of rings.

inbound call center — A call center that receives telephone calls from customers and may answer questions, take orders, respond to billing inquiries, and provide customer support.

incident — The term for different types of customer transactions—that is, problems, requests, and questions; also called issues.

incident data — The details of a problem or request, including incident type (such as a problem or request), channel used to submit (such as telephone or e-mail), category (such as hardware or software), affected component or system (such as a printer or monitor), symptom, date and time incident occurred, date and time incident was logged, analyst who logged incident, incident owner, description, and severity.

incident management — *See* problem management.

incident record — All of the fields that describe a single incident.

incident tracking systems — Technology that typically supports only the problem management process and offers basic trouble ticketing and management reporting capability.

incidents resolved within target time percent — The percentage of incidents resolved within a target resolution time.

individual performance goals — Measurable objectives for analysts that support the help desk mission.

information — Data organized in a meaningful way.

information center — A forerunner of the help desk; a place within a company where employees could receive training and help using personal computers.

information indicator digits (IID) — A service that identifies the origin of a call from the type or location of the telephone being used to place the call, such as a pay phone, cellular phone, hotel phone, and so forth.

Information Technology Infrastructure Library (ITIL) — A set of best practices for IT service management.

inquiries — Customer requests for information, such as "When will the part for my equipment arrive?"

insourcing — When service agency employees are physically located at the facilities of the company that has hired them to provide support services.

instant message systems — Systems that enable two or more people to communicate in real time (chat) over the Internet by typing on a keyboard.

internal customer — A person who works at a company and at times relies on other employees at that company to perform his or her job.

internal help desk — A help desk that responds to questions, distributes information, and handles problems and service requests for its company's employees (internal customers).

internal vendor — A department or a person within a company that supplies information, products, or services to another department or person within the same company.

Internet — A global collection of computer networks that are linked to provide worldwide access to information.

Internet-based training (IBT) — Training systems that people access from any personal computer that has an Internet connection and a browser.

intranet — A secured, privately maintained Web site that serves employees and that can be accessed only by authorized personnel.

inventory management — A process that encompasses only the activities involved in collecting and maintaining information about IT assets, not the relationships that exist among those assets. *See* configuration management.

ISO 9000 — A set of universal standards for a quality assurance system that is accepted around the world.

IT asset — Any product or service that represents a cost or adds value to an IT organization.

Kaizen — A Japanese term that when applied to the workplace means continuing improvement involving everyone—managers and workers alike.

keyword searching — The technique of finding indexed information by specifying a descriptive word or phrase, called a keyword.

knowledge base — A collection of information sources such as customer information, documents, policies and procedures, and incident resolutions.

knowledge engineer — A person who develops and oversees the knowledge management process and ensures that the information contained in the help desk's knowledge base is accurate, complete, and current; also called knowledge base administrator (KBA).

knowledge management — The process of gathering and maintaining a company's information assets (knowledge) in a knowledge base.

knowledge management system — Technology that combines the reasoning capability of an expert system with other information sources, such as databases, documents, policies, and procedures.

large help desks — Internal help desks that have more than 25 people on staff, or external help desks that have as many as several hundred people on staff.

lead time — The amount of time needed to adequately plan and implement a categorized change.

level one — The initial point of contact for customers when they have a problem, question, inquiry, or request.

level one analyst — A person who takes calls (e-mails, faxes, and so forth), logs customer incidents, and resolves incidents when possible; also called help desk analyst, customer support analyst, or help desk technician.

level one resolution rate percent — The percentage of incidents resolved at level one, but not necessarily during the customer's initial telephone call.

level one specialist — A person who researches complex incidents and develops solutions that require more skill—or, in some cases, more time—than a level one analyst typically can devote to a single incident; also called help desk specialist, technical support specialist, or customer support specialist.

level three — The person or group that resolves complex problems that are beyond the scope of level two.

level two — The person or group that resolves problems that are beyond the scope or authority (such as system access rights or permissions) of level one.

location — The physical site of the help desk in the building.

macro — A series of menu selections, keystrokes, and/or commands that have been recorded and assigned a name or key combination.

Malcolm Baldrige National Quality Award — Established by the U.S. Congress in 1987 to recognize U.S. organizations for their achievements in quality and business performance and to raise awareness about the importance of quality as a performance indicator.

mass-healing systems — Systems that enable help desks to detect and repair problems across the enterprise. For example, mass-healing systems provide help desks with the ability to detect and eliminate viruses that may be infecting the company's networked PCs.

medium help desks — Help desks that have between 10 and 25 people on staff; can take on the characteristics of both small and large help desks.

metrics — Performance measures.

mission — A written statement that describes the customers the help desk serves, the types of services the help desk provides, and how the help desk delivers those services.

monitoring — When a supervisor or team leader listens to a live or recorded call or watches an analyst take a call in order to measure the quality of an analyst's performance during the call.

moves, adds, and changes (MACs) — Activities that include moving equipment, installing and configuring new systems, and upgrading existing systems.

multi-level support model — A common structure of help desks, where the help desk refers problems it cannot resolve to the appropriate internal group, external vendor, or subject matter expert.

multivendor support — Support for customers who use products developed by a number of different vendors.

National Institute for Occupational Safety and Health (NIOSH) — A part of the Centers for Disease Control and Prevention (CDC) responsible for conducting research and making recommendations for the prevention of work-related illnesses and injuries; located on the Web at www.cdc.gov.

network monitoring — Activities that use tools to observe and control network performance in an effort to prevent or minimize the impact of problems.

notification — The activities that inform all of the stakeholders in the problem or request management process (including management, the customer, help desk analysts, and so forth) about the status of outstanding problems or requests.

Occupational Safety and Health Administration (OSHA) — An agency of the U.S. Department of Labor that is dedicated to reducing hazards in the workplace and enforcing mandatory job-safety standards. OSHA also implements and improves health programs for workers; located on the Web at www.osha.gov.

off-the-shelf — Personal computer software products that are developed and distributed commercially.

one-stop shop — A help desk that is fully responsible for resolving all problems and service requests, even if the solution requires extensive research or even coding changes.

outbound call center — A call center that makes telephone calls to customers, primarily for telemarketing.

out-of-scope requests — Requests that are beyond the capabilities of the help desk.

outsource — To have services provided by an outside supplier instead of providing them in-house.

overall satisfaction surveys — Customer satisfaction surveys that ask customers for feedback about all calls they made to the help desk during a certain time period.

page hit — A Web page visit.

peer-to-peer support — A practice in which users bypass the formal support structure and seek assistance from their coworkers or someone in another department whom they believe can help.

people — The help desk component that consists of the staff and structure put in place within a company or department to support its customers by performing business processes.

personal digital assistant (PDA) — A small mobile hand-held device that provides computing and information-storage and retrieval capabilities for personal or business use.

physical layout — How the help desk is arranged into workspaces.

portal — A Web "supersite" that provides a variety of services such as a site search where pertinent articles and white papers may be located, a product and services buyer's guide, a discussion center or forum, event calendars, publications, and so forth.

post-sales support — Helping people who have purchased a company's product or service.

pre-sales support — Answering questions for people who have not yet purchased a company's products or services.

priority aging — Increasing the priority of a problem when it is not being resolved in a timely manner.

proactive help desk — A help desk that uses information to anticipate and prevent problems and prepare for the future.

problem — An event that disrupts service or prevents access to products.

problem management — The process of tracking and resolving problems; also called incident management.

problem management and resolution systems — Technology that offers enhanced trouble ticketing and management reporting capability; also may support the request management and asset and configuration management processes.

problem owner — An employee of the support organization who acts as a customer advocate and proactively ensures that a problem is resolved to the customer's satisfaction.

problem ownership — A practice that ensures that when the help desk analyst cannot resolve a problem during the first call or escalates the problem to a person or group outside of the help desk, a problem owner is designated; also known as total contact ownership.

problem priority — Identifies the order for working on problems with the same severity.

problem tracking — Follows *one* problem from recognition to resolution.

procedure — A step-by-step, detailed set of instructions that describes how to perform the tasks in a process.

process — A collection of interrelated work activities, or tasks, that take a set of specific inputs and produce a set of specific outputs that are of value to the customer.

productivity — An efficiency measure that relates output (goods and services produced) to input (the number of hours worked).

profit centers — A help desk that must cover its expenses and, perhaps, make a profit by charging a fee for support services.

push technology — A way to deliver information to Web-enabled PCs. The information is delivered in one of two ways: push or pull. In the push method, the server contacts the client when there is new information to send. In the pull method, the client contacts the server to determine whether new information is available.

quality — A characteristic that measures how well products or services meet customer requirements.

query by example (QBE) — A searching technique that uses queries, or questions, to find records that match the specified search criteria. Queries can include search operators.

questions — Customer requests for instruction on how to use a product, such as "How do I...?"

queue — A line.

reactive help desk — A help desk that simply reacts to events that occur each day.

record — A collection of related fields.

recording systems — Technology that records and plays back telephone calls.

remote control system — Technology that enables an analyst to take over a caller's keyboard, screen, mouse, or other connected devices in order to troubleshoot problems, transfer files, provide informal training, and even collaborate on documents.

remote monitoring system — Technology that tracks and collects alerts generated by a network monitoring system and passes them to a central server where they can be automatically picked up and logged in the problem management and resolution system or displayed on a special monitor or electronic white board.

reopen percent — The percentage of incidents an analyst opens back up compared to the total number of incidents that analyst closed during a given period of time.

reopened percent — The percentage of closed incidents that had to be opened back up within a given period of time.

repetitive stress injuries (RSIs) — Physical symptoms caused by excessive and repeated use of the hands, wrist, and arms; these symptoms occur when people perform tasks using force, repeated strenuous actions, awkward postures, and poorly designed equipment.

request — A customer order or request to obtain a new product or service or an enhancement to an existing product or service.

request for information (RFI) — A form or letter that asks for specific product information relative to the company's requirements.

request for proposal (RFP) — A form or letter that requests financial information as well as product information.

request management — The process of collecting and maintaining information about customer requests.

request owner — An employee of the support organization who keeps the customer informed and is involved in scheduling any installation activities needed to complete the request.

request priority — Identifies the order for working on submitted requests.

requirement — Something that is essential.

resolution — A definitive, permanent solution to either a problem or a request, *or* it is a proven workaround.

resolution data — Details that describe how an incident was resolved, including all fields required to track service level compliance and perform root cause analysis, such as the person or group who resolved the incident, resolution description, date and time resolved, customer satisfaction indicator, date and time closed, and root cause.

resolution percent — The percentage of incidents an analyst resolves compared to the total number of incidents that analyst handled during a given period of time.

resource desk — A reference desk where level one analysts can get help with difficult incidents and training to handle similar incidents in the future.

resource desk specialists — Senior level one analysts or specialists who are dedicated to the resource desk or who rotate between the resource desk and the front line.

response time — The length of time a customer waits for a reply to a fax, e-mail, or Web-based request; comparable to the ASA metric used for telephone calls.

return on investment (ROI) — A business calculation that measures the total financial benefit derived from an investment—such as a new technology project—and then compares it with the total cost of the project.

root cause — The most basic reason for an undesirable condition or problem, which, if eliminated or corrected, would have prevented it from existing or occurring.

root cause analysis — A methodical way of determining why problems occur (the root cause) and identifying ways to prevent them.

rule-based system — A system made up of (1) rules, (2) facts, and (3) a knowledge base or engine that combines rules and facts to reach a conclusion.

screen pop — A CTI function that enables information about the caller to appear, or "pop" up, on the analyst's monitor based on caller information captured by the telephone system and passed to a computer system.

search criteria — The questions or problem symptoms entered by a user.

search operators — Connecting words such as AND, OR, and NOT sometimes used in queries; also called Boolean operators.

self-healing — Hardware devices and software applications that have the ability to detect and correct problems on their own.

self-management skills — The skills, such as stress and time management, that people need to complete their work effectively, feel job satisfaction, and avoid frustration or burnout.

senior help desk manager — A person who typically establishes the help desk mission and focuses on the help desk's strategic or long-term goals.

service agencies — Companies that provide help desk outsourcing services.

Service Level Agreement (SLA) — A written document that spells out the services the help desk will provide to the customer, the customer's responsibilities, and how service performance is measured.

service level management — The process of negotiating and managing customer expectations by establishing Service Level Agreements (SLAs).

service management and improvement — Activities such as monitoring help desk performance and identifying and overseeing improvements to the help desk.

severity — The category that defines how critical a problem is based on the nature of the failure and the available alternatives or workarounds.

simultaneous screen transfer — A function that transfers the call as well as all the information collected in the ticket up to that point.

skills-based routing (SBR) — An ACD feature that matches the requirements of an incoming call to the skill sets of available analysts or analyst groups. The ACD then distributes the call to the next available, most qualified analyst.

skills inventory matrix — A grid that rates each analyst's level of skill on every product, system, and service supported by the help desk.

small help desks — Help desks that have anywhere from one to 10 people on staff.

soft skills — The qualities that people need to deliver great service, such as listening skills, verbal skills, customer service skills, problem-solving skills, writing skills, and the ability to be a team player.

software distribution system — Technology that allows an analyst to automatically distribute software to clients and servers on the same network.

software piracy — The unauthorized use or reproduction of copyrighted or patented software.

speech recognition — The conversion of spoken words into text or mouse emulation commands.

staffing and scheduling systems — Systems that work with ACD systems to collect, report, and forecast call volumes.

status data — Details about an incident that are used to track incidents not resolved at level one, including incident status (such as assigned, awaiting parts, resolved, closed), the person or group assigned, date and time assigned, and priority.

subject matter expert (SME) — A person who has a high level of experience or knowledge about a particular subject.

support — Services that enable the continued use of a system once it is released for distribution.

support center — A help desk with a broader scope of responsibility and the goal of providing faster service and improving customer satisfaction.

taking ownership — Tracking an incident to ensure that the customer is kept informed about the status of the incident, that the incident is resolved within the expected time frame, and that the customer is satisfied with the final resolution.

target escalation time — A time constraint placed on each level that ensures that problem resolution activities are proceeding at an appropriate pace.

target resolution time — The time frame within which the support organization is expected to resolve the problem.

target response time — The time frame within which the help desk or level two acknowledges the problem, diagnoses the problem, and estimates the target resolution time.

technical skills — The skills people need to use and support the specific products and technologies the help desk supports.

technical support — A wide range of services that enable people and companies to continuously use the computing technology they acquired or developed.

technologies — Enable the creation and enhancement of tools.

technology — The tools and systems people use to do their work.

telemarketing — The selling of products and services over the telephone.

template — A predefined item that can be used to quickly create a standard document or e-mail message.

time idle — The average length of time an analyst was idle during a given period of time. *See* idle state.

time robbers — Activities that take up time and do not add value to the work that analysts perform. In fact, time robbers usually decrease productivity and increase stress levels.

tool — A product or device that automates or facilitates a person's work.

total cost of ownership (TCO) — The total amount that a company or person spends on computer technology over its lifetime. A considerable portion of the TCO is technical support.

Total Quality Control (TQC) — The system that Japan developed to implement *Kaizen* or continuing improvement.

Total Quality Management (TQM) — A management approach to long-term success through customer satisfaction.

trend analysis — A methodical way of determining and, when possible, forecasting service trends.

triage — The process of determining a customer's need and routing him or her to the appropriate support group.

ubiquitous computing — An environment in which people have access to their information and computing systems from public shared access points, such as automated teller machines (ATMs), hotel rooms and lobbies, airports, retail stores, and supermarkets.

value — The perceived worth, usefulness, or importance of a product or service to the customer.

voice mail — An automated form of taking messages from callers.

voice response unit (VRU) — A technology that integrates with another technology, such as a database or a network management system, to obtain information or to perform a function; also called interactive voice response unit (IVRU).

wellness — The condition of good physical and mental health, especially when maintained by proper diet, exercise, and habits.

white board systems — Systems that allow two or more users on a network to view one or more user's drawing, or a document or application being projected, on an onscreen white board.

white boards — Smooth, erasable white panels on which analysts write notes and communicate current and future events.

workaround — Circumventing a problem either partially or completely, usually before implementing the final resolution; also called bypass and recovery.

workflow software — Software that allows messages and documents to be routed to the appropriate users; often part of a groupware system.

workspace — An area outfitted with equipment and furnishings for one worker.

world class — A company that has achieved and is able to sustain high levels of customer satisfaction. For example, a world class manufacturing company is considered excellent by its customers when compared to other service companies, regardless of what industry they are in.

World Wide Web (WWW or Web) — A collection of documents on the Internet with point-and-click access to information that is posted by government agencies, businesses, educational institutions, nonprofit organizations, and individuals around the world.

wrap-up mode — A feature that prevents the ACD from routing a new inbound call to an analyst's extension.

wrap-up time — The average length of time an analyst was in wrap-up mode during a given period of time.

Index